ADVANCE PRAISE FOR *THE COSTS OF CONNECTION*:

"A provocative tour-de-force. A powerful interrogation of the power of data in our networked age. Through an enchanting critique of different aspects of our data soaked society, Nick Couldry and Ulises A. Mejias invite the reader to reconsider their assumptions about the moral, political, and economic order that makes data-driven technologies possible."

—danah boyd, Microsoft Research and founder of Data & Society

"There's a land grab occurring right now, and it's for your data and your freedom: companies are not only surveilling you, they're increasingly influencing and controlling your behavior. This paradigm-shifting book explains the new colonialism at the heart of modern computing, and serves as a needed wake-up call to everyone who cares about our future relationship with technology."

—Bruce Schneier, author of *Click Here to Kill Everybody: Security and Survival in a Hyper-Connected World*

"This book is a must-read for those grappling with how the global data economy reproduces long-standing social injustice, and what must be done to counter this phenomenon. With a feast of insights embedded in visceral historical and contemporary illustrations, the authors brilliantly push the reader to rethink the relations between technology, power, and inequality."

—Payal Arora, author of *The Next Billion Users: Digital Life beyond the West*

"This is a deeply critical engagement with the systems that enable 'data colonialism' to extend its reach into the past, present, and future of human life itself. Couldry and Mejias provide a comprehensive and well-considered challenge to the seeming inevitability of this transformative development in capitalism. Theirs is a giant step forward along the path toward rediscovering the meaning and possibility of self-determination. It is not too late to join in!"

—Oscar H. Gandy, Jr., Emeritus Professor,
Annenberg School of Communication,
University of Pennsylvania

"Nick Couldry and Ulises A. Mejias go digging deeply into the digital: its spaces, its layers, its deployments. One of their guiding efforts concerns what it actually takes to have this digital capacity in play. It is not an innocent event: it is in some ways closer to an extractive sector, and this means there is a price we pay for its existence."

—Saskia Sassen, author of *Expulsions*

"Couldry and Mejias show that data colonialism is not a metaphor. It is a process that expands many dark chapters of the past into our shiny new world of smartphones, smart TVs, and smart stores. This book rewards the reader with important historical context, fascinating examples, clear writing, and unexpected insights scattered throughout."

—Joseph Turow, University of Pennsylvania

THE COSTS OF CONNECTION

CULTURE
AND
ECONOMIC
LIFE

THE COSTS OF CONNECTION

How Data Is Colonizing Human Life
and Appropriating It for Capitalism

NICK COULDRY AND ULISES A. MEJIAS

STANFORD UNIVERSITY PRESS
STANFORD, CALIFORNIA

Stanford University Press
Stanford, California

Printed in the United States of America on acid-free, archival-quality paper

Library of Congress Cataloging-in-Publication Data

Names: Couldry, Nick, author. | Mejias, Ulises Ali, author.
Title: The costs of connection : how data is colonizing human life and appropriating it for
    capitalism / Nick Couldry and Ulises A. Mejias.
Description: Stanford, California : Stanford University Press, 2019. | Series: Culture and
    economic life | Includes bibliographical references and index.
Identifiers: LCCN 2019010213 (print) | LCCN 2019011408 (ebook) | ISBN 9781503609754
    (electronic) | ISBN 9781503603660 (cloth : alk. paper) | ISBN 9781503609747 (pbk. :
    alk. paper)
Subjects: LCSH: Information technology—Social aspects. | Internet—Social aspects. |
    Electronic data processing—Social aspects. | Capitalism—Social aspects.
Classification: LCC HM851 (ebook) | LCC HM851 .C685 2019 (print) | DDC 303.48/33—dc23
LC record available at https://lccn.loc.gov/2019010213

Typeset by Motto Publishing Services in 10/14 Minion Pro
Cover design by Christian Fuenfhausen

Contents

Preface

Colonized by Data

The telegraph pole, the Christian cross, and the rifle arrived all at once for the Bororo people of Mato Grosso. The rifle of the soldier and the settler served to seize the Bororo's land in the name of industry and progress, the cross "pacified" and "civilized" them, and the telegraph integrated them into the rest of the newly wired Brazilian republic in the mid-nineteenth century.[1] Some Bororo donned western clothing and moved from communal to single-family dwellings, as the priests told them to do. They learned the settlers' language and were put to work on the construction of the national telegraph network.

Such history is what comes to mind when most of us think of colonialism. Yet we know that the effects of colonialism continue to be felt, as indigenous people even today resist dispossession, cultural invasion, and genocide. Consider next another starting point, the Idle No More movement, a campaign by indigenous peoples in Canada to protect their ancestral resources.[2] Like many activist movements, Idle No More has become a smart user of social media to promote its cause and enlist supporters. The telegraph pole used to link the Bororo into networks of colonial power has given way to a tool on which even the victims of colonization would now seem to depend. Nonetheless, the implications of such tools are, at best, ambiguous. Reflecting on the use of social media during the campaign's protests, Leanne Betasamosake Simpson, a scholar, writer, and artist of the Nishnaabeg people, wrote that "every tweet, Facebook post, blog post, Instagram photo, YouTube video, and email we sent during Idle No More made the largest corporations in the world . . . more money to reinforce the system of settler colonialism. . . . I wonder in hindsight if maybe we didn't build a movement, but rather we built a social media presence that privileged individuals over community, virtual validation over empathy, leadership without accountability and responsibility."[3]

Consider now a third starting point—the question that Irish novelist Sally Rooney, dubbed "the J. D. Salinger of the Snapchat generation," recently asked herself: "Why wasn't I drinking enough water?"[4] Following a series of fainting spells, doctors advised her to increase her hydration because, like many busy people, she sometimes forgets to take a water break. Fortunately, as the cliché goes, there's an app for that. The makers of WaterMinder offer a program to bypass the part of the brain that regulates thirst, reminding you to drink regularly to meet predefined quotas while tracking your progress. Like many apps, the program claims to turn what would otherwise be an insignificant private act into a social celebration, allowing you to earn achievements that you can share with your friends. "Makes water fun again," wrote a reviewer of the app.[5]

The continuity between the first and second starting points is clear, but what of the third? It might seem counterintuitive to imagine that colonialism's sites of exploitation today include the very same West that historically imposed colonialism on the rest of the world. But what if the armory of colonialism is expanding? What if new ways of appropriating human life, and the freedoms on which it depends, are emerging? That is the disturbing possibility that we explore in this book.

Let's look at Sally Rooney's story again. The simple, daily act that every individual body does of monitoring whether it has drunk enough water has suddenly become something that happens in a competitive social space. The human body has been reworked into something that requires a distant infrastructure, from which, incidentally, profit can be made. In Rooney's own words, "I have contracted out one of the essential functions of my body to a piece of software." But this is just one small example of something much bigger: the systematic attempt to turn all human lives and relations into inputs for the generation of profit. Human experience, potentially every layer and aspect of it, is becoming the target of profitable extraction. We call this condition *colonization by data*, and it is a key dimension of how capitalism itself is evolving today.

If colonialism is the problem, you may be thinking, *Isn't the solution as simple as calling for the internet to be decolonized, liberating us all?* After all, there have been calls to decolonize everything from schools to museums and ways of thinking. But uttered too easily, such calls risk making anyone and everyone into *metaphorical* subalterns, serfs, or slaves of Silicon Valley. Such metaphorical complaints leave intact the *social and economic order* that colonialism comprises at its core. It is not enough to "play Indian."[6] As Eve Tuck and K. Wayne Yang remind us, colonization "is not an approximation of other experiences of oppression"[7] but a highly distinctive exercise of power.

Our argument in this book—that human life is being colonized by data and needs to be decolonized—is no approximation. We are not playing Indian. There is nothing metaphorical about the new era of coloniality that we will describe. By tracing continuities from colonialism's historical appropriation of vast territories, such as contemporary Brazil, all the way to data's role in contemporary life, we suggest that although the modes, intensities, scales, and contexts of today's dispossession are distinctive, the underlying function remains the same as under historical colonialism: to acquire large-scale resources from which economic value can be extracted.

If historical colonialism annexed territories, their resources, and the bodies that worked on them, data colonialism's power grab is both simpler and deeper: the capture and control of *human life itself* through appropriating the data that can be extracted from it for profit. If that is right, then just as historical colonialism created the fuel for industrial capitalism's eventual rise, so too is data colonialism paving the way for a capitalism based on the exploitation of data. Human life is quite literally being annexed to capital.

Some Signposts

This book's argument will therefore be a double one. Our first assertion is that our everyday relations with data are becoming colonial in nature; that is, they cannot be understood except as an appropriation on a form and scale that bears comparison with the appropriations of historical colonialism. Our second argument is that this new colonialism does not just happen by itself but is driven by the imperatives of capitalism. Whereas the relations between historical colonialism and what emerged as industrial capitalism became clear only after centuries, the new data colonialism occurs against the background of centuries of capitalism, and it promises to take familiar aspects of the capitalist social and economic order to a new and more integrated stage, a stage as yet too new to reliably name.

Three further aspects of our argument about data colonialism and its relation to capitalism's evolution must be noted at the start. One is that none of this would be possible without radical changes over the past thirty years in communication infrastructures, specifically the embedding of computer systems in human life at many levels. This book's analysis of data colonialism and capitalism's evolution takes very seriously the transformative role of information technologies and the resulting new infrastructures of connection. The second point is that such technological transformation does not change human life by merely existing. Technologies work, and have consequences for human life, only by being woven into what people do, where they find meaning, and how their lives are interdependent. Data colonialism requires the creation of a new *social and economic order* that is potentially as enduring as the order that enabled capitalist market societies from the nineteenth century onward. The third point concerns how the power relations generated by this emerging order work: data colonialism appropriates not only physical resources but also our very resources for *knowing* the world. This means that economic power (the power to make value) and cognitive power (the power over knowledge) converge as never before. Therefore, what is happening with data can be fully understood only against the background not just of capitalism but of the longer interrelations between capitalism *and colonialism*. The exploitation of human life for profit through data is the climax of five centuries' worth of attempts to know, exploit, and rule the world from particular centers of power. We are entering the age not so much of a new capitalism as of a new interlocking of capitalism's and colonialism's twinned histories, and the interlocking force is data.[8]

What do we mean by *data*? If a shopping list is scribbled on a piece of paper, we don't mean that. But if the list is entered on a mobile phone, perhaps on Google's Keep app, then we do mean that. Furthermore, if we consider the algorithms that collect information across all users of Keep to see what people are making lists of, we definitely mean that. For our very specific purposes, the concept of *data* cannot be separated from two essential elements: the external infrastructure in which it is stored and the profit generation for which it is destined. In short, by *data* we mean information flows that pass from human life in all its forms to infrastructures for collection and processing. This is the starting point for generating profit from data. In this sense, data abstracts life by converting it into information that can be stored and processed by computers and appropriates life by converting it into value for a third party.

This book introduces quite a few other concepts and neologisms, which are explained in detail as the chapters unfold. It might be useful, however, to provide some basic definitions and explain their relationships right at the beginning. *Data colonialism* is, in essence, an emerging order for the appropriation of human life so that data can be continuously extracted from it for profit. This extraction is operationalized via *data relations*, ways of interacting with each other and with the world facilitated by digital tools. Through data relations, human life is not only annexed to capitalism but also becomes subject to continuous monitoring and surveillance. The result is to undermine the autonomy of human life in a fundamental way that threatens the very basis of freedom, which is exactly the value that advocates of capitalism extol. These fundamental transformations of human life have dramatic consequences for the social world too. They enable what we call *social caching*, a new form of knowledge about the social world based on the capture of personal data and its storage for later profitable use. As social relations are thus transformed, we see the emergence of the *Cloud Empire*, a totalizing vision and organization of business in which the dispossession of data colonialism has been naturalized and extended across all social domains. The Cloud Empire is being implemented and extended by many players but primarily by the *social quantification sector*, the industry sector devoted to the development of the infrastructure required for the extraction of profit from human life through data.

For now, the good news is that these transformations are in their early stages. That is why an awareness of the historical roots of today's transformations is so vital. We must respect the uniqueness of the struggles of historically colonized peoples, but that doesn't mean we can't learn from them. Today's attempt to extract economic value from human lives through data has a systematic integration and depth that we argue is, in some respects, without historical precedent. But we see its features most clearly through their continuity with past relations between colonialism and capitalism. We fail to learn from that history at our peril.

Introducing the Social Quantification Sector

Some of the main actors in these transformations are already familiar. As just mentioned, we call them the social quantification sector. This sector has been growing for a long time, in part through marketers' accumulation of consumer data, such as credit card data, which began in the 1980s.[9] In the past fifteen years, however, the social quantification sector has achieved a new depth and complexity.

This sector currently includes the manufacturers of the digital devices through which people connect. By this we mean not just well-known media brands such as Apple, Microsoft, and Samsung but also the less-well-known manufacturers of "smart" (that is, internet-connected) fridges, heating systems, and cars through which we never imagined we would communicate. Still less did we imagine that, in the quickly expanding Internet of Things, such devices would communicate with other devices about us. The sector also includes the builders of the computer-based environments, platforms, and tools that enable us to connect with and use the online world, including household names such as Alibaba, Baidu, Facebook, Google, and WeChat. There is also the growing field of data brokers and data processing organizations such as Acxiom, Equifax, Palantir, and TalkingData (in China) that collect, aggregate, analyze, repackage, and sell data of all sorts while also supporting other organizations in their uses of data. And, finally, the social quantification sector includes the vast domain of organizations that increasingly depend for their basic functions on processing data from social life, whether to customize their services (like Netflix and Spotify) or to link sellers and buyers (like Airbnb, Uber, and Didi).

Beyond the social quantification sector is the rest of business, which has also been transformed in the "great data transition."[10] Much of what ordinary businesses now do is crunch data from their internal processes and from the world around them; most businesses also depend increasingly on the work of the social quantification sector to target their ads and marketing. And beyond that is the vast array of everyday contexts in which people are integrating the outputs of that sector into daily life. The Cloud Empire is the larger outcome of this combined growth of the social quantification sector and data practices right across business and social life.

A few words of clarification about the term *social quantification sector* are needed. When we say *social quantification sector*, we use the word *social* to refer to that constantly changing space of relations and interconnections on which the quality of human life depends but whose meaning is endlessly contested in political and civic struggle.[11] When we use the word *social*, we do not necessarily mean a well-ordered or well-integrated way of living together. For at issue in this whole transformation is precisely the *quality* of life that human beings will have together in the new capitalist social order. The capture of personal data through social caching and its storage for later profitable use—normal today but two decades ago barely imaginable—has major implications for our quality of life as human beings.

Social caching is often hidden from users of platforms and internet services under a veneer of convenience ("To use this app, you must first . . ."). Stripped of that veneer, the deal looks rather different. A key consequence of connecting with others in the era of data colonialism is submission to the continuous tracking of human life, a process known until recently as surveillance. As a leading computer-security expert, Bruce Schneier, put it, "The primary business model of the internet is based on mass surveillance."[12] The all-seeing authoritarian state was a standard topic of twentieth-century literary dystopias (from Kafka to Orwell),[13] but Schneier points to an even bigger problem: the building into corporations' *routine* operations of processes that conflict, as surveillance always has, with basic freedoms such as autonomy. The tracking of human subjects that is core to data colonialism is incompatible with the *minimal integrity of the self* that underlies autonomy and freedom in all their forms.

This was the deeper meaning of Edward Snowden's revelations of US and UK security services' data-gathering in 2013. Suddenly, citizens became aware that today's pervasive state surveillance would be impossible without the continuous social-caching operations of commercial corporations.[14] Since then, fears of a new "corporate governance of everyday life" have been growing.[15] But other fears have started to overtake them, including the "fake news" scandals that have gripped politics since late 2016 in the United States, United Kingdom, and elsewhere. There are also fears that, because of polarizing forces online, "social media is ripping society apart";[16] fears from other commentators of a social dystopia driven by platforms' search for advertising income;[17] and, finally, the fear that the targeting of news via social media platforms represents "the most lethal political weapon ever invented."[18] Calls for the regulation of social media platforms and other information technology giants are becoming familiar.[19] But none of these highly charged debates answers the underlying question on which this book will focus: *should human beings in the twenty-first century accept a world in which their lives are unceasingly appropriated through data for capitalism?*

Colonial Echoes

This is where the long history of colonialism's entanglement with capitalism helps us move beyond the sound and fury of contemporary scandals and grasp the longer pattern of resource appropriation that gives shape to today's developments. Long before Karl Marx identified it as a force in the world, capital was already expanding in the sixteenth century, in the period most commonly identified with historical colonialism and the emergence of the Spanish, Portuguese, and British empires. Capital was acquiring new territories from which to extract resources and new bodies from which to extract labor. Those close relations between colonialism and capitalism (indeed, between colonialism and modernity in general)[20] are important to our story; they help us grasp what is distinctive about the current expansionary phase of capitalism.

What do we mean by *expansionary*? Capitalism has been expanding from the start, in the sense of exploiting new resources, finding new ways of making profit, and finding new markets. But until recently, this expansion has been based on the exploitation of human production through labor relations, as classically theorized by Marx, resulting in the ever-greater transformation of physical nature as an input to capitalism. But the appropriation of human life in the form of data (the basic move that we call data colonialism) generates a new possibility: without ending its exploitation of labor and its transformation of physical nature, capitalism *extends* its capacity to exploit life by assimilating new or reconfigured human activities (whether regarded as labor or not)[21] as its direct inputs. The result, we argue in chapter 1, is the expansion of the practical scope of capitalist exploitation, but in ways that can be linked back to Marx's own sense of capitalism's expansionary potential. In this emerging form of capitalism, human beings become not just actors in the production process but raw material that can be transformed into value for that production process. Human life, in the form of profitably abstracted data, becomes more like the seed or manure that Marx noted became factors of capitalist production, having once just been part of human beings' cycle of interaction with the land.[22] This transformation of human life into raw material resonates strongly with the history of exploitation that preceded industrial capitalism—that is, colonialism.

The very concept of raw material has deep colonial roots. *Raw*, in this context, means available for exploitation without resistance rather than a substance that needs no processing. The natural environment itself first had to be reconstructed so that it became available for value extraction.[23] Then, through the practice of slavery (which preceded colonialism but which reached a massive scale under colonialism), human bodies were transformed into a raw material for capitalism in the form of slaves. Historians have warned us against treating slavery—usually imagined as a premodern practice—in isolation from the development of industrial capitalism. The plantation and the factory coexisted for a long time.[24] The treatment of human beings as mere property stimulated the rationalities of profit maximization, accounting precision, and data optimization that we now tend to associate with modern rationality.[25] Here is an eloquent description by the historian of the capitalist slave plantation, Edward Baptist:

So push a button (with the index finger of your *right* hand) on the machine of the trading world, and things happen to benefit the man with sterling bills, a huge pile of cotton, a long roster of slaves, abundant credit that allows him to extend his reach across time and space.[26]

What if comparable processes for abstracting human life are today enabling new, extended forms of economic extraction? Human data is not actually raw,[27] but business often imagines it is. Human life first needs to be configured so as to "naturally" generate a resource such as data. Momentary data about one individual's actions or properties is worthless unless it can be combined with data about *other* individuals, actions, moments, and properties to generate relations between data points,[28] and that is why an infrastructure has been built to ensure this. The world of internet-based connection *is* a world in which new types of corporate power, with privileged access to data streams extracted from the flow of life, can activate a metaphorical button—an apparatus of extraction, whether platform, app, or AI system—that reconfigures human life so that it contributes continuously to the collection of data and thereby, potentially, to the generation of profit.

The result of such data relations is certainly not a new slavery, since nothing can compare to the terrible violence of that institution (the practice of "distinguish[ing] every bad thing by the name of slavery" was already criticized by Frederick Douglass in the mid-nineteenth century).[29] But that should not blind us to what remains a disturbing line of continuity: as happened historically, but under new conditions, human life today is becoming the object of appropriation for extraction and, in the process, enabling capitalism to move to a still higher scale and integration of operation. Our intent is not to make comparisons to the detailed contents or form of historical colonialism but to focus on colonialism's enduring *function*, which we see as enacting illegitimate appropriation and exploitation and as redefining human relations so that the resulting dispossession comes to seem natural. It is such continuities that the term *data colonialism* enables us to grasp.

What Is Data Colonialism?

More explicitly defined, *data colonialism* is our term for the extension of a global process of extraction that started under colonialism and continued through industrial capitalism, culminating in today's new form: instead of natural resources and labor, what is now being appropriated is human life through its conversion into data. The result degrades life, first by exposing it continuously to monitoring and surveillance (through which data is extracted) and second by thus making human life a direct input to capitalist production. Data colonialism is, in other words, an emerging order for appropriating and extracting social resources for profit through data, practiced via data relations. Unlike historical colonialism, whose vast profits helped create the preconditions for what we now know as industrial capitalism, data colonialism emerges against the backdrop of the entire intertwined history of colonialism and capitalism. This means that the basic colonial move of appropriating data from human life (data colonialism) works hand in hand with social arrangements and technological infrastructures, some that emerged during earlier capitalism and some new, that enable that data to be transformed into a commodity, indeed, a direct input to contemporary capitalist production.

Although the site of data colonialism that we most often notice is the social quantification sector, and particularly the personal data extraction practiced by social media platforms, the basic extractive principles underlying data colonialism have been gestating in the business methods of modern capitalism for three decades. The original context was industrial capitalism's progressive globalization in the late twentieth century through trade liberalization and extended supply chains as well as its financialization through an explosive growth of debt (both corporate and personal) and the acceleration of global capital flows. In this general context, the information infrastructures emerged that enabled people and processes to be connected to each other under conditions that facilitate data extraction.[30]

Take an example far from social media: the discipline of logistics. The goal of logistics is to use continuously connected data flows to organize all aspects of production across space and time within global commodity chains.[31] It was enabled, decades before social media, by software inventions such as the relational databases that help businesses find patterns in huge data flows across diverse sources and locations.[32] If logistics aims to rationalize production, the recent growth of the Internet of Things (IoT) aims to incorporate consumption—what we do with products after we buy them—into an extended chain of profit extraction through the processing of data.[33] The bigger vision of the IoT, and of data colonialism as a whole, has been expressed by a company normally seen as the enemy of the entrepreneurs who built social media platforms—IBM. By turning the human environment into a network of listening devices that capture data about all activities, IBM suggests that they can "liquify" areas previously inaccessible to capital. The company put it this way: "Just as large financial marketplaces create liquidity in securities, currencies and cash, the IoT can liquify whole industries, squeezing greater productivity and profitability out of them than anyone ever imagined possible."[34] In this view, every layer of human life, whether on social media platforms or not, *must* become a resource from which economic value can be extracted and profit generated. The processing power of artificial intelligence is a key tool in all these developments.

Far from being a feature of the West only, the growth of the social quantification sector, logistics, and the IoT in the context of rapidly expanding uses of artificial intelligence is a core development and policy goal in China too.[35] The social quantification sector emerges as an arena of commercial and geopolitical competition between the West (particularly the United States) and China.

We can capture the core of our double argument most succinctly by characterizing data colonialism as *an unprecedented mutual implication of human life and digital technology for capitalism.* None of this would have been possible without the emergence in the past three decades of a radically new technological infrastructure for connecting humans, things, and systems, known generally as the internet. We have written this book because it is time to count the *costs* as well as the much-proclaimed benefits of such connection for human life.

The Book's Structure at a Glance

In telling the story of this double transformation (a new colonialism and an extended capitalism), our goal is to equip readers to better see the world that is being built for them and to imagine a different one.

Chapter 1 lays out our argument's foundations: the concepts of data colonialism and capitalist data relations, their contextualization within the twinned histories of capitalism *and* colonialism, and capitalism's recent turn toward the capitalization of human life itself. We will explain how much recent critique of data trends misses two crucial ingredients: the radically reconfigured social world that computer-based connection makes possible and the unprecedented fact that the emerging colonial/capitalist power structure has at least two poles of power in what, until now, we have called the West and in China (with India an important player over the longer term).

Chapter 2 then explains in more detail the workings of the social quantification sector as an economic and organizational transformation within the emerging larger formation of the Cloud Empire. We will map out the relations between the multiple ways in which data is transforming the capitalist economy on the basis of data colonialism's fundamental mode of appropriation. An interlude is offered following chapter 2 for readers who might need a quick overview of colonialism and the critical and theoretical responses to it. Chapter 3 places our overall analysis in the context of the much longer history of *colonial* appropriation, demonstrating the hidden patterns that get missed until we look at the contemporary era through a colonial lens. As a result, we see the recent rise of data as a mode of social and economic ordering within the much longer perspective that decolonial theorists have called *coloniality*: the long-term skewing of the world's economic-resource distribution in favor of particular types of power formations and the justification of this skewing by an equally biased distribution of knowledge resources, loaded until very recently in favor of the "West."

The next two chapters build on the framework established in the first three chapters to examine more closely the social order emerging from data colonialism and what it means for human beings and their quality of life everywhere. Chapter 4 asks what is happening to the social domain in datafied societies and, in particular, what is happening to our knowledge of the social world as it becomes transformed by data relations. Data-driven changes to social knowledge also have major implications for injustice and inequality in the social world. Chapter 5 turns to the implications of data colonialism for the very nature of human subjecthood and specifically for human autonomy. Autonomy may be a compromised concept in some forms, but it is one we cannot do without, because it provides the normative basis for resisting the violence of data relations. Without the notion of autonomy, and in particular the minimal integrity of the self that underlies it, democracy and freedom in *any* form would make little sense.

Chapter 6 brings the book's threads together, assessing where data colonialism and the capitalization of life are likely to head in the foreseeable future and what type of larger social order/disorder this will entail. From there, a postscript suggests ways to imagine forms of human connection that may be free of the costs of data colonialism's regime and to begin orienting ourselves toward possible strategies for resisting data colonialism on the ground.

This book is an attempt to disentangle a historical moment of great complexity. As the first subjects of an emerging data colonialism, we can make sense of this complexity only within the much longer history of colonialism and capitalism. We also need to do a considerable amount of interpretative and analytical work across today's societies and economies. In writing this book, we have been fortunate enough to build on much excellent work within the past decade that has begun to uncover the shape and dynamics of human life's appropriation through data.[36] But in searching for a larger theoretical framework to make sense of the whole sweep of these developments—the framework of data colonialism—we have had to forge some new connections and take an eclectic path in terms of theory. Rather than positioning our argument exclusively within Marxism, postcolonialism, Foucauldian analyses of biopolitics, or critical-information science, our aim is to put these perspectives into conversation, taking the best from each to forge a new starting point adequate to today's complex transformations and their hidden violence.

We hope that, like us, you will find worthwhile the effort to trace the "inner connection"[37] of what is happening with data. It is now urgent to better understand the hidden and not-so-hidden costs of something human beings have until now generally seen as good: connection. Only from better understanding can come the chance of resisting today's terms of connection and the forging of better ones.

THE COSTS OF CONNECTION

Part I

Extracting

.

The Capitalization of Life without Limit 1

"THIS IS WHAT MODERN COLONIALISM LOOKS LIKE." So tweeted Christopher Wylie, the whistle-blower who kicked off the Facebook/Cambridge Analytica scandal in March 2018.[1] Wylie was referring to Cambridge Analytica's plans to expand its operations in India for using social media targeting to influence the political process there. But the scale and scope of data colonialism is much wider than the malfeasance of a few overweening data marketers and their in-house psychologists. It extends much wider even than Facebook's normal practices of data extraction and data licensing that the scandal opened to view.

Yet the scandal was important. It was as though a side deal by Facebook with independent data prospectors had accidentally left open a hole in the ground that allowed the general public, for the first time, to see clearly into an underground anteroom. There, in that anteroom, visible for all to see, was the entrance to social media's real data mine, although few understood exactly what lay behind that subterranean door in Facebook's exclusive domain, let alone the planetary scope of capitalism's data mining. The long-anticipated "techlash" had begun but, as yet, without a map of the wider pattern of exploitation, whose traces had suddenly become visible.

The concept of *data colonialism* helps us draw that map. In this chapter, we unpack further what this term involves and outline its relation to capitalism and to the new social order that is stabilizing in and through capitalism. Along the way, we will also explain certain other key concepts, such as *platform* and *data relations*, while clarifying the similarities and differences that our argument has with other recent analyses of the digital era, for example, the huge recent commentary on the exploitation of digital labor.

To start, we must recall what made historical colonialism distinctive. Colonialism was a form of economic and social organization dominated by major colonial powers such as Britain, France, Spain, and later the United States. It is now usually regarded as historically closed, ended by the decolonizing movements of the later twentieth century, although in politics and other areas, neocolonial forms of power live on (a more detailed discussion of historical colonialism can be found in the interlude following chapter 2). Our interest in this book is in the continuities from that older colonialism to a new form of colonialism—data colonialism.

There were four key components to historical colonialism: the appropriation of *resources*; the evolution of highly unequal social and economic *relations* that secured resource appropriation (including slavery and other forms of forced labor as well as unequal trading relations); a massively unequal global *distribution of the benefits* of resource appropriation; and the spread of *ideologies* to make sense of all this (for example, the reframing of colonial appropriation as the release of "natural" resources, the government of "inferior" peoples, and the bringing of "civilization" to the world).

In describing the transformations underway today as data colonialism, we use the term *colonialism* not because we're looking for a metaphor but because it captures major structural phases within human history and specifically within capitalism. Colonialism has *not* been the standard reading of what is changing in contemporary capitalism.[2] Yet it is becoming increasingly clear that capitalism's current growth cannot be captured simply in terms of ever-more ambitious business integration or the ever-expanding exploitation of workers. Some have characterized today's developments as increasing waves of "accumulation by dispossession," a feature characteristic of capitalism throughout its history.[3] But even this fails to grasp how the *axis* of capitalism's expansion has transformed, through a shift in the supposed "raw material" that capitalism aspires to get under its control.

The discovery of new forms of raw material is what makes the current moment distinctively colonial. If historical colonialism expanded by appropriating for exploitation geographical territory and the resources that territorial conquest could bring, data colonialism expands by appropriating for exploitation ever more layers of *human life itself*. Regarding data colonialism, much debate on contemporary capitalism has been sidetracked by an excessive focus on whether digital labor is being exploited,[4] a significant topic, certainly, but not the most important feature of today's transformations. We will show how data colonialism appropriates many specific aspects of human life—from work to school, from health treatment to self-monitoring, and from basic forms of sociality to routine economic transactions, plus the grid of judgment and direction that we call "governance." When we refer to data practices as colonizing human life, we refer to the appropriation of data, potentially for profit, in any and all of these areas. But we also intend the term *human life* to refer to the as-yet-still-open horizon of exploitation over which data colonialism claims future rights: as ever more of our activities and even inner thoughts occur in contexts in which they automatically *are made ready for* appropriation as data, there is, in principle, no limit to how much of human life can be appropriated and exploited. In this way, Marx's core insight into the expansionary potential of capitalism is actualized in circumstances that Marx himself could not have anticipated.

To be clear, it is not the mere appropriation of data that is colonial. An individual can imagine appropriating the "data stream" of her own life and using it for her own purposes; she can also imagine agreeing to the appropriation of, say, some of her health data by medical professionals for purposes she approves of and on terms that she wholly controls. But these are not typical of the cases we will discuss. Data colonialism is concerned with the external appropriation of data on terms that are partly or wholly beyond the control of the person to whom the data relates. This external appropriation is what makes possible such data's exploitation for profit.

This progressive opening up of human life to externally driven data extraction is what we mean by the capitalization of human life *without limit*. In this phrase, we recognize Marx's long-standing insight that capitalism has always sought to manage human life for the maximization of profit; at the same time, we emphasize that data colonialism absorbs new aspects of human life streams directly into the productive process. It is not that social limits to life's capitalization can no longer be imagined—indeed, the whole point of this book is to argue for the necessity of such limits—but that, as things currently stand, much corporate discourse fails to recognize any limits except those that it sets itself. The result of this convenient failure is not just to renew colonialism but also to expand the scope of capitalism too, that is, the capitalism developed on the basis of historical colonialism. Through data colonialism, contemporary capitalism promises to consume its last remaining "outside," dispossessing human subjects of their capacity as independent sites of thought and action. *Resisting* data colonialism becomes the only way to secure a human future not fused indissolubly with capitalism, indeed, the only way to sustain the value that capitalism claims to promote: human freedom.

The Dimensions of Data Colonialism

Today's technological infrastructures of connection are varied. They include digital platforms such as Facebook and Alibaba that we are familiar with, the whole mass of corporate intranets, and any detailed interfaces for linking up persons, things, and processes for data transfer. Infrastructures of connection enable data colonialism to be more subtle than historical colonialism in how it appropriates resources. Historical colonialism appropriated territories and bodies through extreme physical violence. Data colonialism works through distinctive kinds of force that ensure compliance within interlocking systems of extraction in everyday life.[5] These systems are so many and, taken together, so encompassing that they risk governing human beings in just as absolute a way as historical colonialism did.

Colonizing Resources: The World as Input to Capital

Data colonialism appropriates for profitable exploitation a resource that did not begin to be universally appropriated until two decades ago: data. According to an authoritative definition, data is the "material produced by abstracting the world into categories, measures and other representational forms . . . that constitute the building blocks from which information and knowledge are created."[6] More than that, human life, and particularly human social life, is increasingly being constructed *so that* it generates data from which profit can be extracted. In doing so, ever more of life is required to be continuously monitored and surveilled, removing the boundaries that previously existed between internal life and external forces. In this double sense, human life is appropriated through data, becoming something else, a process tied to external processes of data extraction.

Capitalism can exploit any number of data sources. Any computer, any device with an embedded computer, or any entity readable by a sensor with computing power can generate data for this purpose. Data sources may be processes, things, or people as well as the interactions between any of these sources. The extraction of value from data is equally indifferent to its origin. Capitalism as the systematic organization of value extraction has only one goal in relation to data—to maximize the production of value through data extraction—and so in principle cares little about the sources and types of data exploited.[7]

Contemporary possibilities for data extraction derive from connection between computers. The demand for human beings and things to "connect" is common ground between corporations in the West and the East. Facebook's emphasis on the value of connection is well-known: Zuckerberg, ahead of Facebook's first public share offering, wrote to investors that Facebook "was not originally created to be a company" but "to make the world more open and connected." The 2017 open letter by "Pony" Ma Huateng, CEO of the Chinese company Tencent, is clearer, however, on what is at stake for the wider society: "With the full digitization of the entire real economy and society, we not only need to reduce 'islands of information' through more connections, but also need to achieve continuous optimization of communication and collaboration through better connections."[8] Connection, in other words, generates *societies and economies* that are integrated and ordered to an unprecedented degree.

Data expands the production resources available to capital. If, following Marx, we understand capital not as static accumulations of value and resource but as "value in motion,"[9] then the appropriation of data enables new ways of forming capital through the circulation and trading of informational traces (data). But the trading of data is only part of a larger change whereby capital comes to relate to the whole world, including the worlds of human experience, as its extractive resource. "It seems to me we have squeezed all the juice out of the internal information," said the CEO of US data company Recorded Future.[10] The resulting move to external data sources has changed the rationale of business while seemingly making "organizations smarter and more productive." Human beings cannot remain unaffected since, in the words of Thomas Davenport, a leading US analyst of the data business, "Human beings are increasingly sensored," and "sensor data is here to stay."[11] Sensors can sense all relevant data at or around the point in space where they are installed. "Sensing" is becoming a general model for knowledge in any domain, for example, in the much-vaunted "smart city."[12]

Sensors never work in isolation but are connected in wider networks that cover ever more of the globe. All business relations get reorganized in the process, and new types of business (for selling and controlling data flows and for managing the new infrastructure of data processing and data storage) become powerful. This affects all types of business, not just social media platforms. As one business manager put it, "We make more money selling data to retail data syndication firms than we do selling meat."[13] It is all too easy to see this as simply a shift within capitalism's modes of operation while forgetting that the cost is always the expansion of surveillance regimes that intrude on the autonomy of human beings. As we show in detail in chapter 5, all notions of autonomy, until now, have assumed that individuals have access to a minimal space of the self that is its space of becoming. But the goal of continuous data appropriation intrudes on this space and changes humanity's relations to external infrastructures decisively, erasing, potentially forever, the boundary between the flow of human experience and the environment of economic power that surrounds it.

Operationalizing this move, however, is not simple. First, there is the question of how economic value can be extracted from data. Data can be sold directly, used to enhance the value of sold advertising, or integrated into the organization of other product streams or into production generally. But it is no part of our argument to claim that extracting value from data is automatically successful, only to argue that the goal of doing so is increasingly the goal of business. The impact, however, on how business talks about itself has been profound.

When it comes to access, and this is the second complexity, contemporary business tends to *talk* about data as though it was "just there," freely available for extraction and the release of its potential for humankind. In the history of colonialism, a similar claim was expressed in the legal doctrine of *terra nullius*, land such as the territory now known as Australia that supposedly belonged to "no one" (*nullius*).[14] Today's equivalent metaphor is data as the "exhaust" of life processes.[15] Data is assumed to just be there for the taking:

> Verizon Wireless . . . is no different from other wireless carriers in having a great deal of information about its customer movements. All wireless phones broadcast their location . . . in radio signals, and all carriers capture the information. Now . . . Verizon is selling information about how often mobile phone users are in certain locations and their activities and backgrounds. Customers thus far have included malls, stadium owners, and billboard forms.[16]

But such claims are constructions of how the world is and should be. Meanwhile, the exploitation of data, now that the world has been found to be full of it, is becoming increasingly sophisticated. The use of data analytics is central to whole economies, including cultural and media production once focused mainly on the content itself.[17] Davenport distinguishes three phases in the development of data analytics: whereas early analytics was essentially "descriptive," collecting companies' internal data for discrete analysis, the period since 2005 has seen the emergence of the ability to extract value from large unstructured and increasingly diverse external and internal data sets through "predictive" analytics that can find patterns in what appears to have no pattern. Today's "analytics 3.0" uses large-scale processing power to extract value from vast combinations of data sets, resulting in a "prescriptive analytics" that "*embed[s]* analytics into every process and employee behavior."[18] Once the world is seen by capitalism as a domain that can *and so must* be comprehensively tracked and exploited to ensure more profit, then all life processes that underlie the production process (thinking, acting, consuming, and working in all its dimensions and preconditions) must be fully controlled too. This principle, made possible by technological connection, is the engine that drives the capitalization of human life in its twenty-first-century form, and its remit goes much wider than social media platforms.

Yet the internet was developed against the background of the values of freedom and human cognitive enhancement characteristic of the US counterculture of the 1960s.[19] Unsurprisingly, there has been some pushback against capitalism's apparent new dependence on extracting data from human life. Surveillance is not obviously a benefit to citizens (except as a temporary means to counter serious threats), so it must be repackaged or disguised. Here is the source of data colonialism's most interesting contradictions. It is eerie but not uncommon to find the language of personal freedom melded with the logic of surveillance, as in the motto of facial-recognition software manufacturer, Facefirst: "Creating a safer and more personalised planet through facial recognition technology."[20] Google, meanwhile, is marketing Nest Hello, a video doorbell that includes facial-recognition technology, and Amazon has its own facial-recognition service called simply Rekognition. In China, facial-recognition software is becoming the cool new way for customers to pay for fast food and a (less cool!) way for city authorities to monitor public spaces.[21] But elsewhere, unease at the implications of facial recognition for democracy is growing.

As though in response, Apple, which makes vast profits through a walled garden of devices, proclaims its refusal to collect data on users via those devices.[22] Yet Apple tracks its users for many purposes and so does not contradict the trend of data colonialism, except that its business model does not generally depend on the sale of this data. Indeed, Apple receives substantial sums from Google for allowing it privileged access to iPhone users.[23] A controversy developed when Apple's iOS and MacOS systems were shown to collect information on user location and search activity. Apple's subsequent Privacy Policy states that collected data "will not be associated with [a user's] IP address,"[24] yet iPhone features still support the surveillance needs of marketers. Both the iBeacon service and the iPhone's built-in Wallet app enable push notifications from marketers.[25]

Responsiveness to surveillance concerns is a selling point for other players too, at least outside China. WhatsApp distinguishes itself by its end-to-end message encryption, while Snapchat has its posted messages disappear, at least from the users' view, after a short period. But the actual position is more complex. Although WhatsApp claimed it was "built . . . around the goal of knowing as little about you as possible," a company blog post following WhatsApp's $19 billion acquisition by Facebook admitted that its logbook of customer phone numbers would become connected with Facebook's systems, an admission that led to a European Commission fine for Facebook and a string of legal challenges.[26] WhatsApp's own terms now make clear that users are likely to yield up their entire mobile address book when they use the service, and there is evidence that WhatsApp also stores metadata on the time, duration, and location of every communication.[27] Snapchat's disappearing messages have been mimicked by Instagram, also now part of Facebook, and the US Federal Trade Commission has challenged Snapchat on whether sent images really disappear.[28] Meanwhile, the growing popularity of ad blocking[29] may simply incentivize marketers to find smarter ways of tracking people so that they can be reached with ads. As the CEO of PageFair, a company specializing in such tactics, noted, "Tamper-proof ad serving technology has matured to the point where publishers can serve ads on the blocked web."[30]

Whatever the local resistances and derogations, extracting data from a "naturally connected" world has become basic to the very nature of brands: "Understanding that customers are always connected and consuming . . . allows marketers to think of both their digital and offline touchpoints as one fluid and integrated brand presence."[31] This vision of an economy enhanced by the data-gathering possibilities created by "connection" is shared by both market capitalism and state-led capitalism. In China, it is continuous connection that underpins the government's vision of "a networked, intelligent, service-oriented, coordinated 'Internet Plus' industrial ecology system,"[32] a strategy that serves China's desire to acquire both greater economic independence from the West and greater influence within global digital capitalism.[33] In India, the Aadhaar unique ID system introduced in 2009 is creating huge new opportunities for data exploitation by both government *and* corporations, although it faces greater civil-society opposition than have parallel developments so far in China.[34] Such *costs to human autonomy* are not accidental but intrinsic to emerging logics of connection that treat the continuous monitoring of human subjects as not exceptional but "natural."

Colonizing Social Relations

Like historical colonialism, data colonialism would be inherently unstable if it could not translate its methods into more enduring forms of social relations. As Nick Dyer-Witheford pointed out in an early analysis, capitalism has always approached the internet as a domain in which control over the communicative capacity of individuals would allow capital to appropriate not just labor but also, as Marx himself put it, "its network of social relations."[35] Data colonialism extends this network well beyond communicative capacities, ensuring the continuity of data appropriation across an expanding array of social relations.

At the core of data colonialism is the creation of a new type of social relation that we call "data relations," as defined in detail later. Data relations make the appropriation of human beings' data seem normal, just the way things are. Data relations are of many sorts, but all share one basic feature: they ensure informational resources (data) for capitalism in areas of human life that, previously, were not considered direct inputs to production.[36] Far outside the sphere of normal productive activity, ordinary social interaction is increasingly lived in environments of continuous data collection, behavior prediction, and choice shaping. But this is possible only because social actors now enter more or less voluntarily into data relations that secure regular data flows for capital. The drive to expand data relations explains a lot about contemporary capitalism. So, for example, it is the need to make data relations routine everywhere that drives Facebook's offer of simplified internet connection (Facebook Free Basics) in more than twenty countries with weak or uneven internet infrastructure, principally in Africa. The emergence of data relations increasingly complements labor relations' contribution to capitalism's reproduction.

Meanwhile, existing social relations (including labor relations) for hundreds of millions of people are increasingly datafied—that is, managed through data, including data gathered from the surfaces or insides of workers' bodies. Work, for many, increasingly occurs within the sort of corporate environment of sensors that Davenport imagined; in its absoluteness, this recalls the continuous surveillance, if not the violence, that slave labor endured on a large scale under historical colonialism.[37] Labor relations are becoming more directly and continuously extractive, whatever the formalities that cloak them.[38] This has implications too for inequality, as exposure to (or freedom from) continuous surveillance becomes a key factor that distinguishes lower-status from higher-status jobs.

New forms of labor are also emerging under data colonialism in the "sharing economy." Here data relations are fused with labor relations, although the existence of labor relations is controversially denied by platforms such as Uber.[39] These new *hybrid data/labor relations* encompass a huge variety of more or less formalized work, including data processing.[40] Labor is captured in a seemingly "scale-less" business model that detaches workers from institutional supports but richly rewards platform management. Rhetoric cannot disguise the potential for exploiting low-level work skills at a distance and therefore at a scale and speed without historical precedent (for example, the repetitive coding and data inputting necessary for the training of artificial intelligence in so-called Machine Learning).[41]

The relations between state and economy are also being transformed. Data relations give corporations a privileged window into the world of social relations and a privileged handle on the levers of social differentiation. States have become increasingly dependent on access to what the corporate sector knows about the lives of those states' citizens, reversing the long-subsisting direction of knowledge transfer (from states to corporations). Although the resulting relations have become hugely controversial in the West (consider Apple's high-profile battle with the FBI over the encryption of its iPhones), in other states such as China the government has been heavily involved in encouraging platform development, in part *because of* their surveillance potential. As Jack Ma, CEO of Alibaba, put it, "The political and legal system of the future is inseparable from the internet, inseparable from big data."[42] Meanwhile in India, Paytm, a mobile payment system (or digital wallet) used by 230 million people in which

Alibaba has a 40 percent stake, has faced scandal over its sharing of users' personal data with the government.[43]

Because data reinterprets the traces of the everyday world, large-scale data processing recalibrates social knowledge, with the consequences depending on the type of market society under analysis. In liberal market societies, the new data infrastructure involves for the first time market institutions in producing basic social knowledge. But in state-led market societies, such as China, the state acquires a remarkable new tool to *direct* the production of social knowledge in its own interests. It is now an explicit goal of the Chinese government to use artificial intelligence to "establish [an] intelligent monitoring platform for comprehensive community management." Direct social governance shaped by data colonialism becomes not a distant ideal but a practical reality. The result, as the Chinese government put it with no apparent irony, is "a market improvement of the economic and social order."[44]

New Colonial Corporations

Another way in which capitalism's new interrelations with data deserve to be called colonial is the massively unequal global distribution of economic power on which they are based. Chapter 2 will provide much more detail, but for now, here are the basics.

There is the ownership or control of the processes of data collection, which gives special power to whoever owns or controls the hardware and software that collects and analyzes data. Some analytics companies operate at huge scale: in 2014 Acxiom notoriously claimed seven hundred million customers worldwide and over three thousand pieces of information for every US citizen![45] The most dramatic example is Google, which, even though banned in China, still controlled 82 percent of the global search engine market in 2018, collecting data from us every time we use it.[46] There is also ownership or control of the "ecologies" within which data is collected, such as digital platforms and apps of various sorts. In terms of human users, these processes and ecologies of data collection are vast, and the resulting concentration of advertising power correspondingly huge: 72 percent of global advertising spending is in the hands of Google and Facebook.[47]

From this base, huge investments in data analysis techniques become possible, with so called deep learning increasingly central to the largest IT businesses. From early on, the vision of Google's founders was "AI complete." Much later, IBM announced in 2017 that it "is now a cognitive solutions and cloud platform company," while Microsoft reorganized itself in March 2018 to prioritize its cloud services and AI businesses.[48] The retailers Amazon and Walmart are giant data processing operations. But this is only the start of the layered power concentration that data colonialism enables.

There are many additional layers of colonial-style ownership. One is domination over production of the "tethered" devices through which human beings connect to the infrastructures of data collection (by "tethered," we mean a device whose use ties users to reliance on a particular operating system or set of proprietary products: think of Apple but also of the use restrictions built into most portable devices).[49] Another is power over the computing capacity that enables large-scale processing and storage of data, usually known as the cloud, a mystificatory term.[50] (Amazon by the end of 2017 already had 51.8 percent of global market share, rivaled only by Microsoft with 13.3 percent, the Chinese Alibaba with 4.6 percent, and Google with 3.3 percent.)[51] Important also are the remarkable monopolies in content delivery, whether monopolies over last-mile internet connection or phone spectrum: consider the near monopoly power of broadband providers such as Verizon in the United States, which has driven the recent US net neutrality debates.[52] Finally, as internet content circulation becomes ever more massified,[53] there are new forms of control over the production of content (think of Netflix's growing commissioning power or the pricing power over books and music of Amazon and Apple).

These layers of power concentration offer to citizens and consumers a world that is highly connected, but the quality of connection is distinctly uneven. Beyond questions of individual access, countries vary in the robustness of their internet connectivity, while intercontinental cable laying is becoming a growth area for the social quantification sector itself.[54] Although the exact distribution of the benefits of these power concentrations will no doubt evolve, at this point the global domination of a web of US companies and a small group of Chinese companies is secure.

New Colonial Ideologies

Such profound shifts in how value is extracted, social relations are organized, and economic power is distributed require narratives that reframe them in more acceptable terms. This is another aspect in which today's developments bear comparison with historical colonialism. Data colonialism is producing its own new ideologies.

First, there is the ideology of connection itself, which presents as natural the connection of persons, things, and processes via a computer-based infrastructure (the internet) that enables life to be annexed to capital. Connection is, of course, a basic human value, but the *requirement* to connect here and now—connect to *this particular* deeply unequal infrastructure—means submission to very particular conditions and terms of power. Perhaps the most frank admission of connection's ideological role came in an internal memo, later discounted by its author, that Andrew Bosworth, a Facebook vice president, posted in June 2016: "We connect people. Period. That's why all the work we do in growth is justified. All the questionable contact-importing practices. All the subtle language that helps people stay searchable by friends. All of the work we do to bring more communication in. The work we will likely have to do in China someday. All of it."[55]

There is also the ideology of datafication,[56] which insists that every aspect of life must be transmuted into data as the form in which all life becomes useful for capital. Practically, this means not just attachment to a computer connection but the removal of any obstacles to corporate extraction and control of data once that connection is established. The point is not that data itself is bad but that the compulsion to turn every life stream into data flows removes what was once an obstacle to extracting value from those life streams.

The marketing ideology of personalization makes such tracking and surveillance seem attractive. Who after all would *not* want a service more geared to his or her particular wants and needs? The argument, very simply, is that personally targeted messages require prior information that can come only from . . . targeted surveillance! Yet evangelists for data-driven personalization still feel the need to defend this ideology aggressively, as when Acxiom, in a 2015 opinion survey, characterized acceptance of continuous data collection as "pragmatist" (fair enough) and opposition to it as "fundamentalist" (itself rather an extremist statement).[57]

These specific ideologies are examples of "dataism."[58] They are tools for shaping practice and thus highly specific in their applications. They are often combined with an overarching imaginative claim that we might call myth: the myth that all this is inevitable and that today's infrastructures of connection and data extraction fulfill human beings' collective potential in some transcendent way.[59] The term *community*, as something seemingly inherent to human life, can easily fuel this myth. Think not just of Mark Zuckerberg's frequent appeals to Facebook's "global community" but also of the Tencent CEO's invocation of a "digital ecological community."[60] This ideology of inevitability also has its counterpart in ideas on the anticapitalist left that treat networks as the basis for a leap toward overthrowing capitalism.[61]

Colonialism's and Capitalism's New Embrace

Data colonialism has a distinctive geography. Like historical colonialism, data colonialism is global in its ambitions, but unlike it, it penetrates the life conditions of individuals across all societies, wherever they are, that are being reshaped around digital infrastructures of connection. Data colonialism's expansion is therefore both external (geographical) and internal (social). Given that the drive to appropriate data is fueling China as much as, if not more than, it is the West, it makes no sense to read data colonialism as exclusively a Western project. Seeing today's transformations *bifocally*—through the lens of both capitalism and colonialism—is essential to understanding their complex global dynamics. We cannot clearly see the scale of capitalism's current appropriation of human life without a colonial lens, and we cannot understand the force of this new colonial appropriation without understanding how capitalism operates through processes of social ordering.[62]

Indeed, capitalism's standard ways of understanding itself as a rational order are effective in masking the colonial scale of appropriation that is underway. Much of today's data appropriations are not seen in daily life as appropriation at all but as part of everyday business practice. As such, data relations introduce into business management a new bureaucracy, as first theorized by Max Weber.[63] This bureaucracy is based on the apparent "rationality" of organizations' continuous data extraction. Here, as earlier in history, capitalism expands by operating as a system of meaningful social relations, reading the world this time as a mass of valuable data sources.[64]

Older critiques of historical capitalism can provide valuable insights here. One important idea is that of the "fetish." For Karl Marx, the fetish (classically the "commodity fetish") made the economic relations of capitalism *seem* necessary. Marx delineated a trinity of fetishized objects: interest as the fruit of capital, rent as the fruit of land, and wage as the fruit of labor.[65] Now we can add a fourth object: data as the fruit of life processes.[66] This is exactly how business now speaks (think of the mantra of data as the new oil).[67]

Another deep continuity with classic Marxist accounts comes from the data-driven possibilities of management control over production. The core of how industrial capitalism transformed work was not technological but social. The organization of work came under the exclusive control of management and, as such, became controllable at every stage of performance.[68] Traditional industrial management remained limited, however, to mechanical data collection based in observation or form filling. By contrast, data-driven logistics, built on infrastructures of connection and fueled by artificial intelligence, convert *all* aspects of production—far beyond the factory walls and in every corner and moment of a transnational supply chain—into a managed assembly line. The new infrastructure of data processing that sustains data relations extends so-called scientific management in ways that recall classic diagnoses of industrial capitalism: "The image of the process, removed from production to a separate location and a separate group, controls the process itself."[69] Through data, capitalism begins to govern the *whole social domain* with management logic, another aspect of its annexation of human life.

Having sketched the basic features of data colonialism, let's look a little deeper into the capitalist social order that emerges *through* data colonialism.

Data and the Emerging Social Order of Capitalism

Every aspect of data colonialism can be understood in terms of its contribution to a fundamental principle of capitalism: the drive to *maximize control of the inputs to its production process.*[70] This requires a reasonably ordered state of the social world that makes markets possible and functional. In all societies characterized by increasingly overwhelming information flows, the premium on society's legibility, even its basic countability, grows.[71] In capitalist societies that are not democracies, such as China, capitalism's desire for the control of production inputs works hand in hand with government's unrestrained desire to control all inputs to the social order.

This newly intensified role for both capitalism and governments in managing social life became possible only through the unprecedented technological opportunities for connection that we know collectively as the internet. Their origins lie in investment from the US Cold War military-industrial complex and subsequent massive corporate investment that transformed the internet into a global space for corporate networking and transnational market coordination.[72] Through the internet and its embedding into everyday life and business emerged something else: the possibility of a *new type* of economic and social order.

Note that we are not claiming that this order is completely discontinuous with the past. Certainly, data colonialism builds on the earlier growth of technological systems across most aspects of human life, something that German philosopher Jürgen Habermas metaphorically calls the "colonization" of lifeworld by system. But *that* process has been underway for more than a century and lacks the distinctive order of data colonialism.[73] It is important also, once more, not to just see this as a story about the West. After all, Tencent had already financed its fast-growing online chat platforms by a public flotation in 2004, the year Zuckerberg was launching Facebook. Neither is this just a story about Western values such as possessive individualism with which capitalism's growth has long been associated. For what today's infrastructures of connection make possible is a new economic and social formation in which the orders of "liberal" democracies and "authoritarian" societies become increasingly indistinguishable.[74]

How then is this new type of order being built?

A New Social Order for Capitalism . . . Everywhere

The technological infrastructures of connection that have emerged in the past three decades have enabled a deep reorganization of social space and time, indeed, of social order. As Langdon Winner put it, "Technologies are ways of building order in the world."[75]

The starting point was disarmingly simple. Computers are universal machines in the sense that they can perform an unlimited number of operations; computers are able to model any aspect of the world that can, in principle, be modeled.[76] But computers *work* by capturing and archiving data about their own operations: they capture "changes of state" that follow from a keyboard action or other internal process.[77] Such capture is a form of translation, representing computer actions (and whatever external realities they model) in a language that enables them to be processed by the computer's "grammar" for storing information. This captured data becomes the basis for demanding future changes of state. When computers are inserted into social space (because human beings use them), this capturing facility becomes available to reshape that social space too. Long before the general availability of the internet, sociologist Shoshana Zuboff predicted that the computerization of inputs to production would transform the workplace by changing flows of information and the forms of authority and power sustained by those flows.[78]

Added to such basic data capture came the possibility of interconnection between computers through the internet. In a small network, the implications of data capture would have been limited, but when the push to commercialize the internet came with the World Wide Web, the introduction of commercial browsers (Mosaic and then Netscape), and the US government's decisive transfer of ownership of the internet's infrastructure from the state to commercial hands, decisive consequences for social life were to follow.[79] If the massive increase in popularity of personal desktops and laptops transformed the consumer market, it was paralleled by the growth of computer-based networking in the business world, an expansion in which the United States played a dominant role.[80] All these developments transformed the internet from a bounded "public infrastructure"[81] to an infinitely extendable space of connection across which global capital could freely range, under the auspices of the libertarian policy agenda sweeping the United States in the 1990s.[82] Move forward another ten years, and, through portable devices with connectivity (smartphones and then tablets), the internet stopped being something statically available from particular points in space and became a dimension that overlays social space continuously. As Rob Kitchin and Martin Dodge put it, "Software . . . alters the conditions through which society, space and time, and thus spatiality, are produced."[83] As a result, the internet, understood as an infrastructure of connection, has reconstituted social space in a fundamental way. In one sense, this was always the vision of IT pioneers. Tim Berners-Lee insisted in 1999 that "hope in life comes from the interconnections along all the people in the world."[84] But such connection was only the start of a larger transformation.

Combine vastly extended interconnection with that basic feature of computers (they capture data), and the result is the beginning of a radical new possibility: that each computer's archive of its own history becomes available to be tracked *and influenced* by any other computer anywhere in the internet's vast universe of networks. Human beings themselves, as regular users of those computers and their archives, became, in principle, "trackable and tractable."[85] The actualization of this theoretical possibility resulted from multiple commercial innovations, spurred by various forms of necessity and opportunism. It was marketers, plagued by the perennial difficulty of reaching customers with their messages, who took advantage first with the humble cookie, capable only of tracking people on single devices,[86] and more recently with techniques that link online data with offline behavior or use a social media ID to combine data about various online selves. The invention of social media platforms in which every user move is automatically tracked was a major further step. The data benefit unleashed to social media providers such as Facebook was huge: through its Open Graph program, Facebook gained access to what users did not only on Facebook but also on every platform that users accessed via their Facebook ID—for example, Spotify.[87] The result is what the industry, with-

out irony, calls "people-based marketing."[88] Meanwhile, Google's alliance
in 2008 with online advertising company DoubleClick brought together
Google's mastery of linking search activity to searchers' interests and
DoubleClick's tracking of individuals based on their unique data profiles.
Under Google's control, the combination of the two approaches greatly in-
creased the information that could be matched with unique individuals.

The growth of computer-to-computer monitoring for marketing purposes was only part of a more general growth, starting in the 1980s, in the
monitoring and shaping of life at a distance. Much of this data gathering
requires no subterfuge, because it is a basic mode of operation in corporate
intranets, networks of environmental sensors, and scientific data collection—that is, "new types of sensors are constantly becoming available."[89]
Elsewhere the possibility of generating value through data by tracking users became a taken-for-granted feature of an online world whose resources
were generally "free" but accessible only within a space in which sensing
is built-in: the world of connected computers.[90] The embedding of sensing
into everyday life is not something that users can control, however. Rather,
since those tracking capacities are grounded in the basic software through
which computers run, they introduce an internal form of order that is projected outward onto everyday life. The parallels with political and social
order are not accidental. As Wendy Chun puts it, computer "code is exe-
cutable because it embodies the power of . . . enforcement that has traditionally been the provenance of government."[91]

This power goes far beyond platforms' data gathering, even though it
is the accountability of platform power that attracts the most debate.[92] The
perspective of IBM on what it calls "digital disruption" (the rise of digital
social platforms and infrastructures that were believed to challenge IBM's
power as a long-existing market "incumbent") is striking:

> Many believed that the world's incumbent businesses were at risk of being
> marginalized. We had a different point of view. We did not believe the plat-
> form giants alone would dominate a data-centric economy—in large mea-
> sure because they lack access to the most valuable sources of the world's data:
> the 80 percent that is not searchable on the Web. The world's incumbent busi-
> nesses and institutions own and generate this data.[93]

Much of data colonialism's force in the social world comes from corporations of all types, with or without social media platforms, colonizing the world around them through the extraction of data.

Through these various steps, the capacity *to order the social world continuously and with maximal efficiency* has become, for the first time, a goal for corporate power and state power. Our computers and phones, and even our bodies if they carry trackable devices, become targets of this new form of power.

Two possibilities result that, before digital connection, were literally beyond the imagining of corporations or states. The first is to annex every point in space and every layer of life process to forms of tracking and control. After all, everything is in principle now connected. The second is to transform and influence behavior at every point so that this apparently shocking annexation of life to power comes to seem a natural feature of the social domain. Far from being imposed from above, this double transformation, like industrial capitalism in Marx's understanding, makes sense only as a deeply social transformation in which members of contemporary societies have agency, even if not much power.

From this transformation of the building blocks of social life follow other consequences that earlier social worlds had not foreshadowed.

Social power relations have become reversible in alarming ways. Think of our relations to everyday tools. Tools are basic to our sense of having individual agency in the world. But, as the Internet of Things expands, there will eventually be few everyday tools that do not have the capacity to monitor us, collecting data about how we use them and possibly about other ambient data of value to the tool's makers.[94] One example is Google, the search engine that records our searches in order to "search" us; another is "intelligent personal assistants" such as Amazon's Echo or Microsoft's Cortana[95] that, to work, must record how we interact with them. For now, people are still shocked to hear that their phones have a built-in capacity to listen to them, even when not making a call; in time, we may regard this as normal.

Yet a more connected social world will not necessarily be more secure. Indeed, there is no limit to the *instability* that an interconnected social order can generate. As Bruce Schneier argues, it is a fallacy to believe that more connection generates more security. On the contrary, since the possibilities of bad actors are infinite, more connection must generate more, not fewer, problems of security.[96] The average security robustness of connected space tends to fall as more points get connected. Devices in the Internet of Things (such as those that control fridges or thermostats) simply lack the computing power to have their security repatched remotely, unlike, say, desktop or laptop computers.[97] People cracking the code of baby monitors to speak to and scare children supposedly under digital protection are just graphic illustrations of a much deeper security problem, which in fact *serves* the interests of data extraction.[98]

Whether these things are serious concerns depends, of course, on whether the priority is the security of the individual or the security of the state. For a state like China, a more intensely connected system is likely to be an advantage, making freedom the problem and internal data colonialism potentially the solution. This helps us make sense of China's revolutionary new "social credit system"—rather shocking to the West.[99] The program aims to launch in 2020 and is expected to pool all information about the creditworthiness and social worth of Chinese citizens into a single interlinked system for monitoring and evaluation.[100] China's huge platform growth (especially of Alibaba and Tencent) in the past five years provides the core infrastructure for this project, but those platforms are building their own supposedly separate systems of credit rating (Sesame Credit and Tencent Credit).

In both liberal market societies and authoritarian market states, data colonialism's consequences for social inequality are dramatic. This stems from a basic feature not of computers but of data. The purpose of collecting data is always to differentiate:[101] data's purpose is to generate information that usefully discriminates between entities. Again, discrimination in itself is not bad: we want a heart recorder that correctly distinguishes between a heartbeat and other bodily signals. The issue is how data discriminations are applied within the framework of existing structures of social discrimination. Today's vast infrastructures of connection, like all forms of power, build on existing inequality. But they also create new forms of inequality through various means: inequalities of data capital,[102] exploitation of the human labor that sustains Machine Learning, and the ability of data-driven categorizations to reinforce those existing inequalities. Just as the capitalization of work through labor relations has over time produced a highly unequal distribution of the profits generated by labor, so over time we can expect the capitalization of life through data relations to introduce new forms of inequality into human life itself. We can increasingly expect human beings to be socially managed *in terms* of their data value—that is, their value as data inputs to capitalist production.

Platforms' Role in Stabilizing Capitalism

How, practically, does capitalism, whether in its pure market or state-sponsored forms, try to hold together this emerging social order? Capitalism needs primary relations of data extraction to at least be stable, predictable, and convergent. One key tool for ensuring this is the digital *platform*, whose basic function we outline here.

Platforms are structured online spaces, made possible through elaborate software, that offer services of various sorts: a space to sell things, meet people, share information, find specialist resources, and so on. But they are also fundamentally spaces for data extraction. As Tarleton Gillespie puts it, platforms are "built on an infrastructure . . . for processing data for customer service, advertising, and profit" that makes them "oriented toward eliciting more data, and more kinds of data, from [their] users."[103] Platforms generally operate without explicit payment. The actual "payment" that the platform operator receives is usually based directly on the data extracted, though often also in part on data-driven advertising. The data "payment" is more interesting than the advertising payment. It can be either the value that the operator generates by packaging and selling to third parties the data it gathers about transactions and users (the commodity value) or the value that the operator raises by giving others access to its data (what we might call the rent value). Either way, surplus value is generated, although in a connected space of infinite size; economic success requires platforms to achieve a sufficient scale of operation to realize that surplus value effectively.

As part of their basic business model, platforms operate as multiway data auctions, linking users, data buyers and users, and of course the platform itself. As Julie Cohen explains, the basic structure of platforms gives their operators a remarkable power to organize parallel series of economic relations through adaptable arrangements,[104] with each series arranged through the platform's interface software. This convening power of platforms creates a recentralizing force that requires all actors to make their content "platform ready."[105] That force is based on platforms' power to control the degree and type of data extraction that is the "price" ordinary platform users must pay.

Platforms create an interface without historical precedent: an interchange in which social life in its open-ended variety *interfaces seamlessly* with the forces of economic extraction. This seamlessness is not natural any more than data is naturally raw. It must be constructed through the painstaking removal of barriers to data flow within and between platforms; seamlessness is an achievement, in part, of software that enables platforms to produce "the social" for capital. This explains the deeply ambiguous status of the largest and most successful platforms, such as Facebook, which is expected to speak for and even regulate the social world because of the power that running a platform with two billion users gives it. Major platform power in China (Alibaba and Tencent) is even more ambitious, developing a triple interface across social, economic, *and* financial worlds to provide a new practical infrastructure for the world's largest society. These models of economic power and social order depend on the unspoken principle of seamlessness: every barrier to data flow is a barrier to the unlimited production of social life in forms that can generate data for capital.[106]

The largest platforms distribute their presence across the internet via plug-ins that allow platform users, wherever they are, to link back to the resources of the platform, creating even more possibilities for aggregating data continuously across space and time.[107] These power concentrations depend on the emerging social centrality of these platforms in a genuine sense, for we really *do* go onto platforms because we know others will be there (the so-called network effect). That is why platforms are fast becoming meaningful social infrastructures too.[108] In these various ways, platforms are a principal organizational form through which capitalism's connected social and economic order is being realized.[109] They are a key tool for ensuring that the colonial-scale appropriation of data for human life becomes the norm. As networks, some platforms are larger than most nation-states. The largest platforms conceive of themselves accordingly. As Zuckerberg put it, "In a lot of ways Facebook is more like a government than a traditional company."[110] The longer-term implications for legal, political, and social power are as yet unknown. One key way in which platforms produce the social for capitalism is through a new type of local social relation that stabilizes our habits of connection. Our term for this is *data relations*. Let's look at these relations in a little more detail.

Data Relations

Data relations are the emerging social form through which data colonialism as an extractive process gets stabilized between individuals, groups, and corporations, and so it comes reliably to contribute to capitalism's emerging new social order.[111] By "data relations" we do not mean relations between data but the new types of *human* relations that data as a potential commodity enables. In time, data relations are likely to become as naturalized as labor relations.

Some forms of data relations—for example, within a corporation that has the residual power to collect data across its activities—are operational and require no additional level of social agreement. But in many other cases a relation has to be constituted in such a way that it enables data to flow in the first place. Once constituted, the seeming naturalness of the relation frames the resulting data as something that can be validly extracted from the flow of life. Without the act of extraction there would be no identifiable item of data and thus no separate right to extract that data. It is the stability of data relations that enables data extraction to seem both valid and beyond challenge. This is another consequence of the basic point already noted, that data is not natural but a resource whose extractive possibilities must themselves be socially constructed, just as physical nature had to be reconfigured so that it could be exploited by capital.[112]

Data Relations: Their Key Features
To be an effective foundation for a new type of social order, data relations need not have the solidity we imagine in many work contracts. Indeed, Zuboff plausibly argues that much data extraction today is not a contract

or relation at all, in that data just seems to get extracted at a distance.[113]
But the wider set of arrangements on which data colonialism relies would
be ineffective unless they operated as *something like* a social form that
seems both natural and normal, quite unlike an arbitrary act of theft or
extraction. It is this social form we call data relations; data relations enable the basic processes of social construction on which the stabilization of
data colonialism depends for the long term.

We can expect the varieties of data relations to grow massively as data
colonialism itself expands. To get at the core of what we mean by a data relation, imagine yourself entering a spiral. The entry point is that at which,
for whatever reason, you enter the ambit of computer monitoring. Computer tracking is now so basic to the social world that it might seem hard to
imagine one *not* already being within that ambit, but, even so, at any moment there is always likely to be at least one specific transaction in which
you are engaged that motivates the capture of particular life traces from
you. It could be using a search engine, investigating a particular website,
searching for a product at a good price, using a platform, or dealing with
an institution (say, a school, corporation, or government). Sometimes the
entry point will derive from an extra step you have taken—for example, attaching a tracker to your body or accepting a tracker's presence nearby as
you perform a task.

You have, wittingly or unwittingly, entered the spiral of data relations.
But those relations may or may not be based on consent. Implied consent,
even if unenthusiastic, is common to many platform situations. Often
rolled into this consent is acknowledgment of the platform owners' claim
to thereby own the data, even though this is rarely made explicit; if it was,
it would likely be contested more often. Incorporated also is consent to
other, more subtle conditions that are required to convert the flow of a person's life into material for valuable data extraction in combination with
the parallel flows of data about others' lives. The information that Facebook requests before you join the platform illustrates this: What is your
birthday? What school did you go to? And the like.

In most cases, however, there has been little consent to data collection
as such, although recent European legislation, the General Data Protection
Regulation, seeks to change this, at least in a formal sense. Yet, in agree-

ing to or accepting data collection, people may have a pressing need to secure a service of some sort (just as a labor contract is held together by the worker's need to sell her labor power for money so she can buy the necessities of life). Through data relations, for example, we access connection (platforms where everyone else we know is a user) and services that are basic to daily life, such as insurance. Service providers may claim they need to track us continuously to provide that service, or they may require registration through an identifying feature (say, a social media login) that draws us into releasing even more data.

Sometimes there is no consent to data relations at all, just brute necessity. One example is when people wear a sensor or tracker, on order of their employer, as they move around their work space. Another example is when, as in China's Xianjiang province in February 2017, the government banned petrol sales to anyone without GPS tracking installed in his or her car.[114] The logical limit of consent is when—as is increasingly common in China today—paying for transactions or just walking around public space involves facial recognition by algorithmically enhanced tracking systems linked to national databases. The development of systems that manage these barely consensual relations is a growth area: the Beijing company Face ++ was valued at $1.5 billion *before* its latest fund-raising from the Chinese and Russian sovereign wealth funds.[115]

Not all data is immediately available to be commodified. Indeed, much data gathered by corporations may lack a value until a specific use for it can be found in the context of much larger data sets. But some data—for example, about potential interest in a purchase signaled when a link is clicked—may have a precise value on an advertising auction platform such as Google's Adsense and Alibaba's Alimama. Whether immediately commodifiable or not, the data extracted has potential value in a wider space of equivalence in which the individual's distinctive properties as a data source can be ignored (this abstractness is exactly how Marx understood commodification to operate).[116] The commodification of exchangeable data is the end goal of data relations and is, as Matthew Crain notes, "the root of [their] power imbalances."[117]

The final turn of the data relations spiral comes when categorizations derived from the processing of your data are applied back onto you, the human subject, from whom the data was derived, whether or not you are identified by name. Data subjects often attempt to modulate their behavior in order to influence the algorithm that they believe is categorizing them. But however well meaning, this ignores the basic point: that just by *going on* with the activity that brought us into data extraction's ambit, we confirm data relations' continued force.

Through the regular, compressed repetition of these elements in myriad forms, data extraction starts to become part of the natural order of things.[118]

Updating Marx for the Age of Big Data

There is an echo of Marx in what we have said so far about data relations, but our argument is not in line with orthodox Marxism.[119]

Many remember from Marx the idea that capitalism's social order is based on labor relations: the transformation of what was once just productive activity into labor power. Labor power has the abstract measurable dimension of a commodity that can be exchanged in a market for money. Under capitalism, workers stop being "a part of the conditions of production (as in slavery or serfdom),"[120] and their labor power becomes something they can sell as a commodity. But if that were all there was to Marx's social theory, it would not help us understand a world in which, as we have seen, capitalism's underlying drive to capitalize life itself has taken on new forms that are not all routed through labor—that is, what is understood in some sense as productive activity. We are concerned here with the annexation to capital of life processes *whether or not* they are labor, evidenced when many of the life streams from which data is extracted for value are not seen by those involved as part of any productive activity.[121]

What is core to the new capitalist social order is that ordinary social interaction today contributes to surplus value not as labor but as a factor of production.[122] Human life is being incorporated within a vastly expanded production process and, as such, faces increasing pressure to be commodified, whether as data for which platforms get paid in some form or (in the vision of some reformers) as a form of disguised labor power, for which those reformers propose platform users get paid.[123] The key point is not whether some payment results but that the data traces of our activities are under pressure to be commodified at all.[124] This is the central change underway, and it flows not from the transformation of labor via digital platforms but from something deeper: *an expansion of the whole process of capitalist production and the factors that contribute to it* to encompass the flow of human life in all its open-endedness. In the long run, this expansion of production may develop into an entirely new "mode of production," in Marx's term, but just a decade or so into datafication, it is premature to name this yet.

In arguing this, we are following Marx, but we are doing so in a way that works creatively with his social theory for the age of data colonialism. We draw here on a radical reinterpretation of Marx offered by the late Moishe Postone. This reinterpretation reads Marx as proposing that the fundamental social form of capitalism is not labor relations but rather the commodification that underlies, for example, the transformation of everyday work *into* labor relations.[125] We say "for example" because on this reading of Marx, other transformations through commodification are possible, and not only in the domain of work. Marx himself seemed to envisage just such a broadening of commodification when he wrote that "as capitalist production i.e. capital develops the general laws governing the commodity evolve in proportion."[126] As already noted, Marx discusses how the materials workers use in the labor process themselves acquire exchange value as commodities, and so, for example, seeds and manure become commodities under capitalism, even though before capitalism they were just part of the normal cycle of land use.[127]

On this reading of Marx, at the core of industrial capitalism's long-term transformation of the social world was how work (the everyday productive activities that have gone on since the beginning of time) acquired an abstract dimension that enabled it to be commodified, that is, turned into a commodity that could be exchanged.[128] It is this possibility of *abstracting value from life processes*, even when they are not directly productive activities, that leaves open the prospect of new types of commodified social relations and, through them, a new social order for capitalism.

We know that data is produced by abstracting the processes of human life into measurable bits and types. We know also that data is not simply abstracted from us automatically but through arrangements and relations into which we are assumed to have voluntarily entered at some point, even if retrospectively. Meanwhile, data is being increasingly, though as yet unevenly, commodified. Therefore, our proposal is simple: that just as industrial capitalism, according to Marx, changed society by transforming the universal human activity of work into a social form with an abstract dimension (via the commodification of labor), so capitalism today, in the expansionary phase we call data colonialism, is transforming human nature (that is, preexisting streams of human life in all its diversity) into a newly abstracted social form (data) that is also ripe for commodification.

It is this transformation that is the larger context for the datafication of labor relations that many critics have noted.[129] It is this transformation also that links the appropriations of data colonialism to contemporary capitalism's latest lines of expansion. But the outcome is hardly something to celebrate. For the unwelcome truth is that, just as in Marx's eyes capitalism had disrupted human beings' relations with physical nature, in the era of data colonialism, capitalism risks disturbing humanity's relations to *its* nature—that is, our lives as reflexive, relatively autonomous human beings. Data colonialism interposes infrastructures of data extraction directly into the texture of human life and so risks deforming human experience in a fundamental way, invading the space of the self on which the values of autonomy and freedom in all their forms depend.[130]

Our Argument within the Wider Debate about Data and Capitalism

Why is it that so far we have talked simply of *capitalism* and not *digital capitalism, informational capitalism, communicative capitalism, platform capitalism,* or *surveillance capitalism,* to name some rival terms?[131] The reason is straightforward. No convincing argument has yet been made that capitalism today is anything other than what it has always been: the systematic organization of life so as to maximize value, resulting in the concentration of power and wealth in very few hands. Contemporary societies are marked by the ever-increasing importance of the circulation and processing of information. As we emphasized earlier, this accelerated circulation and extraction of data and information has had profound impacts on the management of business, on the organization of work, and on the integration of social life into the economy. But that is no reason to say that the fundamental drivers of capitalism have suddenly changed; they have not.

Therefore, when we use the term *capitalism* with a contemporary reference, we mean capitalism as it is now developing in societies in which "the production, accumulation and processing of information" is growing.[132] Surveillance is certainly part of this, again as we have emphasized, but not sufficiently to brand today's capitalism as surveillance capitalism. For, within the longer history of colonialism *and* capitalism, surveillance has often been the accompaniment to the direct appropriation of laboring bodies for value (think of the slave plantation).[133] What is new today is not so much surveillance but rather the networks of social relations in which vastly extended modes of appropriating human life through data work to order economic and social life as a whole. That is the larger picture we see by working simultaneously with the concepts of data colonialism and capitalism.

It might also seem surprising that, up to this point, our argument has not referred to neoliberalism. The concept of neoliberalism, most thoroughly developed by Michel Foucault, is enormously important for grasping the cultural, political, and social means by which capitalism has been reproduced and reinforced in the late twentieth and early twenty-first centuries.[134] There is no question of its continuing relevance. Indeed, some recent accounts of neoliberalism, such as Wendy Brown's, come close to ours in their overall diagnosis of what is wrong in capitalist societies.[135] That is because neoliberal politics from the 1980s onward transformed culture and politics by insisting that market functioning should govern all of life, not just formal economic processes, thus justifying many forms of market deregulation and financialization as well as the invasion of market logics into spheres previously protected from them. As such, neoliberalism has contributed to the general *preconditions* of data colonialism and specifically to preparing people for the intimate relation to capitalism that data relations bring. But data colonialism goes beyond neoliberalism by *literally annexing* human life directly to the economy and reorganizing it fundamentally in the process. When data colonialism is complete, there will be no need for the ideology of neoliberalism, since there will be nothing left of human life *except* materials for potential commodification. At that future point, the boundary around social and personal life that neoliberal logics once transgressed will have dissolved, revealing data colonialism as neoliberalism's ultimate horizon.[136]

Finally, what of this book's relation to the many Marxist readings, particularly in the Autonomist tradition, of digital networks and social media platforms as the launchpad for ending capitalism? There are two important points to be made here. First, we acknowledge that some might see in our analysis of the "capitalization of life itself" merely a replay of the Autonomists' 1960s analysis of capitalism's social expansion. Indeed, today's exposure of daily life to capitalist forces of datafication does seem superficially similar to the well-known Autonomist notion of the "social factory," which argued that the capitalist organization of work had extended from the factory to the whole of society.[137] But Autonomists were rather vague about the mechanisms of this general intensification of capitalism's influence over social life, except when they claimed the structure and norms of capitalist work somehow expanded out into social life.[138] That idea gives us no grip at all on data colonialism, which, as we have shown, appropriates life as raw material whether or not it is actually labor, or even labor-like. Our temporal scale for appreciating these developments should be not so much the past half century of socializing capitalism, especially in Europe, but the centuries-long global cycle of colonialism's long intertwining with capitalism.

This takes us to a second key point. Because Autonomist analysis is based on a reading of capitalism's long-term social expansion that was *already* underway in the 1960s, it does not serve us well to assess the sites and potentials for resistance to this century's developments around data. What if human experience is becoming a condition or factor in capitalist production, with no agency *as such* to overthrow capitalism unless this integration into production is itself resisted?[139] What if today's networked social relations herald not a new awakening of the social spirit but capitalism's deepening *through* the reorganization of human life as a whole and not of labor specifically?[140] The latest Autonomist thinking certainly addresses the extraction of data[141] but argues that although the creative capacity of humanity is exploited by the social quantification sector,[142] this capacity remains somehow unaffected by the process, ready to jump into resistive action.[143] This ignores completely the pervasiveness of data colonialism as a form of extraction and the force with which it is being applied, whether in the workplace, in financial and legal transactions, or in our transformed understanding of the social world itself. And it ignores the power of data relations to restructure life for capital in societies such as China and Russia, where data colonialism proceeds under the auspices of an authoritarian state. As Michael Hardt and Antonio Negri write, "Behind the value of data . . . stands the wealth of social relationships, social intelligence, and social production."[144] But there is no "behind" in the space in which data colonialism operates; it is not a stage with a front and back but a force field, as powerful in the long run as the force field of labor relations that transformed the social world two centuries ago.

In this chapter, we have unpacked the double theoretical foundations of our argument: data colonialism and the emergence through data relations of a new capitalist social order. In the next chapter, we look more closely at the Cloud Empire that is emerging through the playing out of data colonialism on a global scale.

The Cloud Empire

2

Everything is free, except the video we capture of you. That we own. . . .
I'm going to sell you your life back.

—Josh Harris[1]

IN 1999, YEARS BEFORE FACEBOOK WAS FOUNDED and just as Google was getting out of a garage, Josh Harris not only predicted but enacted the future of the internet in an art project he called *Quiet: We Live in Public.* Harris was a brilliant yet somewhat disturbed entrepreneur who made a fortune by creating platforms that integrated user content and new media in visionary ways. For *Quiet,* he set up an underground bunker where volunteers lived for a month in hive-like conditions, cameras recording their every moment. Room, board, and amenities were provided free of charge. The experiment, which included Stasi-style interrogations and plenty of sex, drugs, and guns, ended in near catastrophe, but not before Harris had come up with the credo for the social quantification sector, captured in the preceding quotation.

Fast-forward a couple of decades. According to end-of-2017 market-capitalization values, if you are one of the two billion Android users in the world (Android being a "free" operating system), you represent a $363 value to Google. Each Facebook user (using the "free" website) is worth $233 to the company.[2] To parent company Tencent, based in China, each user of the "free" app WeChat represents a $539 value (at least before the significant fall of their stock in 2018).[3] Even when we pay for a service, the data obtained from us has considerable worth. A mobile phone company might record a user's location about three hundred times a day.[4] That company can then turn around and sell the data as part of an industry that generates $24 billion a year.[5] Josh Harris seems to have realized early on that an infrastructure was being created for a system of pervasive yet inconspicuous surveillance that quantified life and extracted profit from it. But how did his vision come to be so perfectly realized?

In this chapter, we are using the image of the Cloud Empire to suggest that along with advancements in the coordinating power of information and communication technologies, often portrayed as progress, we are seeing a regression to blatant forms of appropriation that have a lot in common with the economic logic of historical colonialism. Although the word *empire* has acquired hyperbolic undertones, evoked as a quick and convenient signifier of exploitation on a grand scale, we use it here purposefully and strategically as a way to unpack the organized and ongoing appropriation of social life through data. Unlike earlier forms of imperialism, the Cloud Empire is not founded on a particular state's overt military and political desire for control of territories. Instead, it operates more informally, seeking to make all of life available to capitalization through data not by brute force but by sustaining the expansion of exploitable spaces.

As discussed in the previous chapter, data colonialism is what happens when human life becomes an input for capitalism. That human life should acquire this particular status under a capitalist system is not strange or new. After all, capitalism seeks to commodify everything,[6] so everything potentially becomes its input. But how "everything" is defined at a specific historical moment is what requires attention. What is unique about our historical moment, we argue, is that human life *as organized through data relations* becomes the direct input of capitalism, a condition that we describe as specifically and newly colonial.

One factor that makes the Cloud Empire colonial is the logistical and martial ethos of the enterprise of expansion. Colonialism requires an infrastructure that facilitates the movement of resources, and what makes the Cloud Empire colonial is the scale and scope of this worldwide network of extraction and distribution, which is managed through increasingly sophisticated logistics. And we should not forget the debt that the concept and sometimes the practice of logistics owes to the military spirit.

The smooth movement of resources along global supply chains is a movement in which corporations and armies have often supported each other during colonial times. To be sure, Amazon does not require its own army, like the East India Company did. But as Deborah Cowen argues, logistics "[map] the form of contemporary imperialism,"[7] and as Ned Rossiter points out, "Increasingly, logistics infrastructure is managed through computational systems of code and software,"[8] that is, through data. Thus, we can see data relations as part of a highly organized system of economic extraction and market penetration, a system founded on logistics.

Another factor that makes the Cloud Empire colonial is the enormous role that transnational corporate networks play in keeping the system running. In such an environment, we see the emergence of what Philip Stern called the "company-state":[9] a corporation with immense powers to regulate not just trade but also law, land, and liberty—in short, to regulate life. At the same time, as Immanuel Wallerstein points out, capitalism (and by extension, colonialism) cannot flourish without the active participation of the state, which controls the relations of production by legalizing (or refusing to regulate) certain forms of labor, such as slavery in the past or temporary or gig-based work nowadays.[10] Thus, it is powerful corporations operating *in collaboration* with powerful states that are defining the new colonial geographies and constructing a different social and economic order. The world is conquered and divided roughly along old lines but with new motives. A clear axis is emerging that reflects the divisions of political and economic power and influence in today's world, with China and the United States at opposite ends of that axis but equally engaged in rampant data colonialism.

Before we go into more detail, let us summarize the relationship between our terms. Data colonialism is the *how*, the extractivist processes through which life gets newly appropriated by capitalism. The social quantification sector is the *who*, the consortium of private and public players who engage in data colonialism to achieve their financial and political goals. And the Cloud Empire is the *what*, the overall organization of resources and imagination that emerges from the practices of data colonialism. The colonizing practices of the Cloud Empire are carried out mainly by the social quantification sector but also by segments of other sectors such as finance, science, civil society, and cultural industries. Like older empires, the Cloud Empire is both practiced and imagined. It is a totality that emerges from data colonialism over time to achieve the imperial reality of corporations' domination of life through data.

How the Cloud Empire Came to Be

In chapter 1 we explained some technological preconditions for the emergence of data colonialism. But how can we explain the emergence of the Cloud Empire in terms of the dynamics of capitalism itself? There are two ways of thinking about this.

One is to see the creation of the Cloud Empire and the colonial drive toward data extraction as responses to various contradictions (or at least problems) within late twentieth-century capitalism.

Problem 1: As inequality increases and the majority of people have less money to spend, capitalism needs to find new ways to exploit them that don't involve buying things. Wealth is becoming less evenly distributed, which means most of it is accumulating at the top while the majority of people experience a loss of wealth.[11] If people buy fewer and fewer things, this can become a problem for capitalism. Fortunately (for capitalism), social quantification introduces a new model in which people can generate profit for corporations simply by participating in social activities, without having to buy commodities.

Problem 2: If, as some argue, the rate of profit is falling because of technological advances, social quantification represents a valuable new source of profit, at least for the immediate future. As new technologies are introduced into the production process—or as workers are replaced with machines and artificial intelligence—things can be produced more cheaply, which brings down their prices, reducing the profit that corporations can derive from selling their goods. Although opinions vary on how much effect this is having on the global economy,[12] what is clear is that capitalism seeks opportunities to maximize profit, and the social quantification sector represents an opening, at least in the short term, to exploit new revenue streams.

Problem 3: As natural resources are depleted, social life emerges as the next big reserve of resources available for extraction. The depletion of our planet's natural resources can no longer be denied, and capitalism needs to find new horizons of appropriation. The social quantification sector poses as a "green" form of capitalism because it produces wealth by putting social, not natural, resources to work. Because the resources comprised by data from social life are symbolic and do not represent material wealth to the people from whose lives that data is extracted, it could conceivably but wrongly be argued that people are not dispossessed when corporations use that data. The effect of data colonialism, however, is to give corporations control of resources that can be extracted from social life by installing into people's lives corporate powers and rights of surveillance that did not exist before. The result is to appropriate human life to corporate power and thus dispossess it of its independent agency, which is why we refer to this process as a form of colonialism. Data colonialism completes the process of appropriating life that the expropriation of nature started.

A second explanation of how the Cloud Empire emerged emphasizes not disruptions but continuities. We noted at the end of chapter 1 how data colonialism's social transformations go even deeper than those that stem from neoliberal politics and culture. Whereas neoliberalism has been at war with those parts of social life that remain outside the market, data colonialism literally appropriates all of life for capitalism and therefore for markets. In this sense, data colonialism can be seen as a *culmination* of neoliberal ideology. In another sense, the kinds of changes that—in the West, at least—neoliberalism advocated or celebrated (the "liberalization" of trade and markets, the emergence of global financial markets, and the huge growth of the personal finance sector) were among the practical preconditions for data colonialism.[13] Indeed, the tools of data colonialism (such as Machine Learning) emerged in part as *solutions* to the practical challenges thrown up by the need, for example, to manage complex global supply chains and massively accelerating financial flows.

Both contextualizations are, in our view, important. Whether we see the emergence of the Cloud Empire more in terms of continuities or as a decisive break from what preceded it, its strategic importance in capitalism's history remains clear.

The Cloud: From Metaphor to Episteme

Today's data empires are not necessarily interested in land, but they are interested—at least allegorically—in air. If there is one metaphor that captures the structure of this nascent empire, it is that of "the cloud." Essentially, cloud computing enables on-demand access to a shared pool of computing resources.[14] Because information is stored on third-party servers, not on the owner's computer, the data is said to live "in the cloud." More than just a convenient and evocative metaphor, the concept of the cloud operates at different levels to help shape our social realities.

To understand these different levels of meaning, we can compare the similar ways in which the concepts of "the cloud" and "the network" are used. The concept of the network (a set of *nodes* connected by *links*) can be used in three different ways.[15] First, it can be used as a metaphor to describe any kind of set of interconnected actors. Everything from proteins to terrorists can be said to be organized as a network. Second, networks can be used as a template not just to describe a form of organization but also to enforce it. When Facebook is described as a social network, we are not just using a metaphor to describe a group of nodes; we are suggesting that those nodes are arranged in a particular way by the architecture of the network, an architecture that facilitates some things and makes others impossible. Third, the concept of the network can act as what Michel Foucault called an episteme,[16] a way of imposing a certain structure on the world to make sense of it. For example, to think of social groupings as being composed of connections that can be quantified (analyzed, predicted, and utilized) is a way of using a network episteme to understand and interact with something by forcing an external structure upon it.

The concept of the cloud functions in a similar way. The cloud can be a metaphor to suggest that data is gathered together in a remote location. It can be a template to organize how data is extracted, stored, and analyzed so that it can be managed together "in" the cloud. And the cloud, especially the Cloud Empire, can act as an episteme, a model for knowledge that organizes our social realities—even those that are not datafied—into structures that can facilitate their datafication. When we say things such as "Pics or it didn't happen!" or we participate in weekday memes like

#ThrowbackThursday, we imply that the way to understand life is to package it and distribute it according to models specified by the dynamics of the Cloud Empire.

One Buyer to Rule Them All

One reason the Cloud Empire is so successful at appropriating all of human life is because its biggest corporations can dominate our data relations both as sellers and buyers. Companies such as Google act as *monopolies*, "selling" us (sometimes providing to us for "free") every device or service we need to live our datafied lives. But Google also acts as what economists call a *monopsony*, that is, the single buyer of all the data we produce (the identification of monopsony as the dominant market structure of the internet was made by one of us back in 2013 and has since become commonplace).[17] A monopsony means that although digital tools have empowered us to become producers instead of mere consumers of media, there are limited options for choosing which platforms to participate in. Those of a certain demographic wanting to join a social networking site will probably join Facebook, because that is where their friends are more likely to be. Those wanting to upload videos of cats are highly incentivized to use YouTube, because that is where most users are likely to watch; and so on. We—the producers of data—are legion, but the buyers of what we produce are few. A platform, in particular, is the perfect medium for monopsony, a means to produce social content for capital.

The power of a monopsony rests not so much in its ability to raise prices, like a monopoly, but in its ability to push prices downward.[18] Lower prices might sound like a good thing, except for the fact that the reduction is accomplished not by reducing corporate profits but by paying less to those who supply or work for the monopsony. Because there are no other buyers of the workers' labor, monopsonies are able to effectively set wages to whatever they want.[19] That is why when it comes to participation in platforms, we basically hand over our data to them at no cost, even though without our data these companies valued at billions of dollars (as of 2017, Facebook is valued at $434 billion, Snapchat at $35 billion, and so on) have little to show for themselves. Some might celebrate the power of the internet to subvert capitalism and decentralize cultural production,[20] but this power means little if a handful of corporations control the entire infrastructure of data appropriation and use. The internet, which originally represented a rejection of mass media, is being remassified. On a regular day, Netflix and YouTube account for half of all internet traffic in the United States, with massive implications for their ability to "buy" and distribute content for money or otherwise.[21] The one-to-many model of mass media dissemination has simply been replaced by a many-to-one model, not the democratic many-to-many model we once hoped for.[22]

The monopoly-monopsony hybrids we are describing represent massive concentrations of power. These companies currently exercise a hold over the infrastructure that makes social quantification possible; they control everything from undersea cables to satellites to the "last mile" architecture that delivers internet service to individuals. They also control the environments or platforms in which data is being generated, the design and production of the devices through which data is collected, and the computing capacity necessary to analyze the data, including through increasingly sophisticated machine learning methods that do not require explicit human intervention. Finally, they also control the content. Whether it is user-generated or a corporation's intellectual property, legal and technical mechanisms have been put in place to ensure that these corporations can either co-own it, derive value from it, or at least control its distribution (for example, companies such as Apple and GoPro have been appropriating user-generated content and integrating it into their own marketing campaigns).[23]

In a post-Snowden, post–Cambridge Analytica era, this kind of critique of social quantification monopsonies is no longer difficult to find. We seek to expand this discussion by articulating a theory of data-based social quantification as the key means to install a new method of economic and social power. Our point is that through datafication, social interactions in all their forms become a domain in which market power can be exercised and value can be extracted, sometimes through extended means of labor and other times without any apparent activity on the part of those dominated but always under the rubric of a kind of appropriation and exploitation.

Appropriation and exploitation are the reasons we believe it is still relevant to talk about colonialism in the age of data. They are not outdated features of an old system but relations that newly define our present age. Marx, in an attempt to identify the characteristics of industrial capitalism, differentiated what he was trying to describe from previous modes of production, including those forms of *primitive accumulation* that can be said to include historical colonialism. But as David Harvey points out, the problem with this approach is that it relegates "accumulation based upon predation, fraud, and violence to an 'original stage' that is considered no longer relevant or . . . as being somehow 'outside of' the capitalist system."[24] Our thesis is that primitive accumulation does not precede capitalism but goes hand in hand with it. We follow authors such as Shoshana Zuboff, Julie Cohen, and Saskia Sassen[25] in recognizing an emergent phase of primitive accumulation so unique and historically significant that it deserves treatment as a new stage of history that we call data colonialism.

The Logic of the Cloud Empire

Is the extraction of data like the extraction of bounty minerals, natural riches, or cash crops? Are companies such as Facebook and Google just as responsible as company-states[26] like the East India Company, the Hudson Bay Company, or United Fruit were for devastating their colonies and enriching their empires? We are definitely not arguing that there is a one-to-one correspondence between using an app to share pictures of cute cats and participating in a process that decimated the natural resources and indigenous populations of vast areas of our planet. But if colonialism can be understood, among other things, as a process that allows one party to occupy the living space of another and appropriate his resources, overpowering him through a combination of ideological rationalizations and technological means (which include the use of surveillance and dominance), then we propose that we have entered a new phase of colonialism. To say this is not in any way to forget the racist, sexist, exploitative, and Eurocentric legacy of historical colonialism (which, after all, continues to shape the way we relate to each other today, even online).

With this appropriation comes very specific reorganizations of space. The machines of data colonialism shape and mold the space around us, creating the new geographies of the Cloud Empire. As Lisa Parks and Nicole Starosielski[27] point out, the very infrastructure of digital networks (the wires, servers, and signals that constitute them) are the embodiment and medium of violence, the conduit through which extraction takes place. This infrastructure follows many of the same colonial routes of previous centuries, establishing vertical connections between the colonies and the centers of empire, where wealth accumulates and where the managerial and technical elites of the empire are still educated.

But the issue is not just about the continuity, through digital infrastructures, of old imperial routes. The human and environmental relations of production also remain characteristically colonial. Raw materials for the electronic infrastructure that supports the social quantification sector still come from Africa, Asia, and Latin America, with 36 percent of the Earth's tin and 15 percent of its silver going into electronics manufacturing.[28] Massive energy usage translates into pollution[29] that, along with the dumping of toxic waste from the electronics industry, continues to impact poor communities disproportionately (by 2007, 80 percent of electronic waste was exported to the developing world).[30] And much of the labor necessary for the social quantification sector is still located in places such as Asia, where it is abundant and cheap. In China, manufacturer Foxconn, responsible for about half of the world's electronics production, employs a massive workforce of one million laborers who are managed under military-style conditions.[31] Meanwhile, much of the distressing work of content moderation for platforms (weeding out violent and pornographic images) is done in places such as the Philippines.[32]

How the Social Quantification Sector Works

If data in the cloud is stored in data centers and not in personal computers, this brings up the very important question of who owns it. Whereas earlier models of the internet allowed for distributed ownership of resources that could be used collectively, the cloud centralizes ownership and establishes very specific parameters for how data is shared. Instead of data being stored at each individual computer and each individual node deciding what data to share or not share, the cloud represents a model in which data is stored in "banks" that are owned by private corporations. Owning and maintaining these clouds is the largest-growing IT sector, with $547 billion estimated to be spent worldwide on infrastructure-as-a-service by the end of 2018.[33]

Once data generated by individuals is stored in the cloud, it is the corporations that decide what data other users are allowed to "borrow" from the bank, without those users being able to permanently store it in a way that would let them freely reproduce or transform it. That is why *streaming*—or downloading content in a format intended for short-term storage and access—is the norm instead of storing content locally and permanently. In this model, users are no longer the proprietors of any data they produce or acquire, and they don't get to decide what is collected or shared or for what purposes. From producers and owners, they pass into being renters of data, laborers who generate data to be sent back to the servers or, as earlier discussed, who are the source of life streams from which such data can be automatically extracted. Ned Rossiter argues that "[as] an apparatus that governs the storage, processing, and transmission of data, the data center extracts value from the social and economic life of connection."[34]

The infrastructure of the cloud thus enforces a certain violence of dispossession, which necessitates a broader critique of the political economy of the Cloud Empire. Our use of the label "social quantification sector" is intended precisely to expand the discussion beyond infrastructure and to single out corporations and other actors operating at the intersection of larger regions of the economy, including the information and communication technologies (ICT) sector and the arts, entertainment, and recreation sector.

Although our main focus is companies that seek to profit from the capitalization of our social lives, it is important to keep in mind the relation that the social quantification sector has to the larger ICT sector, and indeed to the wider business world, in its use of ICTs. Plainly stated, without the tools and business models of the ICT sector, the social quantification sector would not exist. A company such as IBM—which predates any social media company by decades—may today be involved in specific aspects of social quantification (IBM owns weather.com, for instance). But its scope is oriented mostly to business applications, including consulting and cloud computing. For these reasons, companies like IBM may not feature prominently in our discussion of social quantification, although this should not obscure the fact that the amount of digital data generated by businesses exceeds the amount of data generated by the social quantification sector (even though the two are intersecting).[35] The point is that the social quantification sector is more of a *sub*sector of the entire ICT business sector, useful in identifying specific activities and approaches that revolve around the capturing of everyday social acts and their translation into quantifiable data, which is then analyzed and used for the generation of profit. The point also is that in the era of data colonialism, the ICT sector is working ever more closely with all forms of business within the wider Cloud Empire.

We can develop an initial image of the social quantification sector by focusing on its biggest and best-known players—the company-states described earlier.

The Big Five

First, there is Amazon, one of the world's most valuable brands, with over 310 million active customer accounts worldwide.[36] As an online store, Amazon captures about half of all the money that people in the United States spend online (around $136 billion in net sales during 2016). Amazon is no longer just an online store but a company engaged in electronics manufacturing and media production/distribution while it prepares to "disrupt" the grocery, health care, shipping, and retail businesses, among others. It is also a huge web-services provider, currently supplying 44 percent of the world's cloud computing capacity, with clients ranging from Netflix to the CIA.[37]

Next there is Apple, which has become known for the high integration of its hardware and its software: its devices use only Apple's operating system, and software from other providers runs on its devices only when Apple allows it. Such a degree of control is seen as authoritarian by some and as the epitome of good design by others. Regardless, this stance allows Apple to distinguish itself from its competitors by, for instance, building ad blockers right into its Safari web browser or claiming that they do not sell any of the data they collect from users.[38] Even if this is the case, Apple must take some responsibility for the labor conditions under which its de-

vices are manufactured, for its collusion with the media industry in ways
that are not favorable to consumers,[39] or for its innovative ways to avoid
paying taxes: the company pays 9.8 percent in taxes, whereas global corporations typically pay around 24 percent.[40]

Facebook's business model is premised entirely on its ability to capture
data from its users and sell it to advertisers. Of the five corporations being
discussed, Facebook is also the one that seeks to profit the most from con-
ditioning users to conduct their social lives on its platforms, which have
extended to include popular services like WhatsApp and Instagram. The
company has come under fire for experimenting on users, targeting ads
to them based on biased criteria, and shirking its responsibility to protect them from harmful or false content.[41] Additionally, Free Basics, a program with fifty million users that promises to bring free internet access
to populations in underdeveloped countries, has been accused of breaking
net neutrality principles by allowing users to access only certain websites,
above all, Facebook.[42]

Google (also known by the name of its parent company, Alphabet) acquired its prominence by becoming the search portal for the internet and,
more importantly, monetizing the search process by including advertisements in the results. Today, Google processes more than 40,000 search
queries worldwide every second, or 1.2 trillion searches every year. Its cloud
products—which include free email, maps, office software, communication
tools, and so on—and its Android phone operating system are used by billions of people all over the world, not to mention the number of users that
watch up to five billion videos a day on YouTube, its most popular subsid-
iary.[43] Its dual dominance in the phone operating system and search engine markets has attracted intense scrutiny from regulators, particularly
the European Commission. It is also a huge player in artificial intelligence.

Finally, there is Microsoft, which was partly successful in transfer-
ring its early dominance in the PC software market to the web market by
bundling its internet browser (Internet Explorer) with its desktop operating system (Windows). Since then, the company has struggled to keep up
with its competitors, although it retains a substantial share of the business
IT market and it currently owns the second-largest cloud service in the
world.[44] It is also restructuring its business toward AI.

What is unique about these big five monopoly-monopsony hybrids is that they have carved out the social quantification space among themselves under an informal *Pax Britannica*–type of noncompetitive agreement. Yes, Microsoft spends about $5 billion a year keeping up with Google Search, and Apple spends about $1 billion[45] competing only with Google Maps (just as Google tried unsuccessfully to launch Google+, an alternative to Facebook). But what this really means is that there are no other corporations out there with the resources to compete at the same scale in this sector.

This is not to say that other large-scale competitors will not emerge in the near future. Walmart, for instance, is currently partnering with Microsoft to attempt to bolster its digital presence to compete with Amazon and has for more than a decade led the retail sector in the adoption of systematic data extraction and processing.[46] And this is also not to say that smaller players are not important.

Beyond the Big Five

The Big Five sometimes interact and mix with other players in the social quantification sector. The operations of these players can be organized into five key (often intersecting) domains: hardware, software, platforms, data analytics, and data brokerage (all of which may also describe some of the actions of the Big Five!).

The hardware area includes manufacturers of digital devices that extract and use social data, from laptops and tablets to phones and watches to gaming consoles, robots, cars, drones, and so on. A manufacturer of a "dumb" television set would not be part of the social quantification sector, but any manufacturer of a "smart" device (a product that collects and analyzes information about its user) would be included. This sector also includes the manufacturers of the infrastructure required to run the social quantification sector (routers, servers, transmitters, and so on) and the service providers that deploy hardware to deliver internet and phone access to individuals. Examples of corporations in this domain include Apple, Cisco, Samsung, Amazon, Microsoft, and Verizon.

Software includes the developers of the programs and environments that support social quantification, including operating systems, websites, applications, services, games, apps, and plug-ins. Examples in this domain include Google, Apple, Microsoft, and Ubisoft.

It is important to note an emerging area at the intersection of hardware and software, the so-called Internet of Things (IoT). By attaching sensors and connectivity features to a host of everyday objects, the IoT is creating a vast network of wired appliances that track, monitor, and report social data (data variously relevant to social actors). It is estimated that the number of connected devices will grow from nearly 27 billion in 2017 to 125 billion in 2030.[47] These devices include everything from cars to electric appliances and smart personal assistants such as Amazon's Echo and Google Home. Some home systems can recognize the age, sex, and weight of people in the vicinity as well as their emotional state, the language they speak, and the activities they might be engaged in.[48]

Next there are the builders of platforms, another distinctive particular combination of hardware and software that, as it were, convenes streams of the social world for profitable data extraction. Any networked service that can collect data from users, via websites or devices, can be defined as a platform. These environments can include not just "free" socialization services such as Facebook, Twitter, and WeChat but also platforms for the provision of paid services such as Uber, Airbnb, and Netflix (which, according to its corporate website, counted on 130 million worldwide subscribers by the second quarter of 2018). Platforms exist across all commercial sectors, including banking, entertainment, finance, insurance, retail, travel, and, of course, romance and sex (from dating to porn platforms).

Digital platforms give gatekeeping power to their owners, much as the navigation routes of historical colonialism empowered the towns near where goods had to land. But because of the connected nature of the online environment, today's gatekeeping power has consequences on a vast global scale, not just a local or national one. All the data generated and captured through hardware and software in platforms is then processed by two other important types of players in the social quantification sector.

Data analytics firms are companies that collect data and analyze it. Hardware, software, and platform companies analyze their own data, of course, but analytics firms provide more specialized services such as psychometrics (large-scale analysis of users' personalities and preferences) and telematics (coordinating production and distribution processes using data collected at multiple points). US examples of marketing-oriented analytic firms include Paxata, Trifacta, IBM, and Google. But there is a wide spectrum of companies that collect and analyze data across many domains of life, including health (Mede Analytics), genetics (23andMe), education (Junyo), crime (Wynyard), and so on. In China, data analytics are concentrated in big corporations such as Alibaba, Baidu, and WeChat. Some of these firms focus on data that can be used for sales and marketing purposes, but they increasingly integrate information about users' social lives into their models and products. This information can also be used for political purposes, as evidenced in the recent case of Cambridge Analytica and Facebook.

Data brokerage firms are also companies that collect data but more with an intention of "packaging" and selling any personal information related to financial, demographic, criminal, political, recreational, and social activities as well as data about general interests, purchase behavior, and the health of individuals. Examples include Acxiom, Datalogix, eBureau, ID Analytics, PeekYou, and Recorded Future. Data brokers take many forms, from those who simply gather data to those who match buyers and sellers of data to specialist data brokers who process data for specific purposes, for example, to advise creditors about debtor risk (such as Experian or the troubled Equifax). There is even the practice of onboarding, which involves matching data from one's *offline* activity (gathered, for example, if you give your email address in the middle of a transaction that you thought was offline) with the much larger amount of data available about one's online activities.[49] The public recently got a rare glimpse of some of the secret practices of the social quantification sector during testimony to the US Senate Committee on Commerce, Science, and Transportation, which revealed that the data broker industry was collecting and selling lists of rape and domestic abuse victims, sufferers of dementia and erectile dysfunction, and payday loan responders, among others.[50]

In theory, all this data collection must work around privacy and consumer-rights constraints, but often it does not. Although some countries offer more protection than others, Katherine Strandburg's observation that "US law for the most part has not regulated the datafication or repurposing of information that is acquired as a byproduct of providing service"[51] is applicable beyond North America and particularly in developing countries.[52] In India, for instance, one can easily buy lists of one hundred thousand individuals (car owners, retired women, or any number of categories) for less than $250; the lists are generated from information collected by mobile companies or even by enterprising individuals working at banks or hospitals looking to make some extra cash.[53] In China, regulation about what data companies can collect and what they can do with it is intentionally relaxed, which the government hopes will make Chinese companies more competitive in the global market.[54] Across the globe, regulation is also difficult because corporations can work across two or more of the abovementioned domains; Google, for instance, is a hardware and software manufacturer as well as a data analyst and broker. In other cases, the operations of one corporation can be intimately tied to another. For example, Acxiom and Facebook were partners until recently, which meant that the latter provided data to the former.[55] The fact that ties were severed in the wake of the Cambridge Analytica scandal suggests that Facebook probably plans to internalize the data-aggregation functions that Acxiom previously provided.

There is great variety in terms of the size, scope, and mission of the players operating in the social quantification sector. Some of them are small (sometimes one-person) developers of programs or services, such as the WaterMinder app mentioned at the beginning of the book. There are also academic, governmental, and nonprofit organizations performing analytics, usually for research purposes but sometimes in collaboration with corporations. And there are powerful contractors that work closely with the government, including the army and police forces. Consider Taser, the company that produces the stun guns used by cops. Taser, through its Axon AI division, provides free body cameras and video storage to police departments and then sells them services that use the data generated by the cameras to perform things such as facial recognition and predictive crime analysis.[56] There are also the rogue players in the social quantification sector: criminal or clandestine entities that engage in everything from manufacturing of knockoff smart devices to pirating of content to stealing and hacking of social data. Given that 2017 saw 1,120 data breaches with more than 171 million records exposed in the United States alone,[57] no one can deny that criminal players are part of the social quantification sector. The role of crime is particularly important when, as noted in chapter 1, the overall insecurity of infrastructures of connection is increasing.

Finally, when considering the size and composition of the social quantification sector, we should also consider its economic impact. In terms of actual revenue, it is important not to overestimate the size of the social quantification sector in the wider economy.[58] Oil and gas, financial services, automotive, and pharmaceuticals are in fact larger sectors than ICT. For instance, in 2016, oil conglomerate Saudi Aramco made $311 billion dollars in revenue, compared to Amazon's $107 billion; Toyota made $237 billion compared to Google's $89.5 billion; Apple posted a revenue of $234 billion, less than Walmart's $482 billion; and Facebook's $27.64 billion and Uber's $6.5 billion of revenue are considerably less than Volkswagen's $237 billion.[59] But it is equally important not to underestimate the prominence of the ICT sector in terms of stock market capitalization and not to underrate the considerable growth in this sector: in the first quarter of 2008, the top four corporations in terms of market capitalization (the value of the shares of a corporation) were Exxon/Mobil ($452 billion), PetroChina ($423 billion), General Electric ($369 billion), and Gazprom ($299 billion). A decade later, in the first quarter of 2018, they were Apple ($851 billion), Alphabet/Google ($717 billion), Microsoft ($702 billion), and Amazon ($700 billion). In that same year, Apple broke the $1 trillion record in capitalization for a brief period.

By itself, the social quantification sector might be less economically significant than others and certainly not as significant as mainstream opinion would lead us to believe. But it plays a key role in the overall structuring of the Cloud Empire and the shaping of the social world around it. Its smaller economic role is more than made up for by its enormous influence on data processing and business models within the wider social order built around data colonialism.

Colonizer Within: The Social Quantification Sector in China

Although the influence of Google, Apple, Facebook, and Amazon is felt throughout the world, the power of non-Western social quantification empires that are regional and internal facing should not be overlooked.

There are important examples of countries that have not been entirely colonized by the Western quantification sector but have instead continued a historical practice of colonizing within their own borders. In Russia, there are companies such as Yandex and Vkontakte operating in the search and social networking markets, companies with close links to the government but which nonetheless compete nationally with Google, Facebook, and the rest of the US social quantification sector.[60] India's approach in the IT sector, meanwhile, has been to leverage cheap labor and engineering expertise to attract global investment. But in contrast with yesterday's image of the Indian call center providing customer support for Western companies, India's current IT sector represents a burgeoning ecosystem of start-ups, technology developers, and service providers of global reach. This infrastructure is being developed in close collaboration with the state through public–private partnerships. For instance, India's data centers, which provide server hosting and colocation services to companies all over the world, are supported by the government through land allotments and tax rebates; furthermore, the IT sector and the government work closely on national data-management projects such as census or citizen-identification programs.[61] Also, India's immense population constitutes an equally enormous market for both foreign and domestic firms, with the digital economy in India soon poised to represent a trillion-dollar market.[62] This is why financers and corporations in Asia and the United States are racing to fund start-ups and acquire companies in India;[63] as of this writing, Walmart is suspected of wanting to buy e-commerce giant Flipkart to compete with Amazon, and Alibaba plans to enter the game through its acquisition of Paytm.[64]

The most comprehensive example of internal colonization is, of course, China, a Cloud Empire in and of itself that is as advanced as the West's and could in the near future surpass it. In fact, it is already extending to other parts of the world not just through hardware but also through cloud computing, financial services, and artificial intelligence.[65] Companies such as Baidu, Alibaba, and Tencent are sizeable conglomerates with more diversification than their Western counterparts. If we take early 2018 values as our vantage point (but note Tencent's subsequent loss of approximately $150 billion), the panorama looks as follows: Baidu, with a market value of

$87 billion, focuses on searches and ads but also provides services such as maps, games, tools for small business, food delivery, and electronic wallets. Alibaba, with a market value of $481 billion, specializes in e-commerce and online shopping but also offers phone payment methods, cloud services, mobile entertainment, marketing, enterprise communication, and its own operating system. Tencent, with a market value of $540.6 billion, showcases mobile chat and social networking, including the ubiquitous QQ and WeChat.[66]

Apart from the diverse scope and reach of each of these companies, the Chinese social quantification sector differentiates itself from the West in a number of ways. First, it is much more integrated with financial and banking operations; corporations are better equipped to track credit scores and offer bank-like services, including mobile micropayments featuring facial ID and various forms of platform-based commerce (innovations that the West is starting to replicate). It is worth keeping in mind that China is the largest e-commerce market in the world, twice as large as the United States. Second, China is much more interested in integrating the rural economy into the whole. Alibaba, for instance, has an extensive network of rural service centers that help farmers and small producers.[67] JD.com (the third-largest tech company in the world, after Amazon and Alphabet) has set up a system of delivery that allows even people in remote rural villages to buy items online and expect them to be delivered quickly and efficiently through a system relying on high-tech means such as drones and more traditional means such as delivery staff recruited from the regional population.[68] This model could be exported to developing countries (in Africa, for instance) as an infrastructure for urban-rural integration that flows into the Chinese economy. There is also a much more concerted effort to invest in artificial intelligence on the scale of the economy and society as a whole.[69] Although Silicon Valley enjoys an early lead, China might quickly surpass it in terms of resources invested in AI-fueled education, research, and development. China's 1.4 billion people, including its 730 million internet users, generate vast amounts of data that can be used to train AI algorithms and can be appropriated with little concern for privacy rights.[70] Third, China's social quantification sector can use its AI technologies to collaborate with the government on ambitious projects such as the Internet Plus plan, which seeks to connect manufacturing, finance, government, agricultural, and medical services into one big information superhighway.

Critics in the West see this close collaboration between government and internet companies as evidence of Chinese authoritarianism.[71] Consider the social credit system (discussed in chapter 1) currently being tested in China that will establish a nationwide data network to track the activities and reputations of every single citizen.[72] Or note reports that facial recognition AI and big data are being used to monitor and control the movement of Muslim ethnic minorities, turning the region of Xinjiang into a "surveillance laboratory."[73] On closer inspection, however, such initiatives are problematic not so much because they are uniquely antidemocratic (the West has its own crises of civil rights) but because they perfectly illustrate where datafication might eventually be headed *everywhere*. In the name of safety and security, other governments will find it easier to claim they must not be left at a disadvantage and will escalate the initiatives already in place (in fact, these governments might find it appealing to import ready-made systems of surveillance along with telecom infrastructure, as some African countries are doing from China).[74] Ultimately, the close collaboration between a government that grants economic and legal advantages to tech companies[75] and companies that help the government conduct its surveillance is a global feature of data colonialism, not one restricted to China, Russia, or the United States.

To reiterate, data colonialism is what happens when life becomes the input of capitalism and becomes organized through data relations. As part of this process, data colonialism comes to depend on an emerging transformation of social relations both within the formal economy and outside of it. Urgent calls for us to submit to this new order are portrayed as inevitable, when in fact they are not. Nonetheless, this alters neither the breadth of the new corporate ambition to transform social life nor the extent of the social inequalities that will emerge from implementing that ambition through the Cloud Empire. We have been clear that data colonialism is transforming social relations beyond the context of labor, and we turn next to an analysis of how some aspects of work are indeed being reshaped by it.

Working in the Cloud Empire

Immanuel Wallerstein observed that "profit is often greater when not all links in the chain are in fact commodified."[76] By this he meant that capitalism has always relied on indirect modes of exploitation that can operate in addition to the direct modes of exploitation related to wage labor. Put differently, unpaid or underpaid work is of utmost importance in capitalism, whether that work is the work of the slave, the housewife, or the selfie poster. Historically, this has served both to externalize costs so that it is members of society, not employers, who have to bear them and to extend capitalism beyond the formal economy. Today, social quantification represents the most extensive attempt to construct a whole economy based on the free ride that capitalism can extract from our lives, so that modes of unpaid and underpaid work that were unimaginable before are legitimized, normalized, and, in the long run, naturalized.

Unpaid Labor

There is a lot of unpaid work performed by humans on social quantification platforms, even when this work provides value to the network and allows the platform owners to enrich themselves. Consider, for instance, all the ways in which users can contribute free labor in the Local Guides program that is part of Google Maps. This program asks individuals to "Review a place," "Rate a place," "Add photos to a place," "Answer questions about a place," "Edit a place's information or Edit a road on the map," "Add a missing place," "Check facts about places nearby," and "Respond to Q&As." In return, the platform offers recognition; working for them can help "your contributions get noticed" and valued in this "gamified" system.[77] The work can also be remunerated not in cash but in perks that can be used to further integrate workers into the platform (such as "3 months of Google Play Music and 75% off a movie rental on Google Play" or something similar). Many social quantification platforms have similar ways of rewarding users, but in general, the more "social" a platform is, the less expectation there is that users will be recompensed for their work, since the joy of social interaction facilitated by the platform is presented as enough payment. Julian Kücklich refers to this phenomenon in which participation *itself* generates value as *playbor* (part play, part labor), suggesting that from the perspective of capitalism, the means of production here are the players themselves.[78]

Companies in the social quantification sector use unpaid labor not only to exploit users but to undermine other competitors in the cultural production sector. For instance, Jonathan Taplin points out that YouTube is the largest music-streaming platform in the world, to which users (unpaid laborers) have uploaded practically every song in existence. At the same time, YouTube has relegated the job of monitoring for copyright infringement to the owners of the underlying intellectual property (the record companies). The result is that artists and record companies collect less revenue from YouTube than from other music-streaming platforms, even though their content is played many more times on YouTube than anywhere else.[79]

Underpaid Labor

Sometimes, participating in the Cloud Empire economy is not an unpaid job but an underpaid one. The Turker is perhaps the quintessential example. Turkers are freelance independent contractors who perform small tasks on Amazon's Mechanical Turk platform, or MTurk, a crowdsourcing marketplace launched in 2005 where Requesters (businesses or individuals) can post tasks that computers can't currently perform or that are cheaper for humans to do. Armies of Turkers can then earn small amounts of money (usually less than one cent per task) to perform the jobs, which might include doing things such as categorizing, sorting, testing, rating, generating content, or training artificial intelligence algorithms that will eventually make the human Turker redundant. Workers are seemingly empowered because, as contractors, they set their own hours and choose their own tasks. But employers are empowered too, since they don't have to pay payroll taxes, can avoid regulations concerning minimum wage and overtime work, and can get millions of microtasks performed that regular employees might resist doing.

MTurk never became a huge success (Turkers have consistently complained it is nearly impossible to earn a living wage), but its real impact has been the inspiration it generated for what is now referred to as the *gig economy.* Also known as the sharing, peer, or on-demand economy, the gig economy continues the trend of replacing salaried full-time work with contingent part-time "gigs." Part-time work now accounts for almost one-fifth of the job growth in the United States since the 2008 recession ended. According to one estimate, currently there are around fifty-three million freelancers in the United States[80] who, like Turkers, don't have the opportunity to earn a living wage or receive essential work benefits through their freelance work. And yet, these trends are paradoxically being hailed—in the words of an Uber executive and former Clinton administration strategist—as "democratizing capitalism" and "driving wealth down to the people."[81]

A Pew report from 2016[82] put the supposedly transformative impact of the gig economy into perspective: 24 percent of Americans in that year reported making money from gig platforms, with only 8 percent (around twenty-six million) doing so from employment, as opposed to other activities such as selling things on eBay. For comparison purposes, in China the sharing economy generated $500 billion in transactions involving six hundred million people in 2015 alone (although "sharing" in this context might simply mean renting a bicycle from one of the forty companies that facilitate fifty million rides every day).[83]

The gig economy, for all its limitations, has significance as an exemplar of where capitalism is heading. Platforms and apps do the work of connecting demand (people looking to hire someone to do a job) to supply (temp workers willing to perform that job for a price set by the platform). Because the economic transactions happen within and through the platform, companies are able to benefit by taking a cut from each transaction, through advertising, or by extracting data from the transactions that they can then sell to third parties, all the while washing their hands of any messy contractual obligations between themselves and the users (some platforms simply charge giggers to bid on jobs, regardless of whether they get the job). This is monopsony in action.

The demographics of the people who employ gig workers (in the United States, at least) seem to skew strongly toward young, white, wealthy urban dwellers.[84] The demographics of the workers themselves (again, in the United States) skew toward those who are young, lower income (less than $30,000 per year), and black or Latino. Of the 8 percent of Americans making money from gig platforms, three-fifths felt that their platform income was "essential" or "important" to them.[85] Anecdotal evidence seems to corroborate the fact that some gig workers do have opportunities to engage in new creative and leisure activities as a result of their unstructured lifestyles. But the system as a whole is designed to maximize platform profit at the expense of workers.[86] Here is just one testimonial from a twenty-six-year-old kindergarten worker, babysitter, and cook:

> It's difficult to think positively about my situation. I keep busy but I have to constantly juggle different gigs every day (sometimes I start working at 7:30 a.m. and I get home after midnight). What scares me the most is that I have no guarantees, no steady pay, no stability. . . . I currently work seven days a week to make €750 (£525) per month and I would earn a lot more doing a more traditional job with a traditional employment contract, but these arrangements are a rarity these days.[87]

Since retirement plans seem to be out of the question, the advice given to gig workers is that they should simply plan to *not* retire![88] What we see is essentially a technologized form of a subsistence economy that seems to be creating a new kind of "reserve army of labor." Marx had described the importance in capitalism of maintaining part of the population in unemployment (the "reserve army") so that they could be easily hired in times when overproduction was necessary.[89] The promise of intermittent work on platforms positions large numbers of people as a reserve army for work outside institutions. Thus, the combined effects of the gig economy and automation will likely be disastrous for most workers—not only will many of them face replacement by machines but those who remain will more likely accept lower wages and worse working conditions as the specter of a reserve army of gig workers, robots, and AI hangs over their heads.

Given all of this, considerable PR maneuvering is required to make such a depressing trend palatable. Here, what in chapter 1 we called the ideology of personalization can do useful work. In its own marketing materials, Airbnb promotes itself as "an economic lifeline for the middle class."[90] An ad for Uber features an African American driver speaking of the economic necessity to have a "side hustle," a necessity Uber allows him to fulfill while also giving him time to "chill" whenever he wants and to spend more time with his family.[91] The reality of Uber in particular, however, paints a less rosy picture. Alex Rosenblat and Luke Stark[92] review Uber's record of economic manipulation through surge pricing and sudden driver deactivation as well as the general opacity of its algorithmic processing from the point of view of its drivers (the company can make it seem as though there are more drivers available in a location than there actually are, simply to push worker wages down). Unsurprisingly, Uber's retention rates are quite low, with 96 percent of new Uber drivers quitting their jobs within their first year.[93] This paints a picture of the Uber driver as the least important part of the equation, truly an expendable member of a reserve army. And yet, until recently, the company was a darling in terms of market valuation, and "uberize" became a widely used verb within investor circles.

Summarizing in a way that is applicable to the whole sharing economy, Melissa Gregg puts it well when she says that "liberation [from employee contracts] frees up Uber from the traditional responsibilities of being an employer. It is ingenious to make employment less predictable, and thus less costly, in the name of independence and choice."[94] As such, regardless of its size or long-term success, Uber remains an important exemplar of a projected direction for global capitalism: it represents the potential to create new forms of exploitative work, to substantially increase the levels of exploitation within established forms of work, and to circumvent human labor altogether (the company is currently investing heavily in driverless cars and trucks). Data-gathering and data tracking are essential to all these functions, the fact of which makes exploitation seem like the "natural" outcome of algorithmic processes. Gone are the narratives of a benign form of capitalism in which institutions still acknowledged a social responsibility. Instead, we have institutions that merely engineer "processes" or "interfaces," and society has to live with the results.

Despite the challenges that gig workers face, those who celebrate the "disruptive" effects that the sharing economy is having on traditional sectors (hotel and taxi companies, for instance) could perhaps be excused for seeing in all this a benefit for society—cheaper services. What is missing from such an analysis, however, is any discussion of long-term effects. The buyers of gig services today may enjoy lower costs, but if more and more of them are forced to become the providers of gig services tomorrow, then the "disruption" that the sharing economy is creating is clearly negative over the longer term.

Surveilled Labor

Not only are workers' conditions becoming more precarious, but their moment-to-moment activities are also becoming increasingly monitored. A large transformation underway is datafication's role in changing how workers are managed, which entails an increasing degree of monitoring. As Larry Catá Backer argues, "Surveillance has become not only a technique of governance, but its substitute,"[95] with assumptions and objectives beyond passive data collection. Extending beyond the workplace to all aspects of a worker's life, this new kind of surveillance is very much a domain of the social quantification sector. Its evolution must be placed in the longer history of surveillance within capitalism, which, as Christian Fuchs points out,[96] was already noted by Marx. Alongside the consumer surveillance, discussed more fully in chapter 3, and the mutual surveillance between competitors that is inherent to market economies, capitalist labor relations have—according to Fuchs—always been characterized by at least three types of surveillance: applicant surveillance, workplace surveillance, and workforce surveillance.[97]

For applicant surveillance, there is an increasing reliance on automated testing rather than on human assessment. By 2014, an estimated 60 to 70 percent of US prospective employees faced online personality tests *before* they could even be seen or spoken to by a human being.[98] Personality testing dates back at least to the 1930s, but greater data processing power has massively increased the capacity to integrate such testing and the results it produces into the categorization of actual and potential workers. One estimate suggests there might be as many as seventy-five-million assessment tests administered to potential employees each year in the United States.[99] A form of anticipatory management, personality tests can flag any criterion an employer chooses—for example, candidates who are prone to join a labor union, who display potential markers for mental illness, or who are likely to ask for salary increases or, conversely, remain on the job without asking for a raise.[100]

Once an employee is recruited, both workplace and workforce surveillance take over. The line between the two is in fact disappearing, as
the workplace becomes any and every site the worker might happen to be
at, while being pervasively measured and monitored through continuous
streams of data collection and processing. Some of the models currently
employed are discussed in the following paragraphs.

Smart scheduling. Work shift-management systems are increasingly
being used by businesses such as retail stores and restaurants to schedule
work periods, allowing corporations to replace a full-time workforce with
a "just in time" army of temps whose schedules are irregular and unpredictable. The benefit for the corporations is that they can increase profits
by avoiding overstaffing and full-time contracts. As with the gig economy,
the benefits to employees are much less clear. As of 2017, only 17 percent of
US retail employees had a set or constant work schedule.[101]

Data-driven micromanagement of workers. This includes methods such
as *voice picking* (short for "voice-directed order picking"), used extensively
in Amazon's warehouses. Whereas other techniques for managing workers (RFID tags on goods, GPS tracking of workers and the machines they
are operating) still leave the worker some autonomy (their position is managed only indirectly), voice picking works to channel surveillance directly
through the worker's body. The worker is instructed through a headset
that relays automated verbal comments—issued not by a person but by a
warehouse management system—while of course simultaneously watching the worker's movements. The system uses voice recognition to understand what the worker is saying.[102] Similar technologies of surveillance are
in use in many other industries, such as retail, and there is evidence of
considerable negative impacts on workers' health as they struggle to keep
up with their AI-driven foremen.[103]

Remote desktop surveillance. This method includes systems such as
those used by online staffing platform Upwork to keep an eye on freelancers doing work from home (about a third of the US workforce). The system,
installed voluntarily by the freelancers, takes pictures of their desktops at
random times and tracks their minute-by-minute activity, including key-
stroke and mouse movement (are they checking personal email? posting
on Facebook?). This is a way for clients to make sure workers are not "wast-

ing time," and freelancers face pressure to accept this level of surveillance because doing so guarantees that they will be paid immediately after the job is done, while refusing might mean having to wait a long time for a client to pay an invoice. In other words, submission to surveillance is directly tied to economic benefits.

Telematics. This management approach involves using data generated by sensors to continuously monitor a worker's performance. A growing sector in which this approach is being applied is transportation, where quantification provides new tools to monitor and control drivers. UPS package-delivery trucks, for instance, are now equipped with around two hundred sensors that monitor everything from location and speed to whether the seatbelt is engaged and, of course, how much time the driver is taking to deliver each package. Likewise, 30–50 percent of the US trucking industry is now using electronic onboard recorders that radically change truckers' relations to their work, fostering competitive individualism and influencing their behavior.[104]

Monitoring work interactions. Models developed and refined in the domain of general *social* interactions are now being applied to the domain of *workplace* interactions, thus normalizing the overall transformation. An emerging $11 billion industry is developing "enterprise social" platforms such as Microsoft's Yammer, Salesforce's Chatter, and (the name says it all) Facebook at Work. These platforms, inspired by social media, function to collect data from a worker's daily interactions and convert them into metrics that can be used to assess job performance, identify interventions to reward or punish workers, or even make hiring and firing decisions.[105]

Bodily surveillance. This includes the use of wearable devices and self-tracking technologies (WSTT), which employ Bluetooth, triangulation algorithms, and infrared sensors to measure and track mental and physical manifestations of arousal and performance, allowing for ubiquitous monitoring beyond the workplace and the workday.[106] McDonald's, for example, has introduced "sociometric badges" that monitor everyday behavior and emotion. Leisure self-tracking devices such as Fitbit are increasingly becoming requirements of employment contracts within the context of "wellness programs." This sudden focus on well-being stems less from humanitarian concerns than from corporations' efforts to reduce the influence of stress on productivity: according to the UK's Health and Safety Executive, the number of days lost due to stress, depression, anxiety, and headaches is rising dangerously.[107] The assumption that the constant monitoring and reporting of health statistics will reduce (rather than increase) stress seems counterintuitive to anyone except the designers and enforcers of such programs. Yet by 2015, a total of 580,000 US companies had already implemented wellness programs involving such devices.[108]

In reviewing some of the methods just discussed, Esther Kaplan observes that

> in industry after industry, this data collection is part of an expensive, high-tech effort to squeeze every last drop of productivity from corporate workforces, an effort that pushes employees to their mental, emotional, and physical limits; claims control over their working and nonworking hours; and compensates them as little as possible, even at the risk of violating labor laws.[109]

In the context of the Cloud Empire, data becomes a core "management" tool[110] that not only facilitates the logistical organizing of production but also monitors, evaluates, and regulates workers' bodies and social interactions to make them both more productive and ultimately more dispensable.

Where Is the Cloud Empire Taking Us?

As Ranabir Sammadar argues, "For capital this is the desirable history of labour—labour at work but not visible, ready at hand but not always necessary, labour living but, whenever required, soon dead."[111] The last part of the quote might sound like an exaggeration, except when we begin to consider the role of automation. The prediction that technology would bring about the end of unfulfilling labor does not seem to be unfolding according to the hopes of economists. Automation and AI technologies, which many corporations in the social quantification sector actively develop and promote, seem to be designed to eliminate laborers, not liberate them. Given the investment in AI of companies such as Amazon, Apple, Facebook, and Google, Scott Galloway argues they should be referred to as job destroyers, not job creators.[112]

With the arrival of the "second machine age,"[113] the destruction of many jobs is a given, even if the scope of the transformation is still up for debate. According to some estimates, digital automation puts up to 47 percent of all US employment at "high risk" of vanishing.[114] In the retail sector alone, this translates into 7.5 million jobs out of a total of 16 million.[115] Other estimates that focus on tasks instead of occupations present a much smaller figure of 9 percent of jobs at risk of disappearing.[116] Looking at historical data instead of predictions reveals that adding one robot to a workforce of one thousand human workers has increased unemployment and reduced wages, even if the shifts are very small thus far.[117] Nonetheless, it is hard to project past trends into the future without accounting for the disruptive power of technology. Most analysts agree that the question of the impact of automation cannot be tackled without looking at wider societal issues such as basic income, tax reform, and educational changes.[118]

As more people become under- or unemployed, social controls for managing discontent need to be tightened. There are two main approaches we are seeing within the Cloud Empire for dealing with this. First, there are, in various countries, increasing alliances between the state and the private sector in supporting each other's goals. We see a similarity in approaches across the political spectrum—from open to closed societies. These approaches include deregulation (if previous regulation even existed) of the media and technology industries in a manner that gives more market power to favored corporations; collaboration between the government and the private sector to develop and implement technologies for surveillance; expansion of the state's power to impose special measures of surveillance during increasingly permanent periods of emergency; and comprehensive secrecy about what governments and corporations do with data collected from citizens, all in the name of security and antiterrorism. These practices are replicated in practically every country with a modern ICT infrastructure, regardless of whether they are democratic or authoritarian in character.

Second, there is a targeting of vulnerable social groups as part of the strategies of data colonialism. One thing that makes the Cloud Empire colonial is the approach of corporations and states to the oppressed. Under the Cloud Empire, everyone contributes as a raw input to capitalism, but as with old forms of colonialism, the poor (always a racialized and gendered category) continue to pay a heavier price. Here we allude to the work of authors such as Oscar Gandy, Seeta Peña Gangadharan, Virginia Eubanks, and Safiya Umoja Noble,[119] who argue that when it comes to the poor and the vulnerable, digital "inclusion" comes at the cost of extensive data profiling, including practices that are predatory, discriminatory, exploitative, or simply degrading. Chapter 4 will look into this further.

The merciless power of the Cloud Empire comes from an overarching rationality in which data shadows—and eventually stands in for—the very thing it is supposed to measure: life. Apps, platforms, and smart technologies capture and translate our life into data as we play, work, and socialize. AI algorithms then pore over the data to extract information (personal attributes from "likes," emotions from typing patterns, predictions from past behaviors, and so on) that can be used to sell us our lives back, albeit in commodified form. Science, technology, and human ingenuity are put at the service of this exploitation, making it likely that, unless resisted, the Cloud Empire will in a few decades seem like the natural order of things. This is indeed a bleak picture, but it is not entirely new. The larger pattern harks back to a previous era of rampant extraction—that of historical colonialism, as we will explore in the next chapter.

Interlude

On Colonialism and the Decolonial Turn

FOR READERS who wish to gain a basic understanding of what historical colonialism was, how it developed, and the postcolonial and decolonial responses that emerged in reaction to it, we recommend reading this interlude before proceeding. Others already familiar with these concepts may want to skip to chapter 3.

Colonialism in Context

Most allusions to colonialism refer to the European colonial period, that period in history from the sixteenth to the mid-twentieth centuries in which nation-states from Western Europe colonized large parts of the African, American, and Asian continents. An immediate question might arise as to why earlier regimes are not considered to be part of this historical period. After all, there are plenty of examples of empires such as the Persian, Roman, Aztec, and Ottoman that engaged in the exploitation of nearby communities before the arrival of Columbus in America in 1492. But two characteristics made early-modern European colonialism unique. The first one is that it extended the scale of empire not just geographically but in having imposed a single universalizing narrative of values, beliefs, and politics, ushering in the beginning of modern globalization. Instead of talking about coexisting worlds, such as the Iberian world, the Aztec world, and so on, we can talk about a single emerging "modern" world system with one Eurocentric world history.[1] The second characteristic, which flows from the first, is that colonialism sought to fundamentally change and reorganize the social and economic order of the societies it colonized, as opposed to satisfying itself with extracting tribute, as did earlier empires.[2]

Historical colonialism required first and foremost an *external* colonizer, a group of people who took land and resources that were not theirs. "Appropriation" implies that the land was already occupied by someone, although these colonized, "primitive" inhabitants were not treated as the real owners of the resources. Speaking in general terms, then, colonialism can be said to consist of a global system in which colonizers use power to dispossess the colonized of valuable resources, sending the wealth back to the metropolis or the motherland and all the while justifying their actions with a discourse of hierarchical differentiation between peoples and cultures.

This discourse was necessary historically because oppression and brutality needed to be rationalized in some manner. As philosophers from Hegel to Paulo Freire have pointed out, oppression dehumanizes not only the oppressed but also the oppressor.[3] In an attempt to rehabilitate his image, the oppressor needs to describe himself as having virtuous principles (religious or secular), even if they are in contradiction with his actions. In this manner, historical colonialism was framed as a worldview in which the colonizer was described as superior (strong, rational, civilized, resourceful, and Christian), and the colonized as inferior (weak, ignorant, savage, lazy, and heathenish).

A dichotomy of *us* versus *them* was established in which the European self was assumed to be a complete individual and the non-European other an incomplete one. The colonizer thus assumed the "obligation"—the "burden," even—of exploiting the colonized in the name of civilizing them. In the eyes of the colonizer, the violent cost of the enterprise to "modernize" the "primitives" was inevitable yet necessary, even if this meant working individuals to death.[4] Indeed, the most inhuman treatment was not seen as unethical because it was not believed to be inflicted on *full* human beings;[5] violence was merely a feature of the economic mode of production.

European colonialism was not a period characterized by the same mode of production from beginning to end (in which "mode of production" is a historically specific arrangement of how things are produced, distributed, and consumed, further discussed in chapter 3). Instead, colonialism involved a period of transition from a tributary mode of production (beginning with the Iberian conquest of the Americas) to something that by the "end" of colonialism looked very different: a modern capitalist mode of production. In a tributary mode of production,[6] a ruling class extracts surplus wealth in the form of labor, goods, or monetary tribute from a subjugated class through the use of force or the threat of such. In the case of Europe, this mode of production corresponded with early-modern feudalism, which from the ninth to the fifteenth centuries resulted in the gradual accumulation of vast quantities of wealth. But the tributary mode of production didn't just disappear from history; instead it simply metamorphosed into other modes. The wealth accumulated during feudalism allowed aristocracies to develop increasingly large courts and armies, eventually giving rise to a mercantile system in which the surplus collected by the state and its agents could be made available to merchants, who would in turn engage in the exchange of commodities with those in other parts of the world. In this manner, trade routes were expanded, eventually leading to the "discovery" and conquest of the Americas—that is, the beginning of European colonialism and, with it, the dawn of globalization and what we understand today as "modernity."

The characteristics that defined this modernity in postmedieval Europe and that became associated with European "superiority"—an emphasis on individualism, rationality, and secularism; the values of scientific and technological progress; and the establishment of the nation-state as primary social form[7]—were all facilitated by processes financed through appropriation. As tribute flowed from colony to metropolis, resulting in increased circulation of commodities and the accumulation of even more wealth, the disparity between colonizer and colonized began to grow. In this sense, sixteenth-century Spain and its viceroyalties can be seen as the first set of "modern" core and periphery states,[8] the former achieving development at the expense of the underdevelopment of the latter. Thanks to resources extracted from its colonies, Spain became a modern unified territory with a national military capable of defeating the Turks in 1571 and ruled in a vernacular language and with an expanding economy. It was the riches in its colonies that financed such progress, establishing a model to be followed by Holland, England, and France.[9] In this sense, modernity—the general mode of organized "progress" that became dominant—was colonial from its starting point.[10]

If the first three centuries of colonialism were marked by territorial conquest, wealth extraction, and an increasingly interconnected global mercantile network, it would take until the industrial revolution of the eighteenth century for a mode of production not directly based on tribute to fully emerge. Colonialism slowly created the conditions for the transition from the tributary mode of production (plantations or mines with slaves) to something different: modern capitalism (factories with workers, developed national markets, and growing international trade cycles). The capitalist mode of production can be described as one in which people are *paid* to work instead of merely *forced* to work. Nevertheless, exploitation is still present in capitalism: workers generate an output value greater than what it costs to hire them, value that is converted by the capitalist into profit. Additionally, workers have no other choice but to sell their labor; since they do not own the means to produce anything themselves, they are obligated to buy what they need to subsist from the capitalist. A geographically extended labor pool—available and willing workers all over the world—was formed. This new labor market was created in large part by advances in manufacturing technologies linked with growth in the transportation, finance, and communication sectors that characterized the industrial revolution, and it allowed factory owners to easily replace skilled workers with interchangeable unskilled workers, which meant workforces could be increased or decreased (hired or fired) in response to fluctuations in the market. The resulting social relations that sustained both labor and commodity exchange in industrial capitalism were radically different from the feudal and family-based forms of production that preceded them.[11] Despite the continuities between colonialism and capitalism, capitalism did indeed transform the social and economic order that had characterized Europe during early colonial times.

An important point in this discussion, however, is that wage labor did not spread evenly across the world. In other words, the capitalist revolution did not look the same or have the same results outside of Europe. The

"coloniality of power," as described by Aníbal Quijano, means that opportunities for labor were always linked to race and geographically differentiated: while wage labor became the norm for white Europeans, their
non-Western counterparts continued to be exploited under earlier models (slavery, serfdom, and independent-commodity production) that were
nonetheless compatible with capitalism.[12] Colonial labor had always had a
racial component added to the other categories of worker classification;[13]
one's place within the system and the kind of labor one engaged in was determined by one's geographical and geopolitical location as much as one's
race, sex, and labor power. This did not stop being the case under capitalism, at least not for the colonies. Although we may speak of a general transition during the colonial period from a tributary to a capitalist mode of
production, the truth is that this transition was not experienced by everyone on equal terms. What defines the history and development of capitalism is, in fact, its ability to simultaneously operate with *multiple* modes of
production: a capitalist metropolis in which workers earn wages can co-
exist with tributary colonies in which workers are enslaved through mercantile systems of exchange, setting in motion large-scale flows of commodities and people that progressively extended across the world the
inequalities inherent in the capitalist system.[14]

Here we should pause to highlight the importance of slavery to the
economic development of the West, both during historical colonialism
and, just as importantly, during the transition to early industrial capitalism. The economic development of the West cannot be understood without slavery, although this reality is neglected in the standard histories of
capitalism.[15] As late as 1800, other nations such as China or Japan could
have emerged to occupy the place that Europe and the United States did
in global capitalism, but it was the advantage provided by slavery that allowed the colonizer nations to emerge as superpowers.[16]

Current scholarly work on "second slavery" (that is, the US-based wave
of slavery in the eighteenth and nineteenth centuries that followed the initial wave of slavery during the European colonial period) invalidates the
view of slave labor as an "archaic institution, incompatible with modernity, that was condemned to extinction after the advent of industrial capitalism, modern political regimes, and liberal ideologies."[17] During this

period, slavery was rehabilitated and redeployed in the creation of new productive zones for the cultivation of cotton, coffee, and sugar, shifting agricultural production from the old colonies of France and Great Britain to the Americas, with the southern United States providing 75 percent of the world supply of cotton from 1830 to the beginning of the US civil war in 1861 and expanding its cotton production from twenty million pounds to over two billion pounds a year during the first half of the nineteenth century.[18] This increase was accomplished not through agricultural innovations but through the systematization of terror that race-based slavery represented, including techniques such as the application of torture (for example, with a "whipping machine" that would turn slaves' backs into "bloody jelly") to increase output; expanded surveillance; decreased breaks; and plantation technologies such as inventory forms detailing the name, age, and value in dollars of slaves as well as spreadsheets for tracking daily cotton picking.[19] The slave plantation thus emerges not as premodern but as a site of the horrors and contradictions of modernity.[20] In the words of Robbie Shilliam, it is "plantation slavery in the Americas, not industrial factories in Europe, [that] epitomise the fundamental relationship between capital and (un)freedom."[21]

Aspects of this relationship have survived to our day, not only in the conditions of slavery under which certain minerals for the production of electronic devices are extracted in places such as the Democratic Republic of Congo[22] but also in the global networks of production that Jack Linchuan Qiu dubs "Appconn" (Apple-Foxconn), a form of "twenty-first-century slavery"[23] that relies on deplorable and exploitative work conditions in China to manufacture the latest consumer technologies. Slavery, as Sven Beckert and Seth Rockman remind us, is a crime against humanity that is never reducible to an economic "externality."[24]

From Neocolonialism to Postcolonialism

Strictly speaking, historical colonialism is over. Most colonies gained their independence by the 1960s. But independence, acquired at a bloody cost, did not overcome dependency. A combination of internal conflict, debt, corruption, and poverty—all direct or indirect legacies of colonialism—

meant that liberated colonies seldom achieved authentic independence in the form of generalized prosperity. Consider the case of the 1791 to 1804 revolution in Haiti, an uprising by black slaves that completely transformed the social and racial politics of the nation. Although the revolution managed to expel the French, it came at a cost of 162,000 lives and the imposition of an external debt of 150 million francs, or around $20 billion by today's standards, a debt that was eventually paid back at huge cost, the effects of which have burdened the country ever since.

The legacy of colonialism explains not only debt and poverty but also other important issues of our times such as racism, migration, lack of educational opportunities, and terrorism. The remnants of colonialism will linger as long as former colonizers continue to try to impose their economic and political models of development as the only worthy goals for the rest of the world.[25] Thus, although historical colonialism might be over, we can still speak of *coloniality*, that is, of legacies of colonialism that have outlived colonial rule per se. Theoretical and critical approaches such as neocolonialism, postcolonialism, and decoloniality have emerged to help us come to grips with that legacy.

Although these terms—*neocolonial, postcolonial,* and *decolonial*—are sometimes used interchangeably to describe similar projects of critique, it is important to locate their roots and differentiate their goals. *Neocolonialism* is a term generally associated with a twentieth-century discourse that assigned to the former colonial powers the blame for the stunted development of newly independent nations.[26] It is also a concept that allowed intellectuals to begin talking about the *internal colonialisms* that divide former colonial societies along ethnic, and not just racial, divides—for instance, with lighter-skinned people having a higher status than darker-skinned people.[27] Today, neocolonialism is used more frequently to suggest a new form of colonialism whereby a powerful country might exercise control not through territorial occupation but at a distance through economic or political domination, cultural monopolization, or the threat of military force. Contemporary US imperialism might be said to be a form of neocolonialism—in other words, a form of military and economic dominance without direct political control.

Since colonized elites played a crucial part in exploiting their own people (even if they did so under the protection of the colonizer), it is too simplistic to assign all the blame to the colonizers. Thus, *postcolonialism* attempts to offer a more nuanced analysis of colonialism and its repercussions, particularly with respect to the ways in which the relationship between former colonizer and colonized continues to shape the realities of both groups in the contemporary world. Postcolonial theory and postcolonial studies encompass many concerns, methods, critiques, movements, and agendas, and a brief overview of these is attempted here in order to relate them to our account of data colonialism developed in other chapters.[28]

Even though it is a response to historical colonialism, postcolonialism can be understood as a political reaction against inequality and exploitation *today*. A postcolonial critique is often adopted as a counterclaim against capitalism, globalization, and neoliberalism in our times, as it seeks to make evident their colonial roots even if those roots are partly obscured by contemporary ideologies. In the words of Sankaran Krishna, "If neoliberal globalization is the attempt at naturalizing and depoliticizing the logic of the market, or the logic of the economy, postcolonialism is the effort to politicize and denaturalize that logic and demonstrate the choices and agency inherent in our own lives."[29] Or, as Robert Young describes it, postcolonialism is an "active transformation of the present out of the clutches of the past."[30]

One of the central themes in postcolonialism is the issue of identity and representation: how the colonizer and the colonized represented themselves and each other. This is an important question because, as postcolonial theories suggest, modes of representation are not just cultural pronouncements; they are used to justify oppressive practices, including racism, enslavement, economic oppression, and even genocide. Postcolonial theories posit that the foundation of colonial modes of representation is *difference*, that is, the way in which the colonizer and the colonized were rendered as belonging to different categories of humanity, with the colonizer represented—as mentioned earlier—in opposition to the colonized by virtue of being strong, rational, civilized, resourceful, chosen by God, and so on. This differentiation is not merely a passive description but a form of symbolic violence,[31] imposing on the dominated a worldview created by the dominant that condemns the former to perpetuate the very structures that oppress them.

Authors such as Aimé Césaire and Albert Memmi, writing in the 1950s, argued that there was no real human encounter in colonialism, only *thingification*,[32] an objectification of the colonized that justifies violence and racism. The colonized were forced to occupy a place in which their culture and the culture of the colonizer were constantly in conflict and in which they not only suffered subjugation but came to accept it as a natural social order (although theorists such as Memmi have always seen in this opportunities for creation, not just destruction). Other writers such as Edward Said have linked issues of representation to the exercise of power. Said argues that "the Orient"[33] was formulated in the minds of Europeans to possess characteristics that were based not in a search for truth but in a desire to dominate, and he was mostly concerned with how these stereotypes, which could serve not only to oppress but also to romanticize or patronize, were projected and reproduced through scholarship and culture.[34]

Postcolonial studies also attempt to examine how history and science were weapons in the quest to use knowledge to subordinate the colonized politically and economically and to get them to accept their subordination. In order to accomplish this, history and science needed first to be portrayed as the domain of Europe, part of the heritage of the Enlightenment that the West deemed necessary to bring to the rest of the world. History (the particular histories and trajectories of colonial appropriation) thus became a universalizing Eurocentric endeavor, describing everything not just from the perspective of European eyes but in terms that made sense only in relation to European values. This kind of historicism situates progress and "universal" principles as emanating from the West and then flowing to the Rest: modernity emerges as a one-directional arrow pointing to Europe, something all "nonmodern" societies must strive toward. The history of human civilization is seen as an evolutionary trajectory that starts with man in a natural state and culminates with European "civilization." Whatever inferior samples are encountered along the way (in the form of non-European humans) can have their differences explained through natural (that is, racial) means and not through a history of power.[35] Whereas all knowledge systems can be said to be ethnocentric, this modern European ethnocentrism is the only one that claims for itself universality across time and space.[36] Postcolonial studies help us see how the language of modernity and universal knowledge, inscribed in historical discourses, becomes a tool of imperialism to civilize and educate colonial subjects.

The military, mercantile, and bureaucratic exploits of colonial Europe would not have been possible without scientific and technological tools. These included new means of communication and transportation (the telegraph and the railroad) as well as new ways of collecting and analyzing information for the purpose of the administration of populations and commodities (statistics, accounting, economic theory, and so on).[37] The success of these inventions in facilitating empire-building was seen as further validation of the superiority of the West.[38] But beyond the creation of tools for managing territories and populations, discussed from a different perspective in chapter 4, colonial science provided its own new rationalizations for conquest. A whole new obsession with classification, particularly during the eighteenth and nineteenth centuries, helped to establish the boundaries not only between human and beast but between perceived higher and lower forms of humans, all in the name of the expansion of science and, through it, the betterment of "man." Immanuel Kant, a central figure in modern Western philosophy, provided the first scientific definition of the concept of race in his 1775 essay "Of the Different Human Races." Subsequently, a branch of anthropology became invested in the elaboration of "racial types," whereby certain physical attributes were linked to certain mental and behavioral characteristics—for instance, skull size and other arbitrary measures were used in an attempt to establish the superiority of white men over people of color and also over white women.

This "scientific" racism and sexism would become essential in colonial governance. Well-meaning white people believed (and continue to believe) that Western science and technology were the only means of improving the condition of the destitute "savages" in the colonized territories. Other less well-meaning individuals saw the absence of "advanced" knowledge in the colonized as a good reason for their annihilation. Frederic W. Farrar (a cleric born in India who became friends with Charles Darwin) argued, for instance, that the extermination of the Tasmanian people was justified because these were people who had not "added one iota to the knowledge, the arts, the sciences, the manufactures, the morals of the world."[39]

Whereas postcolonial debates have given us important ways of critiquing the evolution of Western modes of knowledge production, the relationship between postcolonial theories and Western thinking remains complicated. At times, postcolonialism has been accused of borrowing too much from the West. For instance, postcolonialism shares many research interests with postmodernism, a movement that preceded it and influenced it. These overlapping interests include a questioning of signs and meanings, the negation of universalizing master narratives in favor of narrative multiplicity, the displacement of the subject in language, the conceptualization of the individual beyond a Cartesian framework, and the analysis of how power operates. This has ignited debates about whether postcolonial thinking is too close to the very thing it is trying to critique, but the case can be made that this engagement with Western theory has in fact strengthened postcolonialism's ability to "provincialize" European thinking.[40] By questioning its universality and insisting on its status as partisan historical narrative, postcolonial theory is able to challenge the concept of modernity and engage in telling "a different story of reason,"[41] one that accounts for the different subjects universalism has repressed.[42] Postcolonial theory has played a major role in helping merge our understandings of social injustice and what Santos calls cognitive injustice, which lies at the core of the injustices that data practices generate.[43]

From Postcolonialism to Decoloniality

These are goals that the project known as decoloniality also shares, but its approach to realizing them is somewhat different. To begin with, decolonial thinkers critique certain aspects of postcolonialism. They reject Western traditions more emphatically and instead draw their inspiration from the work of nonwhite and mostly non-Western thinkers such as Frantz Fanon. They accuse postcolonialism of being too aligned with the antihumanist thought of postmodernism: in their broad distrust of narratives, rationality, universalism, and constructs such as freedom and human rights—or, rather, in their association of all of these things exclusively with Western values—postcolonial theorists (the critique goes) become complicit in the continued dominance of Eurocentrism.[44] Instead, decolonial thinkers are inspired by and engaged with grassroots movements such as the Sem Terra (Landless) movement in Brazil or the Zapatistas in Chiapas, gender-equality movements such as Chicana and Muslima feminism, projects such as the Caribbean Philosophical Association's efforts to shift the geography of reason, and the creation of institutions such as the World Social Forum.

Decoloniality thus seeks to provide not just strategies for surviving in a neo- or postcolonial context but also models for articulating an alternative worldview emanating mostly from the Global South, a worldview that challenges and rejects notions of a Eurocentric modernity.[45] Ramón Grosfoguel identifies three central features of a decolonial theory. First, as already mentioned, it seeks intellectual sources beyond the Western canon and is inspired by political movements from the Global South. Second, it is based on a critical dialogue between diverse political and ethical projects that moves toward a *pluriversal* rather than a *universal* worldview (based on an abstract Western universalism). And finally, it recognizes that the decolonization of knowledge can be achieved only through critical thinking "from and with subalternized racial/ethnic/sexual spaces and bodies."[46]

Decoloniality is therefore not simply decolonization, defined as the end of colonial occupation and administration, but a broader rethinking of relations to ongoing coloniality. As postcolonial theorists themselves pointed out, decolonization did not result in the liberation of subjugated peoples but in the continuity of domination through new forms (including, as we argue in this book, in new social relations managed through data). The "coloniality of power," to return to Quijano's concept,[47] means that colonial structures persist everywhere, both in the so-called First World as well as the Third World, in cities as well as slums, in the minds of the oppressor as well as the oppressed. Whereas postcolonial theorists conceptualize capitalism as primarily a cultural phenomenon[48] and Marxists accuse postcolonialists of paying too much attention to culture instead of economics,[49] decolonial theory refuses to prioritize culture or the economy and instead sees the coloniality of power as both an ideological and material phenomenon.

Despite these differences, postcolonial and decolonial theories alike can be used for our purposes to examine the role of data relations in perpetuating modes of oppression. That is our goal for the rest of the book. By aligning our argument with the project of decoloniality, we hope to contribute to the imagining of alternative spaces for understanding and being in the world, spaces that, as Walter Mignolo argues, enable the building of life-affirming communal futures that are different from our pasts.[50]

The Coloniality of Data Relations   3

We are still living out the history of 1492. . . . The possibilities that were overlooked and unseen 500 years ago must re-emerge as humanity's project over the next 500 years.

—Ashis Nandy, Merryl Wyn Davies, and Ziauddin Sardar[1]

IN SID MEIER'S STRATEGY VIDEO GAME *Civilization IV: Colonization*, you—the human—can choose to play Spain, England, France, or the Netherlands in a battle to colonize the New World. The colonized, though, are represented by "nonplayer characters" controlled by the game's algorithms. Your role is to oversee an expanding territory from an omniscient "God view" perspective, allocating resources and squelching insurrections. Meanwhile, the only reason nonwhite people and their lands exist is to be conquered and used, making at least that aspect of the simulation seem authentically colonial. Rated E for "Everyone," the game whitewashes the truly horrendous aspects of colonialism: the slavery, the rape, the genocide.[2] And perhaps because of this level of sanitization, the game-play quickly becomes boring and repetitive, falling into the established 4X pattern that characterizes strategy video games: explore, expand, exploit, and exterminate.

It is not surprising that strategy video games, which are all about the expedient management of resources in the context of colonization, should follow this 4X model. But what of data colonialism? In this chapter, we use the framework of exploring, expanding, exploiting, and exterminating to conduct a transhistorical comparison of dispossession that will reveal continuities between historical colonialism and today's data colonialism. To truly recognize the injustices of today, we need to look at them through the eyes of yesterday. By understanding the detailed parallels, we can uncover fully the *coloniality*[3] of data relations, a concept that points to the broader continuities in how the legacy of historical colonialism resonates in the present—in this case, through social relations as abstracted and commodified by data.

Of course, we know that historical colonialism was anything but a game. On the American continent alone, of the 145 million people living in the hemisphere before the conquest, 90–95 percent had been exterminated by 1691.[4] Most of the survivors were condemned to poverty. Around the time Columbus arrived in America, a typical European had an average per capita income three times that of someone living in what is now sometimes called the Global South. By 1850, that ratio had increased to five to one. By the early to mid-twentieth century, when around 85 percent of the world was under some form of colonial rule, the ratio was fourteen to one.[5] The inequality that plagues us today is not entirely the result of colonialism but at the same time cannot be explained without it. From the perspective of postcolonial and decolonial studies (the disciplines that consider critiques of colonialism and capitalism from the viewpoint of the colonized), it is impossible to understand most aspects of our contemporary world—including, we propose, the role of data in our lives—without considering the unfinished history of colonialism and how it continues to shape former colonizers and the formerly colonized. We will be arguing in this chapter that the social relations embodied in data are part of a broader colonial (and not merely capitalist) legacy. This legacy involves a more extreme degree of alienation than usually recognized within a traditional Marxist perspective, because subjects are estranged not only from the products of their labor but from their own personhood, their basic realities as living beings. They are, in short, dispossessed of something basic that belongs to them, through an appropriation carried out through the extraction of data.

Media studies have occasionally concerned themselves with colonialism but mostly through approaches such as area studies or a critique of media and cultural imperialism. These kinds of efforts examine why, for instance, media has developed in a particular way in former colonies or how Western media culture has saturated global markets. Although our engagement with colonialism is much more direct, we reiterate that we wish to avoid simplistic metaphors when comparing historical colonialism and data colonialism. Rather, what is proposed in this chapter is that the dispossession inherent in data relations can be better understood through a careful analysis of how extraction worked in historical colonialism. Specifically, this chapter will argue that historical colonialism and data colonialism share some fundamental structures that ground the resource appropriations and social relations of each: the way the colonized subject is conceptualized and how colonialism shapes the way the colonized think of themselves; the naturalization of certain modes of ruling subjects; and the legitimation of certain types of knowledge with their associated claims to power, including a specific conceptualization of time and space that ends up universalizing a specific worldview.

If historical colonialism was an appropriation of land, bodies, and natural resources, data colonialism can be understood as an appropriation of social resources, one that represents both a progression of capitalism and its return, potentially, to more brutal forms of exploitation. It is *because* the dispossession of social resources today operates in ways that replicate how the dispossession of natural resources once worked that we argue data relations re-create a colonizing form of power. Data relations—as defined in chapter 1—are new types of human relations that give corporations a comprehensive view of our sociality, enabling human life to become an input or resource for capitalism. In this neocolonial scheme, the colony is not a geographic location but an "enhanced reality" in which we conduct our social interactions under conditions of continuous data extraction. The resources that are being colonized are the associations, norms, codes, knowledge, and meanings that help us maintain social connections, the human and material processes that constitute economic activity, and the space of the subject from which we face the social world.

When speaking in general terms about the exploitation of social resources, we don't mean to imply that the social constitutes a "pure" domain that somehow should exist outside of power and appropriation. As the history of capitalism shows, political and economic forces have endeavored for a long time to dominate different aspects of human life and, in so doing, have produced particular social domains. Thus, under capitalism, social interactions became progressively commodified, with every-day social interactions increasingly embedded in economic relations.[6] The data colonialism of our time expands this commodification by an unprecedented order of magnitude. In this new world, corporations act as colonizers that deploy digital infrastructures of connection to monetize social interactions, and the colonized are relegated to the role of subjects who are driven to use these infrastructures in order to enact their social lives. Just as, to meet the requirements of industrial capitalism, all economic relations were transformed into market relations via the medium of money,[7] today social relations and human life in general are increasingly transformed into potential market relations through the medium of data. Because it is very often the stuff of a subject's own life that is being exchanged, data relations comprise what in the perspective of colonial history can be seen as an embryonic "mode of production," a new form of tributary relationship between colonizer and colonized.

In Marxist theory, a "mode of production" is a concept used to differentiate the way that the economy of a historically specific society is organized in contrast to other societies. Human beings plan and organize their labor—that is, the extraction of sustenance from nature—and in the process shape their reality. Each mode of production thus represents a historically specific organization of labor: a unique arrangement of tools, knowledge, and social structures that constitutes a particular kind of reality. We are not arguing here that data colonialism represents a new, fully formed mode of production. Rather, we are proposing that data colonialism represents a transformation that will *eventually* result in a new mode of production. In other words, we are at the cusp of a radical expansion of the processes of capitalist production and the factors that contribute to it; this expansion will entail, over time, a complete reorganization of social relations and a transformation of what counts as economic resources. Although it is too early to describe the contours of this new mode of production and to predict how exactly it will shape society in the long run, what is already evident is that the shift entails much more than the emergence of digital labor that so many critics have discussed.[8] Just as historical colonialism reorganized all aspects of the lives of its subjects (from the economic and political to the psychological and spiritual), data colonialism makes the entirety of our existence available to capitalism. Capitalism continuously seeks to integrate as many dimensions of life as possible into the production process, but what is concerning at the moment is the speed at which areas of sociality previously cordoned off from capitalism are being commodified.

In order to explain why and how this is happening, we need to rethink how we see colonialism and capitalism as apparently distinct and, indeed, incompatible modes of production. Instead of looking at them as discrete and separate moments in history, it is more productive to look at colonialism as an "uncivilized" mode of production allowed to operate at the margins of a more "civilized" capitalism. Let us then conceive of colonialism and capitalism as two sides of the same coin: one side enacting dispossession in a brutal and rampant manner and the other normalizing this process by relegating it to the *outside* (outside the present, outside the civilized, outside the measurable, and so on). All the while, however, the process of dispossession itself is presented as a necessary and beneficial step in human progress. Various critics of neoliberalism and datafication[9] have already recognized in our times a renewed race to amass wealth through new kinds of dispossession. But to understand why this form of accumulation is a continuation and not a break with the historical arc of the past five centuries, we need to look more closely at the history of colonialism and its role within capitalism.

One of the goals of this chapter is thus to bring critical research on colonialism and critical internet studies into conversation with each other, methodologically and politically. To accomplish this, the chapter begins with an assessment of the continuities and discontinuities involved in the kind of appropriation that is at work in historical and data colonialism. We then proceed to analytically compare the historical correspondences between the past and the present in terms of the aforementioned 4X's of colonialism: exploration, expansion, exploitation and extermination. This will allow us to begin to formulate a framework for theorizing alternatives or what we call "counterpresents" to data colonialism, a task to which we will return more fully in the last section of the book but which we need to start here before analyzing in the second part of the book the threats to human sociality and autonomy that data colonialism poses.

Data Colonialism as Appropriation and Neoextractivism

Colonialism, in its old and new forms, operates through the dispossession of resources. This dispossession happens through the *appropriation* of things that belong to someone else and through the *extraction* of value from the appropriated resources. By doing this, the natural and the social worlds are implicated in new modes of production, transformed into factors in ever-changing capitalist cycles of production. Put differently, appropriation and extraction convert life, particularly human life, into profit centers for capitalism. We will discuss appropriation first and extraction second.

Appropriation frames resources as *naturally* occurring, free for the taking. Let us recall that historical colonialism dispossessed indigenous people of their land *before* they could conceive of it as private wealth in the way that the colonizers conceived of it as private wealth. The colonizers first appropriated the land based on a particular legal and social framing of the land; then they gave the land value by putting it to use in a particular way, that is, as private property. By the time indigenous people understood the concept of private property, it was too late: their land had acquired new value, this value had been stolen from them, and they themselves had been overpowered and enslaved by the new system. In a similar vein, our social lives are not material "wealth" to us, like money and property are. But once they are datafied, they cease to be just life and become a source of wealth.

For personal data to be freely available for appropriation, it must first be rendered as a natural resource, a resource that is *just there*, ready to be extracted. This is where the logic of colonialism comes into play; the idea is reinforced that the depletion of resources by those who find them is natural. There is a parallel here with how capitalism has appropriated natural resources, which is by framing their state of readiness for exploitation through legal, linguistic, and other means. Jason Moore[10] describes how this process has worked, arguing that capitalism has so far depended on the availability of *cheap nature*: natural resources that are abundant, easy to appropriate from their rightful owners, and whose depletion is seen as unproblematic. The resources are not cheap *per se*, but legal and philosophical frameworks are established to rationalize them as such. Exterminating natives and chopping down trees is accomplished "cheaply" only when a certain ideological, legal, cultural, and even religious system of beliefs is put in place.

Today, what we have is a different version of the same fundamental move: the collection of *cheap social data*, an abundant "natural" resource. We can see this rationalization operating in the metaphors used to describe data extraction. A World Economic Forum report stated that "personal data will be the new 'oil'—a valuable resource of the 21st century. It will emerge as a new asset class touching all aspects of society."[11] The allusion to petroleum seemed to be particularly evocative in the early 2010s, as evidenced by the number of times it was employed by CEOs and analysts. The CEO of Tresata said, "Just like oil was a natural resource powering the last industrial revolution, data is going to be the natural resource for this industrial revolution."[12] The vice president of the European Commission responsible for the Digital Agenda claimed that "data is a precious thing. . . . That's why I've called data the new oil. Because it's a fuel for innovation, powering and energizing our economy."[13]

Like oil, data needs to be processed. But unlike oil, data is not a substance found in nature at all. It is the by-product of *social interactions* that are mediated by digital technologies, a by-product that is captured and processed by a third party that is not intimately involved with the people in the interaction and indeed can operate at many removes from them through the market for selling data. The first use of the metaphor of data as the "new oil" is attributed to Clive Humby, the conceptual grandfather of the loyalty shopping-club card, who in 2006 said, "Data is the new oil. It's valuable, but if unrefined it cannot really be used. It has to be changed into gas, plastic, chemicals, et cetera to create a valuable entity that drives profitable activity; so must data be broken down, analyzed for it to have value."[14] Data must thus be presented as an ownerless resource that can be exploited only by certain parties (what Julie Cohen calls data refineries).[15] A few excerpts from a report by the Organization for Economic Cooperation and Development are worth quoting at length.

Data are an intangible asset; like other information-related goods, they can be reproduced and transferred at almost zero marginal costs. So in contrast to the concept of ownership of physical goods, where the owner typically has exclusive rights and control over the good—including for instance the freedom to destroy the good—this is not the case for intangibles such as data. . . . Data ownership can be a poor starting point for data governance, and can even be misleading. . . . The important question isn't who owns the data. Ultimately, we all do. A better question is who owns the means of analysis? Because that's how . . . you get the right information in the right place. The digital divide isn't about who owns data—it's about who can put that data to work.[16]

What is suggested by this kind of discourse is that data "oil" needs corporations to transform it into something useful. Thus, the appropriation of this resource is presented as something natural, with benefits for all of us.

The transformation of "raw" data into a resource from which corporations can derive value is possible only through a material process of *extraction*, the second of the concepts we are discussing. As Naomi Klein observes, extractivism implies a "nonreciprocal, dominance-based relationship with the earth" that creates *sacrifice zones*, "places that, to their extractors, somehow don't count and therefore can be . . . destroyed, for the supposed greater good of economic progress."[17] But extraction has also acquired new horizons. Whereas authors like Alberto Acosta[18] use the term *neoextractivism* to refer to the appropriation of natural resources in neocolonial settings (conducted by authoritarian or even progressive governments stuck in relations of dependency with the Global North), the term can also be used to describe the shift from natural to social resources in the colonial process of dispossession. *Today the new sacrifice zone is social life.* It is this shift that makes data colonialism such a threat to human life, for as Leanne Betasamosake Simpson argues, "The act of extraction removes all of the relationships that give whatever is being extracted meaning."[19] Life, extracted through data relations, acquires a devalued meaning and becomes a mere factor in capitalist production.

Warnings about the perils of data extractivism are not new, as Evgeny Morozov reminds us.[20] But we can now be more specific about how this process unfolds through a series of *extractive rationalities* that further justify exploitation, including

- *economic* rationalities that frame the data we produce and the labor we contribute as valueless because they are generated through socialization and not paid work and therefore are available for capitalization by other parties;

- *legal* rationalities that, as Julie Cohen argues,[21] frame data as ownerless, redefining notions of privacy and property in order to establish a new moral order that justifies the appropriation of data;

- *developmental* rationalities that present data colonialism as a civilizational project, carried out on behalf of underdeveloped subjects in the name of progress and safety;

- *cultural* rationalities that promote "sharing" while lowering the value of privacy and raising the value of competitive self-presentation; and

- *technical* rationalities that frame data appropriation as a legitimate goal of science, entrepreneurship, and human creativity.

These rationalities are more practical and specific than are the broad ideologies of data colonialism mentioned in chapter 1. They help make all the small choices involved with data relations seem rational and common sense.

The 4X's of Data Extractivism

Looking at data relations with colonial precedents explicitly in mind, as we do in this section, helps us see how it is that the extractive rationalities mentioned above are being actualized in the banal habits of data relations. Our goal in doing so is not to provide a conclusive compendium of analogues but rather to select certain moments in the history of colonialism and describe their reverberations today in a way that evokes the persistence of appropriation and extraction. To achieve this, we have organized our analysis in terms of the 4X's of strategy video games mentioned at the beginning of the chapter.

Explore

Extractivism began at the point of contact between the colonizer and the colonized. This initial encounter contained within it the terms of exploitation to be deployed as the colonizers explored and "discovered" new resources. Consider the Spanish *Requerimiento* of 1513, a document read by conquistadors to newly found subjects, who were abruptly informed that their lands belonged not to them but in reality to the spiritual leader of the explorers, someone called the pope, successor to Saint Peter and leader of the Catholic Church:

> Of all these nations God our Lord gave charge to one man, called St. Peter,
> that he should be Lord and Superior of all the men in the world, that all
> should obey him, and that he should be the head of the whole Human Race,
> wherever men should live, and under whatever law, sect, or belief they should
> be; and He gave him the world for his kingdom and jurisdiction.[22]

The document also informed indigenous people that if they willingly subjected to this strange order, their lives, property, and religious beliefs would be respected and left alone. Sensing that not many natives would avail themselves of this option, however, the *Requerimiento* spelled out what would happen to those who refused.

> But, if you do not do this, and maliciously make delay in it, I certify to you
> that, with the help of God, we shall powerfully enter into your country, and
> shall make war against you in all ways and manners that we can, and shall
> subject you to the yoke and obedience of the Church and of their Highnesses;
> we shall take you and your wives and your children, and shall make slaves
> of them, and as such shall sell and dispose of them as their Highnesses may
> command; and we shall take away your goods, and shall do you all the mis-
> chief and damage that we can.[23]

The irony, of course, is that voluntary submission was not even a real option, because this was a document read in Spanish to non-Spanish-speaking peoples. Even if they could have accessed a limited translation, they probably would not have understood the legal and theological concepts by which they were suddenly and forcefully dispossessed of their property, or even understood "property" in the same way as did the invaders. The quick annexation of resources was justified by means of these abstract rationalizations that needed to make some sort of sense only to the colonizer.

The *Requerimientos* of our times are known as end-user license agreements (EULA) or statements of rights and responsibilities (SRR). These documents spell out how newly discovered resources and their presumed owners are to be treated by colonizers. For instance, an earlier version of Google Chrome's EULA stated that "you give Google a perpetual, irrevocable, worldwide, royalty-free, and non-exclusive license to reproduce, adapt, modify, translate, publish, publicly perform, publicly display and distribute any Content which you submit, post or display on or through, the Services."[24] Meanwhile, Facebook's privacy-settings page reassuringly informs users that "you're in charge. We're here to help you get the experience you want."[25] The actual SRR tells a different story, however (the agreement was last revised on April 2018, making the language more clear and accessible but not significantly changing the terms of use). By agreeing to use Facebook's platform, users have little control over things like how their location is monitored, how their behavior is tracked for advertising purposes, or what information about them is shared to companies outside of Facebook. Users can opt out of some of these practices, but by default new accounts are set to share as much information as possible with Facebook.[26] At least according to European law, "opting out" does not meet the requirements for legally valid consent.[27]

Users give Facebook permission to use, for commercial or noncommercial purposes, whatever content they upload to the platform, including photos and videos. What is less well known is that the license that users give Facebook, as specified in the SRR, is transferable (which means companies affiliated with Facebook also own the content), worldwide (which means it applies to all Facebook users, regardless of the laws in the places where they live), and royalty-free (which means users are not entitled to any remuneration). As Van Alsenoy and colleagues argue, this agreement might be in violation of EU laws, including copyright laws and those that the European Court of Human Rights established about the right of individuals to control the use of their images.[28] Arguing that Facebook is bound only by California law is in itself a violation of the EU concept that consumer contracts shall be governed by the laws of their countries of residence. Taking the laws and rationalities of one location and attempting to apply them universally to the rest of the world is a very colonial move, on par with the *Requerimiento*.

But that's not all. The SRR also informs users of the following:

- "Facebook is not responsible for the actions, content, information, or data of third parties, and you release us, our directors, officers, employees and agents from any claims and damages, known and unknown, arising out of or in any way connected with any claim you have against any such third parties."

- "We do not guarantee that Facebook will always be safe, secure or error-free."

- "If you violate the letter or spirit of this Statement, or otherwise create risk or possible legal exposure for us, we can stop providing all or part of Facebook to you."[29]

Such blanket and overreaching clauses—which are standard in the social quantification sector—are not only legally dubious but as full of hubris as the *Requerimiento* was. Companies reserve the right to modify agreements at any time, and users are expected to preemptively agree to any changes, no matter when and how often they are implemented. Because the language is so incomprehensible, most users simply scroll to the bottom of the document and click the "I agree" button without so much as a quick glance.[30]

"Exploration" and territorial annexation in historical colonialism were enacted by advances in the technologies of transportation and the sciences of management. Following the "discovery" of the Americas, a global network for the flow of goods and information began to take shape, a network whose infrastructure continues to be visible today and whose development was part and parcel of the growth of Western science and technology. Francis Bacon, for instance, made an explicit connection between long-distance travel (that is, colonial expansion and the knowledge transfers it unleashed) and the growth of various scientific disciplines.[31] Since the colonies could not be managed directly by the metropolis, they had to be objectified through scientific means and represented through emerging forms of records that could travel through time and space and thus conquer complexity. Principal among these new methods of management were two important technologies: *maps* (representations of the space to be colonized and managed) and *surveys* (mechanisms to extract data that can be analyzed in order to manage colonized spaces). Cartography, of course, had a long history preceding colonialism. But according to Cole Harris, modern maps "conceptualized unfamiliar space in Eurocentric terms, situating it within a culture of vision, measurement, and management."[32]

Like the network visualizations of today, colonial maps illustrated a form of knowledge that can be described as *nodocentric*.[33] The maps showed the location of mines, ports, towns, and other resources that were crucial to the operation of the empire; they isolated and represented the points or nodes that had value and rendered everything else invisible. A network diagram performs very similar functions. Only nodes and their connections are prioritized, giving us a reality in which nodes can only "see" other nodes, and only nodes deserve to be accounted for. In essence, the colonial maps of the past and the network diagrams of the present function as spatial representations of a power structure that in each case submits to a capitalist and a colonialist logic. They connect peripheral resources to processing centers or network hubs while depicting intermediary spaces as empty or dead.[34] Locations that hold no value to the colonial enterprise, just like individuals who are not users of the platform, practically disappear from the map or diagram.

Speaking of processing centers, it is important to note the role in exploration that the metropolis played as the centralized data bank in which information about colonized territories would be collected, analyzed, and used to assemble maps and other documents. Institutions such as the Casa de la Contratación de las Indias and the Consejo Real y Supremo de las Indias in Spain or the Royal Geographical Society in London would function as information repositories and map production centers at which standardized survey data would be organized into chorographic records and reports on the natural and social history of colonized territories. Other institutions such as the Dutch East India Company maintained extensive botanical gardens to collect knowledge about plant species from the colonies. Centers such as the Society of Jesus in Rome served as clearinghouses of new medical knowledge based on remedies made from New World ingredients, knowledge that would then be disseminated through the connections of these centers to universities.[35] Today, data centers serve similar functions by storing data and "mining" it—a pertinent colonial metaphor—to produce new knowledge for the benefit of corporations.[36]

The creation of a global network that facilitated colonial exploration was presented as further proof of the superiority of Europeans over non-Western peoples.[37] This network started to acquire a more familiar shape with the more recent commercialization of the telegraph and the telephone starting in the nineteenth century. As the planet became crisscrossed with an infrastructure that continues to account for 80 percent of global information flows today, the geography of the cable system replicated the mercantile routes established during historical colonialism,[38] and colonial maps continued to exert their influence. For example, Britain forced companies that operated transatlantic submarine cables to use London as their connection hub (after World War I, the epicenter for global communications shifted from England to the United States).[39] Ownership of the new communication infrastructure continued to follow colonial models as well by concentrating it in the hands of a few multinational consortia of state and private-sector corporations. When independence was finally achieved, former colonies simply inherited the infrastructure of the colonizers and in many cases were pressured to allow foreign companies to continue to control and profit from that infrastructure. To attempt to intervene with that model could have potentially disastrous results, as evidenced by the extreme example of Chile, where the US-based International Telephone & Telegraph corporation played a crucial role in the CIA-backed overthrow of the government in 1973 after democratically elected president Salvador Allende threatened, among other measures, to nationalize the telecom industry.

We would do well to remember, however, that even when infrastructure came under the control of independent governments in postcolonial times, it did not necessarily represent gains for the average citizen. As Miriyam Aouragh and Paula Chakravartty[40] remind us, calls by former colonies for the democratization of global media systems often went hand in hand with efforts by those same governments to silence dissent at home. In most cases, the censorship and antidemocratic regulation undertaken by authoritarian regimes was backed by the United States and other Western powers; commitment by the West to "freedom of information" consistently took second place to the support of oppressive regimes that pushed the West's agenda of modernization.[41]

By considering these precedents, we can see that the social quantification sector's exploration of the exploitable regions of our social lives adheres in large part to colonial patterns of infrastructure development and ownership, intelligence gathering, and imperial politics. One need only consider Facebook's Free Basics project. According to its own PR, Facebook is "helping people around the world access impactful local services, including health resources, education and business tools, refugee assistance sites, and more."[42] But the NGO Global Voices calls the program an instance of "digital colonialism" that, under the guise of bringing "free" internet to underdeveloped countries, locks its fifty million users into the company's extraction model. The Global Voices report[43] looked at the success of the program in Colombia, Ghana, Kenya, Mexico, Pakistan, and the Philippines and found that Free Basics is not always customized to feature local content or use local languages. Additionally, the program breaks net neutrality principles by preventing users from browsing the internet openly, and, more importantly, it collects data about *all* the activities of users (restricted as they are), not just those conducted on Facebook. Because most users of Free Basics are people already connected to the internet who merely want to lower their data-plan bills, the report concludes that the program is motivated more by the desire to capture new audiences and less by a desire to help people bridge the digital divide. That is probably why in 2016, civil society in India organized to force the government to prevent Free Basics from being offered in that country,[44] a move that drove Marc Andreessen (cofounder of Netscape and a Facebook investor) to lecture Indian civil society via Twitter on the economic futility of anticolonialism.[45]

Expand

Indians have plenty of reason to be suspicious of foreign corporations. Founded in 1600, the East India Company by the year 1833 controlled five hundred thousand square miles of territory in South Asia, encompassing 93.7 million subjects paying 22,718,794 pounds a year to the British empire in taxation. At its height, the Company controlled about half of the world's trade, specializing in basic commodities such as tea, textiles, and spices. The power of the East India Company was secured by its own military and paramilitary armies, which served not only to protect its interests and enforce compliance with its decrees but also to collect revenue and perform police duties.[46]

Along with military force, the East India Company relied on technological innovation to expand and manage its empire. A perfect example of this is the railroad, which in the nineteenth century came to embody colonialism's hunger and capacity for growth, not to mention its "civilizing" mission. Roads and maritime routes had already established flows of information and wealth even before colonialism, but the railroad was seen as a dramatic representation of the gap between civilized and noncivilized people. British civil servants, for instance, condescendingly joked that all signs of civilization disappeared beyond one hundred yards on either side of the railway track in India.[47] This attitude can perhaps be explained by the fact that the railroad embodied most of what was seen as revolutionary in the industrial era: metal instead of wood as the primary construction material, mechanized power, unprecedented speed (which redefined the scale of distance and time), and a logic of rationality and precise timing.[48] The effect of the railroad on the expansion of empire stemmed from its role not just as transportation technology but also as a means of economic development, state building, and information distribution. The beginnings of cybernetics can be traced to the information-overload crisis that the railroad introduced and that demanded new methods of control.[49] Domestic and international markets emerged thanks to the railroad, and states acquired cogency and identity in part due to the regular connections it made possible. The railroad as transportation and communication technology enhanced colonial governance by improving and extending tax collection and information flows, making centralization more efficient and allowing for the rapid deployment of military resources.[50]

Idealistic colonizers believed that the railroad, by bringing different social groups together as they traveled in proximity, would eventually erode caste divisions and barriers imposed by religious beliefs[51] (although, curiously, this idealism did not extend to the divisions between colonizers and colonized). Karl Marx himself believed the railroad and the newspaper would help to politically unify India.[52] This list of effects and hopes seems to closely mirror those surrounding the internet. During rosier times, many believed that the internet would transform economies by creating and redistributing new wealth, that it would facilitate new levels of intercultural understanding by creating more opportunities for dialogue, that it would democratize governance and topple authoritarian regimes, and that it would lead to a renaissance of journalism.[53]

Other nineteenth-century innovations—surveillance and population-control technologies—also had a profound impact on the expansion of colonialism. Surveillance technologies are complementary to the use of force but are distinct from them. They function as a prelude or threat to the actual use of violence, keeping certain elements of the population in check. In the case of colonialism, they also aimed to shape the modes of living of the colonized and rearrange these modes according to principles based on Western notions of progress. Often, the colonies served as laboratories to experiment with these methods before importing them to the homeland. Surveillance technologies such as the panopticon, which Foucault described as an exemplary illustration of modern disciplinary power, were first tried in India and then imported to the United Kingdom.[54] Fingerprinting was also first applied in South Asia in the mid-nineteenth century by William J. Herschel as a means of controlling prisoners, pensioners, and contractors. Only later did the practice reach England. Along with other forms of identification that were introduced in the colonies, the point of fingerprinting was not primarily to identify unknown subjects (who hadn't been fingerprinted yet) but to extend police power over groups who were already under suspicion and already indexed by the system.[55] Through technologies that made it easier to control the population, colonial power could be expanded to new provinces and social domains and, indeed, introduced at home.

Colonial implementations of these surveillance technologies continue to reverberate today in digital data and privacy issues. Similarly, digital methods of "fingerprinting" (capturing a unique computer identity instead of an impression of unique finger ridges) are an essential component of computer-based surveillance systems that aim to track all activity in order to identify threats.[56] Initiatives such as the Aadhaar system in India (discussed in the next chapter) assign a universal identification number to every citizen based on biometric data, supposedly to improve the distribution of social benefits but also to generate new commercial and security streams of data.[57] Meanwhile in China, where 530 patents were filed in 2017 alone for camera- and video-surveillance technologies,[58] the state is rapidly approaching its goal of providing continuous and total surveillance in public spaces. Even public toilets in some locations are equipped with facial-recognition software to dispense only the allowed amount of toilet paper to users, ensuring they don't go above their quota within a certain time frame.[59]

Of course, no system of surveillance is perfect and all-encompassing, which is why the ultimate goal of a monitoring system is for the subject to *internalize* the disciplinary gaze of the authorities, as Foucault described in his analysis of the panopticon.[60] But even before the panopticon, methods such as taxation and the confession of sins were used during historical colonialism to ensure that colonial subjects felt an obligation to behave as though everything, from their material possessions to their innermost thoughts and desires, was open for scrutiny and auditing and had to be reported to the corresponding secular or religious authorities.[61]

Similarly, obedience to authority in data colonialism is promoted through a quasi-paranoid self-monitoring feeling that "we live in public" but that we need not worry too much about it because everyone else is also being watched. We need not worry, that is, as long as we have "done nothing wrong." If the panopticon effect relied on our inability to tell exactly when we were being watched, so that we behaved all the time as though we were, the "inverse panopticon effect"[62] of pervasive data surveillance relies on us knowing that we are being watched all the time but lapsing into behaving as though we are not, thus naturalizing acceptance of a world in which surveillance and continuous tracking operate unnoted in the background.

In this manner, the technologies of data colonialism become what Ashis Nandy called (in the context of historical colonialism) our most *in-*

timate enemies—internalized overseers that we carry with us even when we are not connected to the network. As Nandy observes, colonialism is a "state of mind" that requires a "shared culture" between the colonizer and the colonized.[63] Our comfortable acceptance, at least until recently, of the extractive rationalities of data colonialism indicates the extent to which our subjectivities had already been utterly occupied by data colonialism's norms and ideologies.

Exploit

Whereas *exploration* and *expansion* involve the "discovery" of new resources and the extension of ideological frameworks for marking such resources as available for appropriation, *exploitation* constitutes the actual work of extraction and formalizes a new type of relation within society, a new social contract.

Natural resources, or *cheap nature,* could be exploited by colonialists and capitalists only through employing *cheap labor,* which framed the productive capacity of a certain class of human beings (first slaves and then workers) as exploitable also. Like cheap nature, cheap social data can be fully capitalized only through the exploitation of cheap labor. But as we argued in chapter 1, data relations are not labor relations in the strict sense of the word. Jason Moore explains that "capitalism must commodify life/work but depends upon the 'free ride' of uncommodified life/work to do so."[64] Similarly, with data colonialism, the exploitation that occurs through social quantification has less to do with the kind of exploitation that happens in a factory and more with the "free ride" that capitalism benefits from when extracting wealth from our broader social lives.

Words such as *exploitation* and *labor* have very specific meanings in Marxist theory, so it is worth discussing how they might be employed in the context of datafication. Strictly speaking, as Nick Srnicek observes, internet users do not receive wages, and their work is not used to lower production costs, increase productivity, and so on, so "it is hard to make the case that what they do is labor, properly speaking."[65] Thus, from a Marxist perspective, internet users cannot be said to form part of a working class, and we can't say they are exploited in the traditional sense. But theorists argue that media consumers are exploited not because they literally work for media companies but because as an audience they become a commodity sold to advertisers without themselves benefiting at all (for researcher and activist Dallas Smythe, for instance, watching advertisements was a form of labor and exploitation).[66]

Our argument is that data colonialism expands the domain of production in our capitalist society in a more fundamental way, giving way to an emerging new order, a new structuring of social relations. Individuals continue to work and sell their labor per the traditional dynamics of labor relations, but now they are implicated in capitalism in other ways that do not even require them to work for anyone. They simply need to participate in social life, as they ordinarily would, in order to generate value for the capitalist. Datafication thus meets Lawrence Crocker's necessary and sufficient conditions for exploitation: "That there be a surplus product [data] which is under the control of a group [the social quantification sector] which does not include all the producers of that surplus [the public]."[67] Capitalists also continue to exploit workers in the traditional way (by collecting more in profit than they pay in wages), but now they are able to exploit individuals who do not even work for them and to whom they do not pay anything. Thus, while the original Marxist definitions of exploitation should be respected, the important point is that the absence of *direct* exploitation (that is, through a regular job) does not mean exploitation is not happening *indirectly* (by workers being "excluded from the means of production and from their benefits,"[68] as Raymond Murphy observes).

For these reasons, the thesis that datafication technologies can have democratic potential must be treated with extreme suspicion. It has become acceptable (even fashionable) to admit that while the platforms of the Cloud Empire are exploitative, they can still be used as ad hoc tools in the fight against capitalism. Although the short-term achievements that platform activism can facilitate are important, we must be vigilant that these technologies do not become what Ellen Meiksins Wood calls *an alibi for capitalism*.[69] When people insist that these platforms are an important "civic" space of resistance against the power of the state and of corporations, they are in fact weakening and corrupting our conceptualization of what a "civic" space must be. As Meiksins Wood argues, this reconstituted civic space is framed from the beginning as a new form of social power "in which many coercive functions that once belonged to the state [are] relocated in the 'private' sphere, in private property, class exploitation, and market imperatives."[70] In that way, platforms are machines for turning the social into a form "adequate to capital," as Marx would put it.[71] Describing the commercialized civic space of 1990s capitalism in terms that might as well refer to the Cloud Empire, Meiksins Wood says of this supposedly civic and public space:

> We are being asked to pay a heavy price for the all-embracing concept of "civil society. . . ." No ancient despot could have hoped to penetrate the personal lives of his subjects—their choices, preferences, and relationships—in the same comprehensive and minute detail, not only in the workplace but in every corner of their lives.[72]

More bluntly, if the price of new tools for "overthrowing capitalism" is to annex all of social life to capitalism, then the deal is a bad one.

As with previous stages of colonialism and capitalism, exploitation creates and exacerbates inequalities between metropolis and colonies, between "developed" and "underdeveloped" worlds. The flow of data between the Global North and the Global South exemplifies the inequalities that still plague neocolonial relations, especially since the circulation of digital data is becoming just as important as the circulation of material goods in international trade. Cross-border data exchanges represented an overall traffic flow of 211.3 terabytes per second (TBps) in 2014 (up from 4.7 TBps in 2005) and were valued at $7.8 trillion in that year alone. But a closer look reveals that exchanges are highly uneven: while flows between North America and Europe jumped from 1,000 TBps to more than 20,000 TBps between 2005 and 2014, the flow between North America and Latin America, for example, increased only from 500 TBps to 5,000 TBps during that time, and the flow between Asia and Africa (to illustrate flows between the Global South) went from less than 50 TBps to no more than 500 TBps.[73] An overwhelming majority of all cross-border data traffic passes through the United States and is subject to whatever surveillance and collection methods that government deems necessary. Thus, the Global North still assumes the role of gatekeeper, as it did in the days of the telegraph and the telephone, and data flows continue to replicate the movement of resources from colony to metropolis. There seems to be, however, an imminent shift in the struggle for global dominance at a time of accelerating ambitions for artificial intelligence. According to the McKinsey Global Institute's Connectedness Index, which measures the size of inflows and outflows of goods, services, finance, people, and data relative to a country's GDP, China has climbed from number twenty-five to number seven in recent years.[74]

The inequalities in terms of data flows can be seen as part of a larger structure of exploitation. In a study on development and growth, Steven Weber[75] describes the economic imbalance that can result when one side (the colonized) provides the "raw" data, and the other does all the capturing, the processing, the analysis, and the creation of value-added products that the colonized cannot develop on their own and which they must buy at a disadvantage. As has been the case throughout the history of colonialism, this results in the colonizers becoming richer and more powerful, and the colonized underdeveloped and dependent. "The users in [disadvantaged] countries get to consume the products but are shut out of the value-add production side of the data economy," Weber writes.[76] He also points out that the distribution of influential platform businesses is anything but balanced. While enjoying global reach, most data empires are concentrated in the United States and China; other countries may contribute a few notable competitors (Spain's travel website ODIGEO and Brazil's e-commerce platform B2W, for example), but their international reach is much more limited.[77] According to 2017 figures, three out of the top four revenue-earning IT companies in the world were US based, and one was Chinese; four out of the top five "traditional" media companies were also US based.[78] The extractive reach of these companies may be global (more so for US companies at the moment, with China close behind), but it is somewhat misleading to think of them as "transnational" corporations: most of their decision power, employment, capital expenditures, and profits are kept close to home.[79] The model of a few global empires dividing the world among themselves seems destined to hold; it is just that the empires are no longer confined to "the West." As Kai-Fu Lee, CEO of a Chinese venture capital firm, says, "All the rest of the world will basically be a land grab between the US and China."[80]

The last area we will discuss in which exploitation becomes visible at a global/neocolonial level is the negotiations around free-trade agreements, especially as they pertain to the regulation of data flows and e-commerce. Not surprisingly, the United States, China, and other developed countries have been pressuring developing and poor countries to open their digital borders in ways that benefit the social quantification sector. This usually means a number of lopsided trade tactics: antilocalization laws that prevent countries from demanding that data should be stored within their boundaries; fewer privacy requirements, which allows companies in the Global North to collect all sorts of information about users in the Global South; strict copyright measures to protect the intellectual property (including media content and proprietary source code) of the companies in the Global North; and tax breaks that allow consumers to buy directly from foreign platforms such as Amazon without having to pay custom duties.[81]

This kind of deregulation is already being proposed in agreements such as the Trans-Pacific Partnership Agreement (TPP) and the renegotiated North American Free Trade Agreement (NAFTA). The rationale is not new and has been ideologically framed since the 1990s in terms of "nondiscrimination" (the Clinton and Obama administrations were enthusiastic proponents of it), meaning that in the name of "free trade," corporations should be allowed to colonize markets in the Global South in order to officially increase competition, provide better services, and incentivize innovation.

This does not mean, of course, that governments have not tried to resist this push. Countries such as China have stringent protectionist policies (not least to protect their homegrown data industries), and others (including Russia, the EU, Nigeria, Vietnam, and Australia)[82] have data localization laws. As Indian policy analyst Anita Gurumurthy and her colleagues argue,[83] the notion that the free flow of data will benefit *everyone* is a myth, as the companies and countries that sign these "free" trade agreements are in very unequal positions. It is a myth we already heard loudly in the nineteenth-century liberal discourse on free trade that was so important to the expansion of industrial capitalism and historical colonialism.

Exterminate

It is estimated that 185,000 kilograms of gold and 16,000,000 kilograms
of silver flowed from Latin America to Spain during the sixteenth and
early seventeenth centuries, coming principally from mines in Bolivia
and, later, Mexico.[84] A Catholic priest described these mines as verita-
ble mouths of hell, in which slave or indentured laborers—men, women,
and children treated "like stray animals"—died from exhaustion, abuse,
or poisoning within four years of arriving.[85] In an ironic and cruel twist,
however, Spanish law (the *Compilations of the Laws of the Indies*) prohib-
ited the exploitation of the "Indians" working in the mines and granted
them the right to own and profit from them.[86] In other words, while in reality indigenous people were being worked to death, the letter of the law
treated them as rightful owners of the mines, explicitly denying the fact of
their extermination.

The mission statements of social quantification companies do not mention anything about extermination of natives, but like Spanish law, they
adopt a very generous and helpful attitude toward those whom they seek
to subjugate. They purport to "bring the world closer together" (Facebook)
and to "enable people and businesses throughout the world to realize their
full potential" (Microsoft). They also aim to "give everyone the power to
create and share ideas and information instantly, without barriers" (Twitter). Google has policies that promote values of transparency, user choice,
and responsibility—including a "responsible manufacturing" policy and
even a "conflict minerals" policy," both of which regulate the sourcing of
manufacturing materials from war-free locations. Amazon wants to be a
place where "customers can find and discover anything they might want to
buy online," and Airbnb imagines a "magical world" in which "everyone of
us can belong anywhere" and we "can be anything we want." Intuit, which
sells financial software to individuals, declares that they want to change
their users' lives "so profoundly, they couldn't imagine going back to the
old way."[87]

Granted, none of these companies is setting out to commit genocide.
But while physical violence is the feature we most often associate with colonialism, economic violence can also have disastrous and lasting effects

on a society. Undeniably, extermination was a key component in the process of extraction and appropriation during historical colonialism. But as the system "evolved" to one characterized by the organized economy of industrial capitalism, the need for applying physical violence was reduced. Systemic violence is a costly strategy, to be applied only when there is a demonstrable "return on investment," (when the costs of the large-scale brutalization of native populations still translates into profits for the empire). But a point can be reached when these costs become too high, economically but also ethically, since empires can present themselves as righteous while engaging in genocide only for so long. At such moments, direct systemic violence is gradually replaced with indirect and interpersonal forms of localized cruelty (as between masters and slaves) and eventually eliminated and replaced with entirely different social relations, such as labor or data relations.

Thus, *extermination* in data colonialism is better understood not as the elimination of entire peoples but as the gradual elimination of social spaces that can exist outside data relations. We know from looking at the legacy of historical colonialism that genocide always entailed the obliteration of cultures, languages, and ways of life. In that sense, data colonialism continues mass media's project of homogenization, a project whereby difference is subdued in the interest of conformity. The actual extermination of subjects becomes unnecessary once the elimination of forms of life that do not exist merely as inputs for capitalism is achieved.

The pervasiveness of data relations does not mean, however, that the subjects of data colonialism are all treated the same. During colonialism, the social relations of exploitation were defined primarily by race in the colonies, by class in the metropolis, and by gender across all locations. One category of subjects, affluent white males, was placed at the top of the hierarchy, and everybody else was arranged below them. Today, it would superficially seem as though we are all *equal* subjects of data colonialism, so that economic violence is diffused almost to imperceptible levels. But in fact we are still unequally positioned by our class, race, and gender in relation to the global infrastructures and categorizing practices of the Cloud Empire, as chapters 4 and 5 explain. Our identity still functions within the new platforms to determine how we are categorized, what information we encounter or is hidden from us, and what we are allowed to do with that information. In other words, class, race, and gender (the whole trajectory of historical exploitation) still determine the extent to which we are exploited through use of the data we create.

The colonial drive for extermination is concealed in ways too subtle even for the masters of the social quantification sector to recognize. Consider Amazon's MTurk, mentioned earlier. The platform that essentially launched the gig economy was named after the Mechanical Turk, an eighteenth-century chess-playing automaton that became somewhat of a sensation in Europe. Walter Benjamin described the contraption as follows:

> It is well-known that an automaton once existed, which was so constructed that it could counter any move of a chess-player with a counter-move, and thereby assure itself of victory in the match. A puppet in Turkish attire, water-pipe in mouth, sat before the chessboard, which rested on a broad table. Through a system of mirrors, the illusion was created that this table was transparent from all sides. In truth, a hunchbacked dwarf who was a master chess-player sat inside, controlling the hands of the puppet with strings.[88]

The fact that the automaton represented a Turk was anything but accidental, since as Jonathan Gil Harris points out, there is a long European tradition stretching back to the Middle Ages of producing Muslim-looking puppets or homunculi to suggest that Islam is an artificial or fake religion and that its adherents are incapable of autonomous thought or action.[89] By reclaiming this imagery, MTurk unconsciously implies that exploitable humans can perform machinelike functions behind the scenes, and that the "puppets" doing this work belong to a subhuman category that can be exploited and economically marginalized.

What the 4X's Will Mean to Digital Natives

Imagine a product designed to enforce the long-distance economic dominance of one group over another, a product that creates passivity and dependence on the part of those who consume it, that can be used to destabilize the economic and political relations within a society, and whose usage entails an exploitative chain of transnational dimensions. The fact that we could just as easily be talking about opium or the latest app from the social quantification sector suggests how much things have *not* changed in colonial relations over the last two centuries.[90]

Around 1800, Britain was consuming a lot of Chinese tea and other Chinese products and was therefore becoming increasingly indebted to that country (while goods flowed from China to Britain, considerable amounts of silver flowed from Britain to China). In order to fix this trade imbalance, Britain decided to try something different. Instead of the territorial colonization they had practiced in India and the Americas, the East India Company was mobilized to attempt a financial conquest of China through the trade of a highly addictive drug that "targeted the biology of the Chinese population."[91] Since opium could not be grown legally in China, the East India Company moved all of its production to India, becoming a monopsony for the poppy plant: "If a peasant decided to be in the business of producing opium, he had no option but to deal with the Company. . . . The entire output of the drug would have to be handed over to the Company through a contractor at a price determined unilaterally for the year."[92] Two wars later, the Chinese had been forced to open their territory to trade and had ceded Hong Kong to the British, and the East India Company had saturated the market with the drug, devastating Chinese society. By 1825 the opium trade was generating enough funds to pay for all the Chinese tea Britain consumed, and on top of material commodities the British were taking large numbers of indentured laborers from China ("coolies") to work in their colonies.

The products of the social quantification sector do not have such visible and dire effects, but we must still question the ways in which they are altering social fabrics and widening inequalities. Although not exactly narcotics, some of the products generated by the Cloud Empire are notorious for their addictive and exploitative nature. Consider the teen drama *Skam*, a social media series that started on Norwegian public TV and is now a very successful Facebook franchise airing in the United States, France, Germany, and Italy (and watched all over the world by millions of teenagers). *Skam* did not invent the use of personal surveillance as a mode of social interaction, but it definitely promotes and rewards it by encouraging viewers to stalk or "play detective" with fictional characters on Facebook and Instagram as a way to drive the narrative forward (Instagram, currently a very popular platform with young people, is owned by Facebook). The fact that Facebook can create realistic profiles for fictional characters, complete with histories and timelines that can be modified by the corporation to augment credibility, illustrates Facebook's ability to manipulate reality for profit. And the illusion proves too hard to resist for many. Events in the drama unfold almost in real time and are highly localized; for instance, characters post updates about getting ready to attend a concert just as the actual concert is about to take place. Characters also comment on real current events as they unfold, and viewers can respond and interact with the characters, which leads many viewers to assume the show is real, at least at the beginning.

The result is a fictional drama inserted into the nonfictional social media realities of teens in a way that risks becoming highly addictive, considering that young people already spend about nine hours per day consuming media. And the formula is very successful. The US launch of the series was viewed 7.4 million times (compared to 2.3 million views for a typical teen TV show such as *Riverdale*).[93] *Skam* is a global phenomenon beyond the countries in which it plays and even beyond Facebook (clips from the Norwegian version were viewed in China 180 million times). Furthermore, it is promoted without any advertising, essentially through word of mouth. The marketing, in other words, is done by users themselves (although "influencers" are hired by Facebook to promote the show to their peers). The designed addictiveness of the show is an attempt by Facebook to retain young users at a time when many are spending more time on platforms like YouTube. *Skam*'s ability to create addiction in vulnerable audiences, reorganize reality for profit, reduce social life to *social media* life, derive value from the resources of users, and mobilize global markets makes it a good example of data colonialism in action.

How can such invasions into our social lives be countered? The project of challenging data colonialism can and must draw inspiration from decoloniality, the study of the legacy of colonialism as it continues to shape modern social relations. Territorial and data colonialisms represent both a continuity and a disruption within capitalism, and as decolonial movements have shown us, the responses must equally take into account the past while going beyond it to imagine alternative presents and futures. If we fail to do that, the term *digital natives* (generations who have always grown up with the internet) starts to take on a more sinister meaning: *those whom data relations have dispossessed.*

From Counterhistories to Counterpresents

In their responses to historical colonialism, postcolonial studies have helped us frame *counterhistories*, or alternative versions of history that reclaim elements erased by Eurocentrism. Similarly, a decolonial approach to data can help us frame *counterpresents*, alternative understandings of our current social realities that allow us to see ourselves as more than mere inputs for capitalism.

In order to articulate these positions, what are needed are methods for denaturalizing the logic of data and critiquing data colonialism. We must then use the results of those methods to reimagine different forms of social and economic relations and connections outside of Western notions of modernity. The project of creating these alternate versions of modernity is what Enrique Dussel calls a "worldwide ethical liberation project"[94] that challenges the universalism of a Western form of reason. In essence, creating counterpresents implies engaging in media practices that question how notions of "progress," "civilization," or "innovation" are equated with data relations as conceptualized by corporate interests. Creating counterpresents would also mean reclaiming the agency of the colonized data subject. The colonial project granted subjecthood to dominated individuals, but it did not grant them equality.[95] Counterpresents would allow the subjects of data colonialism to imagine a different worldview in which they can locate themselves as fully autonomous actors, beyond data's "horizon of totality"[96] and with a fully recognized right to challenge the progress of data colonialism.

An important reason for undertaking all of this urgently is that data colonialism is a period of transition. It is not here to stay; its patterns simply announce an emerging order that is yet to come. As discussed in chapter 1, historical colonialism served as a prelude to modern industrial capitalism. The eighteenth-century abolition of colonial slavery solidified the

British empire's transition in the nineteenth century to a new form of imperialism based on liberal values such as free trade. This in turn allowed the empire to reimagine itself at the center of a global network of commerce in manufactured goods—the beginning of what we would recognize today as modern capitalism.[97] In short, historical colonialism was not just about systematic and global extraction and appropriation but about reimagining those things as *progress* and enforcing a new world order in which colonizers could continue to rule with decreased (yet still prevalent) levels of violence but also with *increased legitimacy*. They would rule, in fact, by disavowing violence and declaring themselves the defenders of human values. In light of this history, we must reassess recent statements made by commentators following the Cambridge Analytica scandal expressing dissatisfaction with the corrupt data extraction system but assuring the public that it can be reformed and salvaged so that the march of progress may continue.

In the next section of the book, we continue the analysis by looking at data colonialism not just as a comparative template but as a specific order of extraction, as a particular process for producing knowledge that redefines the social world and circumvents our capacity to act autonomously in that world. We turn, in other words, to the new social order that is being built all around us through data colonialism.

Part II

Ordering

The Hollowing Out of the Social 4

A self-adjusting market . . . could not exist for any length of time without
annihilating the human and natural substance of society. It would have
physically destroyed man and transformed his surroundings into a wilderness.
—Karl Polanyi[1]

Know your customers better than they know themselves.
—Website for Tresata (a customer intelligence management firm)[2]

AI brings new opportunities for social construction.
—China's "Next Generation Artificial Intelligence Development Plan"[3]

IN THE EARLY 2010S, Uber executives treated attendees at their parties to their
"God view" of all Uber's cars tracked across the surrounding city. As
part of the spectacle, they showed locations of currently active passen-
gers; sometimes, for fun, they removed passenger anonymity. It took three
years for news of this to reach the journalistic mainstream.[4] Most interesting about this story is neither the fact of surveillance power nor Uber
executives' reveling in it—after all, surveillance power is integral to data
colonialism. The most interesting thing about this story is the version of
social knowledge that it implied: an all-seeing, all-encompassing knowledge at a distance, based on the synthesizing capacity of an algorithmic
system. There is a vision here of how the social world *becomes newly know-
able* when data extraction is a basic mode for generating economic value.
In this chapter, we ask what sort of social world is being built as a result
of data colonialism. What will count as social knowledge in that world,
and what older forms of social knowledge may drop out of the picture?
Furthermore, what do those changes mean for social inequality and social justice?

The challenge that data colonialism poses for social life and for critical social research is entirely new and disturbing. Because this new colonialism's mode of operation involves producing the materials from which
information, and ultimately knowledge, are made, its operations cannot

be insulated from how we understand the worlds we share, from our so-cial imagination and even our politics. Data relations generate value in the very same movement in which they redescribe and remap the world, fus-ing knowledge production and value extraction. Because this challenge is new, our goal in this chapter is to delineate the types of problems to which the practices of data colonialism give rise. We cannot possibly be compre-hensive in our coverage of how this is playing out on a global scale. Inevi-tably our narrative will give most weight to the places, such as the United States, where critical scholars and activists have begun to regularly pro-test about the disturbing consequences. But we will find enough examples from other places, including China, India, South Africa, and Sweden, to suggest that the problems are global in reach. Wherever you are reading this, we are confident you will find echoes of the strange new claims, un-covered in this chapter, to know the social world through data.

As a way into this complex topic, we consider social knowledge forms in the North America and Europe of the nineteenth and early twentieth cen-turies. There is a special reason for this comparison. One of the most pow-erful challenges to economics' detachment from the social world was made by the historian Karl Polanyi. In the 1940s, Polanyi rethought how market societies came into existence. The advent of industrial machinery changed everything, requiring long-distance markets to supply the parts that kept machinery moving and sufficient customers to buy what machines pro-duced. Since markets are oriented to exchange for gain regardless of scale, the expansion of national markets across every sector of life severely dam-aged local social relations; far from being natural, human life organized exclusively around markets proved almost unlivable in seventeenth- and eighteenth-century England, the first economy to industrialize, as older ways of organizing resources (for example, the family workplace and the local market) were pulled apart.

Polanyi concluded that "a market economy can only exist in a *mar-ket society*," which must be created through "highly *artificial* stimulants administered to the body social."[5] This happened in the nineteenth and twentieth centuries through what Polanyi calls a double movement; first, a profound institutional reorganization made markets (in particular in la-bor, land, and finance) into social realities, turning "all transactions . . .

into money transactions";[6] second, over time, a countermovement of compensatory mechanisms emerged to control market relations and make them socially livable.[7] Key developments were the regulation of labor, land markets, and the financial sector.

Polanyi's analysis has provocative implications for today.[8] As he makes clear, the market transformation that data colonialism involves will not succeed by itself: it will require *its own social transformation* that, initially, is likely to be violent, or at least dislocating. At the core of any such social transformation will be "the commodity concept."[9] Capitalism, to reap the benefits of data colonialism, must make the social domain into a marketized space whose every point has value and is available for commodity exchange. Data relations, and the new forms of "knowledge" to which they give rise, are the key means to this.

The nineteenth-century countermovement assumed there was still an outside to the economy, a readily understandable world of social struggle from which economic forces could be challenged. But under data colonialism, building on the previous advances of neoliberal politics, capitalism begins to imagine away any outside to the economy. Its distinctive forms of social knowledge describe a social world that is literally coextensive with economic life. This is what we meant in chapter 1 when we said neoliberalism (the injunction to treat social processes *as though* they were markets) may soon become unnecessary as a result of capitalism's new reliance on data relations (which literally turn social processes *into* markets). As the social domain becomes colonized by data relations, the social world gets hollowed out as a site of critical agency.[10] Instead of "social relations [being] embedded in the economic system" (they already have been now for two centuries, as Polanyi showed), social relations *become* the economic system,[11] or least a crucial part of it, as human life is converted into raw material for capital via data.

The value of data colonialism's extractive processes depends on the comprehensiveness of the data generated. As a result, and certainly not by accident, a new form of knowledge emerges that appears to cover the whole of the social world, but only because no part of that world is exempt from processes of data extraction. This new social knowledge begins to override older forms of social knowledge. In making a historical comparison here to North America's and Europe's nineteenth century, we have no wish to romanticize the fierce social and political conflicts of that era, still less to romanticize the term *social*.[12] What is new today is not the quantification of the social or its measurement but the depth at which datafied social knowledge conducts its operations and how the resulting social knowledge is (or is *not*) accountable to the social actors it describes.

The social quantification sector is fast building its own social knowledge. That knowledge is commercially controlled, generally opaque in its production, not open to public debate, and thoroughly oriented first to capitalist drives before it is oriented to the interests of government. It shapes everyday actions quite differently than did earlier forms of social knowledge. The result, as we already hinted in chapter 1, is a different type of social order in which the agency and control of corporations is enhanced and that of individual citizens is reduced and sometimes even erased. The story we tell in this chapter remains, however, only one aspect of how the social quantification sector is shaping society. Also important, for example, are the commercial—indeed, blatantly discriminatory—distortions built into the everyday knowledge that individuals obtain through their online searches[13] and the consequences of the social media platforms for everyday sociality.[14] We do not minimize those developments but seek to uncover here a general dimension of data colonialism's transformation of the social world that has rarely been surveyed.

These developments are masked by the ideology of datafication and the corresponding myth of Big Data.[15] We need to peer back through Big Data's one-way mirror[16] and ask what is going on with the construction of social knowledge today, as data colonialism expands across the world. As preparation, let's explore further that historical comparison with the nineteenth century.

A Brief History of Social Quantification

The role of numbers in shaping our understanding of the social world is easily overlooked. But as the leading historian of statistics Theodore Porter wrote, "The credibility of numbers . . . is a social and moral problem. . . . Power must be exercised in a variety of ways to make measurements and tallies valid."[17] The measurements and tallies required by data colonialism are industrial in scale, even if much of their operation is hidden from view. A history of how, under very different conditions, social numbers came to transform nineteenth-century accounts of the social world will provide a useful comparison.

The notion of "society" is not natural; it had to be constructed at a certain time and place.[18] The nineteenth century's (indeed, also the early twentieth century's) construction of society emerged out of what Max Weber called "the peculiarity of modern culture, its calculability."[19] The history of that period's new forms of measure and statistical calculation has been told often, so we will focus only on the most salient features for understanding today's social knowledge.

The philosopher Ian Hacking has given an elegant account of how in the early nineteenth century, the centuries-long assumption of a hierarchy of individuals marked as socially distinct at the moment of birth began to be replaced with accounts of differentiated human behavior in something called "society." That account was based in measuring groups and individuals by reference to a statistically calculated "norm."[20] While disputes raged for decades about the scientific meaning of the statistical norm and the reality, or abstraction, of the "normal man,"[21] the transformation of the understanding of human variation was dramatic. Not only were people counted, but since counting requires categorization, new ways of "making up people" emerged.[22] From practices of counting and comparing numbers, the discipline of comparative statistics developed, aimed at demonstrating the relative strength and wealth of nations and doing so in public: earlier state-held numbers, generated for tax and other purposes, had remained, at least until the early nineteenth century, within the vaults of the state.[23] And it was states (even if through separate agencies), not private corporations, that collected information such as a population's size and health. Indeed, the state's right and duty to count its population by census was enshrined in article 1, section 2 of the US Constitution as a means of recognizing diversity within the population.[24]

These new practices of counting generated "an avalanche of printed numbers" in Europe and the United States between 1820 and 1840.[25] Talk about human beings became routed through statistics about national societies rather than through the abstraction of human nature. The idea that human behavior could vary in regular ways between nations enabled "the confusion of politics [to] be replaced by an orderly reign of facts."[26] Various actors (not just states but campaigning reformers too) began using statistics to offer rival measures of the well-being of populations. As French data historian Alain Desrosières describes, discussion about poverty in Great Britain was transformed by new statistics on unemployment, health, and housing.[27] Society itself—its dynamics and possibilities for positive transformation—became something debated in public, with the state becoming accountable for data collection and, over time, also for addressing the problems revealed through those numbers. In 1911 the category of social class was for the first time incorporated into the UK national census; meanwhile, health statistics were the subject of lively debate in the medical profession.[28]

Dry details perhaps? Every process of abstracting knowledge from everyday life needs practical tools for formulating it in public as well as devices to disseminate it. This "concrete history of abstraction" is of enormous significance for understanding nineteenth-century Western politics and social reform.[29] Numbers, and the statistical science that developed through them, enabled a model of social control, with the statistical norm operating as an instrument of normalization, within a wider vision of "government from the social point of view."[30] This was the period when the modern psychological disciplines and the practices of social care and urban policy developed.[31] Statistical knowledge brought with it, over time, more complex mechanisms of description, what historian Dan Bouk calls "data aggregates" such as "charts, tables, maps, or even algorithms."[32] For example, Charles Booth's London poverty maps (prints of which can still be seen on the corridors of the London university where one of us works) provided a tool for managing neighborhoods as part of the wider regulation of social life.[33]

These social uses of numbers were a crucial site for contesting power. An emerging social state aimed at the betterment of all created "experts of the social" with new types of professional authority.[34] A key dispute within statistical science was whether "the norm" (for example, the norm of average family size or income) was a real-world reference point around which human variation actually turned or an abstract mathematical point that random variation implied.[35] As Hacking writes, "Normality" emerged "to close the gap between 'is' and 'ought.'"[36] Science apart, statistics' emergence as a forum for debating "the social" did not escape contamination by more sinister dreams of *managing life*—indeed, the evolutionary prospects of the human race. The most scandalous example was eugenics, the pseudoscience of managing births to secure better genetic outcomes for the overall population. Here the apparently objective science of numbers merged with the racial hierarchies between peoples that had already shaped colonialism for centuries.

So far, so familiar, you might think, but differences may prove more crucial than similarities here. Looking back, five points seem distinctive about nineteenth- and twentieth-century forms of social knowledge.

First, the key actors in developing social knowledge and social statistics in this earlier period operated, with few exceptions, at the state's initiative (an exception would be the data-gathering of the commercial insurance industry). It was not until the 1970s and 1980s in the United States that large private companies (marketers) acquired a data-collection capacity to rival that of the state.[37] As a result, the data collectors of that earlier period necessarily faced *some* requirements for public accountability in how data was collected, categories adopted, and results applied.

Second, the forms of discrimination that resulted from data collection were also largely public—and visible as such—resulting, for example, in disputes discussed by historian Dan Bouk about insurance premiums with US commercial insurers.[38] With relatively few variables in play and calculation tasks far less complex than those of today, the reason for someone's higher insurance premiums (often their ethnicity, gender, or "statistical pasts")[39] was clear enough, and the correlation crude enough, to be publicly challenged. In the nineteenth-century United States, African Americans succeeded in lobbying for adjustments in insurance-industry practice.

Third, the search for statistical generality in no sense required an abandonment of the human individual. One of the most intense debates of nineteenth-century intellectual history was about whether statistical laws, operating at the level of the whole society, were compatible with individual free will. Some, like the French social theorist Adolphe Quetelet, insisted the answer was yes; others, like the British historian Henry Buckle, insisted the answer was no, with popular culture (Charles Dickens in his novel *Hard Times*) weighing in to mock statistics' mechanistic view of humanity.[40] Statistics' significance for human self-understanding was debated in public. Perhaps this is unremarkable in itself, but it is sharply different from today's development of Machine Learning tools for computing the social world, largely unobserved and entirely under the control of commercial corporations.

Fourth, social knowledge's role in the wider management of populations competed with other framings of its role: social reform, public justice, economic use of scarce resources, and emerging principles of democratization. Sometimes the resolution of these overlapping claims was disastrous, as in Nazi Germany, South Africa, and other explicitly racist states, although on other occasions it was not. There was, however, no question of social management being reduced to or confused with purely economic or political goals. This was the force of the "*invention* of the social," as Nikolas Rose calls it.[41]

Fifth, and this feature followed from the fourth, was the possibility of developing publicly accountable measures to deepen the description of the social *against* economic and other competing modes of description. The invention of poverty, for example, as a social, not moral, providential, or economic, category—as something based in the unequal social distribution of resources and opportunities—shows how a social dimension to our common knowledge can make a political difference.[42]

Let's bear these points in mind as we consider what's distinctive about social knowledge under data colonialism.

Social Quantification for Data Colonialism

As Theodore Porter put it, "Quantification is a technology of distance." Some distance is inherent to the abstraction involved in producing all quantified knowledge of the social. Such distance is more than a distance from one's subjective opinion—practices of quantification also involve a social separation, the development of "forms of expertise and power relations" that allocate the power to quantify to some actors and not others.[43] It is easy to forget "the social conditions in which science is possible," as French sociologist Pierre Bourdieu once noted,[44] but that is exactly what we must not do in the era of the God view.

A Continuous Private Capacity

The quantification of the social in societies with large marketing sectors (North America, much of Europe, China, Japan, Korea, and to a lesser extent Brazil and India)[45] is the privileged production of private business, even if state power looks on with close interest. Reversing the earlier pattern in which the corporate sector relied on the state's statistics,[46] social quantification today is principally a capacity of the commercial sector, with states the dependent users. Only in this era did it become imaginable that a government might, as the United Kingdom did in 2013, float the idea of abolishing its census and relying instead on privately acquired data.[47] For an authoritarian market-state such as China, however, there is nothing paradoxical here. The growth of a commercial social quantification sector is part of China's wider vision of a modern social order. Meanwhile, the "public-private surveillance partnership" is a feature of most contemporary states.[48]

Underlying this shift has been a colossal growth of computing capacity in private business since the 1980s, linked not just to massively increased data processing capacity within the marketing sector and the new data brokerage sector[49] but also to the vast computing networks necessary to manage commodity chains in the "global factory."[50] As part of the general growth of consumption and competition for market attention,[51] corporations began from the 1970s to invest in tracking entities (human or otherwise) linked to short-term transactions, from stock identification systems to credit-card-transaction histories.

The rhythms and scope of the resulting new social knowledge are highly distinctive. In the predatafication era, the state "enjoyed a unique combination of legal and moral authority to carry out statistical inquiries,"[52] but its exercise was restricted by the frequency with which it could approach its citizens for comprehensive data (for example, a ten-year census) and by the number of permanent categories it could impose (Social

Security number, passport number, and so on). The commercial data collection of our times is continuous and on myriad dimensions.

Opacity, Not Accountability

Today's forms of social quantification present to citizens a very different face than that of predigital data collection by the nation-state. For subjects who interact with it, the social quantification sector's actions are extraordinarily complex, highly distributed, massively comprehensive, continuously updated, and, for these reasons, almost entirely opaque.[53] Social quantification is contestable by individuals or groups only with the greatest difficulty.[54] This is the challenge of "the black box society," in which, as legal scholar Frank Pasquale puts it, "the spaces of our common life that are supposed to be the most open and transparent are being colonized by the logic of secrecy."[55]

The continuity with the nineteenth- and twentieth-century European state's attempt to make society more "legible" is misleading.[56] Unlike the Charles Booth poverty maps of London, no one today can print and put on their wall even a simplified map of how Facebook categorizes the members of a small town or a how a credit rating agency differentiates the customers on its books. Social quantification today produces myriad microcategorizations, but these are privately controlled and largely inaccessible to public view. The social quantification sector exists not to make society generally more legible (that is, readable as and by society as a whole) but to give corporations special and private access to particular forms of knowledge from which economic value can be generated. It is these privileges that giant monopoly/monopsonies such as Facebook and Google can exploit.

There is a strange asymmetry here. Anita Gurumurthy, head of Indian civil society organization IT for Change, writes that "as the citizen becomes more and more legible to the state, the state becomes more and more opaque to the citizen," although we might add corporations to the state in that observation.[57] When the goal of data extraction is the capitalization of human life, we should not be surprised that the resulting knowledges have at best an ambiguous public status.

Opacity is also a practical consequence of operations. Data is collected, processed, and purchased so that particular actors can do particular things. The computing complexes available to corporate and state actors today are capable not just of automatically tracing the relations between large numbers of variables and categories but also of finding patterns in massively large data sets in which no order appears to exist. Underlying the much-hyped Big Data is a new model of knowledge called Machine Learning. Both are often referred to under the heading of artificial intelligence; AI is currently a huge focus of commercial and government investment worldwide.[58]

How does Machine Learning work, in broad terms? The calculative power involved in today's social knowledge is massively greater than that employed in the nineteenth and twentieth centuries; it also operates on different principles. Whereas the earlier social knowledge was built from specific calculations performed on so-called structured data (for example, entries in statistical tables and databases), today's social knowledge can be built from unstructured data, drawn directly from the traces left in the flow of everyday life. The structure of the data has to be found through repeating and gradually refining initial "rules" (guesses) for how to categorize those traces. New rules of categorization are generated in the course of applying those initial rules. As a result, the significance of the analysis is nonlinear, "emergent . . . , [and] consisting of previously unknown patterns and relationships."[59] The end product (the knowledge generated) is not explicable in terms of rules at all; it is just a complex correlation that emerges from a calculative process operating at many different levels.[60] As such, the operations of data analytics are *necessarily* opaque, and no one—not even the engineers who run the process—can account exactly for how that knowledge was generated.[61]

Prediction, Not Explanation

Some, such as *Wired* editor Chris Anderson, turn this opacity into a positive. Anderson argued controversially in 2008 that Big Data (the principle that says N must be all) undercuts the basic idea that historically underlay statistics as a science: that of formulating and carefully testing hypotheses to establish precisely stated correlations and, where possible, causal relations between variables. To imaginary defenders of older social knowledge, Anderson responded:

Out with every theory of human behaviour, from linguistics to sociology. Forget taxonomy, ontology and psychology. The point is that they do it, and we can track and measure it with unprecedented fidelity. With enough data, the numbers speak for themselves.[62]

Instead of nineteenth-century statistician Poisson's "law of large numbers," we have in the early twenty-first century a project whose goals appear to undermine any science: perhaps the old method of science—hypothesize, model, test—is "becoming outdated."[63] The new approach is simply to *process* all data extractable from social life in order to generate discriminations from which value can be optimized.

Big Data practice is in fact considerably more complex than Chris Anderson's cartoon picture. N may well not be all, or anything like all, for many producers of social knowledge, not least because this data is competitively harvested. No one corporation has access to the all, and few, if any, are willing to give up their share of that all to build a collective data pool, although corporate data sets are sometimes shared on a limited basis. In the infinitely large domain of data extraction, each company has a very particular vantage point tied to the functionality and market position of its data-gathering platform. Yet these limitations do not prevent Machine Learning (always based on N = very large) from stimulating *a new social epistemology*. Machine Learning relies on repetitive processing—made possible by the newly abundant computing capacity—to generate reliable predictive proxies for processes whose causal dynamics are not themselves understood. Take any aspect of the social world, even ones for which we currently lack a causal model, and simply generate a proxy for it; there is no limit to what might work as such a proxy, and indeed the vagueness as to what is a "proxy variable" is a problem in legal proceedings that increasingly rely on them.[64] So data scientists may ask: Could visual cues in Google Street View scenes be proxies of the likelihood of nearby crime? Could patterns in the distribution of more-expensive car models in Google Earth pictures be proxy demographic variables (income levels, relative poverty/wealth)? The temptation to pursue such proxy hunts is considerable, especially when public census data is costly and only intermittently collected.[65] The scope for social experimentation that data relations

provide to parts of the social quantification sector is huge but has sometimes proved controversial.[66] Privacy concerns may act as a constraint,
but, if so, China's assumed lower sensitivity to privacy concerns works as a
market advantage for its AI industry.[67]

Collect Everything

If Big Data reasoning relies on the predictive power that comes from repetitive processing of unstructured data, this data can be generated, directly
or indirectly, from whole populations. It no longer relies on the carefully
constructed samples of the general population on which classical statistical knowledge relied. This new model of knowledge requires collecting
data continuously, so that N might as well be all.

Why is that? One reason we have already given: whereas nineteenth-
and twentieth-century smart sampling assumed data collection was expensive and difficult, Machine Learning's challenge is basically not cost
but time (how fast can a potentially infinite series of automated attempts
at pattern recognition produce a usable proxy?).[68] Since it is the size of the
data set (N) over which processors calculate that determines the quality
of the proxies generated, there is no reason to stop collecting data. On the
contrary, one must always try to gather more. This technique can appear
on the ground as little more than wishful thinking, as this employee of the
Los Angeles Police Department put it: "All we're doing right now is, 'Let's
just collect more and more and more data and something good will just
happen.'"[69]

Why in any case would a competing actor hold back from collecting
more data about a human subject when it can do so? The goal of most contemporary data collection is not the production of shared knowledge (with
some important exceptions, such as the discovery of a cure for cancer or
the better understanding of response to crisis). Where, as with the Chinese state, a knowledge interest distinctive from commercial competition
becomes involved, its goal is the processing of all inputs to the social process that might affect its orderly nature, so again: why stop data collection,
and why stop trying to influence behavior on the basis of data collected?
Government and commercial actors intersect around what French legal
scholar Annette Rouvroy has called "data behaviourism."[70] Social knowl-

edge becomes *whatever works* to enable private or public actors to modulate others' behavior in their own interests (not disinterested social knowledge but social capture).

This, in turn, affects what counts as social knowledge. Potential inputs that are not machine readable become irrelevant, since the goal is always to increase N, the aggregate of what can be counted as data. Meanwhile, data subjects are generating material for machine reading all the time. We are constantly encouraged to act in ways that stimulate further counting, gain us more followers, and achieve better analytics.[71] A certain vision of social truth emerges here, expressed by Jeff Malmad, a marketing executive, who says, "The Truth will be present in everything. You'll know everything about yourself and your loved ones if you opt in."[72] This "Truth" is not the truth about society at which nineteenth-century statisticians were aiming—it is a branded, tethered, contract-specific, only conditionally sharable, personally targeted truth that is both the reward and price of continuous connection.[73]

An Intimate Knowledge

What is actually personalized in this new social knowledge is the fit to commercial targeting.[74] The fit is intimate. As Bruce Schneier puts it, data colonialism today offers "a very intimate form of surveillance."[75] Tracking provides an "auto-fitting mould," in Deleuze's prescient phrase from three decades ago.[76] Therefore, why not, as PricewaterhouseCoopers note in their 2014 report on "The Wearable Future," imagine a world of universal wearable processors, linked up to a commercial tracking and messaging system, in which "brands could even tap body cues to tailor messages"? That world would provide marketing opportunities without limit: "Sensor revealing that you're thirsty? Here's a coupon for smart water."[77] Or as a marketing professional more bluntly put it, "Treat your customers like dogs."[78]

There is a deep paradox here. Although quantification is a technology of distance, today's data relations increasingly strive to erase the distance between the social actor's body and the precisely targeted sensor system that serves it (or more accurately, that the body serves). Wearables are likely to be only the start; a Swedish biohacker predicts that "all of the wearables we wear today will be implantable in five to ten years."[79] The gathering and processing of personal data and its conversion into a targeted marketing offer (here's a coupon for smart water, *since* you're sweating) will all have happened *before* we could reflect on any of it. But a real and important distance will remain: the distance comprised by the power of the social quantification sector against which individual actors currently have little or no agency. There is a divergence here from social categorizations as we have known them in the past. As Ian Hacking explained, the distinctive feature of social categorizations, at least until the era of Big Data, was that they were interactive—they operated as categories with which people could interact and negotiate as they were used on them.[80] Humans can interact with today's algorithmic categorization processes, if at all, only derivatively, through an indirect sense of what data *might have already* done to them.

The new social knowledge is designed to target "measurable types" among individuals[81] but not to reflect, let alone understand, a social world in which groups of human subjects live and reflect *together*. We do not need to romanticize the social narratives of the nineteenth and twentieth centuries to realize that something important has gone missing here. At the most basic level, what is missing is consent. As Julie Cohen puts it, consent to the terms of data collection is somehow "sublimated . . . into the coded environment."[82] In addition to consent, choice also gets subsumed by "Big Data's decision-guidance techniques."[83] And if consent *and* choice are bypassed, so too implicitly is the person with a voice whose reflections might have contributed to our understanding of the social world.[84] With so much discriminatory processing controlling how the world even appears to each of us, this new social knowledge gives human actors few opportunities to exercise *choice about the choices* offered to them. There is something disturbing about this for human freedom and autonomy and for the human life environment that is being built here.

Playing the Data Game

Yet people must go on living in the social world. They need to act, interpret, and orient themselves for action; they must be present to others; and they need to find information and resources. All these ways of living in the world are crossed by data relations. We are becoming used to being addressed *as* documentation, *as* data, *as* the bearers of the selective descriptions that databases require. We accept as factual much of the data that computer processing of our tracked activities generates (anyway, what would it be like to operate with total skepticism?).[85] The sheer usefulness of many of the functions that data tracking and data processing support helps to integrate them into the flow of daily life.[86]

Reputation is one example. Many of the accepted infrastructures for valuing people today are managed by platforms and are driven by those platforms' incitements to action and the types of data they do or do not value.[87] Insofar as we care about our reputation (and few people don't), we are continuously oriented to what counts as reputation for platforms. There are in fact many soft incitements toward datafication, including our habits of counting our followers or likes[88] and making sure we click on a friend's latest post. Such soft incitements are formalized in marketers' strategy of gamification. Gamification makes data extraction playful but far from formal—as with games such as Pokémon Go whose playing requires the revealing of location and other data.[89] Gamification, as the president of loyalty marketer Points puts it, creates "a relationship of exchange where consumers are . . . incentivized to share more of themselves: their time, their attention, their information, and ultimately their loyalty."[90] Oracle's Gamification Guidelines break the model down into stages that include not just "feedback mechanisms" and regular "progress indicators" but broad design features to stimulate "larger goal and reward states" and "longer-term engagements."[91] In a similar spirit, NaMo, the social media app dedicated to Indian Prime Minister Narendra Modi, encourages users to "earn badges" by competing "to do tasks."[92]

Some might respond that it is not human beings *as such* that are the objects of data tracking and nudging. In contemporary data relations, the subject is targeted under conditions that need not involve her naming or even her certain identification: people are rather "probabilistically defined customers," reached through a process of "singularization" instead of true personalization.[93] You will be uniquely identified by multiple corporations using different sets of data features, each sufficient to prompt an action, whether a different price or suitability for this or that message. Data scholars call these sets of data points our "data doubles."[94] As management theorists Cristina Alaimo and Jannis Kallinikos note in an analysis of retail fashion platforms, data doubles are the building blocks for new "social objects" that enable corporate actors to refine their influence on users. Media platforms such as Netflix are based on structuring content production and marketing around the data doubles produced through relentless harvesting and processing. The resulting user clusters are not people but "quantitative derivations of an engineered experience."[95] One example is the "communities of other members with similar movie and TV show preferences" that Netflix says it is isolating in an increasingly global strategy of data harvesting.[96]

But there is nothing comforting about this. Even though the new social knowledge is produced through operations that bypass human beings, it is actual human beings who are *tethered to the discriminations* that such knowledge generates.[97] Based on algorithmic reasoning, it is a real person who gets sent to jail, refused health insurance, or offered a favorable price in the supermarket or an opportunity for social housing. Indeed, the gap between the uncertainty of cause and the certainty of personal impact is what makes algorithmic power so unnerving. As Virginia Eubanks puts it, "You get a sense of . . . an electronic eye turned towards *you*, but you can't put your finger on exactly what's amiss."[98]

Let's turn now to the wider presentation of the social world that results from the operations of the social quantification sector.

Caching the Social

From the point of view of the social quantification sector, the new datafied world brims with possibilities of agency. We might even say that the sector has *gained* a social world, bifurcated from the one that social actors can see but massively more tractable to commercial modulation. Data aggregates, for those who produce the new social knowledge, are a live reality[99] on which business advantage depends. The underlying human subject and her perspective on the world remain, much of the time, irrelevant to this process of knowledge extraction.

Everywhere a Data Cache

Almost every time we do something online, and sometimes when we are offline too, a small data packet for later use is grabbed via infrastructures of connection. Let's call those packets "caches." In computing, caches are, as Christian Sandvig notes, stores of content that are held so as to be available for later use; an important practical application of the term *cache* is the stored version of a video on a local server, available when a local customer wants to download it for streaming.[100] The gathering together of data caches and their processing into more useful material generates a live-streamed vision of social reality for the social quantification sector's institutional players.[101] Such *social caching* is data colonialism's extractive dynamic in action.

The retail domain provides good examples. Joseph Turow tells how, increasingly, US retail marketers are targeting highly localized, just-in-time marketing messages and incentives to shoppers as they move around stores and adjacent spaces. Recently, marketers have started messaging people after they have visited a store with a connected mobile device (so-called outdoor retargeting).[102] Fashion retailing is a particular area of growth: "smart garments" enable the tracking of consumer behavior in exchange for the enhanced convenience of the "smart-shop dressing room," in which the coolness of sharing shopping information with friends may well outweigh the creepiness of being followed even as one undresses.[103]

The goal is to cache the social at every available opportunity and then store the cached fragments for use in later targeted messages, offers, or ads. The official justification given by the marketing industry for this deepened personal tracking is not economic advantage but personalization. Because it is now standard to send marketing messages to people's personal devices, it is argued that those messages need to be personalized—that is, adapted to what available data suggests that person wants right then and there. But the logic is circular, and there is no obvious way out of the circle for the consumer. Increasingly, products (from expensive cars to regular consumer goods) go on transmitting information of marketing value about their usage and user *after* purchase. The goal for marketers becomes the "persistently connected product" that maximizes revenue per user throughout its life.[104] Marketers describe this personalization as "one-to-one communication" and "one-to-one dialogue." Yet there is nothing dialogic about the individual's emerging relation to capitalism or the continuous caching of social life on which it relies.[105]

Social caching's role in producing knowledge is likely to increase in scope, and not just in retail marketing. Intelligent Personal Assistants (IPAs) around the home provide a subtle form of social caching. On the pretext of taking on the drudgery of daily life—updating shopping lists, ordering takeout, and so on—products such as Amazon's Alexa (embedded in the Echo and Echo Dot devices), Apple's Siri, and the Google Home suite of devices offer personalized attendance in return for new opportunities to archive personal data. Users are encouraged to treat the assistant as their interface with the world of information, which involves archiving whatever instructions the user gives for machine-learning purposes. The data security implications are unclear (already one US court in Arkansas has ordered Amazon to hand over Echo recordings in a trial).[106] We need to consider not just what the IPA stores but also its interactions with apps on the user's other devices.[107]

The routinization of tracking devices—for example, to track weight loss—makes an important contribution here. To quote two people in a study of users in the UK East Midlands, "When asked why she decided that 1400 calories were the right limit, she explained 'Because that's what it [the app] tells me'; and 'I've put the trust in the app.'"[108] Even if this banal trust in data-hungry devices seems harmless, there is the risk of function creep: the more we become used to tracking as the *natural* way to find out what to do in our personal lives, the more likely we will be to accept tracking as the infrastructure for knowledge in areas of our lives in which we have long expected less control, such as work.[109]

There are indeed plenty of hard incentives to submit to data relations: lower insurance premiums, access to workplace health insurance available only to employees who accept tracking of their health, or perhaps the unavailability of household goods that can function without connection. We have yet to see how far governments will make submission to data relations a precondition for access to various types of services or entitlements. In chapter 1 we noted the social credit system seen by the Chinese government as its route to "the modernization of social governance."[110] Meanwhile in India, the Aadhaar identity-card system is being made a requirement for access to welfare services, tax dealings, and even the online booking of train tickets.[111] Through the operation of social caching, we are increasingly becoming *data subjects* whose responsiveness to data signals is expected, even taken as virtuous.

IoT = LAC? (Operationalizing Life's Annexation to Capital)

The business opportunities from innovative extensions of social caching are multiplying, often in alliance with the state. Consider the cameras with linked data analytics now offered in the United States by Axon AI (formerly Taser) to replace law enforcement officers' crime-scene reports; as one investor said, "Taser wants to be the Tesla or Apple of law enforcement."[112] Even in formal democracies, resource-strapped states will take advantage of these apparently risk-free methods for delegating their knowledge of hard-to-reach areas of the social world to algorithms.

A larger pattern begins to emerge, part and parcel of the Cloud Empire. Continuously caching the social enables corporations and all forms of authority to gain the sense that the social world, or at least selected slices of it, can be continuously streamed *just for them*—not for their entertainment but to enable that world's modulation or management in their interests. When the CEO of Shotspotter, makers of algorithmically processed surveillance mechanisms for the law enforcement sector, was asked to disclose his company's data to the US public, he responded that it would be like "taking someone else's Netflix subscription."[113] So social caching is more than an academic metaphor: it is the practice that de facto—and, increasingly, de jure—authorizes the privileged viewpoint on human life that corporate power claims for itself in the era of data colonialism. Just as historical colonialism installed numerous extractive and other privileges for mining, trading, and other companies, so too data colonialism brings *legibility privileges* for the social quantification sector over the lives of data subjects.

We are not saying that all uses of social caching are bad or misguided. Some uses of social data, perhaps by civic or public institutions, may be responsible, modest, and oriented to organizational self-reflection.[114] At the same time, the normalization of data extraction as the *general means to monitor the world* reinforces the "desire for numbers" (provided they are machine readable). New forms of professionalism and expertise around data capture are reshaping the world of work under data colonialism.[115] Before the internet, however, as Bruce Schneier notes,[116] data sources about social life were limited to company customer records, responses to direct marketing, credit bureau data, and government public records (and, we might add, insurance company data on their insured). Now, a varied universe of data collectors and services within a complex web of data processing functions extracts data from everyday life at a depth far exceeding that found in earlier forms of social knowledge.

It is not that historical types of data collection have disappeared. Indeed, their activities are being reconfigured through datafication. Car insurers are now relying increasingly on continuous surveillance devices installed in cars that tie reduced premiums and other rewards (and possibly even penalties) to the data collected about the driver's performance. An example in the United States is Progressive's Snapshot program.[117] As the Snapshot website puts it, "Snapshot is a program that personalizes your rate based on your ACTUAL driving. . . . That means you pay based on how and how much you drive instead of just traditional factors."[118] This form of personalization gives insurers enormous leeway to vary the criteria on which premiums are adapted to behavior; Snapshot's website lists different criteria for each US state. Snapshot also collects usage data from the phone on which its app is installed, although it claims that it does not "know who you're calling" (the metadata, however, is no doubt still useful in combination with other gathered or acquired data). Note the moral gloss given to this new, more intimate relation between individual and corporation. The Shared Value group of insurers, which includes the South African company Discovery and its product VitalityDrive, claims to change "individual behaviour through incentives for fitness and healthy eating."[119] Beneath the inspiring words is a clear-eyed focus on what Discovery calls "the behavioral nature of risk." Once insurers' risk becomes defined as principally about the insured's *ongoing* behavior (not occasional accidents), the relationship of insurer to insured becomes one that *requires* tracking. But do insurers' commercial interests really make them good life trainers? There are signs—even in the United States, which leads this de-velopment—that many now find this particular type of trade-off unaccept-able.[120] Unacceptable or not, data relations are already becoming for many a compulsory dimension of both labor and life.

Human inputs are only part of the territory that data colonialism seeks to annex to human capital. Machine-to-machine connections significantly deepen the new web of social knowledge production. Consider the fast-growing Internet of Things (IoT). The goal is clear: to install into every tool the capacity to continuously and autonomously collect and transmit data within privately controlled systems. Cisco predicts that by 2022, machine-to-machine connections will be 45 percent of all internet connections.[121] Since machines can communicate with each other continuously, as hu-man beings cannot, we can expect within a few years that the everyday world will have become a communication space in which human beings are minority participants and interpersonal communication a mere sub-set of what gets profitably tracked. The language of capture implies an un-ending series of territorial expansion: from the Internet of Things to "the internet of medical things," from "the internet of services" to "the internet of everything."[122]

Actors in the data sector are not shy about pursuing these opportuni-ties for behavioral influence. Indeed, as one marketer notes, "One of the major value-adds for businesses implementing IoT solutions is the behav-ioural data they unlock. . . . Businesses should be able to segment who is using an object in order to accurately contextualize its usage."[123] A report on "The Internet of Things: Opportunities for Insurers" noted that insur-ers could "use IoT-*enriched* relationships to connect more holistically to customers and influence their behaviors."[124] It is easy to imagine how the evidence of our home life transmitted by fridges, heating systems, and the like could license external judgments and discrimination—all without our knowledge or ability to comment. As Canadian political economist Vin-cent Mosco puts it, "The commodified self is a contested terrain in busi-ness battles that are only just beginning."[125]

The Internet of Things provides the perfect cover for converting all streams of human life into raw material for capitalism, in the process cap-italizing everything and everyone. Simply put, the Internet of Things *oper-*

ationalizes the capitalization of life without limit. We can also capture the Internet of Things through the lens of colonialism. Whereas the extractivism of historical colonialism "relat[ed] to the world as a frontier of conquest—rather than as home,"[126] data colonialism brings extraction home, literally into the home and the farthest recesses of everyday life.

The New "Social Theory"

All models for information processing involve some grid by which they imagine the social world (think of an examination system and its categories of grades). But, as Bernhard Rieder shows in an important analysis of Google's PageRank algorithm, practices of computation cast a particular type of shadow on the social world, imprinting it with their own "theory." Because computers can only process "ideas that can be made computable," a computer model's selection of what it can count shapes how that computer "meet[s] the world." It is *socially* significant that Google tweaked its PageRank algorithm early on so as to give more weight to remote links than might be given otherwise. The result, in Rieder's view, is "a largely conservative vision of society" that interprets content based on accumulated total linkages, downplaying intense new patterns of linkage.[127] The important point is not the details of Google's constantly changing algorithm but that each software system—and every interface built on that software—embeds decisions that encapsulate a particular "theory of the social" on which that software's functioning relies.[128] The wider consequences of this new social theory need to be understood.

Executives in the social quantification sector, whether or not they planned to, are becoming social theorists, or at least trying to sound like them. "Thank you for believing in this community," wrote Mark Zuckerberg in his full-page apology in British Sunday newspapers on March 25, 2018, in the wake of the Cambridge Analytica scandal. But behind the bland term community lay a lot of background theorizing. Certainly executives' habit of speaking like social theorists did not start in the past decade.[129] Just before the 2012 Facebook international public-share offering, Zuckerberg claimed that Facebook is "a fabric that can make any experience online social."[130] In 2010, he had already dubbed the 2007 invention of the social graph (Facebook's way of mapping the network connections between users) "our way of explaining the phenomenon we thought was happening in the world."[131] When Facebook's open graph (which aggregates people's Facebook networks with the wider data Facebook gets from "likes" and via its plug-ins) was launched later in 2010, Zuckerberg speculated more broadly:

> We believe that eventually almost all apps are going to be social but in the world there's a natural spectrum from behaviors that are really naturally social to ones that aren't and the ones that are naturally social are going to be the ones that turn into social apps. . . . [On] the other side of the spectrum are things that are really sensitive and private like health care or finance that I think there probably won't be social apps [for] for a long time. [132]

It is impossible that, as a skilled designer, Zuckerberg was unaware of the amount of technical engineering needed to construct this new social map, yet he talks as though Facebook's engineered model for extracting social data provides a window directly into how the social world really is *and* should be. Software engineering, social theory, and social construction become fused.[133]

The 2017 furor about "fake news" in people's Facebook news feed is just one example of what happens when this abstracted model of the social world collides with the contextualized expectations of real people.

The Hollowing Out of the Social Sciences

Can the human and social sciences correct for the limits of the social quantification sector's emerging model of the world? Or might much of the social sciences already be complicit in this hollowing out of the social? This claim might shock those who see in "datafication . . . an essential enrichment in human comprehension" or "a great infrastructural project that rivals" the Enlightenment's *Encyclopédie*.[134] But let's get beyond the hype and look at what is actually going on in the social sciences today.

A good example is the work of celebrated data scientist Alex Pentland at the MIT Media Lab. Pentland contributed to the World Economic Forum's Global Information Technology Reports in 2008, 2009, and 2014;[135] his research team won the Defense Advanced Research Projects Agency's

(DARPA) prize to commemorate the internet's fortieth anniversary.[136] In his book *Social Physics*, Pentland reaches back to the origins of sociology. But far from reworking classic ideas of the social sciences, Pentland's goal is to replace existing models in sociology and social psychology with the search for "statistical regularities within human movement and communication" that can generate "a computational theory of behaviour."[137] As he put it in the *MIT Technology Review*, "We're not where economics is yet. That will take another 100 years. But we're moving in some very promising directions." The new knowledge source is personal data, the "digital breadcrumbs" each of us leave as we pass through the world. The scale is that of whole organizations, even whole countries. Pentland advocates the wearing in organizations of data-collecting "sociometric badges" (an idea, as we noted in chapter 2, taken up by McDonald's) to scoop up data that would otherwise be lost. His "Data for Development" program collected mobile and demographic data "for the entire country of Ivory Coast."[138] The goal is to "really know ourselves" by understanding the social context that shapes decisions and desires. By "social context" Pentland does not mean the practical settings in which action occurs and desires have meaning; instead, he means "social network effects" culled from Big Data.[139] He offers an adventure in "reality mining" fueled by data as "the new oil of the internet."[140]

To be fair, Pentland cares about data privacy and has developed an "Open Personal Data Store" that separates the sending of information for authentication purposes from the underlying private data that enables authentication, hopefully minimizing risks of reidentification. But what matters more are the silences built into Pentland's redefinition of social science. He says nothing about the close connections between ubiquitous data collection and the new direction of capitalism, and he says little about the familiar ways of understanding the social that this new "social physics" casts into permanent shadow.[141]

Pentland's "social physics" presents in sharp profile what elsewhere is a more diffuse recalibration of social science values. A decade ago a book called *Nudge* by a behavioral economist (Richard Thaler) and a legal theorist (Cass Sunstein) shot up the reading lists of government advisers around the world. The nudge is a basic way of influencing actions by subtle prompts and signals. Whereas critics quickly saw *Nudge* as a way of locking in market-oriented behavior, Thaler and Sunstein claim that the nudge is just a tilting of the "choice environment" that helps individuals reach the outcomes they would want anyway "as judged by themselves."[142] But how many times does an environment have to nudge you before it starts to *govern* what you want?[143] Sunstein's claim that *Nudge* was always about enhancing individual "autonomy" carries little weight when the nudge is continuous, systematic, and opaque. The nudge is also a useful technique for data colonialism, generating at scale not the gentle subtlety Thaler and Sunstein intended but the force of what legal scholar Karen Yeung calls the "hypernudge": dynamic and interactive behavior modulation enabled by continuous connectivity and continuous data flows.[144]

Nudge's guest appearance in social science is just a token in the contemporary battle over economics' explanatory status. Behavioral economics emerged in response to an impasse over the model of rational-choice actor that mainstream economics has assumed for so long. Behavioral economics insists that alongside utility maximization the human subject has another dimension, less rational and more impulsive (in the jargon these are called, respectively, "System One" and "System Two").[145] Behavioral economics is having significant influence in the broader marketing profession, at least in the United States. As Anthony Nadler and Lee McGuigan argue, behavioral economics, through its selective emphasis on the less conscious, less reflective side of brain functioning, "refine[s] marketers' existing conceptions of human nature," which have always sought to tap into the irrational. Such a model of the human subject, when combined with intense data collection, creates the possibility of "persuasion profiling": data-driven persuasion that targets specific cognitive biases that marketers have tracked in data from their target groups.[146] It was persuasion profiling that proved so controversial when it came directly to light in the Cambridge Analytica scandal in March 2018. Underlying persuasion profiling is a crude biologism. Michal Kosinski, the psychologist whose work inspired Cambridge Analytica, said recently that "I don't believe in free will" since a person's thoughts and behaviors "are fully biological. . . . They originate in the biological computer that you have in your head."[147]

Neuroeconomics goes further, using brain science to dismember the model of individual cognitive functioning on which mainstream economics relies.[148] Our concern here is not defending mainstream economics' model of human rationality but rather noticing the tendency among mainstream economics' *critics* to move ever further away from social explanation as previously understood. Neuroeconomics aims to identify the "biological variables which have a large influence on behavior and are underweighted or ignored in standard [economic] theory." Biological evidence is presented to show that economics' concept of preference (the rational actor making choices in the market) must be disaggregated into "the output of a neural choice process." Biology here means brain *imaging*. A leading proponent, Colin Camerer, states that "technology now allows us to open the black box of the mind and *observe* brain activity directly."[149] There is no social dimension to this explanatory universe, just data readings. Whatever the emptiness of neuroeconomics as social explanation,[150] it has growing influence in applied domains such as neuromarketing. Neuromarketing too relies on direct use of neuroimaging,[151] hoping to understand directly the "inner workings" of the brains of consumers without resorting to the "subjective reports" on which market research was previously based. The difficulty of collecting neuroimages without bodily invasion has imposed a practical limit on developing neuromarketing research: some marketers see neuromarketing's claims as unrealistic.[152] Nonetheless, it points toward a possible integration of neuroscience and marketing that bypasses the speaking human subject.

Meanwhile, in the medical sciences there is evidence that an analogous compression of explanatory logic is occurring. Medical and social intervention is increasingly oriented to so-called biosensors: relatively simple bodily signs that are treated as proxies of underlying biological processes or medical reactions, thus bypassing "efforts to identify biological or environmental causes" that consider human subjects in the context of that environment.[153] Here too, the social is being indirectly displaced.

Against this background, there is perhaps no irony when machine-learning techniques are increasingly referred to as "neural," as though they were part of a brain; it has been common practice for some time to call large banks of parallel processing computers a "neural network." We can catch here an echo of the 1960s debates about "mind as machine," a myth whose intellectual thinness does not stop it from having a robust afterlife.[154]

How is critical work elsewhere in the social sciences, say in sociology and socially oriented humanities, positioned to respond? Not well, necessarily. Anthropology and qualitative sociology that still listen to the voices of individual social actors are so fundamentally opposed to this new social knowledge that they risk looking in the other direction as the new model steals up on the social world. No concerted response seems yet to have emerged from qualitative social scientists and humanities-based researchers to neuroeconomics or other applications of neuroscience.[155] Other critical work has registered the new "social knowledge" but in ways that sometimes risk undercutting the notion of the individual reflexive agent that the new social knowledge is only too happy to bypass. It is paradoxical when Bruno Latour, one of the founders of the wonderfully illuminating perspective on human beings' relations with technology called Actor Network Theory, writes that "purposeful action and intentionality may not be properties of objects, but they are also not properties of humans either. They are properties of institutions, apparatuses."[156] Whether this is plausible as an account of human purpose or intention, it is hardly helpful to those who want to defend the role of human agency in our understanding of the social world. Meanwhile the renewed popularity of early-twentieth-century sociologist Gabriel Tarde's concept of "brain memory," which he assumed operated directly between brains in collective contact, would seem to concede important ground to neuroeconomics. In fact, brain memory is just one of a number of concepts popular even in *critical* writing on contemporary power that are distinctly ambivalent in how they treat human beings' reflective agency.[157] One writer on data even celebrates a shift in what it means "to produce a truthful account of the world . . . no longer about hidden truths . . . or psychological depths, but rather about affect and behaviour."[158] Virginia Eubanks concludes that "the presumption that human decision-making is opaque and inaccessible is an admission that we have abandoned a social commitment to try to understand each other."[159] The behavioristic reduction of human experience to what can be tracked serves the capitalization of life perfectly.

There is, however, one bright note: the rise of critical information science that seeks to systematically establish the distortions woven into social caching's presentations of the world. There is now an emerging movement for algorithmic justice, which has raised awareness of many specific issues. The critical movement within data science concerned with "Fairness, Accountability and Transparency" has regular conferences, and a number of universities have focused programs for investigating how algorithms cover the social domain.[160] More generally, an important intersection between critical information science, legal theory, and social theory is opening up the question of how the social qualification sector presents the social world for action by powerful institutions.[161] US civil society has generated some effective campaigning. For example, ProPublica's demonstration that it was straightforward to build implicit racial exclusions into housing advertisements led to Facebook adjusting its practice on monitoring ads.[162]

But the playing field for this crucial work is hardly level: as we write, a legal case is going through the US courts in which researchers from the University of Michigan and Northeastern University are challenging the constitutionality of the US government's interpretation of the Computer Fraud and Abuse Act that prima facie would block researchers from running fairness tests on how platforms present the world.[163] The defense of earlier reference points to social knowledge and critical social research risks becoming engulfed in the disturbing trend in many countries toward political authoritarianism.

Discrimination by Design

This economically driven transformation of social knowledge has major consequences for the distribution of resources in the social world—that is, for questions of social justice.

It is not enough to condemn today's "advances" in social knowledge for not caring about human subjects. Critique must begin from the fact that what now passes for social knowledge is produced through *social relations* that have entirely different power implications from those that underlay earlier forms of social knowledge. Today's social knowledge is produced principally through privately controlled data extraction whose goal is to discriminate between social actors for economic advantage. Algorithms help "fram[e] problems" and provide the classifications on which broader social differentiations are constructed. But "many classifications are now embedded in markets,"[164] a notable example being credit rating systems. Data-driven social classifications have profound consequences for the fairness or otherwise of the social world. Indeed, various entrenched features of the new social knowledge incline it toward enhancing not justice but inequality.

Datafication in the Justice System

"Just because you haven't been arrested doesn't mean you haven't been caught": a Los Angeles Police Department detective is speaking here not about a legal spying operation but about the banal act of noting whether someone's name has frequently been searched for in a police *data system*.[165] Of course, "to classify is human,"[166] but the problem is the sorts of power relations in which today's data categorizations unfold. The social quantification sector exercises considerable power but has few, if any, incentives to make that power transparent (for example, by revealing how an algorithm is "tuned" to weigh one kind of error as more to be avoided than another).[167] There is no competitive advantage either in fairness or in avoiding social harm, but there *is* an advantage in using data discriminations to influence behavior more effectively than competitors do (for example, by playing on people's "pain point," as one marketer put it).[168] So why expect the discriminations that the social quantification sector makes "under the hood" to be motivated by fairness? But unless they are, data classifications are likely to go on producing social harm with cumulative effects that will be extremely hard to track.[169]

This is especially worrying in spheres of social management, such as the law, crime, and social services, in which decision-making is increasingly relying on algorithmic processes that are outsourced to commercial data operations. Software is being used by police to predict reoffending and crime distribution in a number of countries (especially the United States and China, with experiments reported in Israel, Canada, the Netherlands, and the United Kingdom). In the United Kingdom, algorithms are being used by cash-strapped local governments to assess which children need protection from child abuse.[170] Powerful new networks are being built to "connect devices, apps, and people for more than half of the [US's] major city police agencies," with Axon AI being a leading network provider and Palantir (the company of Peter Theil, a Facebook board member) being a leading provider of analytics software.[171]

What are the effects on the ground? US legal theorists Robert Brauneis and Ellen Goodman researched the use of algorithms in US social services departments. They found a toxic mix of complex calculative processes (protected by software developers' legal privilege) and on-the-ground deals to protect the algorithms' workings from accountability even to government. And yet it is these same processes on which the authority of decisions about people's life chances supposedly rely—processes that identify areas of high crime risk for resource allocation or that "[identify] child welfare cases with a high probability of serious child injury or death." Brauneis and Goodman found that a state authority in Alaska "ha[d] no access to the algorithm [on child welfare] that generates the risk assessments and none to the process by which the algorithm is generated and adjusted."[172] Even US criminal courts have difficulty in accessing the algorithms underlying law enforcement practice (something that increasingly concerns US legal commentators).[173] It is disturbing, meanwhile, to read from a recent study of US courts' use of COMPAS software that untrained workers on Amazon Mechanical Turk "are as accurate and fair as COMPAS at predicting recidivism."[174] Opaque algorithms even risk "hollow[ing] out the decision-making capacity of public servants" by creating a distance between public servants' decisions and the evidence-gathering processes on which those decisions rely.[175]

The larger implications for the management of law, crime, and policing are as yet unclear.[176] This radically privatized production of social knowledge compares poorly with the historical processes for generating social knowledge discussed earlier in the chapter.[177] There are growing concerns in the United States that, whatever else it is, algorithmic processing cannot be a substitute for human judges' discretion exercised on behalf of the state.[178] In February 2018, the European Commission for the Efficiency of Justice launched a review of the ethics of using algorithms in justice systems. Meanwhile, a very different vision is emerging in China, that of an "intelligent court" that will use "cloud computing, big data, artificial intelligence . . . to promote modernization of [the] trial system and judgement capability."[179] Contested or not, a new version of social governance is emerging from the daily operations of data colonialism.

Unjust Governance by Proxy

It is not just that many instances of data discrimination occur far from the contexts in which the original data collection was authorized and its meaning shaped. Data's very exchangeability *depends on* abstraction and "the stripping away of narrative" that "facilitates the . . . insertion of numbers in new locations and their adaptability in new contexts."[180] Once in circulation, classifications can generate not just first-order but "second-order corrections," indeed, corrections in any higher domain without limit. Those "corrections" shape the life chances of human subjects. When a person gets categorized as a high-risk loan recipient in one context, it is likely to affect how they are categorized in other contexts.[181]

Such lateral recategorization affects people very differently depending on their status. Disadvantaged groups, such as poor mothers, have always had little control over how state agencies gather and exchange information and judgments about them.[182] Social caching, however, is a powerful but only partly guided new weapon for steering social evaluation and social change, very likely in the direction of greater inequality. This has major implications for how the social world is governed.

There is first the problem, already noted, that decision makers may not understand their data sources. The increasing use of data streams with insufficient contextualization in government decision-making through so-called dashboards has provoked concern in the United Kingdom.[183] The problem is deepened by the distinctive way that data generates knowledge through Machine Learning. Data processing generates proxies—regular correlations that *stand in* for other variables of social knowledge—out of which larger models of the world to be governed are built. The whole point of proxies is to black-box a more complex social domain while facilitating intervention. When an insurer assumes that driving after midnight equates to choosing to take more risk even if a person's working conditions require it or when algorithms treat geographical areas as proxies for levels of crime risk, complexities on the ground become unreadable. [184]

The result is what Israeli legal scholars Niva Elkin-Koren and Eldar Haber call "governance by proxy,"[185] a way of *stopping talk* about those features for which proxies stand in. This can be dangerous. When patterns in current data are assumed to be reliable proxies for future events that may (or may *not*) happen, preventive action will be authorized whose necessity, by definition, never gets demonstrated. The counterfactual—what if no preventive action had been taken?—simply falls out of the picture.[186] And what, as Solon Barocas, Kate Crawford, and colleagues ask, of the processes that generated the proxy in the first place? If they are shaped by patterns in the so-called training data through which Machine Learning generated its proxies, then the nature of those patterns becomes important. There is no such thing as neutral data: training data drawn from and reflective of an already highly unequal world (for example, data that reflects patterns of racial discrimination and racially linked socioeconomic inequality in the raw facts of where people live) risks hardbaking those inequalities into new interpretations and judgments.[187]

The solution cannot be just transparency. Machine Learning's iterative, nonlinear operations, as noted earlier, make transparency in any literal sense problematic.[188] The problem lies with proxy logic itself, which aims to reclassify the social world and its actors via adequate substitutes for categories that *really are meant* to structure the social world, such as the category "should not be given a loan" or "should have benefits withdrawn." Machine learning requires a bridge from its judgments that links them *reliably* back to that world, and that bridge is only as good as the processes that originally generated the algorithms.

There is a bigger danger too. If lack of accountability to context is becoming a *principle* of the new social knowledge, then this serves data colonialism (the mutual implication of human life and digital technology *for* capitalism) rather well. Abstraction means removing from view the textures of social life that might otherwise provide the reference point for social actors to hold social knowledge to account. Above all what risks being hollowed out by the new social knowledge is the space from which human actors could once imagine themselves with a license *to speak truth to power*. When the social world, in all its possible layers of action, thought, and expression, becomes merely an input to capital, the once resounding Foucauldian principle that for every power there is resistance starts to ring hollow. At best, data colonialism will be accountable through its disguises—disguises such as personalization or self-knowledge whose role is to entice people into data relations.

Older concepts of social explanation, based not on tracking sentiments and connections but on evaluating the wider context of people's lives more broadly (or even asking their opinions!), risk being cast into shadow by data colonialism's new social knowledge. How will concepts such as poverty, which in the nineteenth century emerged from sifting many statistical analyses, survive in competition with proxy logic? According to Marion Fourcade and Kieran Healy, older rationales for giving the poor "more favourable terms because they were poor" have now in the United States largely been replaced with "the idea . . . that the terms of credit ought to depend solely on one's prior credit-related behaviour," as tracked by numerous data processes.[189]

This is not the first time in history that numbers have trumped voice, but what if the social narrative that might have corrected this has been undermined too?[190] Voice—the unmodulated, nonpredictive accounting of experience, once valued as part of social life—is by design excluded from Big Data analytics. People's reflections on the world are unlikely to be part of the data that makes up their data doubles. The capacity for voice does not easily scale, and that *is* its point.[191]

But the threat to voice is not the greatest danger that data colonialism poses to the quality of the social world. What if governance by proxy provides an effective way of deepening the poverty, deprivation, and discrimination that voice might want to protest about? US policy expert Joseph Jerome writes that "most of the biggest concerns we have about big data—online discrimination, profiling, tracking, exclusion—threaten the self-determination and personal autonomy of the poor more than any other class."[192] This is for many intersecting reasons. First, as already noted, the poor have always been more vulnerable to surveillance, and the collection of data has been more prejudicial to them. The poor are also less likely to have the ability to take control of their personal data, whether through lack of bargaining power (if your power is low, opting out of system demands is really not an option), exclusive reliance on a smartphone for connection, or poor literacy. Second, though, the historical tool for *governing* the poor ("guilt by association") is ideally suited for the era of social media, when platforms' data about people's associations is already being analyzed to make decisions about awarding jobs, credit, and university places and to predict who is most likely to commit a criminal offense.[193] And yet it is particularly hard to unpick the contribution of social media data in decision-making—for example, in relation to employment.[194] Third, Big Data collection is already fueling the creation of algorithmic categories perfectly suited to target the poor for predatory marketing of products, such as emergency loans, likely to enhance their poverty and vulnerability (categories such as "Fragile Families" and "At Risk Populations").[195] Fourth, since it requires money and skill to contest errors in vast opaque data sets, the poor are particularly unlikely to be able to challenge any unfairnesses that emerge from all of the above.

A social world governed by proxy and informed by social caching is perfectly arranged, in sum, to ensure what Thomas Pogge called "politics as usual": the continued exploitation of the poor.[196] If so, the social consequences of data colonialism are likely to converge with the legacies of historical colonialism that, in many countries, have not only sustained poverty but skewed poverty and general disempowerment toward ethnic minorities, particularly those formed from dominated colonial populations.[197] This is where the scandalous evidence that algorithmic sorting reinforces racialized discrimination[198] takes on an even more disturbing long-term implication. Could data colonialism's technical tools be the means to lock in ever more securely the unjust settlement of historical colonialism in supposedly postcolonial societies?

Data extraction—data colonialism's basic mode of operation as the implication of human life and digital technology for capitalism—is the medium for a "savage sorting" of the social world. Or as Douglas Merrill, Google's former chief information officer, put it, "All data is credit data, we just don't know how to use it yet."[199]

A Rising Injustice

Let's return for a moment to Karl Polanyi's vivid account of the social unfolding of industrial capitalism. Data colonialism, it is clear, still awaits
its *counter*movement: there is as yet no major change in social thinking
or government policy to challenge its cruelties, as those of industrial capitalism were challenged in the nineteenth century. Recent calls for more
openness about data practice offer only the very start of this change.

If no resistance is forthcoming, the capitalization of life is destined to
reconstruct Hobbes's "state of nature"—a battle of all against all—via an algorithmic simulation that preserves, indeed stimulates, social appearances
while regrounding them in capitalism's general drive to profitable extraction. The process will be heavily disguised. Popular narratives of "smartness" (for instance, the smart city) are an example: in the smart landscape,
there are *only* connected individuals, natural and willing targets of commercial messaging and sources of commercially useful data, functioning
within the larger cycle of capitalized life.[200] Everyone else is *by definition*
invisible. As smartness starts to drive urban regeneration, it will become
harder to hold on to the forms of knowledge lost through the capitalization of life. New urban environments will emerge, such as the proposal by
Google's Sidewalk Labs for downtown Toronto's waterfront district, built
on personalization ("really smart, people-centered urban planning") and
iron corporate control of the "intelligent signals" generated by a datafied
environment.[201] To have a chance of resisting this, we must hold onto earlier forms of social knowledge: voice, public accountability and the public value of social understanding, visibility rather than opacity, contextual
social explanation, and above all a concern with the role of these values in
challenging injustice.

Recall that the whole trajectory of data colonialism started out from
the banal fact that to function, computers must capture data about their
changes of state.[202] It is a curious irony that B. J. Fogg, a leading devel-
oper of unconscious behavioral influence through online choice architec-
tures, named his new science of intervention "captology."[203] Knowledge
by capture, influence by appropriation. When the cutting edge of social

knowledge is a tool kit for achieving *power* at scale (or what Walmart more comfortably calls "personalization at scale"),[204] then the stakes of the social-knowledge game just got higher and its potential contribution to social justice more tenuous.

Data colonialism's new social knowledge generates a deep form of injustice in the very construction of the social and political domain. Philosopher Nancy Fraser calls this sort of problem "meta-political injustice":[205] justice in who or what *counts as* someone to whom or something to which questions of justice apply at all. One way to open up these issues is ethics. As Tristan Harris, one of Fogg's former students and a founder of the Truth About Tech campaign in the United States, asked, "What responsibility comes with the ability to influence the psychology of a billion people? Where's the Hippocratic oath?"[206] As yet, we simply don't know.

But ethics must start out from an understanding of the self. What if the boundaries of the self too are under sustained attack by data colonialism? If so, we may require philosophical resources to identify with precision the violence that data colonialism does to the self and, by extension, the social world as well. That is the topic of the next chapter.

Data and the Threat to Human Autonomy 5

I'm not going to work under conditions where I'm treated like a child, a child who doesn't have enough [sense] to know when to go to bed and when to get up; or when to stop and rest while rush hour traffic clears and then proceed when rested and safer.

—US truck driver[1]

Surely the most wretched unfreedom of all would be to lose the ability even to conceive of what it would be like to have the freedom we lack, and so dismiss even the aspiration to freedom, as something wicked and dangerous.

—Allen Wood[2]

WHAT DOES IT MEAN to be human—to remain distinctively human—in the twenty-first century? A decade and a half ago, it still made sense for one of the United States's leading privacy advocates, Philip Agre, to assert that "your face is not a barcode."[3] But in May 2018, the black rap artist Donald Glover, a.k.a. Childish Gambino, released a video that went viral called "This is America." As the song fades, he sings, "You just a barcode." The chasm between these two sentences says much about the recent trajectory of poverty and race relations in the United States, already touched on in the last chapter. But it also opens an even larger story about the violence that data colonialism does *everywhere* to the core human values of freedom and autonomy.[4] That larger story is the focus of this chapter.

"Transport is becoming a data business," says Hakan Schildt of Swedish truck company Scandia.[5] Yet *driving* a truck used to symbolize the type of work that brought a certain freedom, at least for its male workforce. The first quote at the beginning of the chapter is the voice of a driver interviewed by Karen Levy about the impact of the Electronic On-Board Recorders (EOBRs) now installed in many US trucks. Clearly, he is troubled. A trucker from the same study went further and insisted that "any piece of electronics that is not directly hooked up to my body cannot tell me [when I am tired]."[6] But other employees have been "hooked up" to devices that monitor at least their external movements for more than a decade (for example, store and distribution-center workers of the UK super-market chain Tesco).[7] If the second trucker's imagining comes true, it will not be his body telling him he is tired but a calibrated data system linked up to the bodies of a whole workforce. That system will monitor working bodies through their contracted activities and much of their off-work activity, using the latter as evidence for judging the former. There is a long history of surveillance at work, disproportionately affecting low-paid jobs and disadvantaged populations, but the intimacy of monitoring in today's datafied workplace is without historical precedent. It fits well, however, with the colonial approach to social knowledge that chapter 4 uncovered in which individual reflection and voice matter little, and only aggregated data counts.

What are the implications of all this for human life? The second quote at the beginning of the chapter offers a clue, capturing chillingly the fate for all of us to which the first quotation points. The source is a leading commentator on nineteenth-century philosopher Georg Wilhelm Friedrich Hegel. Hegel was unique among European Enlightenment philosophers in anticipating moments of breakdown when social formations based on certain values come to be organized around practical goals and institutions that directly undermine and oppose those values. The result is the deepest form of alienation.[8]

Could data colonialism be ushering in such a conflict for all its subjects?[9] If so, how might we begin to confront it? Can philosophical concepts such as autonomy help us formulate what is going wrong? Or is the term *autonomy* (so often used metaphorically now for, among other things, IT systems, weapon systems, and even cars) itself at risk of being appropriated by data colonialism?

Although the term *autonomy* raises its own complexities, we will find it more useful than *freedom*. The term *freedom* gives no hints as to what freedom *is for*, whereas *autonomy* specifies the desired state that is its goal. In a strong form,[10] it involves, as the German philosopher Beate Rössler puts it, an actor being "self-*determined*"—"able to act in accordance with desires and actions which are authentically hers."[11] There remain many ways of specifying what self-determination actually means, and some versions of autonomy have, without question, become associated with the Western colonial project. It will be important therefore to hold onto a notion of autonomy that is not a form of aggressively individualistic self-rule but rather refers to the *socially grounded* integrity without which we cannot recognize ourselves or others as selves. Only gradually will we move toward the question of *privacy*,[12] the term through which debates over autonomy normally reach a wider public. In doing so, we will focus less on the many interpretations and extensions of autonomy and more on the idea at its core: the self's minimal integrity, or boundedness, without which the self would not be a distinct site of experience at all.

Before we explore these questions, let's be clear about what drives the problems that data colonialism causes for human autonomy. Complex power relations are involved, as we have seen, but for simplicity's sake let's call the root cause "surveillance." We must immediately note that our standard image of surveillance—a person, generally representing the state, watching or listening in to the full stream of another person's life—is unhelpful for various reasons. Today it is generally corporations, not the state, doing the tracking. The medium of corporate tracking is unlike a human sense (seeing or listening). It is, instead, the accumulation of data from multiple sources, what scholars have called "dataveillance."[13] At any one point in time, the surveiller is unlikely to have a full "picture" of the surveilled; only over time and through aggregation does a sufficiently detailed picture accumulate to motivate action.[14] Finally, as noted in chapter 4, the target of surveillance is not the whole person but rather a montage of data doubles that probabilistically identify a real individual. Yet it *is* that real individual who is tethered to the discriminatory actions taken on the basis of the data gathered. And it is because of the consequences of this tethering that we must retain the term *surveillance*[15] even while acknowledging that its connotations derive in part from historical forms of tracking very different from today's. The reason both traditional surveillance and datafied tracking conflict with notions of freedom derives from something common to both: their invasion of the basic space of the self on behalf of an external power.

The notion that surveillance in this extended sense does damage to human life does not depend on a property claim. The argument is not that the data extracted from me is already my "property" or "possession" and *as such* must not be appropriated by another. For until the act of extraction

there was no boundedness to the information relating to my life stream—
as we have noted many times, data itself is not raw material. What previously was just part of the flow of my activity becomes separately identifiable and so potentially transferable only through the act of extraction. This
transformation has nothing to do with whether the individual is already
identified. Rather, since life (like land in Karl Polanyi's historical account
of industrial capitalism) is not the sort of thing that is naturally commodified, data requires for its creation institutional processes of extraction and
demarcation, from which potential commodities can be generated.[16]

The issue with continuous tracking therefore goes much deeper than
whether by some appropriate legal fiction we do or do not cede ownership
of data to the individuals to whom the data relates.[17] The issue goes deeper
even than the damage done by particular discriminations that flow from
the data's use, discussed in chapter 4. The deepest problem is the violence
that the *very fact* of data collection through surveillance does to the minimal integrity of the self. We derive this latter notion from the concept of
autonomy.

The self's minimal integrity is the boundedness that constitutes a self
as a self. Often that boundedness is experienced in defending a minimal
space of physical control around the body, but it can also be invaded without physical incursion—for example, by acts of power that intimidate,
shame, harass, and monitor the self. By "the space of the self" we mean the
materially grounded domain of possibility that the self has as its horizon
of action and imagination. The space of the self can be understood as the
open space in which any given individual experiences, reflects, and pre-
pares to settle on her course of action.[18] Hegel describes this space as both
external and internal, like a circle that never-endingly turns in on itself.
This, he says, is what makes "the free will . . . truly infinite, for it is not just
a possibility, a predisposition; its external existence is its inwardness, its
own self."[19] It is this continual interplay between internal and external, self
and other, that enables the deeply social understanding of the self that, as
a philosopher, Hegel advocated.[20] From this understanding of the self, we
salvage some ideas in this chapter as tools for challenging data colonialism. Whatever the problems associated with Hegel's profoundly colonial
view of history and his ambiguously conservative view of the nineteenth-

century state, Hegel is unique among European philosophers in seeing so clearly the social grounding of philosophical concepts such as freedom.

Insight into this social concept of freedom (or autonomy) is not unique to Hegel, however, if we look to philosophical traditions outside Europe and North America. Argentinian-Mexican philosopher Enrique Dussel's philosophy of liberation has as its goal the need to articulate a concept of human freedom from *outside* the West's power centers. Freedom, for Dussel, is the substance of a person with "all its uniqueness, its proper indetermination, its essence of bearing a history, a culture; it is a being that freely and responsibly determines itself" and so is always situated "beyond" what Dussel calls "the horizon of totality."[21] In insisting on a space of the self *beyond* any horizon of totality, Dussel goes one step further than Hegel did, explicitly defending the space of the self against any attempt of power to own and absorb it.

When, as in the era of data colonialism, capitalism seeks to absorb human life into an external totality—the apparently self-sufficient world of continuous data processing—it is ultimately freedom in Dussel's (but also Hegel's) sense that is at stake. The need to defend the minimal integrity of the self holds whether one advocates the individualistic freedom guaranteed by a competitive economic order or (as do Hegel and Dussel) a more socially grounded notion of freedom, based in the mutuality of social life. Defending the minimal integrity of the self exposes contradictions within capitalism's own (individualistic) version of freedom while providing a basis to defend the social values that help us *think beyond* that notion and beyond data colonialism too.

Double Consciousness 2.0

In the hollowed-out social world of data colonialism, data practices invade the minimal space of the self by making submission to *tracking* a requirement of daily life, retrofitting the self's domain of action onto a grid of data extraction, a grid only minimally regulated by law.[22] The extractive social relations that underlie data colonialism impose a fundamental form of dispossession. A continuously trackable life is a dispossessed life, whose space is continuously invaded and subjected to extraction by external power.

It has been fashionable to forget this and to feign indifference. Some question the "special" moral status of human beings and even compare them to ants and bees, whose collective life has certainly fascinated humans for millennia.[23] Insect metaphors have long been adopted into the technical language of computing; we have *swarm robotics, registry hives,* and the like. Perhaps there is some force to such analogies when infrastructures of connection enable the aggregation of human-data traces on a vast scale. But there is a danger in such metaphors. No one has yet shown that human beings *are* collective animals in a zoological sense; pretending they are may divert attention from the human costs of capitalism's new social order.

Philosopher Luciano Floridi goes further, renaming the very stuff of the self in terms of information. To him, we are not exactly humans anymore but hybrid creatures that Floridi calls "inforgs."[24] Although Floridi uses this as a starting point for new approaches to the privacy of the "informational body," the convenience of the inforg concept for data colonialism is obvious. Inforgs are the perfect creatures for the hypernudge to rule when they have been refashioned to always be open to data flows and so continuously available for modulation. But by what? Presumably by some form of intelligence? We could bet everything on artificial intelligence, but few have taken this step. Perhaps modulation by human intelligence exercised at the collective level? US West Coast evangelist Kevin Kelly comes close to this when he celebrates the "technium" (his term for the supposed collective "autonomy" that develops from "the feedback loops in the technological system").[25] But why believe humans are intelligent at a collective level while ignoring or recklessly overriding humans' ability to be independently intelligent at the individual level?

Implicitly, a new notion of the subject is being fashioned, meaningful at the collective scale on which data processing flourishes but occluding older understandings of the individual subject. Conflicts between notions of the self characterized earlier phases of colonialism too. W. E. B. Du Bois called the outcome "double consciousness," a situation in which the self is forced to describe itself in *another's* language, one that overrides the language in which the colonial subject might otherwise choose to describe herself.[26] Seen from the point of view of capital, the contradiction is unimportant and certainly not painful, because capitalism's language generally wins! Seen from any other point of view (including that of most human subjects), something important is lost. We must name that "something" that capitalism is not hearing and data colonialism is not registering.[27] But this requires philosophical resources that can salvage something from previous views of the human subject. By salvaging the concept of the minimal integrity of human life—the bare reality of the self as a self—[28]we identify something that we cannot trade without endangering something essential to ourselves. This "something" underlies all the formulations of privacy and autonomy from culture to culture and period to period.

Before we explore in more detail the minimal integrity of the self, we must remember that when the self's autonomy is damaged, individuals are affected in very different ways. Whereas the violence of data colonialism affects all subjects, it also offers new opportunities for human beings to exploit each other by *redistributing* the resulting costs. Even if under data colonialism we are all destined to become data subjects—that is, parties to regular data relations—what this means for one person will be very different from what it means for another. We are not simply talking here about the difference it makes whether you are a chief executive of a data extraction platform or its most junior employee. There is unevenness also in how the consequences of datafication are distributed.

As we noted in chapter 4, the poor are likely to be particularly disadvantaged. Digital platforms, apps, and sensors provide infrastructures for seamlessly installing data-derived performance monitoring into all aspects of work, but they are being installed most energetically in lower-status and low-wage work. Employees such as truck drivers or warehouse workers already have continuous surveillance installed as a basic feature of their lives. There may soon be no workers left in those sectors who remember what it was for their bodies and their every action to be unmonitored.[29] In higher-status jobs, the intensity and continuity of surveillance may be limited to aspects of the recruitment process in which a candidate's social media history is now pored over. In today's "fissured workplace," those in powerful positions will seek privileged control over who is surveilled (and how much) and who is not surveilled. Social power may come to mean, in part, being a net *controller* of the benefits and costs of surveillance, just as under industrial capitalism management power meant controlling the flow of knowledge and information that made up work.[30]

The consequences of how people are surveilled and evaluated will also vary depending on how much a person's role retains zones of discretion. Being "judged by results" means something very different if you are a call-center worker tracked from moment to moment (in real time and/or retrospectively) rather than the director of a stock-exchange-listed company or university professor judged by end-of-year results. Direct, on-the-body, moment-to-moment surveillance and correction is likely to be closely correlated with lower status.

People are also differently placed to repair the costs inflicted through surveillance systems. Imagine the costs when every object, most processes, and much of one's work and other life opportunities are managed through automated monitoring. You may need to buy a new tool when its built-in tracking system breaks down; you may need to find alternative sources for education, health care, or insurance when denied them on algorithmic grounds; or you may need to correct inaccurate data held about you in a system—for example, a credit rating. People's ability to bear those costs will depend, as ever, on a preexisting (likely unequal) distribution of resources. And the more opaque the processes of data sorting are, the more resources will be needed to contest them effectively.

The threat that data colonialism poses to the minimal integrity of human life is therefore both a *universal* issue affecting everyone and the driver of new forms of social and economic *inequality between* people. The two are connected. Data colonialism enacts at scale a major change in how power shapes the life-space of human subjects: this is the universal issue. An immediate consequence is that individuals, institutions, and systems acquire the means to discriminate against and dominate others in new ways. But to have a chance to deal effectively with this more specific problem, it is essential to grasp the underlying universal problem, which is the goal of the rest of this chapter. Once again our survey of the problems data colonialism poses for human life will not pretend to be comprehensive but, at most, suggestive.

We will certainly not be claiming that all forms of damage to the space of human autonomy are the same. There is a world of difference between slavery's direct and violent ownership of bodies and minds and the more indirect forms of surveillance and dataveillance that characterize contemporary data relations. Still, they have something crucial in common. We seek to identify what that is, building on excellent work done by many authors in sociology, communications, and legal theory, including Mark Andrejevic, Julie Cohen, Oscar Gandy, Karen Levy, and David Lyon.

Data Colonialism's Assault on Human Autonomy

It is often said that people, in rich countries at least, have made a trade-off between their privacy (or some aspect of it) and security of service, economic benefits (such as "personalized" prices), and convenience of connection. But the evidence is that, at least in the United States, people feel resigned and powerless to influence invasion of privacy.[31] This does not mean people think that issue is unimportant. A 2015 Pew study found that 93 percent of US adults surveyed thought it was important to be in control of "who can get information about them," with 90 percent feeling that it was important to control "what information is collected about them."[32] Meanwhile, there is evidence of rising concern about data privacy in Southeast Asia, according to a *Financial Times* survey.[33]

Our argument, however, tries to go deeper. The minimal self-integrity under threat is not the sort of thing that human beings can trade without losing touch with what constitutes them as selves rather than as inputs to a collective intelligence or information-processing system. Two senses of self are in play here.[34] Capitalism affirms, for sure, the uniquely identifiable reference point on which all notions of the self hang (it is, after all, this bodily subject whose market potential gets traded in proxy form). But at the same time, capitalism invites us to lose control over a core element in the content of that identified self whose continuity (and change) we value with time. By installing automated surveillance into the space of the self, we risk losing the very thing—the open-ended space in which we continuously monitor and transform ourselves over time—that constitutes us as selves at all.

In the face of this, we find, as already suggested, a surprising ally in a deeply compromised figure: the philosopher Hegel, who fascinated the critics of both capitalism and colonialism (Marx and Fanon). Hegel is known for his theory of "world-spirit," or *Geist*, in terms of whose unfolding he interpreted the whole of history. One might therefore have expected Hegel to be an ally of Big Tech; it was, after all, Ray Kurzweil, now director of engineering at Google, who wrote that "the singularity will ultimately infuse the universe with spirit."[35] But Hegel was a complex philosopher and also one of the most searching investigators into the nature of human freedom. In the words of his main interpreters, Hegel saw freedom as "possible . . . *only* if one is also already in a certain (ultimately institutional, norm-governed) relation to others." In other words, freedom is actualized through our social relations, which means that the loss of freedom is actualized through distortions in social relations. This argument, for the first time, opened up philosophical thinking to sociological evidence and, at its most radical, acknowledged that at particular historical moments, institutional forces may come to undermine the inherited values and norms that govern social relations. When this happens, people start to feel themselves "part of a practice that has either gone dead . . . or requires of [them] further commitments incompatible with others necessary within some form of life." Put bluntly, when our form of life starts to conflict with our underlying values, "the lives in a form of life become uninhabitable."[36]

This is just the sort of normative crisis that a character in a recent novel by US author Don DeLillo sees playing out today:

> [The] world . . . is being lost to the systems. To the transparent networks that slowly occlude the flow of all those aspects of nature and character that distinguish humans from elevator buttons and doorbells. . . . Haven't you felt it? The loss of autonomy. The sense of being virtualized. All the coded impulses you depend on to guide you. All the sensors in the room that are watching you, listening to you, tracking your habits, measuring your capabilities. All the linked data designed to incorporate you into the megadata.[37]

Something, in other words, is going wrong with human autonomy. But, you might ask, isn't the notion of autonomy (the self's ability to govern its own life, deriving from the Greek words *autos* for self and *nomos* for law or rule) itself problematic? What self is really able to *rule* itself, independently of others and of institutions? Haven't doubts about the sovereignty of the individual self driven the popularity of behavioral economics that we discussed in chapter 4?

Crucially, however, it is not *that* notion of autonomy (or freedom) that Hegel defends. For Hegel challenged Western notions of liberal individualism in a key respect, insisting that freedom (*freiheit*), his preferred term, is always grounded in *social processes*, in which individuals interact with and depend on each other. As we have seen, the notion of the minimal integrity of the self goes far beyond Hegel. The integrity of the self that makes choices in a complex world is essential to most liberal notions of freedom. It is implicit in the concept of humanity's "species being"[38] that underlies Marx's theory of alienation. The self's minimal integrity is essential also to Dussel's philosophy of liberation conceived precisely to operate *beyond* the dominance of Western models of power. How else indeed to conceive of a human life beyond the definitional power of the West except by building on what Dussel calls the "natural substantivity of a person," the basic "fact that each individual is distinct and not merely different"?[39]

Let's explore, then, what sorts of problems data relations pose for this fundamental core of autonomy: the natural substance of the person.

Data Risks

When an external power uses data against a person's interests, there are clear potential harms to the subject and her ability to control her sphere of action. These harms can be considered on various levels.

First, there are direct harms through the use of data. We most commonly think here of the state as the important external power—the state that exercises surveillance power to terrorize its citizens or, in more subtle ways, undermine their interests. But equally important is corporate power. There is no reason to assume that a corporation, unless specifically checked from doing so, won't use the personal data it collects or buys in its own interests and against an individual's interests. Many forms of personal data are the source of validly competing interests: when individuals insure against risks to themselves, the interests of insurers and insured are often, quite legitimately, opposed. There are risks of data being misused from which individuals need protection; all the corporate and policy literature about Big Data acknowledges this point in some form.[40]

Automatic data collection poses a danger to autonomy at a second, deeper level, not because its actual uses are always harmful (indeed, some might be beneficial) but because the *possibility* of harmful use distorts the space in which individuals live and act. This is what some writers call the "chilling" effect, which is the impact that the power to collect and hold data on a large scale has on individuals' ability to think of themselves as free actors.[41] Political theorist Quentin Skinner's comment on the Snowden revelations is decisive: "Not merely by the fact that someone is reading my emails but also by the fact that someone has the power to do so *should they choose* leaves us at the mercy of arbitrary power. . . . What is offensive to liberty is the very existence of such arbitrary power."[42]

The chilling effects of corporate watching in practice are so far less clear, but they must be taken seriously. To see why, we must go beyond familiar debates about the authoritarian state or about whether trading part of our autonomy for wider benefits (for example, greater security and the massive convenience of connectivity) is worthwhile. There is a deeper issue toward which the "chilling" argument points: that the constant watchability of our every thought and action by external forces changes the field of power in which we exist,[43] transforming a supposed order *of individuals* into a collection of living entities plugged into an external system.[44]

Datafication and the Space of the Self

This takes us to a third and more fundamental disruption to autonomy. What if capitalist data relations trouble the very basis of autonomy, the minimal boundedness that underlies the very possibility of being a self? What if datafication, not just potentially but *in principle and by design*, interferes with the self's space of movement that is its "own"?

Dave Eggers's fable, *The Circle*, highlights this deeper problem.[45] The Circle is a corporation that is something like a hybrid of Google and Facebook. Eggers's concern in the novel is not that the Circle, which seeks to gather all human data into a seamless "circle" accessible to individuals using just one password, will use that data for bad purposes. Neither is it how the power relations involved in continuous data sharing impact the families and friends of Circle employees (the chilling effect just discussed). Eggers reserves his sharpest criticism for the impact on employees who work inside the corporation and so benefit from its power. Two characters, a keen young recruit (Mae) and her more experienced mentor (Annie), each want to live a life that harmonizes with the surveillance practices on which the Circle's business model depends. They want to but cannot—at least not without a sanity-threatening struggle. At risk is not just the ability of these characters to direct their lives but their basic sense of themselves as selves: the minimal integrity without which they fail to be selves at all.

This comes out clearly at a point in the novel when a senior Circle employee criticizes Mae for hand-writing an entry in her diary about a walk she took down to San Francisco Bay (a typical unstructured individual pleasure). The employee says, "My problem with paper is that all communication dies with it. It holds no possibility of continuity [. . .]. It ends with you. Like you're the only one who matters [. . .] but if you'd been using a tool that would help confirming the identity of whatever birds you saw, then anyone can benefit. [. . .] Knowledge is lost every day through this sort of shortsightedness."[46] The problem was that Mae chose to reflect her experience "only" back to herself rather than relay it to the Circle's data pool. Her choice of recording technology (paper versus smartphone or tablet) and the refusal to connect to wider data systems that this choice implied, is interpreted back to her in moral terms when Mae is told that "knowledge is lost every day through this sort of shortsightedness." The senior Circle employee who criticizes Mae believes that there is no space in which an individual is free to reflect on herself that is not *already* a space over which her corporation, acting in the name of social knowledge, has right of access.

Eggers captures here the fallacy at the heart of dataism. Using the cover of the self's continuing moral obligations, data evangelism overrides the space of the self from where it faces others. This is the space, as Rössler puts it, in which "processes of self-description, self-definition, self-discovery, or indeed self-invention" take place, all of them "dependent upon a person bringing herself face-to-face with herself in conditions in which she can really be sure that she is protected from the eyes of anyone else."[47] The liberal philosopher Charles Fried had anticipated the problem when in 1970, with what would now be a primitive surveillance technology in mind, he imagined a parolee kept under constant and total monitoring *in case* he commits another crime; is this, he asks, consistent with any notion of freedom? Fried argues no, because such an arrangement overrides the basic element of interpersonal trust fundamental to human life: trust that respects the independence of the other person, as *an other* person, to make his own errors. If trust, he argues, were just a matter of risk management, we would probably delegate it to "cheap and efficient surveillance," but "man can't know he is trusted unless he has a right to act without surveillance" and so prove he is worthy of trust.[48] This is exactly the sort of trustless social order toward which data colonialism is taking us. Here China shows the way most clearly. As Jack Ma, founder of Alibaba, put it, in "the political and legal system of the future . . . bad guys won't even be able to walk into the square," because their every movement and action will have been watched.[49]

In response, we must recall that there can be no genuine self (no mutuality between selves) without the self having a space that is its own. The self must control what passes through that space and whether it "ends with" the self or not. It is this space of minimal self-integrity that concentration camps and torturers through the ages have tried to crush. It is this space whose integrity, in less violent but equally persistent ways, becomes collateral damage in the growth of data-driven capitalism.

Capitalist data relations redraw the boundaries around the subject's space of action and reflection, dismantling the effective limits on which depends the very possibility of a self that can trust itself and others. When we strip down autonomy to this minimal space whose integrity is necessary for the self to be a self at all, we touch on the roots of the many and varied forms that privacy takes across the world and that human beings have defended throughout history.[50] This is the philosophical and practical core of contemporary debates about privacy. Privacy, according to surveillance expert David Lyon, is "a pivotal concept that helps to throw light on what is wrong with mass surveillance."[51] Privacy is a matter of the self's minimal integrity whose necessity persists beneath all cultural constructions. But before we can return to the question of data and privacy, we must make one more point about the philosophical roots of the approach to autonomy we are taking.

Defending the Space of the Self

"Freedom is this," Hegel wrote: "To be *with oneself* in the other."[52] Probably no phrase of Hegel's captures what is ethically troubling about data colonialism better than this statement. It is the possibility of being "with oneself" and with no other thing or self that underlies all specific forms of freedom. And it is just this that capitalism is bent on dispossessing under data colonialism. Hegel could never have imagined that this minimal integrity would be routinely threatened, least of all by the wider system of property relations on which capitalism is based. But today that is the contradiction between values and power that we are living.

Hegel's position was that for any person to be "free," he must have access to an "external sphere of freedom" that defines him.[53] The term *external* is curious, since it includes anything "external to my freedom," that is, external to my free will, including even the "goods" of "my body and my life," the substance of my self.[54] Two points are crucial: first, that these goods are and must be "exclusive"; and second, that this right to exclusivity is "inalienable": it *cannot* be given up without giving up on the self as such.[55] It is this space that continuous surveillance over time damages by entering it persistently and insistently, often if not always with a view to modulating its behavior.

Working under the influence of the European ideology of possessive individualism,[56] Hegel calls this space of freedom a "property," a property that is inalienable and nontradable. But we can challenge data colonialism in a way that does not depend on possessive individualism by reformulating Hegel and defending the minimal *space* without whose boundedness the self would not be a distinct self at all. This is the space from which the self listens out and experiences the world. We fear the moment when that space is ruptured; George Orwell's novel *1984* provides the most famous example of this in literature.[57] Hegel himself discusses slavery as an external capture of this space and insists on "the slave's absolute right to free himself."[58] Continuous surveillance of the self from the outside is not as absolute and violent as slavery—it does not amount to the direct transfer of all control of the self's space of freedom—but it unquestionably violates that space.

The Illusion of Autonomy through Self-Measurement

Why is data colonialism's threat to this most basic component of autonomy not the subject of daily angry protest? The most fundamental reason is not ideology, or even the fetishism of data discussed in earlier chapters. The reason is that, as part of the reshaping of social knowledge described in chapter 4, *autonomy itself is being reconfigured* by capitalist data practices. Data relations are becoming the means to a supposed new autonomy, bringing into conflict two aspects of the self, as subject and as object, while co-opting precisely the socially grounded notion of freedom (autonomy) that Hegel defended.

Evangelists of technological connection such as Kevin Kelly see things differently. In his recent book *The Inevitable,* he names tracking as one of the twelve dimensions of technology's transformation of society. By attributing this transformation to "what technology wants" (the name of his previous book), Kelly seeks to quarantine today's profound transformations from ethical critique. His goal is to help us "work *with* [technologies'] nature, rather than struggle against it."[59] The entire edifice of data colonialism and capitalist data relations is obscured by this rhetorical move. For Kelly, datafication on capitalism's terms provides a new form *of* autonomy, because all human costs have been shifted off-balance-sheet. Or rather, the balance sheet that might have tallied the costs to individual human beings has been replaced by a collective settlement in which the whole species supposedly wins. Extreme though positions such as Kelly's are, they have considerable influence at the level of daily practice.

"Know Thyself" through This Device
Consider the plethora of data-based devices for "self-tracking" championed by the Quantified Self movement.[60] These devices encourage three of the levels of data relations outlined in chapter 1: capture, continuous connection, and data release. Since it is the abstracted, commodified form of data relations that binds us into capitalism, it hardly matters that self-tracking relations are often voluntary.[61]

What are the larger transformations at work here? Consumer activity has rarely been exempt from some form of observation, even in the traditional open-air market. But the decisive shift came in the 2010s with the convergent growth of social media platforms, connected mobile devices, and ever more sophisticated "smart environments" that made possible something close to "autonomous" surveillance.[62]

We are increasingly told that human beings *need* to track themselves—for example, to maintain their health. Self-surveillance mirrors the retail and work landscapes of continuous tracking described in the last chapter. You may buy an Apple Watch or iPhone for all sorts of reasons, many unrelated to health, but if you do, you will have easy access to a health app that integrates data about your activity, sleep, mindfulness, and nutrition.[63] Continuous automated data collection can be justified for the social benefits that data relations supposedly involve. When self-trackers celebrate their "community," they do not mean the community of corporate managers who profit from the data stream they generate but the unseen constellation of users encouraged by those corporations to openly share their experiences of self-tracking. Self-tracking *is* often a social process,[64] and that social aspect may, of course, be meaningful, just as our uses of social media are. There is a link here to the wider value of "sharing" in contemporary culture. As Nicholas John points out, what is most striking about sharing as a metaphor is the extendibility of what is to be shared: from thoughts and pictures to information sources and life histories to everything and anything. Sharing our *lives* has come to imply a broader value of "openness and mutuality" but at the risk of mystifying the communities we supposedly form online.[65] In a world in which we are constantly induced to share personal information, data collection becomes part of a social life within which, somewhere, we assume that autonomous subjects still exist.

Can we rely on ourselves to judge whether sharing key portions of our personal data proves, on balance, to be "productive" for us and not just for the platforms? There is evidence that we are often unable to make this judgment,[66] but our confusion is certainly beneficial for the corporations that depend on our sharing. As John puts it, "Sharing produces the data that constitutes the hard currency of Web 2.0 business."[67]

"Know thyself" is one of the oldest ethical maxims, but it has been used to market self-tracking devices ever since the days of the humble bathroom scale.[68] As life becomes capitalized, "know thyself" morphs from philosophical principle to profit center. No doubt specific knowledge can be gained from some forms of self-tracking, and there is much to be gained sociologically in better understanding how individuals use such technologies.[69] But what in the long run constitutes *valuable* self-knowledge here— valuable for whom? The goods generated by capitalist data relations are profoundly ambiguous. They offer us, apparently, the chance to be more autonomous—in the sense of regulating ourselves more intensely—but at the cost of submitting to an external data system whose functioning requires the integration of *its* devices permanently into the space where, until now, we imagined we were truly, and only, ourselves.[70] There is no limit to the freedom that the social quantification sector seeks for its delegated agents, as Microsoft CEO Satya Nadella comments on the digital personal assistant, Cortana: "It will know your context, your family, your work. It will also know your world. It will be unbounded."[71] The resulting forms of self-reflection and community exchange are, as Taina Bucher puts it, "force-relations,"[72] relations with external entities and processes that intimately expose us to the economic forces of capitalism.

Even when we choose to install apps such as Foursquare and thus share data about where we are, the background data aggregation that goes on through Foursquare's API is largely outside end-user control. Foursquare, at least until the introduction of the European Union's General Data Protection Regulation, had tended to treat information, for example, about the web pages accessed through the app and users' locations "as non-personal information" except when required otherwise by law; Google's location API operates, however, without any need for user participation or knowledge.[73] Yet such data acquisition is offered as an enhancement of "experience," echoing the personalization doublespeak that retail marketers use to justify their intrusion into consumers' lives.[74]

Philosophical Challenges to Self-Quantification

Let's imagine, however, that self-quantification's proponents call Hegel's notion of freedom to their aid. Couldn't Hegel's social reading of freedom (autonomy) allow us to argue that the self's development today *requires* tracking devices as a way to enable selves to "determine the aims of their own actions"?[75] We might counter by asking defenders of datafication to deny that some measure of control over data relations is important for autonomy,[76] and indeed the Quantified Self movement has been ready to cede individual property rights in data.[77]

The real problem with the Quantified Self and similar visions, however, goes deeper. For Hegel, it is the reflective relation to oneself that is essential to the development of a free will. Therefore, a free life needs to be a self-sufficient life in which "nothing from outside, nothing not-me, determines my actions."[78] Hegel does not deny—indeed, he emphasizes—that the individual lives a life that is *not* free from external constraints; it is a life lived *through* mediations (lived "in the other," as Hegel puts it). But at the core of freedom for Hegel (the core of autonomy, in our terms) is the notion of an inner life that remains under one's own reflexive control. This inner life is what enjoying one's "right of subjectivity" means.[79] The very thing Quantified Selfers and the social quantification sector see as a benefit (that our moment-to-moment existence is understood better by external data processing systems than by us) collapses the space of subjectivity in which the self enjoys its freedom.

The problem is not that we have relations with external systems or that we delegate certain actions to those systems. We have done both throughout modernity and with increasing regularity and intensity; such processes are rightly the object of the self's reflection.[80] But contemporary data relations involve more than just relations; they involve systems that insinuate themselves within "the self's needs, desires and other choices."[81] This is what Hegel in his discussion of free will called the problem of arbitrariness. The data infrastructure on which the self-tracker relies to augment herself contains elements and dynamics that are troubling because they are arbitrary, driven by goals that are not hers, and operate in ways that remain largely opaque and so can never be reflexively integrated into her goals.[82]

There was something deeply paradoxical in the proposal of a marketer of body sensors at the Digital Health Summit in January 2014: "Our cars have dashboards, our homes have thermostats—why don't we have that for our own bodies?" Natasha Dow Schüll's comment is acerbic: "Instead of aspiring to autonomy, they wish to outsource the labor of self-regulation to personal sensor technology."[83] The attempt at self-regulation (or self-legislation, as Kant and Hegel called it) is basic to what a self is[84] and so cannot be delegated to algorithms without giving up on the basic fabric of the self.

An unease with such an unacceptable deal may explain why many self-trackers give up after a while. Some ex-self-trackers report losing their "ability to self-regulate." Other testimony suggests unease that "getting good data" had become the overriding driver of submission: "From a mental health point of view, one of the things I realized about myself was that I was only really happy when numbers were trending in the right direction." In Hegel's term, this person felt he was not really "with himself" in the data, only emotionally tied to the stimuli that the system generated. A self-tracker can find herself genuinely puzzled about whether, as one put it, self-tracking got her "closer in contact or further away from [herself] and the world."[85] Here, the externality introduced by data relations into the space of the subject emerges in the self's sense of feeling "further away" from what, until then, had seemed closest: the space of the self.

Parallel doubts are emerging in people's sense of dislocation when they find platforms' algorithmic processes reflecting back to them an image that jars with their own sense of self.[86] One response to Facebook's "algorithmic errors" is to start acting differently for Facebook's algorithmic gaze—to "obfuscate" its view,[87] perhaps by sending signals that confuse the system. But this only risks entering the loop of self-counting more deeply, evading the question of whether the relentless conversion of human action into data is itself desirable.

Capitalism knows no limits to the expansion of its datafying logic. Apps are a key means whereby capital extends that logic even further. So too is the fashion among some so-called biohackers to embed microchips under their skin, whether to replace ID cards or for other purposes.[88] Can philosophy help us imagine limits here? Would we be relaxed, for example, about an app that compared our personal processes of creativity against established measures of creative inspiration? Can we imagine installing an app or a chip that measured whether one was really in love with someone? Or an app that compared the depth of one's grief for a loved one against the grief of others for the same, or for a different, person? When exactly does our expanding submission to the self's datafication come up against something that we feel we must be protected from at all costs? As yet, we do not know. The risk is clear, however: that since we have no choice but to go on acting in a world that undermines the self's autonomy, one consequence is that we may progressively *unlearn* the norms associated with it. As the second quotation at the beginning of the chapter head suggests, data colonialism's subjects may come to unlearn freedom in time.

The Personal Data Appropriation Spectrum

We are not denying that some measurement practices might fulfill a greater good and thus be something individuals and groups could choose *for themselves*. The health and education domains provide useful, if contrasting, examples.

Medicine—that is, preventative health care—offers a complex case in which we can certainly imagine making collective decisions to have our personal medical data gathered, provided it was in anonymized form. The UK Labour Party's Digital Democracy Manifesto from 2016 imagines something like this, and why not applaud Harvard's Laboratory System Initiative, which uses Machine Learning to identify patterns in observational data systematically missed by even the best doctors?[89] When the cure for a major disease is the issue, who would deny that science needs more data in order to avoid the "consent bias" whereby those who agree to release their data are untypical of the general population?[90] The historical medical data of the whole population of Iceland was pooled in this way under an arrangement with the US's Department of Health and Human Services.[91]

There are issues here for sure. What does it mean to obtain the consent of a whole population (in Iceland, the data deal was done in secret, without consulting Iceland's citizens explicitly, which proved highly controversial)? Barbara Evans, a leading scholar of health and data law, argues that we need elaborate processes for collective management of data gathered in this way.[92] The risks increase when we realize that frequent claims that medical data is securely anonymized may be unreliable.[93] Under any political system, the security of health data must depend on how far its collection can be insulated from market dynamics (since values such as patient confidentiality are not, after all, market values).[94] Health data is, in any case, quite specific and highly contextual. A proposal for everyone to submit to *continuous* collection of *all* their health data would be very different in its implications for the self's minimal integrity than would be specific individuals sharing specific health data for a specific beneficial purpose. Legal scholars fear that it is exactly such large-scale aggregations of health data that risk escaping the legal protections that have long been integral to medical ethics and law.[95]

The collection of genetic information (the complete data set of an individual's genome) raises even more disturbing questions. Philosopher and physician Daniel Sulmasy argues that a person's genome is not just any personal information but information that is "partly constitutive of who and what [a person is]."[96] To lose control of such data would already be to lose something of oneself. As Gina Neff and Dawn Nafus put it, "There is only so much of oneself that a person can alienate away"[97]—without, that is, ceasing to be a person.

Even if the immediate problems of health-data sharing could be solved, other issues remain. What is there to prevent data originally collected for the purposes of preventive medicine or science from being reused to meet the commercial interests of the pharmaceutical industries? When we turn to health-related data (fitness monitoring and the like), the problems multiply. Such data is generally exchanged without the intense confidentiality safeguards normal in the institutional-health sector. And what is health-*related* data anyway? A highly rated start-up in the health-app sector, Ginger.io, which markets various forms of automated digital health monitoring, reserved the right back in July 2016 to collect a wide range of "User Interaction Data" including, bizarrely, a comprehensive list of *phone* metadata.[98] The chief technologist of the US Federal Trade Commission Latanya Sweeney discovered in a study of twelve apps and two wearable devices that together their "information was transmitted to no less than 76 different third companies."[99] Indeed, gathering one's own health-related data may not be a leisure option but a requirement of one's employment, so what is there to prevent its non-anonymous use by that same employer, or at least the chilling fear that this *might* happen?

In the education sector, by contrast, the principle of confidentiality is less heavily ingrained, and the logic of automated data collection operates with fewer initial constraints. Few roadblocks exist to stop intensified surveillance of students through datafication, and education has always involved monitoring in some form.[100] So-called adaptive learning is today being offered by commercial providers as a "personalized" advance on the education of the predatafication era. Older, pre–Big Data education is depicted now as a "factory-model" under which all children had to receive the same content in the same manner (IBM Education), impeding "a deliberate and continuous approach to the improvement of learning and teaching" (Pearson).

In a recent report, Pearson Education employs the metaphor of a "digital ocean" to capture this new approach, which can record every "fleeting experience" of individuals for monitoring, processing, and evaluation.[101] The costs of continuous surveillance are not even acknowledged here as a risk. Unlike in the case of health care, personalized surveillance is presented as *inherent to* the educational process, not just necessary (as marketers say) for its further "personalization." It is not that privacy is exactly forgotten; rather, the monitoring needed for personalized data collection and storage is not acknowledged to be surveillance at all but instead offered as the basis of a new "digital citizenship":

> Real-time monitoring is not about policing kids. Rather, it's about providing opportunities for mentorship, teaching and learning. . . . This allows students to be responsible, safe and good digital citizens—both in school and out in the world.[102]

The links between continuous surveillance and the education of children are so deeply naturalized here that the panoptic notion of teachers using continuous real-time monitoring is presented as neither chilling nor threatening. On the contrary, it is a selling point, giving teachers "a full bird's eye view of the entire classroom" (Impero Education), which enables them to "immediately intervene in a highly personalized way" (Blackboard). Data collection is imagined to "create a virtuous circle of real-time data that solves issues relating to student leavers lacking necessary skills."[103]

But again, what if the educational-tracking data on particular children becomes aggregated with other data, or even traded by the system provider *after* the student has left the school or university? What would the implications of this be for education, which is understood as a period of rehearsal for adult life? Even more fundamentally, what is happening here to the space of imaginative freedom that education has long been thought to be?[104] In the brave new world of datafied education, surveillance becomes not the enemy, but paradoxically the guarantor, of educational freedom:

> The idea [of digital monitoring] is to allow students the online freedom they need to grow, learn and survive in a digital world, with the safety net of keyword monitoring to protect against the risks.[105]

Yet this new model of "more personalized education"—the mantra of the leading developers of AI in education, such as Pearson—assumes a pedagogic relation that at no point allows the young subject to go unsurveilled. The new model is praised in hyperbolic terms: "One to one human tutoring has long been thought to be the most effective approach to teaching and learning (since at least Aristotle's tutoring of Alexander the Great)."[106] But it is being developed with absolutely no attention to the power issues it raises or to its consequences for young human subjects and their basic autonomy.

Across the health and education sectors runs a common danger, that of the uncontrolled reuse and aggregation of data sets that, even if still anonymized, risk dismantling the functional boundaries within which these institutions were until recently organized. This new "ecology" of data collection and processing, far from enhancing individual freedom, risks offering ever more personally targeted forms of control and management, driven by system imperatives that human subjects cannot fully know or control.

Legal Battles for the Self's Minimal Integrity

Can anything be done to challenge any of this? One place to look for help might be the law. What is law's perspective on data colonialism's threat to the integrity of the self?

Privacy is a protected term in most legal jurisdictions. For that reason, privacy seems the most practical route for defending the self against the incursions of data colonialism. But the growth of data relations, the insertion of surveillance into every conceivable moment of life, and the huge growth in the privatized capacity to aggregate, process, and rework personal and other data pose huge challenges, especially if privacy is confined to the negative understanding of the term (mere freedom from interference) on which liberalism and capitalism have often relied.

Some business figures celebrate this, arguing that publicity, not privacy, is becoming the default setting of our lives online, as though that settled everything; "we," it is implied, have already "moved on" from outdated notions such as privacy.[107] Here, more cautiously, is a White House report from 2014 to which many authoritative experts contributed:

> The physical sanctity of the home's papers and effects is rapidly becoming an empty legal vessel. The home is also the central locus of Brandeis' "right to be left alone." This right is also increasingly fragile . . . [as] people bring sensors into their homes whose immediate purpose is to provide convenience, safety, and security.[108]

If the contexts of data use are becoming irreducibly blurred, then one important early proposal to update privacy for the data age—Helen Nissenbaum's argument that privacy is always based in more specific "informational norms [of] contextual integrity"[109]—is no longer sufficient to stem the tide. Indeed, Nissenbaum herself has recognized that the links between corporate data use and "a subtle erosion of autonomy" go beyond contextual norms.[110] So how can we build a stronger legal framework for challenging data colonialism?

Abandoning the concept of privacy here would be a fundamental mistake, since it still retains some reference to the minimal integrity of the self. Privacy, as leading US privacy campaigner Marc Rotenberg argues, remains "an extraordinarily powerful and comprehensive human-rights claim."[111] But what would effective protection of privacy look like within a broader challenge to data colonialism? The route to legally protecting the self's minimal integrity, as defined in this chapter, is long and complex.

The Historical Legacy of Privacy Protection

There is a growing global debate about whether the existing frameworks for regulating data processes need strengthening and about how this might be done. Some see little hope for any practical intervention that could halt the expansion of market forces, but such pessimism can be understood as the symptom of neoliberal culture's success in enforcing the dominance of market reference points,[112] particularly in the United States and United Kingdom. The increasingly popular business argument that data collection is so pervasive that it should be exempted from legal regulation, and regulation should be focused entirely on use (an argument Helen Nissenbaum calls "Big Data Exceptionalism"), reflects that US market context, though it also echoes much global business rhetoric—for example, from the World Economic Forum.[113] It is possible that the fallout of the Facebook/Cambridge Analytica scandal has fatally undermined this position, but this as yet is unclear.

Here the historical legal context in the United States is interesting. Legal scholarship has for more than a century debated the need to protect the physical, communicative, and virtual space of the self. Samuel Warren and Louis Brandeis in the late nineteenth century proposed a "right to be let alone" in response to the incursions of the yellow press and early paparazzi.[114] This "negative"[115] form of liberty was extended in the twentieth century to connect with "positive" forms of liberty such as informational privacy and decisional privacy—respectively, the right to control over one's personal information and over the process of one's decision-making.[116] Capitalism's broader drive to extract value from personal data is clearly in tension with such inherited notions of privacy and the philosophical values that underpin them. While recent claims in Big Data discourse that individuals do *not* own data about themselves seek to muddy things, they cannot resolve this tension.[117]

The United States lacks a comprehensive legal regime for regulating data ownership or, indeed, privacy more generally,[118] with the US Constitution throwing up conflicting signals. The Fourth Amendment *may* impose limits on the ability of corporations and states to invade the space of the individual, if not on single occasions, then, according to the so-called Mosaic theory, through a cumulative series of actions.[119] According to many commentators, however, its usefulness remains uncertain and highly contingent.[120] Meanwhile, the famous First Amendment, which guarantees freedom of speech (compare article 10 of the European Convention on Human Rights), has recently been interpreted by the US courts to protect data-gathering and data use themselves as forms of *corporate free speech*.[121] It is clear, therefore, that regulatory action is needed to supplement the US Constitution. A major potential advance in privacy protection would have been the FCC's rules extending the protections of the US Communications Act to broadband providers. These rules insisted that customers "must be empowered to decide" how providers may "use and share their data." But they were repealed by Congress in 2017, and the possibility of reviving them is uncertain.[122]

Major legal innovation is needed if we are even to begin to address the consequences of data colonialism, and here the legal traditions of the United States and Europe are differently placed.

Reinventing the Law of Privacy?

US constitutional lawyer Neil Richards offers one route to clarifying the issues, claiming that the First Amendment already provides protection for something like the minimal integrity of the self, even if in little-noticed form. He argues that if the First Amendment protects not just freedom of speech but freedom of thought (for example, freedom of religious belief), then it must also protect the practices from which thinking freely emerges (for example, our rehearsals of ideas, as when reading a book).[123] To be implemented, however, it would require a shift in US legal practice to make corporate actors fully accountable in relation to US constitutional rights.[124] In any case, "intellectual" privacy does not capture data colonialism's challenge to freedom of the intellect and to the self's basic integrity in all its aspects (not just intellectual but also perceptual and affective). Given the current political turmoil in the United States at the federal level, the best hope would seem to be state legislation, such as California's 2018 Consumer Privacy Act, which passed despite opposition from big tech.[125]

The European legal tradition offers a more fundamental challenge to data colonialism. Article 8 of the European Convention on Human Rights already recognizes privacy (including privacy of what it quaintly calls "correspondence"), but the question is how this should be interpreted for an environment in which "correspondence" hardly captures the scale of data-gathering that is built into every transaction and action in connected space.[126] German law provides a basis for going further. Since World War II, German law has recognized the "right to personality," that is, protection for the free development of individuality. This right derives directly from Hegel's and Kant's concept of freedom[127] and is set out in article 2 of the German *Grundgesetz* (Basic Law).[128] Without the security of such a right, German legal thinking argues, the citizen is not able to exercise "unbiased participation in the political processes of the democratic constitutional state."[129] It is no accident that such a principle was established in Germany in the wake of World War II and the collapse of Nazism. What an irony that it is now, in the age of apparent internet freedom, that this anti-chilling principle finds echoes in wider debates about data rights in Europe and beyond![130]

The European Data Protection Legislation (known as the General Data Protection Regulation, or GDPR), which came into force in May 2018,[131] and which the recent California law partly mimics, offers the most significant legal challenge so far to the discourse and practice of data colonialism. The very first sentence of the GDPR challenges the idea that markets and technologies have made privacy irrelevant in the age of Big Data. It states that "the protection of natural persons in relation to the processing of personal data is a fundamental right."[132] The GDPR requires data collectors to give an ordinary-language account to every user of what data they hold and for what purpose. This approach assumes that *lack* of such information damages the underlying right of each person to control her information boundaries, hence the need for an immediate alert when any activity potentially breaches those boundaries. The GDPR's practical requirements interrupt the supposed "naturalness" of data collection from individuals by requiring individuals to be informed of what is going on with their data.

It remains unclear, however, whether this will disrupt data colonialism in practice. The GDPR changes the rules under which data colonialism operates but leaves unchallenged the commercial purposes for which data is

collected. There is also a question about the limits of the "informed consent" principle on which the GDPR relies; this principle is dependent on
how situations of consent are configured in everyday life.[133] It is hard to
see how this, or any similar general framework that we might imagine,[134]
would challenge an environment in which consent to data collection and
processing is overridden by the bargaining power of employers or insurers. Meanwhile, it is super-powerful incumbents such as Google that are
arguably best placed to bear the costs of adjusting their business to GDPR
rules.[135]

Caveats also apply to the legal framework for internet regulation known
as the *Marco Civil*, which was developed by Brazilian civil society and government in the year following the Snowden revelations. The *Marco Civil*
challenged US hegemony over the internet's regulatory structure and incorporated the right to personality as a fundamental principle, but it remains at the level of principles, not detailed regulation.[136]

Perhaps it was naive to expect the legal institutions of market societies
to be the site at which general resistance to capitalism's expansion could
take practical form. In China, where data platforms have emerged in close
alliance with the state, there are signs of the state intervening to insist on
some privacy standards,[137] but at the same time, it is well-known that platforms consistently give the Chinese state access to their data. We should
not forget, however, that the law was a site of extensive conflict over how
industrial capitalism's early excesses could be corrected (this conflict oc-
curred as part of the double movement that Polanyi analyzed, discussed
in chapter 4).[138] And there is no doubt that geopolitical battles over competing regimes of privacy and regulation of data flow—for example, between the European Union, the United States, and China—could be a major factor in how data colonialism *develops* on a global scale over the next
decade.[139] Therefore, it is worth digging a little deeper into contemporary
debates in legal theory to see whether they help us expose the normative
contradictions within capitalism that data colonialism generates.

Privacy and the New Contradictions of Capitalism

Two complex problems overlap here. The first is the radical reconfigura-
tion of how personal data collection works practically under data colonial-

ism in a way that far outstrips how the legal concept of privacy has traditionally been configured. The second problem concerns the philosophical depth at which privacy needs to be rethought in response to these new practical challenges. The later philosophical issue will take us back to the chapter's philosophical starting points.

Today's environment of data collection and processing far exceeds in complexity, continuity, and depth the single violations that were once understood to threaten a subject's privacy. If data colonialism works through an "ecology" of data collection, as the social quantification sector consistently tells us it does, then any response must be environmental too.[140] Driven by private corporations much more than by states, today's "autonomic smart environments,"[141] as Dutch legal theorist Mireille Hildebrandt calls them, are saturated with automated agents that have the power to shape the contexts in which human agents can make choices. So pervasive is this shaping and so unpredictable to human beings are its outcomes that the social environment stops being formed through mutual expectations between people and becomes driven exclusively by the goals of data-driven manipulation.[142] This unsettles the individual freedom of choice that is core to all liberal notions of privacy. How then can *privacy* be rethought to answer this deep challenge that the long-term capitalization of life throws up?

One route passes through the language of human rights. We might look for individual rights deeper than the right to privacy, such as the right not to be deceived.[143] But it is unclear how this would work in an environment that is continuously deceptive, in the sense of not fully disclosing its processes and goals. A better alternative, proposed by various legal scholars, is to move beyond traditional liberal framing of privacy toward a relational understanding of privacy.[144] This relational approach sees privacy as a feature of the mutuality of social relations, a condition that must be collectively sustained if selves and others are to flourish at all. This approach flows directly from the socially grounded approach to the minimal integrity of the self that we found in Hegel and Dussel. This approach also emphasizes not just control over one's process of making choices but also *second-order control*: the ability to manage to some degree one's choices about choices, that is, one's values.[145] This is precisely the level of freedom that is damaged, as Hegel predicted, when a social order starts to be organized around practical principles that no longer fit with the values its members thought were theirs.

Even within this relational (and profoundly social) interpretation of privacy, however, there are complexities. All values, such as privacy, are socially negotiated.[146] But there is something distinctively complex about privacy and, specifically, the importance of privacy to autonomy (understood as the capacity to "find one's own good in one's own way").[147] We cannot find that path if we lose the "breathing-room" in which to develop *as* our selves.[148] In what entity or process exactly are these new, more social notions of privacy or autonomy *themselves* grounded? Some suggest that "the self has no autonomous, precultural core" to be defended,[149] but if values such as privacy and autonomy are *entirely* relational, containing in themselves nothing essential, then what entity exactly is it "whose" autonomy is to be protected? Today's new practices and norms of data collection and processing are themselves surely social and cultural contexts too, but that does not mean that something fundamental for human beings is not at stake in the damage data relations do to privacy.

Although there is no essential form that privacy or autonomy takes across all cultures,[150] each form must always, as we have emphasized throughout this chapter, involve a *minimal* notion of the self's integrity. To be "with oneself" means to be reflexively engaged in one's process of development without—and this is Hegel's crucial emphasis—the direct interference in that reflection of any other entity and its goals. This notion of autonomy is too deep to be traded away for local gain or temporary convenience, perhaps too deep even to be formulated as a right. The underlying core of autonomy is what grounds the possibility of selves having *anything like* rights that protect their integrity in practice.[151]

There remains, however, a deep paradox that both Julie Cohen and Mireille Hildebrandt note: that practices of data colonialism are potentially eroding the very notion of the rational, reflexive, law-respecting human subject on which the legitimacy of law itself depends. Meanwhile, courts in various countries have become early adopters of algorithmic processing, and much of the power to regulate infringements of autonomy is now delegated to commercial platforms,[152] with dangerous practical and normative implications. In the age of datafication, legal institutions need to defend some version of the principle of autonomy for their own survival.

Toward a Larger Vision

Data colonialism works to dismantle the basic integrity of the self, dissolving the boundaries that enable the self to be a self. It is the self in this bare sense that must be salvaged from data colonialism, using all available legal, political, and philosophical means.

This makes the stakes of our argument very clear. None of the ideals desired in today's societies—their democratic status, their freedom, their health, or otherwise—make any sense without reference to an autonomous self in the minimal sense defended in this chapter. Autonomy in this basic sense is the core value underlying any human social order that has the potential to be good. Yet, when all the complex detail of data practices has settled, it is this value that is being threatened today, not by technology itself but by the mutual implication of life and technology *for* capitalism that we call data colonialism.

We can go further. Moving decisively away from individualistic notions of autonomy, freedom, and privacy, we can argue that the datafied social governance and incursions into the self's minimal integrity discussed in part II of the book *together* constitute an environment that is toxic for human life. The way forward lies less in the detail of legal regulation and more in defending an ecology of human life that connects with the visions of those who have resisted colonialism and capitalism for centuries. Exploring this is the task of the next and final part of the book.

Part III

Reconnecting

Decolonizing Data ⬡ 6

Anti-colonialism has been economically catastrophic for the Indian people for decades. Why stop now?
—Mark Andreessen, Facebook board member[1]

THE BIG TECH BACKLASH, we are told, has already begun.[2] Even before the eruption of the Facebook/Cambridge Analytica scandal, there were signals of a growing willingness of regulatory bodies, especially in Europe, to challenge the great powers of data colonialism (for example, Google and Facebook). But the Cambridge Analytica scandal provoked a crisis of higher intensity: instability in tech-sector share prices, a popular movement (on social media, of course) to #leavefacebook, calls in the mainstream press to learn again the lesson of how the nineteenth century restrained the raw injustices of early capitalism (shades of Polanyi), and even an editorial in the *Financial Times* that entertained the case for "everyone . . . to leave Facebook."[3]

Time, you might say, to step aside and let the more enlightened forces of capitalism fix the problem, with the help of robust regulation. That approach would certainly chime with the long-accepted myth that historical capitalism solved the problems of historical colonialism. Data extraction would in this view be at worst a "cryptocolonialist system"[4] whose dispossessive violence is manageable and can be kept hidden from view.

But this response risks missing the bigger picture entirely. Suppose regulators *did* tame the raw force of data colonialism into a more measured pattern of data extraction. Suppose that users generally *did* become less trusting of data corporations' motives, puncturing the more obviously self-

187

serving ideologies of the social quantification sector (for example, the notion of Facebook's "global community"). Suppose that Facebook or even Google's data harvesting power *was* opened up to various forms of public use and benefit.

What these changes still would not touch would be the strategy of data colonialism as a whole to build a new social and economic order based on data appropriation. Untouched also would be the basic fact stressed throughout this book that capitalism's data-driven order is being built globally, not just in the West. It is an order that has behind it the full force of the world's two most powerful states (the United States and China), who are competing for leadership of the social quantification sector and its AI hinterland.[5]

It is this larger narrative of transforming life through data that we are told is impossible to halt, because it is driven by a "technological momentum" that is "inevitable."[6] The notion that datafication is inevitable is, as we noted in chapter 1, a myth of data colonialism. But how to resist it? In this final part of the book, we try to wrest the narrative back from those who celebrate this transformation, and we question whether data colonialism's emerging social and economic order is what human beings actually want.

Our Argument So Far

Before we think more concretely about what is at stake here, we need to review all the strands of our argument.

In part I of the book (chapters 1 through 3) we laid out the building blocks of our argument. After we introduced in the preface the basic idea of data colonialism and the social quantification sector that drives it, we argued in chapter 1 that what is going on with data is best understood through a double process of renewing colonialism and expanding capitalism.

Colonialism is about appropriation; whereas historical colonialism appropriated land, resources, and bodies, today's new colonialism appropriates human life through extracting value from data. We uncovered the basic features of data colonialism: the processing of ever more personal data, the universalization of logistics as a mode of management, the datafication of most aspects of labor, and the creation of data relations that draw us into arrangements whereby data is gathered and value extracted from it, regardless of whether we are at work or somewhere else. Platforms play a key role in making our participation in data relations seem natural, but pressures at work and elsewhere also play a part. We argued that underlying these was something even more fundamental: the drive to capitalize human life itself in all its aspects and build through this a new social and economic order that installs capitalist management as the privileged mode for governing every aspect of life. Put another way, and updating Marx for the Big Data age, human life becomes a direct factor in capitalist production. This annexation of human capital is what links data colonialism to the further expansion of capitalism. This is the fundamental cost of connection, and it is a cost being paid all over the world, in societies in which connection is increasingly imposed as the basis for participating in everyday life. The resulting order has important similarities whether we are discussing the United States, China, Europe, or Latin America. The drive toward this order is sustained by key ideologies, including the ideologies of connection, datafication, personalization, and dataism. The result is not a new type of capitalism but certainly a new means by which and a new scale on which capitalism is operating; this result transcends earlier diagnoses of neoliberalism or the social factory and may, in the long run, provide the basis for an entirely new mode of production.

Chapter 2 outlined how, from the workings of the social quantification sector and the adoption of its products, the Cloud Empire came to be, how it works, and what its emergence might mean for citizens, workers, and individuals. The monopsony/monopoly power of giant digital platforms and the huge growth of the social quantification sector in its many forms were discussed in their global dimensions. This growth is aided by various extractive "rationalities" that together make the capitalization of human life feasible. The result is a rearrangement of life so that it is configured directly under the "hand" of capitalist management and its infrastructures of connection; the goal is, literally, to annex life to capitalism. It is the absoluteness of this ambition to order a world made tractable to capitalism's operations that gives data colonialism its simplicity: the mutual implication of human life and digital technology *for* capitalism. A capitalism without limitation, obstruction, or remainder. A capitalism that encompasses every scale of human life (across space) at every layer (in depth) of individual and collective experience, all unfolding without limitation or interruption (in time).

Chapter 3 looked back at all these changes through the reverse mirror of historical colonialism's long trajectory of oppression. Datafication today represents a new phase of colonialism, as the concept is normally understood. But this new phase also represents continuities in terms of the strategies for extraction that colonial powers employed in the past. Instead of the appropriation of cheap natural resources and cheap labor, the new colonialism is premised on the "natural" availability of "cheap" social data. As corporations engage in new forms of exploration, expansion, exploitation, and extermination, a new capitalist mode of production emerges (just as industrial capitalism emerged during the colonial era to replace earlier tributary modes of production). Because we are only at the start of this new colonialism, we cannot be sure what this mode of production will eventually look like. We can, however, borrow from postcolonial and decolonial thinking tools to articulate not just counterhistories but counterpresents, or alternative understandings of contemporary social orders. These counterpresents will allow us to challenge, within a radically new global distribution of colonial power, the version of modernity and the model of human knowledge that dataism has inherited unproblematically.

In part II of the book (chapters 4 and 5) we looked at the consequences for social and individual life that flow from data colonialism and the new capitalist order it is unfolding. The result, we argued in chapter 4, is a new, datafied social world, in which earlier forms of social knowledge that had in various ways been under public production and control become devalued. A new "social knowledge" emerges that lies entirely under corporate control. We call this "social caching." This "God view" of the social world, though parceled out among many corporations, coalesces in a corporate social imaginary that justifies new ways of governing everyday life for the benefit and convenience of corporate power (think of insurers' expanded power to demand self-tracking as a condition of service). In state-led market societies (for example, the People's Republic of China), a similar process is dubbed the "modernization of social governance." However framed, the transformation of publicly oriented government into "governance by proxy" has profound implications for societies' power relations. This new social order relies increasingly on hidden forms of categorization and discrimination, implemented at many layers of an automated process. New forms of injustice inevitably result: even accidental discriminations remain opaque to subjects and system operators alike and so are likely to go uncorrected. But datafication also provides the perfect cover for older forms of inequality and discrimination to be reproduced and amplified. The voice of individual citizens becomes hard to hear in the relentless drone of data-fueled power, as an older public knowledge gets outsourced to corporate processes.[7] Meanwhile, much of the social sciences has aligned itself with this devaluation of social knowledge and so provides a poor site from which to resist data colonialism.

The consequences of data colonialism for individual freedom and autonomy are just as serious, as chapter 5 showed. Whereas *specific* human subjects face danger from the new social hierarchies that are being built through managing extracted data, *all* human subjects face a threat to the minimal integrity of the self from data colonialism's reliance on everexpanding mechanisms of surveillance and tracking. Lower-status work brings higher exposure to surveillance, with zero discretion, while higherstatus work enjoys more protection from surveillance and greater discretion. The general social exploitation to which data colonialism gives rise is inseparable from particular battles against data-driven injustice. At the heart of both general and specific battles is the need to salvage the self's autonomy in some form—what we called the "minimal integrity of the self"—not as a luxury for the few but as the key term around which resistance to data colonialism's social order can start for everyone. It is exactly this minimal integrity on which continuous exposure to corporate monitoring and data collection intrudes, thus harming it irreparably. Although legal frameworks have in some cases made important challenges to the norms of data colonialism, they are insufficient to eradicate the damage that data colonialism does to human autonomy.

To sum up, the problem and challenge of contemporary data practices is neither data nor simply the particular platforms that have emerged to exploit data. The problem is the interlocking combination of six forces, unpacked in the previous chapters: an *infrastructure* for data extraction (technological, still expanding); an *order* (social, still emerging) that binds humans into that infrastructure; a *system* (economic) built on that infrastructure and order; a model of *governance* (social) that benefits from that infrastructure, order, and system and works to bind humans ever further into them; a *rationality* (practical) that makes sense of each of the other levels; and finally, a new *model of knowledge* that redefines the world as one in which these forces together encompass all there is to be known of human life. Data, in short, is the new means to remake the world in capital's image.

Tactics Are Not Enough

So what next? Many have been tempted to say that the way forward is more of us ditching our social media accounts.[8] But in the face of a new capitalist order, "boutique" forms of individual resistance must be inadequate. Data colonialism is a *collective* problem.

Inadequate too are collective versions of those individual responses that select only part of the problem to reform. For a new order is just that: a comprehensive and effective way of organizing *everything* that cannot be opposed by people thinking or acting "otherwise" in this or that context. It is not enough to opt out of the bits of data colonialism we don't particularly like.

But confronting data colonialism as a whole is seriously inconvenient. That is because data colonialism's model for organizing things underlies countless business models and everyday resources. That is why, as Mark Andreessen inadvertently implied (in the chapter's opening quote), the point of opposing colonialism was never immediate economic success. Worse, over the past two decades, billions of people have started to organize much of their personal lives around the infrastructures of digital platforms and other services that depend, or seem to depend, on seamless flows of data.

The problem of inconvenience drives the temptation toward partial solutions—for example, the idea that we just need better networks, perhaps networks with an element of public purpose or, indeed, that we should follow big tech's own proposals for how to use their products in ways that enhance "digital wellness."[9] "Better" data-driven networks will not save us, however. For by attempting to reform a particular network within a wider system of platforms, we are not challenging the foundations of the system but merely finding alternative ways to replicate it. There is a danger here of repeating the error of those early nineteenth-century political economists, mocked by Polanyi for their "mystical readiness to accept the social consequences of economic improvement, whatever they might be."[10]

Resisting an emerging social order must mean being realistic about the necessity of sometimes using, hopefully to our own ends, the means that that order provides to us. Nineteenth-century workers used markets to purchase books, take trains and carriages, and hire meeting halls while forming new types of associations that seriously challenged the power of markets. We need to think carefully about what in the twenty-first century might be equivalent uses of today's infrastructures of connection that, on balance, take more from those infrastructures than they give up to them. But this is where things get difficult. Smart analysts of political movements for major economic and social change have realized for some time that the benefits (of scale and speed of mobilization, for example) that come from commercial infrastructures of connection such as Facebook or Twitter exert a heavy price. The fact that communication systems of established power extract something from those who want their campaigns to be heard via those same systems is no surprise. But how do we make any progress when our target is precisely the wider economic, social, and political order *built through* our use of those same systems?

It is no part of our argument to suggest that people should instantly and completely disconnect from the infrastructures of connection that have been built over the past two decades: we could not have written this book across two continents without using email and the internet! Hundreds of millions of people have adapted their lives in response to the existence of platforms, and much use of social media and data processing is productive and well-meaning. But if the larger outcome of data infrastructures' use *of us* is a wider order that over time dismantles human autonomy, there can be no neutral use of those tools; there can be no benefits from the use of platforms that don't at the same time reproduce, at root, the very power we want and need to oppose. We certainly respect the valiant attempts of developers to create platforms and search engines that do not rely on the centralized collection of data,[11] but they cannot by themselves amount to a rival ecology of social networking and information tools. Here the depth at which data colonialism's social order operates hits home. Data relations do not offer a space of freedom separate from capitalism but are rather the means whereby capitalist relations are formed and extended—literally, as we connect.

We must acknowledge that we are, most of us, deeply complicit in the order of data colonialism, whether we like it or not. Remember that it was only in the present era—and based on today's emerging grid of surveillance and data extraction—that a social and political order on this truly global scale began to be imagined *at all*. It is therefore the very idea of a comprehensive and integrated life order achieved through the processing of data that must be abandoned, on the grounds that its rationality is corrosive of human life itself. As that new order builds a differently configured life around it, the goal is to imagine the most radical opposition to its order while inevitably continuing to live in and with it. That said, there are many specific proposals that may be of use, even if they can never be sufficient.[12]

Take, for example, proposals for media literacy. There is an emerging industry dedicated to advising us how to better deal with social quantification technologies: Take breaks (unplug)! Talk to your kids about it! Change your privacy settings! We do not deny that media literacy may have some benefits in the immediate term, but we should not pretend that media literacy is a means to resist data colonialism; at most, it enables us to live more at ease with it, thus normalizing it for the longer term.[13] Worse, like all notions of literacy, media literacy relies on the virtuous "disposition" of the subject, which misses how the new order works to dismantle the autonomy of the subject. In any case, media literacy soon comes up against some practical limits. When US sociologist Janet Vertesi applied her media literacy by leaving no data traces during her pregnancy, she found basic economic activity increasingly difficult, until, finally, her husband's attempt to buy cash vouchers to pay for a baby stroller on Amazon was arbitrarily blocked by a store algorithm.[14]

Another important area of agency is regulation and legislation. The European legislation on privacy (the GDPR) represents a serious practical challenge to the details of data colonialism's existing business models. As a result, parts of those models may get reconfigured and rerouted, and the principle of obtaining consent for personal data use is at least now being embedded as a norm of daily practice, even if opportunities to refuse consent to powerful platforms of convenience often remain highly constrained. But even a broken-up and redistributed order of data power is still an order. The problem, as always, is bigger: how to live differently, knowing what we know and having seen the offer of a datafied order, with its benefits and costs.

Still another area of intervention is civic activism. Without a doubt, some types of protest (the provocative hacktivism of Anonymous, for example)[15] are radical enough to challenge, at least temporarily, the legitimacy of large-scale power built through data. But the disruption that hacktivism brings to its targets always risks spilling over into a general disorder that damages those who would otherwise support it. Hacktivism cannot be a generalizable model for living with data power; if generalized, the result would be a data war whose consequences are incalculable. Other forms of activism, though avowedly local, may yet be important exemplars of change. Inspiring examples of resistance will come from places some of us don't like or in forms we find inconvenient, and that's probably a good thing. Some neighborhoods are banning Airbnb (in Detroit, for instance), putting other public values above platform profit and short-term consumer convenience. A Muslim cleric in Indonesia declared selfies *haram*, saying, "If we take a selfie and upload it on social media, desperately hoping for views, likes, comments or whatever—we've fallen into the OSTENTATIOUS trap."[16] But the fatwa backfired: thousands of reaction selfies promptly posted under the hashtag #selfie4siauw (the name of the cleric). One day, however, another fatwa against a social media company may come along, and people will take it as a battle cry; maybe whole communities will start to feel that particular platforms are no longer for them.

This and similar endeavors are being explored by artists, scholars, and activists from within emerging fields such as postcolonial digital humanities and indigenous digital studies.[17] Such work can provide a window onto a different space, what First Nations writer and academic Leanne Betasamosake Simpson calls a "productive place of refusal."[18] For Simpson, a place of refusal is productive if it generates a "grounded normativity," a place from where we feel entitled and empowered in a sustainable way to say no to what we are told is "necessary" and yes to what for now seems impossible. But the danger is that such solutions are accessible only to certain groups, not to everybody. After all, vulnerable populations may lack the choice to refuse the networked systems of surveillance through which come their opportunities for work and financial support.[19]

Our point is certainly not to negate the value of such experiments in resistance to data colonialism. But if we already know that as partial actions they cannot be sufficient, we must set our sights higher; we must develop a wider vision of resistance, a vision for connecting with one another *on different terms* that might provide possibilities for solidarity with resistant data subjects, wherever they are. Who knows, after all, where data colonialism's great wall will break in the end?

A Decolonial Vision for Data

What is at stake when any of us try to refuse data colonialism? What would it mean to articulate a vision of how individuals, communities, and nations can know themselves other than through the tools of data colonialism? A vision that rejects a rationality that claims to bind all subjects into a universal grid of monitoring and categorization and instead views information and data as a resource whose value can be sustained only if *locally* negotiated, managed, and controlled. We might call this a socialism of data because of the primacy it gives to social choices over data, but this is not a vision for a global socialist data-state; we must certainly reject the vision of an integrative social order exemplified by the data-driven market socialism of China today.

Defending the Ecology of Human Life

Capitalism has always sought to reject limits to its expansion, such as national boundaries. But now, as not only human geography and physical nature but also human experience are being annexed to capital, we reach the first period in history when soon there will be no domains of life left that remain unannexed by capital.

And yet this seemingly inevitable order has a fundamental flaw from the perspective of human subjects. That flaw is its incompatibility with a different kind of necessity, the most basic component of freedom, which we call the minimal integrity of the self. The emerging colonialist and capitalist order is therefore, under whatever disguise it operates, incompatible with every political structure built on freedom, including democracy in all its forms, liberal or otherwise.

Vision and imagination become the *most* practical starting points when we are faced with a social transformation so large, so ordered, and so multilayered. We need a vision that does not turn its back on the future but asserts the possibility of a different future, a vision that does not subordinate human autonomy to system autonomy.[20] We will suggest here some practical steps toward this reimagining of our relations to data and data colonialism, a potential new social imaginary about data and our relations to data.[21]

How does this vision start? It begins by rejecting in principle the premises of the new social and economic order and, for example, insisting at every opportunity that corporations—indeed all actors—who use data can do so *legitimately* only if that broad usage is based on respect for the human subjects to whom that data refers and for the goals and awareness of those data subjects. For it is not just individuals' right to control their data that is at stake if we don't reject data colonialism's premises, but also the freedom of social subjects to exist without being tracked, indeed, the right for everyone to live in a world that still holds the possibility of freedom for human subjects in general. Defending this possibility of freedom means defining, more fully than we have done so far, the danger that data colonialism poses to human life.

The order of data relations relies on the unlimited possibilities of data processing generated by the infinite connectivity of the contemporary world. Data relations rely on removing all limits to data appropriation and thus building an expanding, knowledge-based social and economic order. From simple starting points (computer's data capture, the connectability of computers, and the information processing and monitoring that together they enable), institutions and systems are acquiring the capacity to govern life in a completely new way. But is this a good way of ordering life? What power relations does it bring with it, and how can they be moderated?

It is first essential to grasp, as noted in chapter 4, that under data colonialism what is extracted for value *from* social life is not incidentally but intimately linked to the production of knowledge *about* social life. Resisting data colonialism draws us inexorably into the sorts of epistemological questions (about what constitutes knowledge and what its preconditions are) that we might normally delegate to philosophers. What sorts of data should be collected? What sorts of data should be combined with what other sorts of data? When do we need to impose a limit on algorithmic decision-making? Our answers to these questions will shape the social worlds in which we live over the coming decades. We can go even further: because order is the basis of all forms of life, the social and economic order being built through data colonialism raises questions about the future of human life itself.

It is important also to reject rather than accommodate the forms of ideology surrounding data that were identified in earlier chapters. The unlimited targeting of persons by marketing messages is *not* personalization. The pursuit of continuous automated surveillance does *not* really bring the democratization of health or the educational promotion of digital citizenship. It is *not* true that limits to connection are always bad or that flows of information *must* be "seamless": what if particular forms of data flow cause harm (it is easy enough to think of examples)? We should also reject the implication, in metaphorical claims that data creates "ecologies" or "ecosystems," that data processing is somehow natural.[22] Certainly, data gathered in vast accumulations across many sources may have a complexity comparable to known ecosystems, but that does *not* mean that such processes are natural or must be left unrestricted, let alone protected and legally endorsed.

This reimagining of our existing relations to data is much more than *saying no*. Rejection of the idea that no obstructions must be allowed to the flow of data can be formulated positively as the affirmation of what Janet Vertesi calls the principle of *seamfulness*.[23] This is the idea that, instead of prioritizing the seamless movement of data, transfers of data must first always be responsible and accountable to those affected by that data; otherwise, such transfers should not proceed. To put this at its simplest: if data can cause harm, as we know it can, and if individuals and institutions still care about avoiding harm, then the principle of seamfulness in relation to data is surely more "natural" than seamlessness!

Affirming seamfulness as a positive principle suggests also the wider possibility of building a whole set of ecological principles that would challenge the naturalness of data colonialism's so-called ecology. These would include defending the possibility of autonomous human agency and human relations, on which data practices have relentless effects. If, as we saw in chapter 5, dataism's principle that every life process *should* generate data through permanent connection and openness to monitoring and surveillance damages the integrity of the human self, then it is the latter principle (the self's integrity) that should be affirmed, and not dataism.

The growing conflict between data's supposed ecology and such underlying human values is not just a clash of values; it is *itself* a clash of ecologies. Data colonialism proposes a connected world that appears to know itself through its absolute connectability and through unfettered data flows between all its points (whether living or not). Indeed, dataism claims to find a higher force than human life, the force of information processing or algorithmic power, which appears to know human life better than life can know itself. But this ideology clashes with a much older vision of how human life should be, an ecological view of human life, unchallenged until very recently, which assumes that human life, like all life—whatever its limits, constraints, and deficits—is a zone of open-ended connection and growth. This view of human life understands life (my life, your life, the life of the society we inhabit) as something that *finds its own limits* as it continuously changes and develops, even as forms of human power seek to manage and control it.[24]

Reflecting on the meaning of the term *ecology* enables us to take this point further. The order of data colonialism damages the minimal integrity of the self as a space of self-relation. Yet human beings' possibility of being "at home" with themselves depends on having access to that space of the self. The damage done by data colonialism is therefore ecological in its nature and not just in its scale. Recall the ancient Greek roots of the word *ecology*: the task of gathering together a home (*legein* + *oikos*).[25] The social order of data colonialism is, in a precise sense, an *anti*ecology that disrupts the basic space of human autonomy and conviviality in a process that might be compared to what biologists call "dysbiosis." This is the opposite of the successful forms of interdependency between life forms that we call "symbiosis."[26] Data colonialism disrupts the ecology of human life not for some higher purpose but in the name of pure instrumentality: to support capitalism's drive to profit.

Insisting on boundaries to the continuous flow of data (the principle of seamfulness) means insisting that human reason should always be able to impose limits on that flow, because data's goal should ultimately be to serve human, not artificial, life. Nothing we have argued in this book rules out the search for social uses of data that genuinely remain under the control and monitoring of citizens themselves. We have instead offered ample evidence that the emerging social order built from seamless data flows in the interests *of capital* is becoming toxic to human beings through two means: (1) the highly targeted but almost entirely opaque forms of inequality that it authorizes in the name of greater social knowledge and resource efficiency and (2) the uncontrolled surveillance of human life on which it is premised. External systems for seamless data processing provide the means for power (states, corporations, and powerful alliances between the two) to achieve ever more fine-grained and integrated forms of discrimination.

The principle of seamfulness therefore becomes a potential tool for resisting social worlds that are less accountable, harsher, and characterized by ever higher levels of inequality, mistrust, and despair. It also alerts us to the danger that *without* seamfulness, the social costs that data colonialism generates will simply be passed down to the most vulnerable, quite possibly on the basis that they somehow "deserve" it, exactly the form of "moral behaviorism" that has for two decades characterized neoliberal societies. Indeed, we already see signs of *punitive* connectivity and *punitive* data extraction emerging as the dark side of data seamlessness.[27] All the while, the new social knowledge generated by algorithmic processes is silent on these problems, notwithstanding the best efforts of critical information science. In daily life, the winners in the data game will go on reaping the benefits while finding their success largely opaque too. Their path through life will just be smoother, more empowered, and more seamless.

Here, as Boaventura de Sousa Santos has noted, questions of "global social injustice" become "intimately linked" with questions of "global cognitive injustice." Capitalism's grip on the world, through the mechanism of connection, creates a new modality of injustice, indissolubly both social *and* cognitive, that is derived from data processes.[28] Data colonialism's true violence is to make human beings the *objects* of external control through data, together with everything that, until now, has passed for their lives' interior.

If this is the challenge human beings face over the longer term, how should we begin to address it?

A Different Rationality

At this point, two questions—about social/political order and rationality—risk becoming knotted together. We must disentangle them.

The answer cannot be to reject order. Human life, like all life, is sustainable only on the basis of a certain degree of order that conforms to the physical and psychic needs of human beings. Whereas the word *order* has acquired certain negative connotations within the ambit of Western rationality, as something implying imposed structures, it can also mean "balance," as in harmony, and beneficial forms of interconnectedness and living well *together*. Order is the abstract term for many elements of human life we are truly thankful for: routine, expectation, the security of knowing that people generally act as they say they will. But one must always ask: Order for whom? Order on what terms?

If justice is any part of quality of life, we can ask whether data colonialism's order is compatible with human quality of life. The philosopher and economist Amartya Sen has deeply challenged the dominance of mainstream economic thinking and its divergence from basic considerations of ethics. At the core of Sen's challenge to economics' narrow instrumentalism—and the political thought that mimics it—is his insistence on the actual complexity and variety of human reasoning. How can human beings exercise freedom of choice in societies in which processes of discrimination and opportunity segregation operate in an algorithmic shadow zone? Any account of freedom starts, for Sen, from the question of whether daily life gives to an individual "the actual ability . . . to achieve those things that she has reason to value."[29] Economic thinking, he argues, assumes away much of the complexity of individual reasoning, just as do the hollowed-out models of human agency in much contemporary social science (as we saw in chapter 4). Sen argues that we need a better and more inclusive model of human rationality if we are to avoid endangering "the conditions and circumstances that ensure the range and reach of the democratic process."[30] Could data science, and the wider "science" of Big Data, be in need of a similar challenge?

There is in fact a lot at stake in our *conception* of rationality. The Peruvian decolonial theorist Aníbal Quijano proposes a much broader critique of the European paradigm of rationality/modernity than Sen does.[31] Having seen throughout the book that the rationality of datafication is today more global than European and is as celebrated in China as elsewhere, we might wish to downplay Quijano's emphasis on the term *European*, but this does not make his broader analysis any less profound.

> It is necessary to extricate oneself from the linkages between rationality/modernity and coloniality, first of all, and definitely from all power which is not constituted by free decisions made by free people. It is *the instrumentalization of the reasons for power*, of colonial power in the first place, which produced distorted paradigms of knowledge and spoiled the liberating promises of modernity.[32]

The method and goal, then, is not to abandon the idea of rationality (or order) but to reanimate it in terms of different values. What is needed is an "epistemological decolonization" that "clear[s] the way for . . . an interchange of experiences and meanings, as the basis of another rationality which may legitimately pretend to some universality." The goal is not to abandon rationality, order, or even the claim to universality but to reject the highly distinctive claim to *absolute* universality that characterizes European modernity.

We reach here the core of what is wrong with data colonialism's order: its vision of *totality*. Connection—a potential human good in itself—is always offered today on terms that require acceptance of a totality, a submission to a universal order of connectivity. Data colonialism is, after all, not the only vision of human order—indeed, of the human uses of data—

that is possible. But its way of "covering" the world—of compelling us to believe there is no other way to imagine the world unfolding and becoming known to us—is part of its power and its danger. Data colonialism provides a "*horizon* of totality" (in Enrique Dussel's useful phrase) that it is difficult but essential to resist and dismantle.

We must hold on to a different vision of order. An order that understands humanity in a nontotalizing way, that rejects the equation of totality with sameness and the imposition of *one reading* of how the world and its knowledges should be organized. Quijano's voice is inspiring in this respect.

> Outside the West, virtually in all known cultures . . . , all systematic production of knowledge is associated with a perspective of totality. But in those cultures, the perspective of totality in knowledge includes *the acknowledgement of the heterogeneity of all reality*; of the irreducible, contradictory character of the latter; of the legitimacy, i.e. desirability of the diverse character of the components of all reality—*and therefore, of the social*. The [better, alternative] idea of social totality, then, not only does not deny, but depends on the historical diversity and heterogeneity of society, of every society. In other words, it not only does not deny, but it requires the idea of an "other"—diverse, different.[33]

The West's much heralded liberal "pluralism" has always, as Quijano explains, ruled out the pluralities that it found inconvenient.[34] The ideologies of data colonialism are no different, insisting that the whole world—every part of the social world, on every possible scale, and at every possible layer of meaning—can be organized in accordance with *a single* integrated scheme or totality that categorizes all people, acts, and possibilities singly and in opposition to one another. There is no empirical test that could verify this vision of social knowledge: it has authority only by virtue of being imposed on a world reconfigured to its own image. As we learned in chapter 4, measures "recreate social worlds."[35]

The practical starting point for resistance to data colonialism at last becomes clear. It is to articulate a vision that, against the background of Big Data reasoning, will appear counterintuitive to many, *a vision that rejects the idea that the continuous collection of data from human beings is a rational way of organizing human life.* From this perspective, the results of data processing are less a natural form of individual and societal self-knowledge than they are a commercially motivated "fix" that serves deep and partial interests that *as such* should be rejected and resisted.

It may help here to listen to those who have fought for centuries against capitalism and its colonial guises. Leanne Betasamosake Simpson reflects on rationality but from the perspective of human meaning. She affirms a meaning that "is derived not through content or data or even theory . . . but through a compassionate web of interdependent relationships that are different and valuable because of difference." Why difference exactly? Because only by respecting difference do we stand any chance of not "interfer[ing] with other beings' life pathways" and *their* possibilities for autonomy.[36]

Living with an Intimate Enemy

It is difficult to imagine any general adjustment more likely to interfere with human life than the continuous tracking and nudging that is data colonialism's basic practice. The sheer intimacy of contemporary corporate/state surveillance (the depth to which it penetrates and messes with our lives) makes it particularly hard to resist: resisting such an intimate enemy[37] must seem, at least at first, like giving up part of ourselves. If and when we collectively decide to dismantle our attachment to Facebook, for example, it will be a messy operation. It is, after all, the minimal integrity of the self, the very space in which each of us has the possibility of existing *as a self*, that must be restored to integrity now that it has been damaged. That will take work, and we must be very clear about the principles that will guide us.[38]

There is no place in this alternative rationality and vision of social order for the default collection of data or its collection under vague forms of consent.

There is no place for the reuse of data for purposes not consented to by those to whom the data refers.

There is no place for systems of, and approaches to, data collection that are not specifically chosen by human subjects to meet purposes that they too have chosen.

It is time to call out the contradiction between capitalism's current business models (based on default data harvesting) and the value of freedom that capitalism's representatives claim to espouse.

There is, however, nothing nostalgic about our argument. Nostalgia is pointless under data colonialism, since there is no unchanged point of origin to which we can return. Dreaming otherwise misses entirely the significance of the data-driven order that has been carefully, if only so far partly, built over the last two decades. It is a different future that must be created.

A Vision for Data Subjects Everywhere

So far this is still an abstract vision, but it is important to try to make it a little more concrete. Resistance to data colonialism does not mean gestures made for effect (such as quitting Facebook) that leave the order of data colonialism intact. But it does mean saying no to practices that normalize the order of data colonialism in everyday life. We need to find ways of collectively unsettling our identification with data colonialism's requirements. Power is always social in the end, so discovering new powers of resistance must emerge from the social world too.

That means offering a vision that can be useful to the sorts of colonized data subjects we have invoked in the course of the book, and many others besides: the truck driver angry at being directed and overseen by the tracker placed on his dashboard; the Amazon warehouse worker whose every movement is pushed and tracked through a voice-picking system; the family who must face the illness of loved ones without essential health insurance but with no idea why they have lost their hard-earned protection; and the First Nations activist who enthusiastically adopted social media platforms only to wonder what, by the same token, she has given up.

How should we think about the emerging social space from which resistance begins? In an earlier book, one of us introduced the concept of the "paranodal"[39] as a way to think about how we can disidentify from the social pressures of digital networks. Looking at a network diagram, what is rendered visible are the nodes and the links connecting those nodes. The space between them would seem to be barren, unconnected, a great useless void. But this space is not empty. It is inhabited by multitudes who do not conform to the organizing logic of the network, whether by choice, by accident, or by exclusion. This paranodal space is the space that lies *beside* the node and *beyond* the rationalities that bind nodes together.

If the order of data colonialism depends, in the end, on connection (the act of being "plugged in" to networked infrastructures of connection), then it is only when we inhabit the paranodal space, standing to one side of the nodes of digital connection, that decolonized ways of thinking and acting can emerge. Since digital isolation is becoming increasingly impossible to enact, paranodality offers a model for being outside the network even while remaining formally inside (redefining therefore what it means to be effectively "inside" the network). It is not a matter of saying no to Facebook but saying no to data colonialism and no to the rationality of the whole Cloud Empire. Saying no to Facebook only perpetuates the illusion that the rest of social life has suddenly thereby been decolonized when it hasn't. Saying no to the Cloud Empire by contrast acknowledges the totality that must be rejected but denies the legitimacy of that emerging order *as a whole* while admitting our continuing complicity in the practical relations of data colonialism.

More positively, it also means intensifying the pleasures of sociality (solidarity, even) that not even datafication has been able to suppress. One reason we all flocked to social media platforms originally was because they reminded us of the joys of collectivity at a time when mass media seemed to offer only individualistic isolation. That pleasure risks being extinguished now as we become ever clearer that social media outlets are managed by vast commercial interests. But we don't need to forget everything that has been learned during our time on digital networks. We can develop forms of solidarity that extend what we have learned online but turn them toward values that are no longer aligned to data colonialism.

Recall for a moment some of the actions whose partial nature we criticized earlier: media literacy campaigns, withdrawal from this or that platform, and legislation requiring data companies to actually obtain something like consent for using personal data. What if we approached them not merely as individualistic acts or as technical fixes but as part of a collaborative attempt to build a different social world than the one data colonialism promises us? Acquiring media literacy might then include citizens

learning to help one another become less reliant on systems whose negative effects we all know. Withdrawing from a particular platform might
involve learning with others how to distinguish between forms of forced
coordination that benefit platforms and forms of collaboration that genuinely benefit people and then, on the basis of that understanding, building
new communicative forms that prioritize the latter over the former. Legis-
lating for a better data environment might involve going beyond attempts
to "tame" data companies and affirming positive principles on the basis of
which future social uses of data could be organized for collective benefit
and not corporate privilege.

In short, we need a way to tie together the isolated acts of resistance and
technical fixes we have criticized so far and organize them into a larger
project for dismantling data colonialism by collectively acquiring knowledge about its manifold manifestations and the alternatives they suppress.
What is at stake here is the possibility of new ways of knowing and organizing our shared world that support rather than undermine fundamental shared values. We develop this possibility in the next and final section.

Tools for Common Knowledge[40]

The Indian anthropologist Arjun Appadurai recently made an important
call to rethink research beyond the walls of academia. He proposes that we
think of research in terms of the "right to the tools through which *any citizen* can systematically increase the stock of knowledge that they consider
most vital to their survival as human beings and to their claims as citizens."[41] Could the perspectives we have brought together in this book—
critical internet studies and computer science, decoloniality, and critical
social theory—converge to help build for all subjects of data colonialism
some tools and opportunities to investigate how the artifacts and ideologies of the Cloud Empire come to bear on their lives? If so, we might have
the beginnings of a *social laboratory* for disentangling our communicative
and social practices from the profit-seeking motives of corporations. Call
it, if you like, a new kind of research project, but it would be one with deep
continuities to previous decolonial research projects that questioned who
generates new knowledge and who or what that knowledge is for. Those

were not research projects for a narrow elite. Paulo Freire's pedagogy of the oppressed, Jorge Sanjinés's cinema with the people, and the various experiments of what is loosely called Participatory Action Research[42] tried to reimagine research as a decolonial tool, a tool in the hands of the subjects of colonial oppression.

Gayatri Spivak once famously asked, "Can the subaltern speak?"[43] Similarly, today we might ask: Can data colonialism's subjects speak up against the structures that dispossess them? An affirmative answer is possible if we take seriously the temporal dislocation that postcolonial theory grasped so well when it defined itself as an "active transformation of the present out of the clutches of the past."[44] Except that today the dislocation is subtly different. Even though we have explored the roots of data colonialism in the *past*, the debates started here must address the kind of *future* that is already being created in the clutches of the *present*. This, incidentally, is what distinguishes the universalizing involved in our argument from the universalizing that colonialisms have helped shape, indeed, the universalizing that underlies the whole vision of Big Data. Decolonizing data means speaking now from the position of data's colonized and imagining a common future for humanity beyond the contemporary project to reduce human life to the inputs and outputs of data processing. There is a key role, as Raewyn Connell points out, that theory's generalizations can play in challenging what is presented to us as data and thus "reveal[ing] the dynamics of a given moment of history." The strength, however, of theory's generalizations depends on the extent to which they can link back to the specific contexts of human life that data practice wants to write over.[45] This vision for a collective process of research—this project for *thinking together in multiple contexts* about what data colonialism means for human life today—is more political, more interdisciplinary, more practical, and less respectful of the boundaries of academia than are the domains supposedly leading the way in engaging with data, such as the digital humanities.

Research on data colonialism cannot take place exclusively in corporate research labs or corporate-funded universities. It needs to be accessible to everyone and from everywhere while avoiding essentialisms about who can or cannot engage in it; we are addressing a collective problem for humanity, after all. Borrowing from indigenous methods of inquiry, as Linda Tuhiwai Smith[46] proposes, the project of thinking collectively about what it would mean to decolonize data relations can draw citizens and groups into a variety of tasks: *reframing* (shifting the terms of discourse about what data is for), *restoring* (reclaiming forms of well-being eroded by data relations), *naming* (articulating new worldviews that resist datafication), *gendering* (uncovering the hidden and not-so-hidden politics of gender self-determination in data transactions), *protecting* (identifying the social arenas that should exist beyond datafication), and *creating* (channeling creative collectivity to form new social relations around and beyond data). Each of these tasks remain oriented to social goals, not the goals of the corporate infrastructures that underlie data processing.[47] In short, critical research on data colonialism requires new ways of using and sharing data that, as Aníbal Quijano says, "clear the way for new intercultural communication, for an interchange of experiences and meanings, as the basis of another rationality which may legitimately pretend to some universality."[48]

Decolonizing data's role in explaining the social world means rejecting the assumption that only data can explain data—that is, that only quantitative methods based on Big Data methodologies can accurately describe the world from now on. While it should not reject the idea of gathering data as such (for example, for clearly defined social purposes), the evolving project to think together about the consequences of data colonialism must insist on close attention to those "aspects of social life that remain unseen, unheard, uncounted or unacknowledged within prevailing understandings of capitalism," as Johnna Montgomerie argues.[49] Put differently, our understanding of the social world needs to be rescued from a narrow understanding that equates it with large data sets and abstract models with "only fantastical links to actual human experience or observation."[50] The resulting social knowledge will be complicated and perhaps difficult to resolve into a single neat perspective, as with much research carried out on the ground about the uses of digital media or of countermapping technologies by indigenous populations.[51] But that is precisely its strength. Abandon our willingness to listen to this complexity, and, as Virginia Eubanks warned, we abandon our "social commitment to try to understand each other."[52] The project of thinking about data through listening to the experiences of others can benefit from both successes and failures, many of them far outside the corporate mainstream.

As an example of the kind of research we are envisioning, consider the Algorithm Observatory that one of us is building. Part media-literacy project and part citizen experiment, the project's goal is to give the general public simple and accessible resources to understand how social-computing algorithms categorize us (find it at algorithmobservatory.com). These tools can be used to engage critically with the technologies that are shaping our daily lives in profound—but not always transparent—ways. Although at the time of this writing the project is only in the prototype stage, focusing exclusively on Facebook advertising algorithms, eventually the Algorithm Observatory will allow anyone to design an experiment involving any social-computing algorithm. This is because the site does not require direct access to the source code (which corporations are unlikely to share with the public) but instead relies on empirical observation of the interaction between the algorithm and different kinds of volunteer participants. We offer this project as an example of what thinking together about the consequences of data colonialism within and outside the university might look like.

Those who formulate critiques, such as the ones contained in this book, are often asked how to solve the problems they have identified. Although solutions to problems that have taken centuries to unfold must necessarily be partial, incomplete, and tentative, this is indeed our most concrete proposal: *that anyone who feels dispossessed by the Cloud Empire should have opportunities and spaces to participate in collective research about the shared problems that data now poses for humanity.* Where will these spaces emerge? We cannot exactly know yet. But we do know that the decolonization of data relations will require an explosion of creativity in many places and networks. What it does not require is a central blueprint or unified vision of an alternative "order." How else can an emerging social order and its power structures be challenged at each step of the way?

The Cloud Empire's myth that the only way to harness new social resources is to surrender to platforms' control of how and where we make knowledge, organize resources, or even just express solidarity and connection must be unlearned, and even more rapidly than it came into being.

Recent infrastructures of connection have facilitated new forms of collectivity, but this does not mean that we must accept the forms of exploitation that are indissolubly tied to the data relations associated with those infrastructures. If we disown the corporate dream that the world's rich diversity can and must be ordered for profit, we may find that other forms of connection are possible.

Postscript

Another Path Is Possible

TO POWERFUL INSTITUTIONS, the forward path of development that in this book we have called data colonialism seems so clear and so necessary that people tend to accept it as though it was the future already told back to us as settled history. Or, as Microsoft CEO Satya Nadella expressed it, "We retrofit for the future."[1] Indeed, we have become used to social media platforms telling us the story of our future (their future!), and until recently, their narratives of global community seemed comforting to many.

But as we have seen, there is a darker side to the social quantification sector, whose narratives of the future are just as bold. In its March 2017 annual report, Axon—previously Taser International—announced a strategy for "creat[ing] connected technologies for truth in public safety."[2] A month before, Taser had renamed itself after its video camera/AI division, Axon AI. Axon exemplifies well the new social knowledge that is emerging from the Cloud Empire and its growing economic power. Think of it: a stun-gun manufacturer now makes a quarter of its substantial income from data analytics and cloud services that maintain automated cameras and bypass human interpreters. Hear the note of triumph in the words of Axon's CEO: "To the world at large: it's time for change."[3]

Axon's triumphal rise is just a small part of the increasing datafication of the US law-and-order sector, which is, in turn, just part of the wider transformation of social governance and individual self-governance in the United States and many other nations. Governed this way, the social world stops being a space of dialogue and debate, let alone of democratic change, and becomes what the data industry calls a propensity and probability spectrum,[4] governed by knowledges that are largely in corporate hands. Yet this huge social transformation, as noted in chapter 6, is only part of the global battle for leadership of the social quantification sector and AI generally. Such momentous national interests and global financial investments are involved that it makes sense to assume that this general path will extend at least into the foreseeable future. It also makes sense to assume that the economic and social inequalities associated with these changes will overlap with an even deeper inequality in who and what can influence the terms on which we come to know the world around us. This is the twinned legacy of data colonialism and the capitalism that is emerging from it.

More bluntly, we can see the road of data colonialism marked out ahead across the social landscape that data relations are steadily hollowing out. But the concept of the paranodal helps us grasp that there is also a space on the side of that road[5]—an unmarked space that is not yet a path (or anything), headed nowhere in particular except, we can imagine, *away* from data colonialism. This side-space is where we must start to affirm a new direction of travel based on a different rationality and based on different possibilities for order and security, for solidarity and human organization. A space in which we feel no reason to bind ourselves into relations that achieve only what capitalism wants (stable processes of data extraction). A space in which we can recover the idea that human beings might know themselves and choose the relations that organize their lives without delegating this choice and that knowledge to an algorithm.

It would be the worst sort of irresponsibility to conclude fatalistically that the path toward data colonialism is already fixed. Is our only choice really to downsize our freedom to fit the datafied future that is coming? That choice is surely intolerable, and there is nothing dignified in staying silent about it.[6]

Rather than silence, it is better, as we stand to the side of data colonialism's road, to affirm what we know: that the minimal integrity of the self cannot simply be delegated or outsourced to automated systems; that the new social order being built through data will produce patterns of power and inequality that corrode all meaningful practices of freedom; and that these contradictions with important values can still, for now at least, be seen for what they are.

The representatives of data colonialism try to convince us that there is nothing hollow in our assent to their order, that we are choosing familiar values of connection and human solidarity when we choose this datafied social order. They tell us that we need to go on connecting with and through them. But that is a ruse. The ruse depends on inducing human beings to forget ways of living that were left behind when we came to spend so much time servicing the social quantification sector.[7] We are, all of us, part of the ruse. The greatest threat that data colonialism poses is that, in time, it works too well for us to want to live any other kind of existence, so that our complicity in losing hold on the possibility of freedom becomes complete.

The path away from data colonialism will start when we reclaim the capacity to connect that human beings have always possessed, and we decide that today's costs of connection are neither necessary nor worth paying. The struggle is a global one: it matters for humanity as a whole, not just for market democracies, and it confronts capitalism as a whole, not just social media. The shape of the path is uncertain, but this book has tried to imagine at least its starting points. The path will form when, individually and collectively, through rediscovered lines of connection, human beings find a place and a strength from which living uncolonized by data seems not just right but something they would always have chosen.

Acknowledgments

The idea for this book emerged in 2014, and much has happened since then, particularly in the period since writing began in January 2016 and intensified in September 2017. Each of us separately, and together as a writing team, owe a lot to various people who have made this book possible.

From Nick: I would like to thank Jun Yu, scholar at the London School of Economics and Political Science and researcher on the Price of Connection project, for his extremely useful work that provided background material for chapters 3 and 5. That project and my three research visits to meet Ulises in Ithaca were financially supported by the Enhancing Life research program led by Bill Schweiker of the University of Chicago and Gunther Thomas of the University of Bochum and funded by the John Templeton Foundation. The program's financial support is gratefully acknowledged. I would also like to thank Miriam Rahali of LSE for research that contributed to the discussion of privacy in chapter 5 as well as for her terrific research assistance generally during the book's beginnings.

A crucial period of reading and writing for me in the fall of 2017 was made possible by Microsoft Research Lab in Cambridge, Massachusetts, where I was a visiting researcher from September to December. This provided an extremely hospitable place for me to focus and listen. I would like to thank Jennifer Chayes and Christian Borgs for their overall support and to thank Nancy Baym, Tarleton Gillespie, and Mary Gray for being the most terrific hosts. Thanks also to Kelly Buckley, Sharon Gillett, Sarah Hamid, Adam Kalai, Dylan Mulvin, Gen Patterson, Moira Weigel, and particularly Daniel Greene and Glen Weyl for many useful and inspiring discussions. Harvard's Berkman Klein Center for Law and Society, where I was associate faculty in 2017–2018 and 2018–2019, provided a wonderful alternative venue for discussion; thanks to Urs Gasser, Becca Tabasky, and Carey Andersen for their generous support and to Elettra Bietti for her solidarity. Thanks to Bruce Schneier and Shoshana Zuboff for inspiring conversations at that time. And thanks to Mary Ann Hart for the rent of her apartment in Cambridge, Massachusetts, which provided a wonderful space in which to think, read, and write and where much of this book was made.

More generally, working on this book would simply not have been possible without me having been able to step down as head of LSE's Department of Media and Communications in August 2017. I am hugely grateful to Robin Mansell for her grace and kindness in taking over the department, once more, for a year to enable that.

My growing interest in data has emerged through the inspiration and encouragement of particular friends and colleagues at LSE and elsewhere, above all, Mark Andrejevic, Seeta Gangadharan, Myria Georgiou, Andreas Hepp, Jannis Kallinikos, Andrew Murray, Ioanna Noulou, Jean-Christophe Plantin, Alison Powell, Clemencia Rodriguez, Joseph Turow, and, at the very start, the Storycircle team at Goldsmiths that I had the honor of leading from 2010 to 2013 (Wilma Clark, Luke Dickens, Aristea Fotopoulou, Richard Macdonald, and Hilde Stephansen). I would also like to thank Sarah Bianchi, Andrea Bieler, Ruth Farrell, Barbara Rossing, Christopher Scott, Daniel Sulmasy, and Ruben Zimmermann, fellow members of the Enhancing Life program, for illuminating discussions and insights.

As ever, my work on this book would have been impossible without the love and support of my wife, Louise Edwards, my *sine qua non*. Particular thanks to Louise for tolerating my long absences, obsessions, and distractions during what for both of us and for multiple reasons has been a very challenging time. I would like to dedicate my part in this book, in order of age, to my dear nieces Lois Edwards, Isobel Edwards, and Mira Michels Couldry in the hope that not all of what this book senses to be underway will come to fruition.

From Ulises: Among other things, this is a book about social relations, and I would like to acknowledge those relationships that made my work possible. These include the authors I read and learned from, the colleagues

I discussed things with, the staff at various institutions whose work facilitated mine, and the beloved friends whose company I enjoyed while writing this book. They are too numerous to list, but I do want to mention
Patty Zimmermann, always a mentor and friend, who provided encouragement and useful tips on writing.

I am grateful for the teaching-release time I received from SUNY Os-
wego to work on this project. I would like to especially thank my students in China, India, Russia, and the United States; it is their engagement and their questions that inspire me to keep thinking and reading and
struggling.

My efforts on this book are dedicated to my parents, Manuel and Elizabeth, whose support made me who I am and who have always been proud
of my accomplishments. I lost my dad during the course of working on
this project, and his memory shaped my writing in very personal ways. I
continue to discover to this day the many ways in which he is with me.

Finally, I want to thank Asma, my wife. The motivations, inquiries, politics, and passion behind my ideas are inspired in great part by her. She
has shaped this book through conversations and discussions, through
critiques, through travels (both intellectual and geographic), and simply
through our daily routine of spending time together. I am forever grateful
and devoted to her. "Swear by the night forever; Reach for a faultless land;
You may touch what the blinding brightness / Refuses to understand."[1]

From us both: There are a number of people whom we must thank
jointly. We particularly want to thank Joao Carlos Magalhaes, Nick's research assistant at LSE, for his outstanding work in researching topics and
gathering materials and sources for the book, particularly for chapters 2
and 4, and for his general assistance on many practical matters. His intellectual passion is reflected in this book, and we strongly want to acknowledge that. We are also grateful to audiences at Cardiff University and Tam-
pere University in 2018, and before that at the preconference on Big Data
from the Global South at IAMCR 2017 in Cartagena, Colombia, for responses to presentations of parts of our argument. Our thanks go also to
those who took the time to give careful readings and comments on various chapters of our manuscript: Mike Ananny, Asma Barlas, Julie Cohen,
Mary Gray, Daniel Greene, Naeem Inayatullah, Richard Stallman, and

Stanford's two anonymous readers who commented on a complete version from April 2018. The book has benefited greatly from their insights. We are also very grateful to Alison Rainey for her subtle and detailed copy edit of our manuscript, which brought many improvements. Needless to say, we take responsibility for all errors and opinions represented here.

Last but certainly not least, we thank Kate Wahl and our editor Marcela Maxfield of Stanford University Press. Marcela has been the most supportive critical friend of this project that we could have wished for, while Kate's support and belief as publishing director have been crucial from the start.

NICK COULDRY   ULISES MEJIAS
Islip, UK   Ithaca, US
September 2018

Notes

Preface

1. Langfur, "Myths of Pacification."
2. See http://www.idlenomore.ca/.
3. Quoted in Simpson, *Always Done*, 222–23.
4. Rooney, "Fainting Spells."
5. Deleon, "Review of WaterMinder."
6. Deloria, *Playing Indian.*
7. Tuck and Yang, "Not a Metaphor," 3.
8. This is the core difference between our argument and other influential critiques of what is happening with data, such as Zuboff, "Big Other."
9. Gandy, *Panoptic Sort.*
10. Turow, McGuigan, and Maris, "Making Data Mining," 468.
11. We draw here on William Sewell's definition of the social as "the various 'mediations' that place people into 'social' relations with one another . . . [as] interdependent members of each other's worlds" (*Logics of History*, 329).
12. Schneier, "Surveillance Partnership."
13. Increasingly, political scientists see these dystopias as being actualized, for example, Villasenor, "Recording Everything."
14. Kunelius et al., *Journalism.*
15. Christl and Spiekermann, "Networks of Control," 56.
16. Chamath Palihapitiya, quoted in Wong, "Society Apart." Two days later he posted a statement reaffirming his belief in Facebook as "a force for good in the world" (https://www.facebook.com/chamath/posts/10159808356105644).
17. Tufecki, "Building a Dystopia"; and George Soros, quoted in Solon, "A Menace to Society"; see Kollewe, "Unilever Threatens to Pull Ads," on the concerns with social media of Unilever, the world's second largest buyer of advertising.
18. Tom Baldwin, interviewed on BBC Radio 4 *Today* program, July 28, 2018. The fine imposed on Facebook for breaching data laws by the UK information commissioner is a signal of a wider fear of social media's threat to democracy. For

a useful summary of the rising tide of proposed Facebook "reforms," see Thorn-hill, "How to Fix Facebook."

19. Dayen, "Big Tech." These calls reached a climax in the wake of the Face-book/Cambridge Analytica scandal of March 2018.

20. Bhambra, *Connected Sociologies*, 7.

21. We appreciate that Marx himself had an extremely broad understanding of "labor" to encompass not just productive activity but also the wider activities and pleasures of human life (Berki, "Nature and Origins," 36) or, as Marx put it, "Life activity, productive life itself" (*Manuscripts*, 113). But this unusually expan-sive notion of labor risks obscuring the transformation underway whereby new forms of exploitation emerge through the collection and transformation of data from countless human activities that are not understood by human beings as in-volving any productive activity at all (for example, just chatting online, looking at things other people show us, or monitoring oneself).

22. Marx, *Capital*, vol. I, 950, 952.

23. Moore, *Capitalism*.

24. Williams, *Capitalism and Slavery*; and Blackburn, *New World Slavery*. Williams writes, "By 1750 there was hardly a trading or a manufacturing town in England which was not in some way connected with the triangular or direct colo-nial trade. The profits obtained provided one of the main streams of that accumu-lation of capital in England which financed the Industrial Revolution" (*Capitalism and Slavery*, 52).

25. For a pioneering version of this argument in management studies, see Cooke, "Denial of Slavery."

26. Baptist, "Toward a Political Economy," 40.

27. Gitelman, *Raw Data*.

28. Arvidsson, "Facebook and Finance"; and Thatcher, O'Sullivan, and Mah-moudi, "Data Colonialism," 995.

29. Quoted in Delbanco, "Frederick Douglass."

30. For contrasting accounts, see Schiller, *Digital Depression*; and Martin, *Empire of Indifference*.

31. Cowen, *Life of Logistics*; and Schiller, *Digital Depression*.

32. Bogost, "Welcome."

33. Iyengar and Rayport, "Like Software."

34. IBM, "Device Democracy."

35. China's 2015 "Internet Plus" policy describes itself as "the profound inte-gration of the innovation achievements of the Internet in all areas of the economy and society." It puts special emphasis on the "smartification of the manufacturing sector" and "high efficiency logistics" (see China Copyright and Media, "'Internet Plus' Plan"). China's "Artificial Intelligence Development Plan" proposes "indus-

trial intelligentization," including "smart logistics" (China Copyright and Media, "Artificial Intelligence").

36. In particular, the work of Julie Cohen, Vincent Mosco, Bruce Schneier, Joseph Turow, Shoshana Zuboff, and, in the world of fiction, Dave Eggers.

37. Marx, *Capital*, vol. I, 102.

Chapter 1

1. Wylie, "I've Been Getting a Lot of Requests."

2. For rare anticipations of this colonial reading, see Cohen, "Biopolitical Public Domain"; Thatcher, O'Sullivan, and Mahmoudi, "Data Colonialism"; Shepherd, "Measured and Mined"; and Shepherd, "Neocolonial Intimacies." Although the analysis done by Thatcher, O'Sullivan, and Mahmoudi is consistent with ours, their usage of the term *data colonialism* is explicitly metaphorical; rather than *colonial*, Cohen uses the term *"postcolonial"* and Shepherd the term *"neocolonial."* There are also growing debates about neocolonial influence in the technology sector and in the use of data by development and humanitarian agencies; see https://globalstudies.trinity.duke.edu/volume-31-decolonizing-thedigitaldigital-decolonization. Particularly interesting is the work of Joanne Radin ("Digital Natives") on the unreflexive use of health data from First Nation peoples in the United States in the "training" of artificial intelligence. For an analysis of AI practices that opens up a neocolonial perspective and was published as we completed this book, see Crawford and Joler, "Anatomy," especially pp. 17–18. But none of these writers or approaches argue, as we do, that data practices literally represent a new stage of colonialism.

3. Harvey, "Accumulation by Dispossession."

4. Scholz, *Digital Labor*; and Fuchs, *Digital Labour and Karl Marx*.

5. See Grewal, *Network Power*, on how interlocking forms of consent within digital networks can amount to force. Compare Bratton, *The Stack*, 43; and Chun, *Programmed Visions*.

6. Kitchin, *Data Revolution*, 1.

7. Zuboff, "Big Other," 80. As Marx put it, "Capital is in itself indifferent to the particular nature of every sphere of production" (*Capital*, vol. I, 1012).

8. Mark Zuckerberg, letter to potential investors, https://www.sec.gov/Archives/edgar/data/1326801/000119312512034517/d287954ds1.htm, quoted in Somini Sengupta and Claire Cain Miller, "Zuckerberg's 'Social Mission' View vs. Financial Expectations of Wall St.," *New York Times*, February 3, 2012; and Huateng, "Open Letter."

9. Harvey, *Marx*, chap. 1; Marx (*Capital*, vol. I, cited in Harvey, *Geography of Difference*, 63) wrote that "value . . . becomes value in process, money in process, and, as such, capital."

10. Christopher Ahlberg of Recorded Future, quoted in Davenport, *Big Data*, 21. On the implications of relying on external unstructured data, instead of internally generated corporate data, for business strategy, see Constantiou and Kallinikos, "New Games, New Rules."

11. Gartner's research vice presidents quoted in Taylor, "Business Opportunities"; Davenport, *Big Data*, 11, 12, 198.

12. Gabrys, *Program Earth*. Compare Cohen, "Biopolitical Public Domain," 8, which says that the "communication environment has become a sensing environment."

13. Quoted by Davenport, Harris, and Morison, *Analytics at Work*, cited in Degli Espositi, "When Big Data." On the reliance of social media platforms on data rather than on advertising for profit, see Gillespie, *Custodians*, 19.

14. Cohen, "Biopolitical Public Domain," 4. In other colonies, the legal justification for appropriation could be more complicated; for example, in British North American colonies, Locke's argument that common land was not meant by God to go undeveloped forever (Hsueh, "Cultivating"), and in Spanish American colonies, the fiction of the *requerimiento* discussed in chapter 2. Nonetheless, as Julie Cohen points out ("Biopolitical Public Domain," 4), even Locke wrote at times as though America was a *terra nullius*.

15. World Economic Forum, *Personal Data*.

16. Drawn from Davenport's case study "Big Data at Verizon Wireless" (Davenport, *Big Data*, 196).

17. Manovich, "Media Analytics in the Early 21st Century."

18. Davenport, *Big Data*, 197–202.

19. Turner, *Counterculture to Cyberculture*.

20. Strapline on web page: https://facefirst.com/.

21. Russell, "Smile to Pay."

22. Greenberg, "Selling Point."

23. Waters, "Cook Is Right," quoting an unnamed industry analyst.

24. Apple, "Privacy Policy," accessed December 5, 2017, https://www.apple.com/uk/legal/privacy/en-ww/.

25. Soltani and Timberg, "Apple's Mac Computers"; and Turow, *Aisles Have Eyes*, 121.

26. Griffin, "Facebook Is Going to Start."

27. See "Privacy Policy," WhatsApp Legal Info, WhatsApp, accessed February 12, 2018, https://www.whatsapp.com/legal/?l=en#privacy-policy-information-we-collect; and Fox-Brewster, "This Is the Data." For a revealing interview with WhatsApp cofounder Brian Acton, who has parted ways with Facebook, see Olson, "Exclusive."

28. Peterson, "Snapchat Agrees."

29. Apple included ad blocking in its 2015 iOS; Google is currently considering some form of ad blocking to counter "intrusive ads." For discussion, see Wu, *Attention Merchants*; and Warren, "Google Starts Testing."

30. PageFair, *Global Adblock Report*, 1. For discussion of Facebook's strategy to counter ad blocking, see Ryan, "Facebook's Hackproof Ads."

31. PricewaterhouseCoopers, "Wearable Future," 12.

32. See China Copyright and Media, "'Internet Plus' Plan," par. 1 (3).

33. Hong, *Networking China*, 11, 151.

34. Gurumurthy, "Big Brother."

35. Marx, *Capital*, vol. I, 1056; and Dyer-Witheford, *Cyber-Marx*, 122.

36. Our term "data relations" overlaps with the work of Helen Kennedy on "new data relations" (*Post, Mine, Repeat*, 11, 232–33). Kennedy's analysis usefully explores various new uses of "number" in daily life within businesses not normally thought of as in the social media sector, but it does so without some of the detail and, particularly, the wider theoretical links to labor relations, as understood by Marx, that we provide later in this chapter.

37. Browne, *Dark Matters*. We are not claiming datafied labor relations (or data relations) *are* slavery; such hyperbole would be offensive. We are making a comparison in terms of the degree and continuity of surveillance that is normal in various regimes of labor.

38. On the expansion of extraction, see Mezzadra and Neilson, "Frontiers of Extraction"; and compare Morozov, "Will Tech Giants Move" on "data extractivism."

39. That claim was rejected in a landmark European Court of Justice ruling in December 2017 (Bowcott, "Stricter EU Regulation").

40. As first noted by Terranova, "Free Labor." A huge debate followed that we cannot summarize here, but see Hesmondhalgh, "User-Generated Content"; and Jarrett, "Women's Work" for perspectives.

41. Roberts, "Silent Filter."

42. Quoted in Lin and Chin, "Tech Giants."

43. Dixit, "India's Largest Digital Wallet."

44. Quotations from China Copyright and Media, "Artificial Intelligence"; and from China Copyright and Media, "Social Credit System."

45. Cited by Crain, "Limits of Transparency" from Acxiom's website as it was in 2016. By December 2017, such claims had been removed.

46. Its only significant rivals were the Chinese search engine Baidu at 11 percent, Bing at nearly 5 percent, and Yahoo! at 3 percent. https://www.netmarketshare.com/search-engine-market-share.aspx.

47. Waters, "Four Days That Shook the Digital Ad World."

48. Larry Page, "Envisioning the Future for Google," lecture, Stanford University, May 1, 2002, cited in Foer, *World without Mind*, 38; IBM, *Annual Report 2017*; and Martin, "Microsoft Is Launching."

49. See Zittrain, *The Future*, for a pioneering insight on "tethering."

50. Mosco, *To the Cloud*; see chapter 2 for a deconstruction of this term.

51. Gartner, "Gartner Says Worldwide IaaS Public Cloud Services Market Grew."

52. McChesney, *Digital Disconnect*, 111–20, on "the ISP cartel."

53. Sandvig, "Anti-Television."

54. Blum, *Tubes*; Starosielski, *Undersea Network*; and Miller, "Google's Latest."

55. Published in Mac, Warzel, and Kantrowitz, "Growth at Any Cost."

56. Term first used by Mayer-Schonberger and Cukier, *Big Data*; but for a more critical discussion, see Van Dijck, "Datafication, Dataism"; and boyd and Crawford, "Critical Questions."

57. Reported in Acxiom, *"Personalisation."* For the origins of the terms *pragmatist* and *fundamentalist* in Alan Westin's industry-funded surveys on attitudes to privacy and a critique of them, see Hoofnagle and Urban, "Privacy *Homo Economicus*."

58. Van Dijck, "Datafication, Dataism."

59. Kurzweil, *Singularity*; and Kelly, *Inevitable*. For a useful critique, see Mosco, *Becoming Digital*, 120–23.

60. Zuckerberg, "Global Community"; Klein, "Facebook's Hardest Year"; and Huateng, "Open Letter."

61. Mason, *Postcapitalism*; and Williams and Srnicek, "#ACCELERATE MANIFESTO."

62. Put differently, we must avoid eliding "colonialism . . . to capitalism" (Bhambra, *Connected Sociologies*, 7) and, we would add, vice versa.

63. See the perceptive account by Fourcade and Healy, "Like a Market."

64. Recall Marx's argument that commodity works like a "social hieroglyphic" (*Capital*, vol. I, 167).

65. Marx, *Capital*, vol. III, 48.

66. Compare Fourcade and Healy, "Like a Market," 19. Polanyi (*Great Transformation*, 78–79) had a similar formulation when he analyzed industrial capitalism in terms of "fictional commodities": the transformation of work into "labor," land into "real estate," and exchange into "money." Building on Polanyi, Zuboff ("Big Other," 84) argues that "reality" is now being turned into tracked "behaviour."

67. The Economist, "Data Is Giving Rise to a New Economy," May 6, 2017.

68. We are condensing here the three principles of "scientific management" in Braverman, *Labor*, 78–82.

69. Braverman, *Labor*, 87.

70. Capitalism here aims at the state in which, as Marx (*Capital*, vol. I, 952) put it, "All the means of labour . . . now also serve as ingredients in the valorization process. Where they are not converted into actual money, they are converted into accounting money." We are arguing, however, that the "means of labour" include both labor itself, with its means of reproduction, *and* the expanding conditions, or factors, of production.

71. Scott, *Seeing Like a State*.

72. Schiller, *Digital Capitalism*, 8, 13–24; and Panitch and Gindin, *Global Capitalism*, 148, 189, 191, 288.

73. Habermas, *Communicative Action*, vol. 2, 196, 305, an argument developed in relation to social media platforms by Valtysson, "Facebook as a Digital Public Sphere." The closest Habermas comes to unpacking the metaphor of "colonization" is on page 355, where he says system imperatives "make their way into the lifeworld from the outside—like colonial masters coming into a tribal society—and force a process of assimilation upon it." But this idea is not developed as a theory of colonialism, and its starting point—the *separation* of technological systems from lifeworld—is hard to reconcile with life in most, if not all, contemporary societies. More recently, and in a similar vein, Adam Greenfield has written about the Internet of Things as "the colonization of everyday life by information processing" (*Radical Technologies*, 32).

74. MacPherson, *Possessive Individualism*.

75. Winner, "Do Artifacts Have Politics?"

76. Priestley, *Science of Operations*, 1.

77. Agre, "Two Models."

78. Zuboff, *Smart Machine*; see especially pp. 9–10 on the consequences of information becoming "data."

79. Kelly, "New Rules." On the transfer of ownership of the internet's infrastructure, see McChesney, *Digital Disconnect*, chap. 4, 104–9.

80. Schiller, *Digital Capitalism*, 13–24.

81. Plantin et al., "Infrastructure Studies."

82. Schiller, *Digital Depression*; for a good popular history, see Keen, *The Internet*. For a brilliant anticipation of the trend towards data exploitation online, see Schwartz, "Internet Privacy and the State." For caustic comment on the long-term costs of the libertarian agenda, see Lepore, "The Hacking of America."

83. Kitchin and Dodge, *Code/Space*, 13.

84. Berners-Lee, *Weaving*, 209.

85. Fourcade and Healy, "Like a Market," 19.

86. Turow, *Daily You*. See also Arvidsson, "Pre-History"; and Pridmore and Zwick, "Rise of Commercial Consumer Surveillance."

87. Vaidhyanathan, *Anti-Social Media*, 58.

88. Quote from David Jakubowski, head of Adtech Facebook, in eMarketer, "Bye-Bye, Cookies—Atlas Tracks Consumers Online and Offline Via Facebook IDs," December 5, 2014, https://www.emarketer.com/Article/Bye-Bye-Cookies Atlas-Tracks-Consumers-Online-Offline-via-Facebook-IDs/1011661. The term is also used by Acxiom (see, for example, its 2017 annual report). On Facebook, see Marshall, "What Marketers Need." On Acxiom's cross-device consumer identifier, see Steel, "Master Profiles."

89. Davenport, *Big Data*, 198; compare Gabrys, *Program Earth*.

90. Kennedy, *Post, Mine, Repeat*; and Zuckerberg, "Original Sin" (Ethan Zuckerberg was himself an inventor of the pop-up ad).

91. Chun, *Programmed Visions*, 27.

92. Gillespie, *Custodians*.

93. IBM, Chairman's Letter, "*Annual Report 2017.*"

94. We generalize here the concept of "tool reversibility" from Couldry and Hepp, *Mediated Construction*, 132. "Tool reversibility" was already anticipated in nineteenth-century workers' analysis of the factory as making the craftsman into "an animated tool of the management" (cited in Braverman, *Labor*, 94). In a broad way, today's critique of tool reversal echoes Illich's critique of modern tools (*Tools*, 34–37) and Marx's account of humankind's alienation from their productive lives under capitalism (*Manuscripts*, 112–13). But there is something distinctly shocking about contemporary smart tools' direct use of their users.

95. On Echo, see Stucke and Ezrachi, "Subtle Ways."

96. Schneier, *Goliath*.

97. Schneier, "Click Here to Control Everyone."

98. Owens, "Stranger Hacks."

99. It is important, however, not to exaggerate the polarity between the so-called "liberal" West and authoritarian "East." There are important interactions underway between Chinese and Western versions of data-driven capitalism, and China increasingly depends on a liberal global trade regime. See Hong, *Networking China*, 6; and Meng, *Politics of Chinese Media*.

100. For discussion, see Creemers, "Cyber China."

101. Gandy, *Panoptic Sort*.

102. Fourcade and Healy, "Like a Market."

103. Gillespie, *Custodians*, 18–19.

104. For the user, this is via the platform's "terms and conditions," for the business user of the data, its application programming interface, or "API"; see Co-

hen, "Biopolitical Public Domain"; and Cohen, *Truth and Power*. On multisided platforms generally, see Nieborg and Poell, "Platformization."

105. Helmond, "Platform Ready."

106. On seamlessness, see Cohen, "What Privacy Is For," 1928. Platforms play a key role in ensuring seamlessness through the "managed continuities" that they construct between multiple actors and data types (Couldry and Hepp, *Mediated Construction*, 200).

107. Helmond ("Platform Ready") calls this "the platformization of the web."

108. Plantin et al., "Infrastructure Studies."

109. For a pioneering analysis, see Gillespie, "Politics of 'Platforms.'"

110. Kirkpatrick, *Facebook Effect*, 144.

111. We acknowledge, of course, that the division between social and technical is murkier in practice and that both sides are more helpfully called "sociotechnical."

112. Moore, *Capitalism*.

113. Zuboff, "Big Other," 79, 81.

114. Phillips, "China Orders GPS Tracking."

115. Yang, "China Pours Millions."

116. As Marx wrote in a manuscript note to *Capital* that Žižek reproduces, "The reduction of different concrete private labours to the abstraction of the true human labour is accomplished only through exchange which effectively posits the products of different labours as equal to each other" (quoted in Žižek, *End Times*, 213).

117. Crain, "Limits of Transparency," 2. See also Skeggs and Yuill, "Capital Experimentation."

118. For naturalization, see Marx, *Capital*, vol. I, 168.

119. For more orthodox recent approaches to Marx and information, see Fuchs and Mosco, *Age of Digital Capitalism*; Fuchs, *Digital Labour*; and Timcke, *Capital, State, Empire*.

120. Marx, *Capital*, vol. I, 951.

121. One respected analyst of people's use of fitness trackers seems to recognize the problem with orthodox Marxism but draws the wrong conclusion, claiming that, while not intuitively labor, such activities *must nonetheless* be understood as *really* labor. He says, "Regardless of how we might like to conceptualize exercise activities that are tracked, they are labor, because the corporations are treating them as such. Surplus value will be extracted from these activities by corporations, as if they were work" (Till, "Exercise as Labour," 452).

122. Marx's term is "condition of production" (*Capital*, vol. I, 950, 952).

123. Lanier, *Who Owns the Future?*; Malgieri and Custers, "Pricing Privacy"; and Tene and Polonetsky, "Big Data for All." Most recently, see Posner and Weyl, *Radical Markets*; and GenerationLibre, *My Data*. We acknowledge that Posner

and Weyl's proposal is part of a wider vision that involves *claiming* platform data practices as labor while rethinking capitalist property relations generally. Our argument starts out more pessimistically, but we also believe more realistically, from the current capitalist drive to treat the human activities that generate data as raw material for production. Being paid for one's data would, in any case, do nothing to address the damage done by the continuous surveillance on which data collection is built (see chapter 5). The same goes for Morozov's proposal for collective ownership of data assets ("After the Facebook Scandal").

124. Contrast the wages-for-housework argument of 1970s and 1980s feminists (Federici, *Wages*, 4; Delphy, *Close to Home*), which had the goal not of commodifying that work but of "denaturalizing" capitalism's wider social relations so as to challenge them for the longer term. So it is today with platforms: the key issue is not securing payment but denaturalizing the abstraction of social relations through data whereby capitalism is able to expand ever deeper into the social world.

125. As Postone ("Rethinking Marx," 7) put it more precisely, the commodity for Marx is a "structured form of social practice that is a structuring principle of the actions, worldviews, and dispositions of people." See also Žižek, *End Times*, chap. 3, especially p. 205.

126. Marx, *Capital*, vol. I, 950.

127. "Only then," Marx writes—that is, when all such things have become commodities—"can it be said that production has become the production of commodities *through its entire length and breadth*" (*Capital*, vol. I, 950, changed emphasis, compare 951, 952).

128. Postone, "Rethinking Marx," 7.

129. An important precedent for this was Jason Moore's insistence that traditional Marxism's account of capitalism be expanded to include the appropriation of "the life-making capacities of human and extra-human nature" (Moore, *Capitalism*, 70–71). As Moore says, "appropriation" represents a productive activity every bit as much as "exploitation" (Moore, *Capitalism*, 70); see further in chapter 2. Here Moore builds on Marx's (*Capital*, vol. I, 954) point that "objectified labor" incorporates into the production process both paid and unpaid labor. Whereas Moore focuses on correcting traditional Marxism's neglect of physical nature's appropriation, our interest is in the appropriation of *human* nature. We acknowledge also that the underlying process of abstraction through datafication may produce effects that seem like "reification" (Bewes, *Reification*). "Reification," however, is a more absolute term, so it is less suitable to capture many overlapping processes of abstraction. People and processes do not need to be made into "things" to be effectively abstracted.

130. We echo here an important theme of environmentalists' recent commentary on Marx's discussion of the "metabolic rift" (Marx, *Capital*, vol. I, 637; for development, see Bellamy, "Metabolic Rift").

131. Respectively, Schiller, *Digital Capitalism*; Castells, *Network Society*; Cohen, *Truth and Power*; Dean, *Neoliberal Fantasies*; Srnicek, *Platform Capitalism*; and Zuboff, "Big Other."

132. Cohen, *Truth and Power*, Chapter 1. Occasionally, where we refer exclusively to capitalism's informational dynamics, we will use the term *informational capitalism* for shorthand.

133. Browne, *Dark Matters*.

134. Foucault, *Biopolitics*; Brown, *Undoing*; Harvey, *History of Neoliberalism*; and Dardot and Laval, *The New Way*.

135. Note that, reflecting perhaps Foucault's own divergence from Marx, commodification has a curious role in Brown's book. It is generally absent as a term, and Brown notes Foucault's dismissal of its importance (Brown, *Undoing*, 66), but it also reappears at certain points, at least as an accompaniment to her main arguments about neoliberalism as a model for valuing the world in economic terms (Brown, *Undoing*, 45). By contrast, Han (*Technologies of Power*) reads neoliberalism as a direct manipulation of the psyche ("psychopolitics"), bypassing questions of social order entirely.

136. A similar point can be made about the term *biopolitics*, which also derives from Foucault's work (see especially Cohen, "Biopolitical Public Domain"). One can read our entire argument as the extension of biopolitics; how could one not, given we argue that capitalism's new goal is the capitalization of *life*? But in our view, the term *biopolitics* puts the emphasis in the wrong place. Yes, "life" is at stake—absolutely and distinctively—in the transformations of data colonialism. But what drives this is not politics—or the goals of government, even in Foucault's extended sense of "governmentality" as "the conduct of conduct" (Lemke, "Michel Foucault's Lecture," 191). What drives this are the fundamentals of economic organization and how capitalism as an extended social form works for the maximization of profit; "*capitali*zation of life" gets the emphasis right.

137. Tronti, *Operai e Capitale*; Terranova, "Free Labor"; Gill and Pratt, "Social Factory"; Hardt and Negri, *Assembly*; Negri, *Marx Beyond Marx*; Lazzarato, *Signs*; and Berardi, *Soul at Work*.

138. As Gill and Pratt ("Social Factory," 7, emphasis added) put it, "From [the social factory] perspective *labour* is deterritorialized, dispersed and decentralized so that 'the whole society is placed at the disposal of profit.'" Negri, *Marx Beyond Marx*, 1992, 79. Marazzi (*Capital and Language*, 50, emphasis added) analogously argues that "today the capitalist organization *of work* aims to . . . fuse work and worker, to put *to work* the entire lives of workers."

139. Compare Caffentzis, "Immeasurable Value?" Neither Berardi nor Lazzarato say anything in detail about data relations, except to assimilate them into the general reading of the social factory.

140. Autonomists draw on Marx's early notebooks and single out his comments there about the role that human beings' general productive and creative capacity (the "general intellect") can play in the development of capitalism (for a more popular version of this argument, see Mason, *Postcapitalism*, 164–67). Autonomists propose that, as humans become increasingly part of the social factory, particularly online, they become able to turn their creativity against capitalism. But Marx's words even in the *Grundrisse* were more ambiguous: "The development of fixed capital indicates to what degree general social knowledge has become *a direct force of production*, and to what degree, hence, the conditions of the process of social life itself have come under the control of the general intellect and been transformed in accordance with it" (*Grundrisse*, 706, emphasis added). If by "the general intellect" we mean the organizational and creative power within capitalism (think of Google's leadership), then Marx's comment allows for a radically different conclusion from that which the Autonomists draw: "the general intellect" might be the means for capitalism to *appropriate* social life. For other critiques of the Autonomist reading of Marx, see Postone, "Rethinking Marx"; Heinrich, "Crisis Theory"; and Pitts, "Beyond the Fragment." For important perspectives on labor, see Freedman in Curran, Fenton, and Freedman, *Misunderstanding*, 95–121; Hesmondhalgh and Baker, "Creative Work"; and Skeggs and Yuill, "Capital Experimentation." Our reading is also more consistent with Marx's later reading of how commodification transforms the whole of social life *for* capitalism (Postone, "Rethinking Marx"). Braverman writes that "every line Marx wrote on this subject makes it clear that he did not expect from capitalism or from science and machinery as used by capitalism, no matter how complex they become, any general increase in the technical scope, scientific knowledge, or broadening of the competence of the worker, and that he in fact expected the opposite" (*Labor*, 160).

141. Hardt and Negri, *Assembly*.

142. For example, our searches' input to Google's PageRank algorithm (Hardt and Negri, *Assembly*, 169).

143. As they put it, "Exploit yourself, capital tells productive subjectivities, and they respond, we want to valorize ourselves, govern the common that we produce" (Hardt and Negri, *Assembly*, 123).

144. Hardt and Negri, *Assembly*, 169.

Chapter 2

1. Timoner, *We Live in Public*.

2. Using figures from 2017, calculations were performed by dividing the market capitalization (the market value of a company's outstanding shares) by the number of users. Market caps and approximate user numbers on December 29, 2017, were as follows: Alphabet—$731.90B, 2B users; Facebook—$512.76B, 2.2B users; and Alibaba—$727.04B, 488M users.

3. Hannam, "Chinese Giant." The market value for Tencent was $519 billion in November 2017, and the number of users in quarter 2 of that year was 963 million. There was a 25 percent fall in the value of their stock in the first half of 2018, however. Regardless of these adjustments, the fact remains that each of these companies benefits greatly from each of their users.

4. Cohen, "Every Move."

5. Kaye, "Data Business."

6. Wallerstein, *Historical Capitalism*.

7. Cowen, *Life of Logistics*, 8.

8. Rossiter, *Software*, xv.

9. Stern, *Company-State*.

10. Wallerstein, *Historical Capitalism*.

11. Piketty, *Capital*; and Pfeffer and Schoeni, "Wealth Inequality."

12. Marx believed technological advances are always making production more efficient, which in turn lowers costs and makes it more difficult for capitalists to maximize profit. Periodical crises can restore some degree of profitability by allowing successful corporations to absorb the resources of failing corporations. The problem, according to some theorists, is that recent government bailouts are preventing that process from fully unfolding. There is a diversity of opinions on this topic: Kliman, *Failure of Capitalist Production*; Carchedi and Roberts, "Roots of the Present Crisis"; and Carchedi, "Crisis of Profitability?" argue that Marx's law of the tendential fall of the return of profit (LTFRP) along with other factors such as government bailout of banks and corporations, are responsible for recent economic woes; Basu and Vasudevan ("The Rate of Profit"); and Duménil and Lévy (*Crisis of Neoliberalism*) find weak evidence of the decline of profits or its impact on recent economic crises. See also Heartfield, "Book Review," for a critique of Kliman from a Marxist perspective.

13. Arvidsson, "Facebook and Finance."

14. Mosco, *To the Cloud*.

15. Mejias, *Off the Network*.

16. Foucault, *The Order of Things*.

17. For the original occurrence, see Mejias, *Off the Network*. Subsequent applications of the concept include Posner and Weyl, *Radical Markets*; Arrieta Ibarra et al., "Should We Treat Data as Labor?"; Mosco, *Becoming Digital*; and Lanier, *Ten Arguments*.

18. Taplin, *Move Fast*, 81.

19. Manning, *Monopsony in Motion*.

20. Pitts, "Beyond the Fragment."

21. Sandvig, "Anti-Television," 237.

22. Mejias, *Off the Network*.

23. Hunegnaw, *The Future of User-Generated Content*.

24. Harvey, *The New Imperialism*, 74.

25. Zuboff, "Big Other"; Cohen, "Biopolitical Public Domain"; and Sassen, *Expulsions*.

26. Stern, *Company-State*.

27. Parks and Starosielski, *Signal Traffic*, 12.

28. Maxwell and Miller, *Greening the Media*, 93.

29. It is estimated that data centers will use 3 to 13 percent of all global electricity by the year 2030, compared to the 1 percent they used in 2010. Water is another resource gobbled up by data centers. The surveillance facility constructed by the National Security Agency in the United States, the third largest on the planet, consumes 1.7 million gallons of water daily to operate its servers. Maxwell and Miller, *Greening the Media*, 95, 104; and Velkova, "Data That Warms," 4.

30. Meanwhile, the tons of electronic waste generated by the Cloud Empire's infrastructure accumulate in the poorest communities, endangering life. By 2007, 80 percent of electronic waste had been exported to Asia, Africa, and Latin America, where populations near dump sites have seen an increase in brain damage, deterioration of vital organs, and disrupted development in children. Half a million computers from the Global North are dumped every month in Nigeria alone, three quarters of which end up in toxic-waste dumps (Maxwell and Miller, *Greening the Media*, 95). For more recent statistics, see the work of the Basel Action Network, www.ban.org.

31. Qiu, *iSlave*.

32. Chen, "Laborers."

33. Sallomi and Lee, "Predictions."

34. Rossiter, *Software*, 20.

35. IBM, *Annual Report*.

36. Statista, "Amazon: Statistics and Facts," accessed February 5, 2018, https://www.statista.com/topics/846/amazon/.

37. Mitchell, "Infrastructure of Our Economy."

38. Wu, *Attention Merchants*, 335.

39. For an overview of these critiques, see Wikipedia Contributors, "Criticism of Apple Inc." accessed February 5, 2018, https://en.wikipedia.org/w/index.php?title=Criticism_of_Apple_Inc.

40. Rhode, "Biggest Innovation."

41. For an overview of these critiques, see Wikipedia Contributors, "Criticism of Facebook," accessed February 7, 2018, https://en.wikipedia.org/w/index.php?title=Criticism_of_Facebook.

42. Global Voices, "Can Facebook Connect?"

43. All figures come from Google's own corporate reports.

44. Krazit, "Public Cloud."

45. Schiller, *Digital Depression*, 81–82.

46. Turow, *Aisles Have Eyes*.

47. IHS Markit, "Internet of Things: A Movement, Not a Market." 2017. https:// ihsmarkit.com/Info/1017/internet-of-things.html.

48. Khatchadourian, "We Know."

49. Christl and Spiekermann, "Networks of Control," 82–83.

50. *Congressional Testimony: What Information Do Data Brokers Have on Consumers, and How Do They Use It?, Statement of Pam Dixon before the Senate Comm. on Commerce, Science, and Transportation*, 113th Cong., 1st sess. (December 18, 2013), https://www.worldprivacyforum.org/2013/12/testimony-what-information -do-data-brokers-have-on-consumers/.

51. Strandburg, "Monitoring, Datafication," 29.

52. DLA Piper, "Data Protection Laws"; and Frontier Technology, "The Differences between EU and US Data Laws," October 12, 2015, http://www.frontier technology.co.uk/about-us/news/differences-between-eu-and-us-data-laws/.

53. Sarkhel and Alawadhi, "How Data Brokers Are Selling."

54. *The Economist*, "In China, Consumers Are Becoming More Anxious about Data Privacy," January 25, 2018.

55. Kurt Opsahl and Rainey Reitman, "The Disconcerting Details: How Facebook Teams Up with Data Brokers to Show You Targeted Ads," Electronic Frontier Foundation, April 22, 2013, https://www.eff.org/deeplinks/2013/04/disconcerting -details-how-facebook-teams-data-brokers-show-you-targeted-ads; and Rai, "Acxiom Shares."

56. Kofman, "Body Camera Videos." See chapter 3 for a fuller discussion.

57. Identity Theft Resource Center, *Data Breach Year-End Review*.

58. The value that the information and communication technologies (ICT) sector contributes to national gross domestic product (GDP) reveals relatively small figures, which are at odds with the enthusiasm exhibited by market capitalization. This sector (of which the social quantification subsector would only be a subsegment) has added merely 6.8% of value to the US economy in recent years. In a report that pools data for 2006 and 2014 from developed countries in the European Union, North America, and Asia, only Taiwan and South Korea had percentages in excess of 6% (13.3/15.9% and 9.2/8.9%, respectively). Between 1994 and 2014, ICT was only 2.6% of GDP in twenty countries surveyed by the OECD, with an average growth across those countries of 16.7%. In both the United States and the United Kingdom, two supposed leaders of the digital transformation, ICT investment as a percentage of GDP actually fell in this period, to 3.15% and 2.17%, respectively (OECD, "Share of ICT"). As far as the industry's impact on employment rates, it is calculated that worldwide the ICT sector and the consumer electronics sector together employ nearly two hundred million workers, with an-

other two hundred million if we add mining and labor-intensive work (Maxwell and Miller, *Greening the Media*, 106.). This might sound like a lot, but when we isolate the social quantification sector, the overall picture changes. Figures for the year 2000 show that the industries involved in the ICT sector accounted for only 3.9% of employment in the European Union and 4.9% in the United States (Doogan, *New Capitalism?*, 59), with those numbers in fact decreasing over time. According to the OECD report, by 2014 the figure for the European Union had gone down to 2.5%, and the report identifies only Taiwan as showing an employment rate in this sector above 10%. A look at how many full-time employees were actually employed by social quantification corporations reveals a very small number: Airbnb—1,917 employees in the United States, according to 2016 reports; Apple—approximately 123,000 as of September 2017; Facebook—23,165 as of September 2017; Google (Alphabet)—72,053 as of December 2016 (keeping in mind that half of Google's workers are contractors who don't receive full benefits: cf. Bergen and Eidelson, "Inside Google"); Instagram (a Facebook company)—450 as of January 2017; Snapchat—1,859 as of December 2016; Twitter—approximately 3,860 as of June 2016; and Uber—approximately 12,000 as of June 2017 (all figures comes from corporate websites). It should be noted that both Google and Facebook are adding about 10,000 employees each to act as moderators in the aftermath of the fake news scandal (Naughton, "Dirty Work"). Of course, these figures do not take into account all the workers involved in datafication both inside and outside the social quantification sector, including part-time and freelance workers. But to put things in perspective, Walmart and McDonald's each employ about two million people worldwide. Only Amazon comes close to that magnitude, with 541,900 employees as of October 2017.

59. Statista, "The Leading Companies in the World in 2016, by Net Income."

60. Mejias and Vokuev, "Disinformation and the Media."

61. Samaddar, *Marx and the Postcolonial Age.*

62. NASSCOM, *The IT-BPM Sector.*

63. Dvorak and Saito, "Tech Dominance."

64. Sender and Mundy, "Walmart Nears Deal."

65. *The Economist*, "China's Internet Giants Go Global," April 20, 2017.

66. Greeven and Wei, "China's New Tech Giants."

67. Alibaba Holdings, *Annual Report 2016.*

68. Fan, "How E-Commerce Is Transforming Rural China."

69. Knight, "China's AI Awakening."

70. Sacks, "New China Data Privacy Standard."

71. Denyer, "Beijing Bets on Facial Recognition." Although there are occasional signs of tensions, compare Lopez, "Signs China Is Turning against Alibaba"; and Reuters, "China Chides Tech Firms."

72. Hvistendahl, "China's Vast New Experiment in Social Ranking"; and Botsman, "China Moves to Rate Its Citizens."

73. Bloomberg, "China Uses Facial Recognition"; see also China Security and Protection Industry Association, "Background of the National 'Sharp Eyes.'"

74. Hawkins, "Beijing's Big Brother."

75. Lin and Chin, "Tech Giants."

76. Wallerstein, *Historical Capitalism*, 17.

77. Lardinois, "Google Maps"; and Plantin, "Politics of Mapping."

78. Kücklich, "Michael Jackson and the Death of Macrofame." See also Mejias, *Off the Network*.

79. Taplin, *Move Fast*, 99.

80. Newman, "UnMarginalizing Workers," 24.

81. Heller, "Is the Gig Economy Working?"

82. Smith, "Gig Work."

83. Larmer, "China's Revealing Spin."

84. Smith, "Gig Work."

85. Smith, "On Demand."

86. Field, "Inside the Gig Economy."

87. Elan et al., "Inside the New Gig Economy."

88. Mulcahy, *Gig Economy*.

89. Marx, *Capital*, vol. I, chap. 25.

90. Heller, "Is the Gig Economy Working?"

91. Uber, "Earning/Chilling."

92. Rosenblat and Stark, "Algorithmic Labor," 27.

93. Efrati, "Driver Churn"; and McGee, "Only 4 Percent."

94. Gregg, "Doublespeak."

95. Backer, "Global Panopticism."

96. Fuchs, "Political Economy and Surveillance," 671–87.

97. Fuchs, 678.

98. Newman, "UnMarginalizing Workers," note 34.

99. Newman.

100. Featherstone, *Selling Women Short*.

101. Kaplan, "The Spy."

102. Kanngieser, "Tracking and Tracing," 601.

103. Kaplan, "The Spy."

104. Levy, "Contexts of Control."

105. Kaplan, "The Spy."

106. Moore and Piwek, "Regulating Wellbeing."

107. "Statistics—Work Related Stress, Depression or Anxiety," Health and Safety Executive, 2017, http://www.hse.gov.uk/statistics/causdis/stress/.

108. Cf. Hamblen, "Wearables for Workplace." For a broader discussion, see Lupton, "Domains of Quantified Selves" on "forced self-tracking"; and Rosenblat, Kneese, and Boyd, "Workplace Surveillance."
109. Kaplan, "The Spy," 136.
110. Braverman, *Labor*.
111. Samaddar, *Marx and the Postcolonial Age*, 4–5.
112. Galloway, *The Four*.
113. Brynjolfsson and McAfee, *Machine Age*.
114. Frey and Osborne, "Future of Employment."
115. Vanderzeil, Currier, and Shavel et al., "Retail Automation."
116. Arntz, Gregory, and Zierahn, "Risk of Automation."
117. Acemoglu and Restrepo ("Machine and Man") calculate that adding one robot to every one thousand workers "reduces the employment to population ratio by about 0.18–0.34 percentage points and wages by 0.25–0.5 percent."
118. West, "What Happens."
119. Gandy, *Panoptic Sort*; Peña Gangadharan, "Data Profiling"; Eubanks, *Automating Inequality*; and Noble, *Algorithms of Oppression*.

Interlude: On Colonialism and the Decolonial Turn

1. Dussel, "Eurocentrism."
2. Blaut, *Colonizer's Model*; Wolf, *People without History*; and Young, *Postcolonialism*.
3. Hegel, *Phenomenology*; and Freire, *Pedagogy*.
4. Quijano, "Coloniality of Power," 538.
5. Dussel, "Eurocentrism," 473; and Lugones, "Heterosexualism."
6. Amin, *Le Développement*; and Wolf, *People Without History*.
7. While these features characterize "early" modernity, Giddens suggests that "late" modernity (post-1900) is characterized by capitalism (competitive markets and commodification of labor power), industrialism (use of machinery in production processes and the social relations implied by this), the nation-state and the organization as the dominant social forms, surveillance as a mode of supervision and control of populations, and the creation of an abstract and universal idea of time and space (as opposed to a sense of time and place experienced locally). See Giddens, *Modernity*. The influence of colonialism can also be traced in these characteristics, as argued in the rest of the chapter.
8. Pomeranz, *Great Divergence*.
9. Dussel, "Eurocentrism," 471.
10. Quijano, "Coloniality of Power," 548.
11. Polanyi, *Great Transformation*, 60–61.
12. Quijano, "Coloniality of Power," 537, 550; and Lugones, "Heterosexualism," 191.

13. Quijano, "Coloniality of Power," 373.

14. Wolf, *People Without History*.

15. Beckert and Rockman, *Slavery's Capitalism*, 1.

16. See Blaut, *Colonizer's Model*; Acemoglu, Johnson, and Robinson, "The Rise of Europe"; and Pomeranz, *Great Divergence*. Pomeranz argues that "slavery helped make Euro-American trade unlike any between Old World cores and peripheries" (267) by making "the flow of needed resources to Europe self-catalyzing in ways that consensual trade between Old World regions was not: it anticipated, even before industrialization, the self-perpetuating division of labor between primary products exporters and manufacturing regions in the modern world" (24).

17. Tomich and Zeuske, "Second Slavery," 91.

18. Baptist, "Political Economy," 40.

19. Rosenthal, "Slavery's Scientific Management"; and Baptist, "Political Economy."

20. Tomich and Zeuske, "Second Slavery."

21. Shilliam, "Redemptive Political Economy," 51.

22. Bartley, "Hidden Costs of Computing."

23. Qiu, *iSlave*, 11.

24. Beckert and Rockman, *Slavery's Capitalism*, 1.

25. Sa'di, "Colonialism and Surveillance," 151.

26. Krishna, *Globalization and Postcolonialism*, 66.

27. Maldonado-Torres, "Coloniality of Being."

28. Consistent with our eclectic approach, we are dealing with this field selectively and not including all important thinkers in the area.

29. Krishna, *Globalization and Postcolonialism*, 2.

30. Young, *Postcolonialism*, 4.

31. Bourdieu, *Symbolic Power*.

32. Césaire, *Discourse*, 42; and Memmi, *The Colonizer*.

33. Said, *Orientalism*.

34. Although Said's work has been critiqued for denying agency to the Other (the one who is the object of representation, as opposed to the Self who does the representing) and for somewhat reifying Eurocentrism by situating colonialism as a transhistorical and universalizing force, within postcolonial studies Said opened up avenues for thinking about the historical relationship between knowledge and power and about the specific ways in which colonialism sought to produce "truth" and knowledge, and not just ideology, in order to subjugate. See Yegenoglu, *Colonial Fantasies*.

35. Quijano, "Coloniality of Power," 542.

36. Dussel, "Eurocentrism," 471. See also Fabian, *Time*.

37. Bishop, "Western Mathematics."

38. In response, postcolonial examinations of science and technology have, according to Harding ("Convergences and Dissonances"), encompassed four general areas: (1) they have put forth counterhistories of Western progress, providing a critical reevaluation of their development and impact; (2) they have sought to reclaim and recontextualize non-Western forms of knowledge, which were eradicated or appropriated during colonialism; (3) they have examined the ways in which colonial science and technology continue to shape societies even after their independence; and (4) most importantly, they have promoted the development of alternative science and technology projects using decolonized methodologies, even in the difficult conditions of a neocolonial context. Even mathematics, the ultimate universal discipline, has been deconstructed to show that different cultures have generated mathematical ideas and that it is truly a pancultural phenomenon (Bishop, "Western Mathematics," 72).

39. Adas, *Machines*, 204.

40. Chakrabarty, *Provincializing Europe*.

41. Chakrabarty, 236.

42. Ashcroft, Griffiths, and Tiffin, *Reader*, 356.

43. Santos, *Epistemologies*.

44. To complicate matters, some decolonial thinkers see the debates within postcolonialism as an academic performance that is part of the same cultural logic of capitalism, taking attention away from "authentic" leftist struggles based on class rather than identity. Some might even question the limits of postcolonial theory as critique, pointing out that more than a form of criticism, it has become a routine method that is simply replicated across new contexts and locations (cf. Chibber, *Specter of Capital*, 26; and Krishna, *Globalization and Postcolonialism*, 119).

45. See, for example, Santos, *Epistemologies*; and Maldonado-Torres, "Colonialism, Neocolonial."

46. Grosfoguel, "Epistemic Decolonial Turn," 212.

47. Quijano, "Coloniality of Power."

48. Grosfoguel, "Epistemic Decolonial Turn," 218.

49. Thus failing to truly account for capitalism's structures of exploitation outside the West. Cf. Chibber, *Specter of Capital*.

50. Mignolo, *Darker Side*, 141.

Chapter 3

1. Sardar, Nandy, and Davies, *Barbaric Others*, 3.

2. Owens, "Sid Meier's Colonization."

3. For an extended discussion of coloniality, see Lugones, "Heterosexualism"; Mignolo, "Delinking"; Grosfoguel, "Decolonial Turn"; and Maldonado-Torres, "Coloniality of Being."

4. McKenna and Pratt, *American Philosophy*, 375. For the term's basic context, see the preceding interlude.

5. See Krishna, *Globalization and Postcolonialism*, 9; and Loomba, *Colonialism/Postcolonialism*, 15.

6. See, for example, Lefebvre, *Everyday Life*; and Zaretsky, *Personal Life*. See also the references cited in chapter 1, under the section "Our Argument within the Wider Debate about Data and Capitalism."

7. Polanyi, *Great Transformation*, 44.

8. Scholz, *Uberworked and Underpaid*; Scholz and Schneider, *Ours to Hack and to Own*; and Scholz, *Digital Labor*.

9. See Schiller, *Digital Depression*, 246; Thatcher, O'Sullivan, and Mahmoudi, "Data Colonialism"; Sassen, *Expulsions*; Zuboff, "Big Other," 75–89; and Cohen, "Biopolitical Public Domain."

10. Moore, *Web of Life*.

11. World Economic Forum, *Personal Data*.

12. Haupt, "A Ludicrous Proposition."

13. World Economic Forum, *Personal Data*.

14. Palmer, "Data Is the New Oil."

15. Cohen, "Biopolitical Public Domain."

16. OECD, "Data-Driven," 195–97.

17. Klein, *This Changes Everything*, 103.

18. Acosta, "Extractivismo y Neoextractivismo."

19. In Klein, "Dancing the World."

20. Morozov, "After the Facebook Scandal."

21. Cohen, "Biopolitical Public Domain."

22. Council of Castile, "Requerimiento."

23. Council of Castile, par. 7.

24. Google, "Terms of Service," accessed April 16, 2007, https://tools.google.com/dlpage/res/webmmf/en/eula.html.

25. Van Alsenoy et al., "Advertising Network."

26. Van Dijck, *Culture of Connectivity*.

27. Van Alsenoy et al., "Advertising Network," 16.

28. Van Alsenoy et al., 39, 49.

29. Facebook, "Terms of Service." *Facebook*, January 30, 2015. https://www.facebook.com/terms.php.

30. Obar and Oeldorf-Hirsch, "Biggest Lie."

31. Harris, "Long-Distance Corporations," 61. For a parallel explanation of how modern networks have served the military and economic interests of the ruling class, see Mattelart, *Networking the World*.

32. Harris, "How Did Colonialism Dispossess?," 175.

33. Mejias, *Off the Network*.

34. The purpose of maps has always been to make it possible to locate the most efficient paths of circulation. Colonial expansion was facilitated by the pioneering of mercantile routes that mapped newer and faster channels of commodity exchange, creating wealth for European colonizers and merchants by enabling price differentials based on differential access to the assets that the maps represented (see Wolf, *People without History*, 88).

35. Harris, "Long-Distance Corporations."

36. The knowledge produced through maps and surveys, and collected and analyzed in the metropolis, would eventually contribute to the wider scientific project that could be exported back to the colonies to be diffused through education as further evidence of European superiority. For example, Catholic missionaries would not hesitate to teach scientific concepts to the natives in order to demonstrate the supposed dominance of the Christian God over the heathen beliefs of the locals. The Reverend John Cumming remarked that "we can upset the whole theology of the Hindoo by predicting an eclipse" (Adas, *Machines*, 207). But when the religious connotations of this indoctrination would prove too socially disruptive, secular forms of education could be relied on to spread the colonial ideology to the native ruling classes (Sa'di, "Colonialism and Surveillance," 155).

37. Adas, *Machines*; and Young, *Postcolonialism*.

38. Beniger, *Control Revolution*.

39. Winseck, "Communication and the Sorrows of Empire," 164.

40. Aouragh and Chakravartty, "Infrastructures of Empire."

41. Alhassan and Chakravartty, "Postcolonial Media Policy."

42. Solon, "It's Digital Colonialism."

43. Global Voices, "Can Facebook Connect."

44. For a discussion of the impact of Free Basics, see Couldry and Rodriguez et al., "Chapter 13 on Media and Communications."

45. Tweet by Mark Andreessen (@pmarca), cited in Bowles, "Zuckerberg Chides."

46. Bowen, *Business of Empire*.

47. Adas, *Machines*, 228.

48. Marx, "Watched Trains"; Adas, *Machines*; and Innis, *Pacific Railway*.

49. Beniger, *Control Revolution*.

50. Singha, "Settle, Mobilize, Verify," 157.

51. Adas, *Machines*, 225.

52. Adas, 240.

53. Curran, Fenton, and Freedman, *Misunderstanding the Internet*.

54. Kaplan, "Panopticon in Poona."

55. Singha, "Settle, Mobilize, Verify," 188.

56. Butt, "Algorithmic Governance."
57. Cohen, "Biopolitical Public Domain."
58. Lucas, "Patent Filings."
59. Chun, "China's New Frontiers."
60. Foucault, *Discipline and Punish*.
61. Sa'di, "Colonialism and Surveillance," 154–55.
62. Bratton, *Stack*, 363.
63. Nandy, *Intimate Enemy*, 2, 3.
64. Moore, *Web of Life*, 192.
65. Srnicek, *Platform Capitalism*, 41–42.
66. Smythe, "Audience Commodity."
67. Crocker, "Concept of Exploitation," 205 (our additions in brackets).
68. Murphy, "Exploitation or Exclusion?," 233.
69. Meiksins Wood, "Uses and Abuses."
70. Meiksins Wood, 73.
71. Marx, *Grundrisse*, 694.
72. Meiksins Wood, "Uses and Abuses," 65, 73.
73. Manyika et al., "Digital Globalization."
74. Manyika et al., 11.
75. Weber, "Data, Development, and Growth."
76. Weber, 12.
77. Weber, 18.
78. Data derived from annual reports and industry rankings.
79. Panitch and Gindin, *Global Capitalism*, 289.
80. Dvorak and Saito, "Tech Dominance."
81. See Burri, "Trade Agreements"; Aaronson, "Digital Trade Imbalance"; and Martin and Mayeda, "Amazon Would Gain."
82. Bowman, "Data Localization Laws."
83. Gurumurthy, Vasudevan, and Chami, "Grand Myth."
84. Galeano, *Open Veins*, 33.
85. Galeano, 51.
86. Walton, *Civil Law*. For example, see book IV, title XIX of the Compilations, in particular the first law, which allows all subjects (including Indians) to benefit from the mines, and the fourteenth law, which specifies that Indians can own mines. Nevertheless, the fifteenth law allows Spaniards to "manage" the mines on behalf of the "naturally lazy" Indians, who do not know how to exploit them.
87. All quotes are from the corporate websites of the respective companies. The quote from Airbnb is from blog.atairbnb.com/open-letter-to-the-airbnb-community.

88. Benjamin, *Illuminations*, 253.
89. Harris, "Untimely Mammet." Harris notes that automata such as the Mechanical Turk were referred to as mammets, a word deriving from the proper name Mohamet or Mohammed. He adds that "medieval Christian theologians used the word 'mechanicum' as a synonym for Muslim sorcery: they regarded Islam as a mechanical religion incapable of true life and of a meaningful future, and thus consigned it to a dead, unusable past. Benjamin's Turkish chess-playing machine eerily replays this typological gambit."
90. The cultivation and commercialization of sugar, based on slave labor and the creation of global markets for its consumption, could tell a similar story. See Moore, "Early Modern World-Economy."
91. Lowe, *Intimacies*, 103.
92. Prakash, "East India Company," 14.
93. Max, "SKAM."
94. Dussel, "Eurocentrism," 473.
95. Chatterjee, *Nation and Its Fragments*.
96. Dussel, *Philosophy*.
97. Lowe, *Intimacies*.

Chapter 4

1. Polanyi, *Great Transformation*, 3.
2. Tresata, "Solutions," 2017, http://tresata.com/solutions/.
3. China Copyright and Media, "Artificial Intelligence."
4. Hill, "God View."
5. Polanyi, *Great Transformation*, 74, 60, emphasis added.
6. Polanyi, 44.
7. Polanyi, 79.
8. For discussion, see Fraser, "Triple Movement."
9. Polanyi, *Great Transformation*, 75.
10. For a contrasting account of this process that opposes data knowledge to value extraction, see Cohen, "Biopolitical Public Domain."
11. Drawing on Polanyi, *Great Transformation*, 60.
12. See discussion on "the social" in chapter 1.
13. Halavais, *Search Engine*; and Van Couvering, "Search Engines"; and on the interaction between race and search algorithms, see Noble, *Algorithms*.
14. Van Dijck, *Connectivity*; Bucher, "Imaginary"; Bucher, *If . . .* ; and Gillespie, *Custodians*.
15. boyd and Crawford, "Critical Questions."
16. Pasquale, *Black Box*, 9.
17. Porter, *Trust in Numbers*, 11, 33.

18. Porter, 37.

19. Weber, *Economy and Society*, 975.

20. Hacking, *Social Construction*; and Porter, *Rise of Statistical Reasoning*.

21. The key concept posited by leading French statistician and founder of "social physics," Adolphe Quetelet.

22. Hacking, *Taming of Chance*, 6.

23. Hacking, 2, on the contrasting practices of secret statistics-gathering in France and Germany in the pre-Napoleonic era.

24. Kelman, "Political Foundations," 288.

25. Hacking, *Taming of Chance*, 2.

26. Porter, *Rise of Statistical Reasoning*, 27.

27. Desrosières, *Politics*, 255–61.

28. Desrosières, 261, 277.

29. Desrosières, 323.

30. Rose, *Powers of Freedom*, 130.

31. Rose, *Our Selves*.

32. Bouk, "Economy of Personal Data," 86, 106.

33. See Schulten, *Mapping*, for a parallel US history.

34. Rose, *Powers of Freedom*, 114, 130.

35. Hacking, *Taming of Chance*, chaps. 13 and 20; and Desrosières, *Politics*, 7.

36. Hacking, *Taming of Chance*, 163.

37. Alonso and Starr, *Politics of Numbers*; and Gandy, *Panoptic Sort*.

38. Bouk, *Numbered*.

39. Bouk, 32–33.

40. Porter, *Rise of Statistical Reasoning*, 63–64; and Hacking, *Taming of Chance*, 117–19.

41. Rose, *Powers of Freedom*, 112.

42. Desrosières, *Politics*, 253–60.

43. Porter, *Trust in Numbers*, ix, 34.

44. Bourdieu, *Theory of Practice*. We need more attention to "the social relations that render data mining itself opaque" (Andrejevic, Hearn, and Kennedy, "Introduction," 84).

45. Largest shares of global media ad spend were in 2016: United States (35.6%), China (14.5%), Japan (6.6%), United Kingdom (4.5%), and Germany (3.9%), with Brazil at 2.6% and India at 1.3%. eMarketer, "Worldwide Ad Spending: EMarketer's Updated Estimates and Forecast for 2015–2020," October 26, 2016, https://www.emarketer.com/Report/Worldwide-Ad-Spending-eMarketers-Updated-Estimates-Forecast-20152020/2001916.

46. Starr and Corson, "Rise of the Statistical Services."

47. Dorling, "Ending the National Census."

48. Schneier, *Goliath*, 92. See also McChesney, *Digital Disconnect*, 162.

49. Turow, *Daily You*; and O'Neil, *Weapons*.

50. Schiller, *Digital Depression*, especially p. 30, citing Barnet and Müller, *Global Reach*.

51. Wu, *Attention Merchants*.

52. Starr and Corson, "Rise of the Statistical Services," 446.

53. Opacity is a complex area (Ananny and Crawford, "Limitations of the Transparency Ideal"; and Selbst and Barocas, "Inscrutable Systems"), but the overall point stands. See Gillespie, *Custodians*, 198–99.

54. Cohen, *Networked Self*.

55. Pasquale, *Black Box*, 2.

56. Scott, *Seeing*, 2.

57. Gurumurthy, "Big Brother."

58. China's goal is to be "the world's leading AI innovation centre by 2030" (China Copyright and Media, "Artificial Intelligence Plan").

59. Amoore and Piotukh, "Little Analytics," 35.

60. For a useful explanation of Machine Learning, see Posner and Weyl, *Radical Markets*, 213–20.

61. As Vaidhyanathan puts it, data analytics generate not so much a panopticon as a cryptopticon (*Anti-Social Media*, 67).

62. Anderson, "End of Theory." For an early critique of Anderson, see Andrejevic, *Infoglut*.

63. Mayer-Schönberger and Cukier (*Big Data*, 61, note 10) appear to endorse this.

64. Brennan-Marquez, "Plausible Cause," 1287.

65. Khosla et al., "Looking Beyond"; and Gebru et al., "Car Detection."

66. Sandvig, "'Not Our Fault' Study."

67. Denyer, "China's Watchful Eye"; and Yang and Yang, "Smile to Enter."

68. Other constraints, such as the capacities and willingness of the reserve army of human piece-workers who adjust the automated system's early attempts to sort and code unstructured data, are generally treated as below the line and so as not affecting the proxy's validity for knowledge. See Gray and Suri, *Ghost Work*.

69. Brayne, "Big Data Surveillance," 20.

70. Rouvroy, "End(s) of Critique," 143.

71. Grosser, "What Do Metrics Want?"

72. From the Mindshare media and marketing agency, cited in PricewaterhouseCoopers, "Wearable Future," 42.

73. This is the large-scale correlate of how the "personalized" results that individuals receive when they search the online world are skewed by Google's back-

ground calculations of what "someone like them" would want to see. Feuz, Fuller, and Stalder, "Personal Web Searching."

74. Hal Varian, Google's chief economist, makes that clear in a much-quoted paper (Varian, "Beyond Big Data").

75. Schneier, *Goliath*, 1.

76. "Un moulage auto-déformant." Deleuze, "Postscript," 179; and see translator's note at 202–3.

77. PricewaterhouseCoopers, "Wearable Future," cited in Turow, *Aisles Have Eyes*, 226.

78. Martin, *Habit*, 247, cited by Nadler and McGuigan, "Impulse to Exploit," 2.

79. Hannes Sjöblad, founder of Bionyfiken, quoted in Ma, "Thousands of People."

80. Hacking, *Social Construction*. Compare Espeland and Sauder, "Rankings."

81. Cheney-Lippold, *We Are Data*.

82. Cohen, "Biopolitical Public Domain," 9.

83. Yeung, "Hypernudge," 121.

84. "If the recorded individual has come into full view, the recording individual has faded into the background, arguably to the point of extinction" (Fourcade and Healy, "Like a Market," 11).

85. Day, *Indexing*, 10.

86. Day, 60; and see Cheney-Lippold, *We Are Data*.

87. Gerlitz ("What Counts") calls this an adjustment to the platforms' "backend grammatization" (28).

88. Gerlitz and Helmond, "Like Economy."

89. Pokémon Go was developed by Niantic, formerly a lab of Google.

90. Cohen, "Surveillance—Innovation Complex"; and Kristina Knight, cited in Turow, *Aisles Have Eyes*, 161. See, generally, Whitson, "Quantified Self."

91. http://www.oracle.com/webfolder/ux/Applications/uxd/assets/sites/gamificaiton/index.html, cited in Christl and Spiekermann, "Networks of Control," 61–62.

92. Kazmin, "Indians Sound Alarm."

93. Cohen, "Biopolitical Public Domain," 9, 21.

94. Haggerty and Ericson, "Surveillant Assemblage."

95. Alaimo and Kallinikos, "Computing the Everyday," 186.

96. Gomez-Uribe, "Global Approach."

97. Adapting the language of Zittrain, *Future of the Internet*.

98. Eubanks, *Automating Inequality*, 5.

99. Desrosières, *Politics*, 101. Cf. Zuboff, "Big Other" on the "reality business."

100. Sandvig, "Anti-Television," 234.

101. For an excellent review of how this vision is accumulated by Austrian privacy experts, see Christl and Spiekermann, "Networks of Control."

102. Turow, *Aisles Have Eyes*, 202.

103. Wissinger, "Blood, Sweat, and Tears."

104. Iyengar and Rayport, "Like Software."

105. Turow, *Aisles Have Eyes*, 179, 180, 185.

106. Alexa, for example, gives the user the opportunity to empty the archive but at the risk of "degrading" the service. Wikipedia Contributors, "Amazon Alexa," accessed February 26, 2018, https://en.wikipedia.org/w/index.php?title=Amazon_Alexa&oldid=828449372. For US privacy concerns, see Manikonda, Deotale, and Kambhampati, "What's Up with Privacy?"

107. Chung et al., "Alexa."

108. Didžiokaitė, Saukko, and Greiffenhagen, "Beyond the Metaphor," 9.

109. Lupton, "Domains of Quantified Selves," 1.

110. China Copyright and Media, "Artificial Intelligence."

111. Gurumurthy, "Big Brother."

112. Investor quoted by Weise, "Will a Camera."

113. Quote from Tashea, "Should the Public," cited in Joh, "Influence of Surveillance," 119.

114. This is the area one of us has called "real social analytics." Couldry, Fotopoulou, and Dickens, "Real Social Analytics."

115. Kennedy, *Post, Mine, Repeat*, 223.

116. Schneier, *Goliath*, 27–28, discussed in Christl and Spiekermann, "Networks of Control," 83.

117. Christl and Spiekermann, "Networks of Control," 54–55.

118. From Progressive, "Snapshot Means BIG Discounts for Good Drivers," November 16, 2017. https://www.progressive.com/auto/discounts/snapshot.

119. Jais, "Insuring Shared Value."

120. Rainie and Duggan ("Privacy and Information," 4) found that 55 percent of the US population surveyed would reject a thermostat that collected "basic" data about activities in their house in return for regulating the house's temperature efficiently.

121. Bradley, Barbier, and Handler, "Internet of Everything."

122. For the internet of "medical things," see Topol, *Patient Will See You*; for the internet of "services," see Ward, "Internet of Services."

123. Adelman, "Identity of Things."

124. Cited in Christl and Spiekermann, "Networks of Control," 71, emphasis added.

125. Mosco, *Becoming*, 106.

126. Klein, *This Changes*, 170.

127. Rieder, "PageRank."

Notes to Chapter 4

128. Rieder, "PageRank"; and Rieder and Röhle, "Digital Methods," 121–23. Compare Rieder, "Paradox of Diversity," on "accounting realism."

129. For earlier phases of this history, see Turner, *Democratic Surround*; and Streeter, *Net Effect*.

130. Quoted in Van Dijck, *Connectivity*, 67.

131. The Zuckerberg Files, "D8 All Things Digital."

132. The Zuckerberg Files, "F8 2011 Keynote."

133. Hoffman, Proferes, and Zimmer, "Construction of Facebook and Its Users."

134. Mayer-Schönberger and Cukier, *Big Data*, 96.

135. See e.g. Bilbao-Osorio, Dutta, and Lanvin, *Technology Report 2014*.

136. MIT Technology Review, "Social Physics." For an interesting account of the relations between the broader history of "social physics" and the nineteenth-century origins of Big Data's assumptions of an isomorphism between natural and social worlds, see Barnes and Wilson, "Big Data."

137. Pentland, *Social Physics*, 6–7.

138. Pentland, 8, 14, 220.

139. Pentland, 14, 57–59, 194, 199.

140. Pentland, 8, 122.

141. As Annette Rouvroy puts it, the knowledge about "society" that data generates arrives as an "always already given" feature of the "digitally recorded world" (Rouvroy, "End(s) of Critique," 147). Compare Rieder, "Paradox of Diversity," 42, 43.

142. Thaler and Sunstein, *Nudge*, 5, 76–77.

143. For critiques using Foucault's concept of "governmentality," see Hull, "Successful Failure"; McMahon, "Behavioral Economics"; Pykett, "New Neuros"; and Wright and Ginsburg, "Behavioral Law and Economics."

144. Sunstein, "Ethics of Nudging"; and Yeung, "Hypernudge," especially p. 122. For a philosophical anticipation of the hypernudge idea, see Stiegler's discussion of "social engineering" via "the grammatisation of the social relation itself" ("Relational Ecology," 13), discussed by Gehl, "What's on Your Mind?"

145. Kahneman, *Fast and Slow*. Some interpretative sociologists have challenged the idea that individual economic calculations are irrational and are reinterpreting them not in terms of numbers but of the complex moral relations in which economic transactions are in fact embedded (Zelizer, *Economic Lives*, discussed in Wherry, "Relational Accounting"). Yet the rise of behavioral economics continues unimpeded. For a lively if controversial critique, see Shaw, "Invisible Manipulators."

146. Nadler and McGuigan, "Impulse to Exploit," 7; compare Padios, "Mining the Mind" on "emotional extraction."

147. Quoted in Lewis, "What If He's Right?," 30.

148. See, for example, Camerer, Loewenstein, and Prelec, "Neuroscience."
149. Camerer, "Neuroeconomics," C28, emphasis added.
150. For critique, see McMahon, "Behavioral Economics."
151. Ariely and Berns, "Neuromarketing." We also found inspiring a paper by Oscar Gandy and Selena Nemorin, "Political Economy of Nudge."
152. Murphy, Illes, and Reiner, "Neuroethics."
153. Singh and Rose, "Biomarkers."
154. See, for example, Arora et al., "Visual Concept Detectors," 1. For critiques of the original "Mind as Machine" argument, see Weizenbaum, *Computer Power*; and Edelman, *Bright Air*. For a broad account of how models of the computer "mind" in the "cyborg sciences" destabilized economics' model of rationality, see Mirowski, *Machine Dreams*. For the origins of the metaphor of computer processing as "neural nets," see Chun, *Programmed Visions*, 140–43.
155. For an exception in philosophy, see Berker, "Insignificance of Neuroscience." For a general defense of the "Enlightenment" conception of the rational subject against misreadings of the new psychology, see Pinker, *Enlightenment Now*.
156. Latour, *Pandora's Hope*, 192.
157. Other examples are "noopolitics" and "affect." For helpful reflections on the ambiguity of the tradition from Tarde that underlies the concept of noopolitics (or noopower), see Terranova, "Attention, Economy and the Brain." For an important critique of "affect" theory, see Leys, "Critique." See also Andrejevic, *Infoglut*, chaps. 3 and 8.
158. Halpern, *Beautiful Data*, 84, cited in Beer, *Metric Power*, 115.
159. Eubanks, *Automating Inequality*, 168.
160. https://www.fatml.org/; the Auditing Algorithms project run by University of Michigan, https://www.si.umich.edu/node/15002; and the Algorithmic Justice League run at MIT, https://www.ajlunited.org/.
161. See, for example, Barocas and Selbst, "Disparate Impact"; O'Neil, *Weapons*; and Cheney-Lippold, *We Are Data*.
162. Angwin and Parris, "Advertisers Exclude Users."
163. ACLU, "Judge Allows ACLU Case Challenging Law Preventing Studies on 'Big Data' Discrimination to Proceed," April 2, 2018, https://www.aclu.org/news/judge-allows-aclu-case-challenging-law-preventing-studies-big-data-discrimination-proceed.
164. Sandvig et al., "When the Algorithm," 4975; and Fourcade and Healy, "Classification Situations," 61.
165. Brayne, "Big Data Surveillance," 16.
166. Bowker and Star, *Sorting Things Out*, 1.
167. Neyland and Möllers, "IF . . . THEN"; and Ananny, "Ethics of Algorithms."
168. O'Neil, *Weapons*, 10. See, generally, Gandy, *Panoptic Sort*, 15.

169. Crawford, "Trouble with Bias."

170. McIntyre and Pegg, "Council Algorithms."

171. PR Newswire, "Two Acquisitions"; and Brayne, "Big Data Surveillance."

172. Brauneis and Goodman, "Algorithmic Transparency," 31.

173. Joh, "Influence of Surveillance," 125.

174. Dressel and Farid, "Limits of Predicting Recidivism."

175. Brauneis and Goodman, "Algorithmic Transparency," 5, 18.

176. Greene and Patterson, "The Trouble with Trusting AI"; Joh, "Policing by Numbers," 67.

177. For a broader critique of the use of algorithms in the management of everyday life, see Greenfield, *Radical Technologies*.

178. Brennan-Marquez, "Plausible Cause."

179. Chief Justice Zhou Qiang, quoted in Xu, "Chinese Judicial Justice," 62.

180. Espeland, "Narrating Numbers," 56, cited in Beer, *Metric Power*, 79.

181. Chun, *Updating to Remain*, 56.

182. Madden et al., "Privacy," 63; on poor mothers in the United States, see Bridges, *Poverty*.

183. See Bartlett and Tkacz, "Governance by Dashboard," on national government; and Kitchin and McArdle, "City Dashboards," on city government.

184. For the first, see Snap Inc., "Terms of Services" (last modified September 26, 2017, https://www.snap.com/terms/); for the second, see O'Neil, *Weapons*; and Brauneis and Goodman, "Algorithmic Transparency."

185. Elkin-Koren and Haber, "Governance by Proxy."

186. Amoore, *Politics of Possibility*.

187. Crawford et al., "Problem with Bias"; and Fourcade and Healy, "Classification Situations," 570. For a vivid example of how racially shaped input data (general referrals to social services) can distort a well-meaning attempt at an algorithmic warning system against actual child-abuse risk, see Eubanks, *Automating Inequality*, 153–55.

188. Ananny and Crawford, "Limitations of the Transparency Ideal."

189. Fourcade and Healy, "Classification situations," 566.

190. Meanwhile, the social quantification sector claims to champion voice: "10 years from now, people will look at the net effect of being able to connect online and have a voice and share what matters to them as just a massively positive thing in the world" (Zuckerberg in Klein, "Facebook's Hardest Year"). Compare Airbnb's statement that "we characterize data as the voice of our users at scale" (Williams et al., "Democratizing Data").

191. Couldry, *Why Voice Matters*.

192. Jerome, "Buying and Selling," 51, quoted by Madden et al., "Privacy," 65n57.

193. For a brilliant assessment of the situation in the United States, see Madden et al., "Privacy," 66, 79–113.

194. Barocas and Selbst, "Disparate Impact," 707–12.

195. Madden et al., "Privacy," 77, 81.

196. Pogge, *Politics as Usual*.

197. Amaya, *Citizenship Excess*, 62–63.

198. Noble, *Algorithms*.

199. On "savage sorting," see Sassen, *Expulsions*, 4; and compare David Lyon's prophetic book, *Surveillance as Social Sorting*. Douglas Merrill, quoted in Peppet, "Regulating the Internet of Things," 87.

200. Greenfield, *Radical Technologies*.

201. Daniel Doctoroff, CEO of Sidewalk Labs, quoted in Bozikovic, "Google's Sidewalk Labs."

202. Agre, "Two Models."

203. Leslie, "The Scientist."

204. Walmart, *Annual Report 2017*, 9.

205. Fraser, "Global Justice."

206. Leslie, "The Scientist," 9. For the Truth about Tech campaign, see https://www.commonsensemedia.org/digital-well-being#.

Chapter 5

1. Quoted in Levy, "Contexts of Control," 166.

2. Wood, *Ethical Thought*, 51.

3. Agre, "Not a Barcode."

4. Other writers who are starting to question this include Foer (*World without Mind*, 200), on big tech's threat to "autonomy"; Lanier, *Ten Arguments*, especially argument one; Taplin, *Move Fast*, chap. 11; Wu, *Attention Merchants*, 351, 353; and Frischmann and Seliger, *Reengineering*, especially pp. 227–28 on the "degeneration of autonomy into simple stimulus-response behaviour."

5. Quoted in Beattie, "Data Protectionism."

6. Quoted in Levy, "Contexts of Control," 166.

7. Wilson, "Wearables in the Workplace."

8. Pinkard, *Naturalism*, 117, 118, 148.

9. Jean-Francois Lyotard, in a book that noted the rise of information technologies and data, hinted at this possibility already in 1991: "What if what is 'proper' to human kind were to be inhabited by the inhuman" (Lyotard, *Inhuman*, 2)?

10. For a discussion of different more or less minimal notions of autonomy, see Yeung, "Choice Architecture." A strong notion of autonomy as self-control might be vulnerable to the argument that we already *know* there is a degree of arbitrariness in our so-called "inner" selves, a point that both Nietzsche and Freud

developed. True, it can be argued, following Ricoeur (*Freud and Philosophy*), that the point of psychoanalysis was to expand the domain of what, finally, is open to interpretation *as one's own* within the process of the self (compare also Honneth, *I in We*, chap. 11). But our argument depends only on defending the minimal integrity of the self, so it does not need to defend the stronger form of autonomy that is vulnerable to this possible line of attack.

11. Rössler, *Value*, 53.

12. For the relation between autonomy and privacy, see Rössler, *Value*, 9–10: "Autonomy can only be lived in all its aspects and articulated in all its senses with the help of the conditions of privacy and by means of rights and claims to privacy."

13. Clarke, "Dataveillance."

14. "The target often emerges from the data" (Eubanks, *Automating Inequality*, 122).

15. Against this, see Nissenbaum, *Privacy in Context*, 22; and Elmer, *Profiling Machines*, 5. But for counterpositions (close to our own) that defend the term *surveillance*, see Cohen, "Biopolitical Public Domain"; Richards, "Dangers of Surveillance"; Schneier, *Goliath*; and Zuboff, "Big Other."

16. Two writers independently draw here on Polanyi's account of "fictional commodities" (*Great Transformation*, 75–80): Cohen, "Biopolitical Public Domain;" and Zuboff, "Big Other."

17. We do not therefore deny that property-based arguments (for example, legal fictions of ownership) can be developed that *might* support privacy and autonomy; for an interesting US argument along these lines, see Fairfield, *Owned*. There are also proposals for developing, even within the big-tech industry, some form of personal data portability; see the Data Transfer Project sponsored by Google, Microsoft, and Twitter, at https://datatransferproject.dev and http://data portability.org. See also Tim Berners-Lee's proposal for a new web infrastructure that would support data portability: https://solid.inrupt.com. But for caution against this type of argument, see Gurumurthy and Vasudevan, "Societal Need."

18. We borrow here the notion of "settling" on a course of action from Steward, *Metaphysics for Freedom*.

19. Hegel, *Elements*, 54, par. 22.

20. Compare Ivan Illich's notion of conviviality as "individual freedom realized in personal independence" (*Tools*, 25) and Arturo Escobar's call for "a reconceptualization of autonomy precisely as an expression of radical interdependence" (*Designs*, 21).

21. Dussel, *Philosophy*, 158.

22. For commentary on the US legal situation, see Peppet, "Regulating the Internet of Things"; and Federal Trade Commission, *Staff Report*. We discuss the emerging new data regulation later in the chapter; meanwhile, note the begin-

nings of US state regulation of the largely unregulated data broker sector (Coldewey, "Vermont Passes").

23. For recent examples, see Parikka, *Insect Media*, in media theory; and DeLanda, *New Philosophy*, in social theory. The fascination goes far back in literature to Virgil's bees simile in Book Four of the *Georgics* and to Mandeville's *Fable of the Bees*. Note, however, that Thomas Hobbes based his political philosophy in *Leviathan* on insisting that human beings are *not* like bees and ants because they "are continually in competition for Honour and Dignity" (*Leviathan*, 225).

24. Floridi, Fourth Revolution.

25. Kelly, *Technology Wants*, 12, 187.

26. Du Bois, *Souls*.

27. Compare Dussel, *Philosophy*, 113: "The only free being that has a world is the other."

28. We recall here Agamben's highly provocative notion of "bare life" (*Homo Sacer*).

29. Levy, "Contexts of Control." Generally, see Madden et al., "Privacy," 60.

30. Weil, *Fissured Workplace*; and Braverman, *Labor*. For interesting recent work on how this plays in the context of domestic work, see Ticona and Mateescu, "Domestic Workers."

31. Turow, Hennessy, and Draper, *Tradeoff Fallacy*.

32. Madden and Rainie, "Attitudes about Privacy." Compare Lee and Duggan, "Privacy and Information." See also Turow, *Aisles Have Eyes*.

33. Reported in FT Confidential Research, "Data Worry."

34. We draw here on philosopher Paul Ricoeur's (*Oneself as Another*) reflections on the self and otherness that build on the distinction between the Latin words *ipse* (meaning "self") and *idem* (meaning "the same").

35. Kurzweil, *Singularity*, 389.

36. The first two quotes are from Pippin, *Practical Philosophy*, 4–5; the last is from Pinkard, *Naturalism*, 118. For a recent reading of Hegel that tries to restore his status as a radical thinker of social transformation, see Honneth, *Freedom's Right*. For an argument within postcolonial theory, that it is important not to abandon but to reassemble what can still be used within modern Western philosophy, particularly Hegel, see Lowe, *Intimacies*, 147, 175.

37. DeLillo, *Zero K.*, 239. DeLillo's reference to Big Data is made in passing; for novels that focus exclusively on autonomy/privacy and the internet, see Flannery, *I Am No One*; and Kobek, *I Hate the Internet*.

38. Marx, *Manuscripts*, 112.

39. Dussel, *Philosophy*, 112, and compare 158.

40. For recent discussion, see Neff and Nafus, *Self-Tracking*, chap. 2; and Lupton, *Quantified Self*, chap. 5.

41. Cohen, "Privacy," 1912. Compare Joel Reidenberg: "Data privacy is a societal value and a requisite element of democracy," quoted in Solove, *Understanding Privacy*, 179.

42. Skinner, "Historic Overview," emphasis in original. Compare US justice Sonia Sotomayor's remark that "awareness that the Government may be watching chills associational and expressive freedoms"; cited by Joh, "Policing by Numbers."

43. Compare Nissenbaum, "Deregulating Collection," 8.

44. For a novel that reflects on this, see Flannery, *I Am No One*.

45. Eggers's novel is only the latest in a long line of imaginative critiques of corporate life, starting perhaps with Kafka, but it gains a particular force by having been written in San Francisco, close to the physical location of the power appropriations and work cultures that Eggers dissects. China's data platforms have yet to attract a novelistic treatment.

46. Eggers, *The Circle*, 187.

47. Rössler, *Value*, 146.

48. Fried, *Anatomy of Values*, 144.

49. Quoted in Lin and Chin, "Tech Giants."

50. Altman, "Privacy Regulation"; and Prosser, "Privacy." Counterarguments are unconvincing. For example, Richard Posner relies on a curiously postmodern relativism about privacy, repeating the crude myth that "primitive people have little privacy" and ignoring even the evidence he cites that suggests that where spatial privacy is scarce, people evolve linguistic means to protect the space of the self. See especially Posner, "Right of Privacy," 402. Once again, this argument can be defended not only for human beings but for all complex animals whose environment (in German, *umwelt*) is focused around the space of "critical distance" from other species members from which all its movements start; see Von Uexküll, *Animals and Humans*; and Hediger, *Man and Animal*, cited in Hildebrandt, "Balance or Trade-Off?," 365.

51. Lyon, *After Snowden*, 92. See, more generally, Solove, *Understanding Privacy*; Cohen, "Privacy"; and Schneier, *Goliath*.

52. Quoted by Pippin, *Practical Philosophy*, 186, from Hegel's *Encyclopedia* (the book on *Science of Logic*). Compare Hegel, *Elements*, 42, discussed in Wood, *Ethical Thought*, 45–51.

53. Hegel, *Elements*, 73, par. 41, discussed in Wood, *Ethical Thought*, 99–101, and in Honneth, *I in We*, 26.

54. Hegel's term is the self's *substantial determinations* (Hegel, *Elements*, 95, par. 66). In this term, Hegel explicitly aligns his thinking to Spinoza's fundamental point that spirit is "that which is what it is *only through itself* and *as infinite return into* itself," from which everything else, including even the body and the

will that inhabits that body, must be distinguished (Hegel, *Elements*, 96, par. 66, Hegel's italics, commenting on the opening paragraph of Spinoza's *Ethics*).

55. Hegel, *Elements*, 95, par. 66.

56. Although MacPherson (*Possessive Individualism*, 200) shows the roots in John Locke of the idea that "every man has a Property in his own person," Locke's individualistic view of freedom is actually very different from Hegel's socially grounded view.

57. Discussed in Rössler, *Value*, 146.

58. Hegel, *Elements*, 97, par. 66.

59. Kelly, *Inevitable*, 7, emphasis in original.

60. For the manifesto of the Quantified Self movement, see Wolf, "Data-Driven Life." For useful reviews of the recent history of self-tracking, see Crawford, Lingel, and Karppi, "Our Metrics, Ourselves"; Lupton, *Quantified Self*; and Neff and Nafus, *Self-Tracking*.

61. Lupton, Quantified Self, 2.

62. Hildebrandt, "Balance or Trade-Off?," 367.

63. Apple, "Apple Special Event."

64. Neff and Nafus, *Self-Tracking*, 3, 8.

65. John, "Logics of Sharing." For the wider mystification, see Couldry, "Necessary Disenchantment."

66. See Brake, *Sharing Our Lives*; and Debatin et al., "Facebook and Online Privacy."

67. John, "Logics of Sharing," 117.

68. Crawford, Lingel, and Karppi, "Our Metrics, Ourselves," 486.

69. For recent studies, see, for example, Lupton et al., "Personal Data Contexts"; Pantzar and Ruckenstein, "Living the Metrics"; and Schüll, "Data for Life." For a view of social media use that insists on its embedding in multiple qualitative contexts, see Humphreys, *Qualified Self*.

70. For this reason, we are not convinced by accounts of self-tracking that celebrates its "situated objectivity" (Pantzar and Ruckenstein, "Living the Metrics"), let alone its potential as resistance to corporate data practices (Nafus and Sherman, "This One Does Not Go Up to Eleven"). Yes, these practices are richly contextualized, but as data relations they are part of the means to *reproduce* the new data-driven capitalism.

71. Nadella, *Hit Refresh*, 156.

72. Bucher, "Algorithmic Imaginary."

73. Barreneche and Wilken, "Platform Specificity," 506; and Foursquare Labs Inc., "Privacy Policy," last modified February 1, 2018, https://foursquare.com/legal/privacy.

74. Compare Shopkick CEO Cyriac Roeding: "We inject digital juice into the physical world, and make the offline, touchable world a more interactive experience." Quoted in Turow, McGuigan, and Maris, "Making Data Mining," 474.

75. Honneth, *I in We*, 26.

76. Hildebrandt, "Balance or Trade-Off?," drawing on Phillip Agre, "Introduction," 7.

77. As Lupton notes, the Quantified Self movement itself is now starting to prioritize concerns over at least access to, if not ownership of, personal data (Lupton, *Quantified Self*, 134). Meanwhile, according to Neff and Nafus (*Self-Tracking*, 117), there is no consensus among data companies that service the self-tracking sector on whether they or their customers own the data stored in the mechanisms they provide.

78. Pippin, *Practical Philosophy*, 136

79. Pippin, 167.

80. We acknowledge the literatures on Actor Network Theory, social construction of technology, and sociomateriality (for a useful summary for the data context, see Lupton, *Quantified Self*, chap. 2). As Philip Napoli notes in a helpful synoptic article, "Algorithms in many ways *epitomize* the complex intermingling of human and nonhuman actors" ("Automated Media," 344, emphasis added).

81. Wood, *Ethical Thought*, 48.

82. As Neuhouser puts it, autonomy for Hegel is a relation between a free individual and "things." Things do not have goals. Freedom consists in "having at [the individual's] disposal a portion of the external world, made up of will-less entities of 'things' (*Sache*) within which [the individual's] own arbitrary will has unlimited sovereignty *and from which other wills are excluded*" (Neuhouser, *Hegel's Social Theory*, 25, emphasis added). See also Wood, *Ethical Thought*, 49.

83. Schüll, "Data for Life," 13.

84. Pippin, *Practical Philosophy*, chaps. 3 and 4.

85. Quotations from Lupton, *Quantified Self*, 80–81.

86. Bucher, "Algorithmic Imaginary," 5.

87. Brunton and Nissenbaum, *Obfuscation*.

88. Ma, "Thousands of People."

89. Labour Party, Digital Democracy Manifesto, August 2016, available from https://d3n8a8pro7vhmx.cloudfront.net/corbynstays/pages/329/attachments/original/1472552058/Digital_Democracy.pdf?1472552058 (see paragraph on "Digital Citizen Passport"); and Laboratory for Systems Medicine, "This Is the Idea." See also Obermeyer and Emanuel, "Predicting the Future."

90. Evans, "Data Ownership"; and Evans, "Patient Ownership."

91. For history, see the document in the National Institutes of Health, "Iceland's Research Resources: The Health Sector Database, Genealogy Databases, and Biobanks," June 2004, https://grants.nih.gov/grants/icelandic_research.pdf.

92. Evans, "Barbarians at the Gate," last section.

93. For doubts, see Evans, "Barbarians at the Gate," 5; Kaplan, "Selling Health Data," 8–9, 20; and Caulfield et al., "Review of the Key Issues," 108; for claims that deidentification of health data is secure, see Faden et al., "Ethics Framework," S23.

94. See, for example, Rodwin, "Patient Data"; and Evans, "Barbarians at the Gate."

95. Terry, "Health Privacy Exceptionalism."

96. Sulmasy, "Naked Bodies," 3.

97. Neff and Nafus, *Self-Tracking*, 66.

98. https://www.ginger.io/, privacy conditions, as consulted on July 6, 2016.

99. Sweeney, "Health Data," cited in Christl and Spiekermann, "Networks of Control," 64.

100. Williamson, "Calculating Children."

101. DiCerbo and Behrens, "Impacts."

102. Impero Software and Digital Citizenship Institute, "Digital Citizenship."

103. IBM, "Personalized Learning"; and Blackboard website, http://www.blackboard.com/.

104. Dewey, *Experience and Education*.

105. Impero Software and Digital Citizenship Institute, "Digital Citizenship."

106. Luckin et al., "Intelligence Unleashed," 1, 24.

107. Kelly, *Technology Wants*; and Rifkin, *Zero Marginal Cost*. Posner ("Right of Privacy") attempts to reduce privacy to a derived form of economic utility (for a critique, see Ajunwa, Crawford, and Schultz, "Limitless Worker Surveillance").

108. Executive Office of the President and President's Council of Advisors on Science and Technology, *Big Data and Privacy*, 15.

109. Nissenbaum, *Privacy in Context*, especially 140.

110. Nissenbaum, *Privacy in Context*, 84; Nissenbaum, "Deregulating Collection," 28. For us, the term "*informational* norms" seems not, in any case, to capture the deeper aspects of autonomy as a value (DeCew, *Pursuit*).

111. Bennett, "Defence"; Lyon, *After Snowden*, 92; and Rotenberg, quoted in Shaw, "Watchers." Arguing that *privacy* remains a necessary term is not meant here to imply that it is *sufficient* to address many of the forms of exploitation through data that occur, which is why we spend time on the notion of autonomy and its basic preconditions. We disagree therefore with Gilliom ("Response to Bennett"), who appears to reject the term *privacy* on that unnecessary ground.

112. Brown, *Undoing*.

113. Nissenbaum, "Deregulating Collection."

114. Warren and Brandeis, "Right to Privacy."

115. Berlin, "Two Concepts."

116. Westin, *Privacy and Freedom*; and Cohen, *Regulating Intimacy.*

117. World Economic Forum, *Personal Data.*

118. Kaplan, "Selling Health Data," 10; and Evans, "Barbarians at the Gate," 14. See Balkin, "Information Fiduciaries," on the complexities this causes in the area of data holding.

119. Kerr, "Mosaic Theory."

120. Farahany, "Searching Secrets"; and Evans, "Patient Ownership." For more positive readings of the Fourth Amendment's uses, see Joh, "Policing by Numbers," 55–67; and Fairfield, *Owned*, 123.

121. Kaplan, "Selling Health Data"; Cartwright-Smith and Lopez, "Law and the Public's Health," 64–66; and Cohen, "Surveillance—Innovation Complex," 10.

122. Federal Communications Commission, "Protecting the Privacy of Customers of Broadband and Other Telecommunications Services," par. 9, November 2, 2016, https://apps.fcc.gov/edocs_public/attachmatch/FCC-16-148A1.pdf.

123. Richards, *Intellectual Privacy.*

124. Thanks to Julie Cohen for explaining this point.

125. Wakabayashi, "California Passes."

126. The full wording is "respect for private life, family, home and correspondence" (article 8).

127. Wood, *Ethical Thought*, 99; and Hornung and Schnabel, "Data Protection in Germany."

128. Hornung and Schnabel, "Data Protection in Germany."

129. Hornung and Schnabel, 86.

130. Cohen, "Privacy," 1912, 1918.

131. Other countries are introducing parallel legislation, for example, Brazil with its Data Protection Law (August 2018). As a major power, the European Union may be in a position to seek to impose GDPR as a standard on its trading partners. Scott and Cerulus, "Europe's New Data Protection Laws."

132. General Data Protection Regulation (GDPR), "Recital 1."

133. Barocas and Nissenbaum, "Big Data's End Run"; and O'Neill, *Autonomy and Trust*, 154–59, for useful philosophical discussion on the limits of the concept of informed consent.

134. The United Kingdom is already proposing to copy the GDPR, and there is a live debate in the United States on whether it needs regulation similar to the GDPR.

135. Waters, "Google Plays Down."

136. For discussion, see Couldry and Rodriguez et al., "Chapter 13 on Media and Communications," sec. 6.3.

137. Reuters, "China Chides Tech Firms."
138. Polanyi, *Great Transformation*.
139. Beattie, "Data Protectionism."
140. Cohen, *Networked Self*, 272.
141. Hildebrandt and Koops, "Profiling Era," 428.
142. Hildebrandt (*Smart Technologies*, 15) expresses this as a shift from the normal "double contingency" of human social reality to a world driven by a "single contingency," what systems and their drivers want. On the challenge through datafication to mutual expectations assumed by classical phenomenology, see Couldry and Kallinikos, "Ontology."
143. Yeung, "Hypernudge," 127.
144. Schwartz, "Internet Privacy and the State"; Cohen, "Privacy"; Solove, *Understanding Privacy*, chap. 4; and Hildebrandt, *Smart Technologies*. The roots of this move are already there in Fried, *Anatomy of Values*, chap. IX. Rössler (*Value*), while staying within the liberal tradition, comes close to this relational approach.
145. Hildebrandt, *Smart Technologies*, 92. Compare in the earlier literature Dworkin, *Autonomy*, 20.
146. For an interesting discussion of what privacy means among app developers, see Greene and Shilton, "Platform Privacies."
147. Rössler, *Value*, 50.
148. For related approaches, see Cohen, *Networked Self*, 149; Hildebrandt, "Balance or Trade-Off?," 365; and Hildebrandt, *Smart Technologies*, 80, drawing on Agre, "Introduction." Both writers take positions that are fully consistent with a Hegelian approach. So too do the authors of the Onlife Manifesto, which also adopts a "relational" view of the self (Floridi, *Onlife Manifesto*).
149. Cohen, "Privacy," 1908.
150. Solove, *Understanding Privacy*; Altman, "Privacy Regulation"; Fried, *Anatomy of Values*; and Schoeman, *Privacy and Social Freedom*. It is clearly true, however, that the *forms* that privacy takes vary depending, not least, on the technological environment. Ong, *Orality and Literacy*, 130; and Hildebrandt, "Balance or Trade-Off?"
151. Rouvroy and Poullet, "Informational Self-Determination," 16.
152. Cohen, "Biopolitical Domain"; Couldry and Rodriguez et al., "Chapter 13 on Media and Communications"; and Elkin-Koren and Haber, "Governance by Proxy."

Chapter 6

1. Tweet by Mark Andreessen (@pmarca), cited in Bowles, "Zuckerberg Chides."
2. Kuchler, "The Man"; and Doctorow, "Demanding Better."

3. Ball, "Facebook Scandal"; and *Financial Times*, "Four Simple Questions." For a book that caught the moment, see Lanier, *Ten Arguments*.

4. To repurpose the term coined by Herzfeld, "Absent Presence."

5. We agree with Evgeny Morozov that hopes of a breakup of Facebook or Google ignore such geopolitical realities (tweet by @evgenymorozov, April 12, 2018).

6. Kelly, *Inevitable*.

7. Noble, *Algorithms*, 13.

8. Most dramatically, Lanier, *Ten Arguments*.

9. So, for example, Srnicek (*Platform Capitalism*, 158), who argues that "rather than just regulating corporate platforms, efforts could be made to create public platforms—platforms owned and controlled by the people." On Apple's and others' digital wellness programs, see Perez, "Apple Unveils."

10. Polanyi, *Great Transformation*, 35.

11. See, for example, the proposed new platform Openbook. Kuchler, "Privacy Pioneers."

12. We hold here onto the term *tactical* while acknowledging that the underlying distinction from French theorist Michel de Certeau (*Everyday Life*) between strategy and tactics may have outlived its usefulness. De Certeau argued that within every large-scale structure of strategic power (government, markets, rituals, the order of space itself) there are places for tactics: empty zones, such as the corner of a market square, to which the eye or hand of power doesn't penetrate. In tactical places, the possibility subsists of "free" activity with real benefits for the actors, benefits that are not envisaged or controlled by strategic power. De Certeau's notion of tactics, however, assumed some limits to how far power can penetrate into space—a reasonable assumption about every form of generalized power *until now*. But what if the new order being built is an order *beyond tactics*, an order that appropriates almost all resources from which tactics might be fashioned except the short-term local gaming of the system that, by its own admission, "*plays the game*" and so cannot challenge it?

13. Compare Madden et al., "Privacy," 118.

14. Vertesi, "My Experiment."

15. Coleman, *Coding Freedom*.

16. Thornhill, "Muslim Cleric."

17. See Duarte and Vigil-Hayes, "#Indigenous"; and Olsen and Risam, "Postcolonial History."

18. Simpson, *Always Done*, 176.

19. Madden et al., "Privacy."

20. Mansell, *Imagining the Internet*.

21. Taylor, *Modern Social Imaginaries*.

22. So Axon, in its 2017 financial report (the section "Investor Relations," 2018, http://investor.axon.com/about-us), refers to "Connected Ecosystem—From capture to courtroom, securely share and track digital evidence across public safety stakeholders"; and the Alibaba Holding Group Limited in its 2017 report refers frequently to "our ecosystem" from which data is collected and where user activities occur. The notion of treating information as an ecology goes back a long way; see, for example, Davenport and Prusak, *Information Ecology*.

23. Vertesi, "Seamful Spaces." Compare Cohen, *Configuring*, 224–25, on the importance of requiring semantic *dis*continuity in information systems, endorsed by Fleischmann and Seliger, *Reengineering*, 275–76.

24. The result is a profound clash between AI practice and important human goals, even before we confront the fears that AI may become a "superintelligence" capable of overriding human control (see Bostrom, *Superintelligence*).

25. The Greek word *legein* means both "to gather" and "to speak"; *logos* (the related noun) can therefore mean an "account" in two senses: (1) what is said/thought, and (2) what is gathered together in a reckoning or story.

26. Yong, *Multitudes*, 110.

27. For a disturbing survey that suggests that, in the United States at least, narratives about how the burdens and penalties of surveillance should be distributed are building in line with polarized political positions, see Turow et al., *Divided We Feel*. On punitive connectivity among the US poor, see Madden et al., "Privacy." On the longer history of "moral behaviorism," see Wacquant, *Punishing*, 302.

28. Santos, *Epistemologies*, especially 124. We can find an interesting parallel in comments by the prominent, if controversial, figure of Pope Francis in his recent encyclical, where he warned about the "technocratic paradigm," criticizing a way of thinking about technology "as if the [technological] subject were to find itself in the presence of something [the world] formless, completely open to manipulation." The result, he suggests, is to authorize a new and powerful subject "who, using logical and rational procedures, progressively approaches and gains control over an external object" (*Encyclical*, 66).

29. Sen, *Rationality*, 10.

30. Sen, *Development*, 158.

31. It is worth noting that Quijano himself, in making his argument, draws from various prior traditions and thinkers, as Grosfuguel ("Del 'Extractivismo Económico'") points out.

32. Quijano, "Coloniality and Modernity/Rationality," 177, emphasis added.

33. Quijano, again emphasis added.

34. Compare Escobar, *Designs*, 68, on "the invisibility of the pluriverse" and the argument of Santos (*Epistemologies*, 13) that "unity lies in no essence."

35. Espeland and Sauder, "Rankings and Reactivity," 1.

36. Simpson, *Always Done*, 156.

37. Nandy, *Intimate Enemy* (see discussion in chapter 3).

38. As philosopher Giorgio Agamben sees clearly when he writes of "the liberation of *that which remains captured* and separated by means of apparatuses, in order to bring it back to a *possible* [new] common life" (*Apparatus*, 17, emphasis added).

39. Mejias, *Off the Network*.

40. We echo here the title of Ivan Illich's book *Tools for Conviviality*. We acknowledge also the resonances with J. K. Gibson-Graham's project for "building community economies," which works to revise large-scale economic relations through reviving common knowledge and practice (Gibson-Graham, *PostCapitalist Politics*, chap. 7).

41. Appadurai, *Future as Cultural Fact*, 270, emphasis added. We would want, however, to take issue with Appadurai's emphasis on "value-free" knowledge, which somewhat fails to account for the nature of power.

42. Freire, *Pedagogy*; Sanjinés, *Theory and Practice*; and Fals-Borda and Rahman, *Action and Knowledge*. For interesting reflections on Participatory Action Research and contemporary theory, see Cameron and Graham, "Participatory Action Research."

43. Spivak, "Can the Subaltern Speak?"

44. Young, *Postcolonialism*, 4.

45. Connell, *Southern Theory*, 207.

46. Smith, *Decolonizing Methodologies*. There is an interesting parallel here with Santos's advocacy of "a new emancipatory common sense" that rejects the automatic cognitive privilege of "the West" and its institutions and frameworks and respects the integrity of local knowledge everywhere (*Epistemologies*, 158).

47. Couldry, Fotopoulos, and Dickens, "Real Social Analytics."

48. Quijano, "Coloniality and Modernity/Rationality," 77.

49. Montgomerie, *Critical Methods*, 6.

50. Montgomerie.

51. Budka, "Indigenous Articulations"; and Wainwright and Bryan, "Cartography, Territory, Property."

52. Eubanks, *Automating Inequality*, 187.

Postscript

1. Nadella, *Hit Refresh*, 209.

2. Axon, *Annual Report*, March 2017, https://investor.axon.com/financials/sec-filings/sec-filings-details/default.aspx?FilingId=11912252.

3. Founder and CEO of Axon, Rick Smith: https://uk.axon.com/info/future.

4. Tresata, "Solutions," 2017, http://tresata.com/solutions/.

5. Stewart, *A Space*.

6. "Hopelessness," Paulo Freire wrote, "is a form of silence, of denying the world and feeling from it. [But] the dehumanization resulting from an unjust order is not a cause for despair but for hope, leading to the incessant pursuit of the humanity which is denied by injustice" (*Pedagogy*, 64).

7. Simpson (*Always Done*, 17) writes of the capacity called Biiskabiyingan in the Nishnaabeg language: "The process of returning to ourselves, a reengagement with the things we have left behind, a re-emergence, an unfolding from the inside out." For the idea of "returning to ourselves," compare what H. S. Bhola (*Literacy*) calls the ontological reintegration of the individual to the world.

Acknowledgments

1. Crane, Swear by the Night, 13.

Bibliography

Aaronson, Susan Ariel. "The Digital Trade Imbalance and Its Implications for Internet Governance." *Centre for International Governance Innovation (CGI)*, February 3, 2016. https://www.cigionline.org/publications/digital-trade-imbalance-and-its-implications-internet-governance.

Acemoglu, Daron, Simon Johnson, and James Robinson. "The Rise of Europe: Atlantic Trade, Institutional Change, and Economic Growth." *American Economic Review* 95, no. 3 (June 2005): 546–79.

Acemoglu, Daron, and Pascual Restrepo. "The Race Between Machine and Man: Implications of Technology for Growth, Factor Shares and Employment." Working Paper 22252, *National Bureau of Economic Research*, 2016. http://www.nber.org/papers/w22252.

Acosta, Alberto. "Extractivismo y Neoextractivismo: Dos Caras de la Misma Maldición." *EcoPortal.net* (blog), July 25, 2012. https://www.ecoportal.net/temas-especiales/mineria/extractivismo_y_neoextractivismo_dos_caras_de_la_misma_maldicion/.

Acxiom. *Personalisation: Hanging in the Balance.* May 2017. https://www.acxiom.co.uk/wp-content/uploads/2017/05/Acxiom-Privacy-Personalisation-Hanging-in-the-Balance.pdf.

Adas, Michael. *Machines as the Measure of Men.* Ithaca, NY: Cornell University Press, 1990.

Adelman, Ashley. "The Identity of Things." *Janrain* (blog), December 18, 2017. https://www.janrain.com/blog/identity-of-things.

Agamben, Giorgio. *Homo Sacer.* Stanford, CA: Stanford University Press, 1998.

———. *What Is an Apparatus and Other Essays.* Stanford, CA: Stanford University Press, 2009.

Agre, Phillip. "Introduction." In *Technology and Privacy: The New Landscape*, edited by Phillip Agre and Marc Rotenberg, 1–28. Cambridge, MA: MIT Press, 1997.

———. "Surveillance and Capture: Two Models of Privacy." *The Information Society* 10, no. 2 (1994): 101–27.

————. "Your Face Is Not a Barcode: Arguments Against Automatic Face Recognition in Public Places." UCLA, 2004. polaris.gseis.ucla.edu/pagre/bar-code.html.

Ajunwa, Ifeoma, Kate Crawford, and Jason Schultz. "Limitless Worker Surveillance." *California Law Review* 105, no. 3 (2017): 735–76.

Alaimo, Cristina, and Jannis Kallinikos. "Computing the Everyday: Social Media as Data Platforms." *The Information Society* 33, no. 4 (2017): 175–91.

Alhassan, Amin, and Paula Chakravartty. "Postcolonial Media Policy Under the Long Shadow of Empire." In *The Handbook of Global Media and Communication Policy*, edited by Robin Mansell and Marc Raboy, 366–82. London: Wiley-Blackwell, 2011.

Alibaba Holdings. *Alibaba Holding Group Limited Annual Report 2016.* 2016. http://www.alibabagroup.com/en/ir/pdf/agm160524_ar.pdf.

Alonso, William, and Paul Starr, eds. *The Politics of Numbers.* New York: Russell Sage Foundation, 1988.

Altman, Irwin. "Privacy Regulation: Culturally Universal or Culturally Specific?" *Journal of Social Issues* 33, no. 3 (1977): 66–84.

Amaya, Hector. *Citizenship Excess.* New York: New York University Press, 2013.

Amin, Samir. *Le Développement Inégal.* Paris: Les Éditions de Minuit, 1973.

Amoore, Louise. *The Politics of Possibility.* Durham, NC: Duke University Press, 2013.

Amoore, Louise, and Volha Piotukh. "Life Beyond Big Data: Governing with Little Analytics." *Economy and Society* 44, no. 3 (2015): 341–66.

Ananny, Mike. "Toward an Ethics of Algorithms: Convening, Observation, Probability, and Timeliness." *Science, Technology, & Human Values* 41, no. 1 (2016): 93–117.

Ananny, Mike, and Kate Crawford. "Seeing Without Knowing: Limitations of the Transparency Ideal and Its Application to Algorithmic Accountability." *New Media & Society* 20, no. 3 (2018): 973–89.

Anderson, Chris. "The End of Theory: The Data Deluge Makes the Scientific Method Obsolete." *Wired*, June 23, 2008.

Andrejevic, Mark. *Infoglut.* London: Routledge, 2013.

Andrejevic, Mark, Alison Hearn, and Helen Kennedy. "Cultural Studies of Data Mining: Introduction." *European Journal of Cultural Studies* 19, nos. 4–5 (2015): 379–94.

Angwin, Julia, and Terry Parris. "Facebook Lets Advertisers Exclude Users by Race." *ProPublica*, October 28, 2016.

Aouragh, Miriyam, and Paula Chakravartty. "Infrastructures of Empire: Towards a Critical Geopolitics of Media and Information Studies." *Media, Culture & Society* 38, no. 4 (2016): 559–75.

Appadurai, Arjun. *The Future as Cultural Fact: Essays on the Global Condition.*
    London: Verso, 2013.
Apple. "Apple Special Event." Filmed September 12, 2017. Video. https://www
    .apple.com/apple-events/september-2017/.
Ariely, Dan, and Gregory S. Berns. "Neuromarketing: The Hope and Hype of
    Neuroimaging in Business." *Nature Reviews Neuroscience*, March 3, 2010.
    https://doi.org/10.1038/nrn2795.
Arntz, Melanie, Terry Gregory, and Ulrich Zierahn. "The Risk of Automation
    for Jobs in OECD Countries." *OECD*, 2016. http://www.oecd-ilibrary.org
    /social-issues-migration-health/the-risk-of-automation-for-jobs-in-oecd
    -countries_5jlz9h56dvq7-en.
Arora, Sanchit, Chuck Cho, Paul Fitzpatrick, and Francois Scharffe. "Towards On-
    tology Driven Learning of Visual Concept Detectors." *arXiv* preprint, 2016.
    arXiv:1605.09757. https://arxiv.org/abs/1605.09757.
Arrieta Ibarra, Imanol, Leonard Goff, Diego Jiménez Hernández, Jaron Lanier,
    and E. Glen Weyl. "Should We Treat Data as Labor? Moving Beyond 'Free.'"
    Social Science Research Network, December 27, 2017. https://papers.ssrn.com
    /abstract=3093683.
Arvidsson, Adam. "Facebook and Finance: On the Social Logic of the Derivative."
    Theory Culture & Society 33, no. 6 (2016): 3–23.
———. "On the 'Pre-History of the Panoptic Sort': Mobility in Market Research."
    Surveillance & Society 1, no. 4 (2004): 456–74.
Ashcroft, Bill, Gareth Griffiths, and Helen Tiffin, eds. *The Post-Colonial Studies
    Reader.* New York: Routledge, 1995.
Backer, Larry Catá. "Global Panopticism: States, Corporations, and the Gover-
    nance Effects of Monitoring Regimes." *Indiana Journal of Global Legal Stud-
    ies* 15, no. 1 (2008): 101–48.
Balkin, Jack M. "Information Fiduciaries and the First Amendment." *UC Davis
    Law Review* 49, no. 4 (2016): 1183–1234.
Ball, James. "The Facebook Scandal Isn't Just about Privacy. Your Economic Fu-
    ture Is on the Line." *Guardian*, March 23, 2018.
Baptist, Edward. "Toward a Political Economy of Slave Labor: Hands, Whipping
    Machines and Modern Power." In *Slavery's Capitalism*, edited by Sven Beck-
    ert and Seth Rockman, 31–61. Philadelphia: University of Pennsylvania Press,
    2016.
Barnes, Trevor, and Matthew Wilson. "Big Data, Social Physics and Spatial Analy-
    sis: The Early Years." *Big Data & Society* 1, no. 1 (2014). https://doi.org/10.1177
    %2F2053951714535365.
Barnet, Richard J., and Ronald F. Müller. *Global Reach: The Power of the Multi-
    national Corporations.* New York: Simon and Schuster, 1974.

Barocas, Solon, and Helen Nissenbaum, "Big Data's End Run Around Anonymity and Consent." In *Privacy, Big Data and the Public Good*, edited by Julia Lane, Victoria Stodden, Stefan Bendo, and Helen Nissenbaum, 44–75. New York: Cambridge University Press, 2014.

Barocas, Solon, and Andrew Selbst. "Big Data's Disparate Impact." *California Law Review* 104, no. 1 (2016): 671–729.

Barreneche, Carlos, and Rowan Wilken. "Platform Specificity and the Politics of Location Data Extraction." *European Journal of Cultural Studies* 18, nos. 4–5 (2015): 497–513.

Bartlett, Jamie, and Nathaniel Tkacz. "Governance by Dashboard: A Policy Paper." *Demos*, March 2017. https://www.demos.co.uk/wp-content/uploads/2017/04 /Demos-Governance-by-Dashboard.pdf.

Bartley, Tim. "Electronics: The Hidden Costs of Computing." In *Looking Behind the Label*, edited by Tim Bartley, Sebastian Koos, Hiram Samel, Gustavo Setrini, and Nik Summers, 179–208. Bloomington: Indiana University Press, 2015.

Basu, Deepankar, and Ramaa Vasudevan. "Technology, Distribution and the Rate of Profit in the US Economy: Understanding the Current Crisis." *Cambridge Journal of Economics* 37, no. 1 (2013): 57–89.

Beattie, Alan. "Data Protectionism: The Growing Menace to Global Business." *Financial Times*, May 13, 2018.

Beckert, Sven, and Seth Rockman, eds. *Slavery's Capitalism*. Philadelphia: University of Pennsylvania Press, 2016.

Beer, David. *Metric Power*. Basingstoke, UK: Palgrave Macmillan, 2016.

Bellamy, John. "Marx's Theory of Metabolic Rift: Classical Foundations for Environmental Sociology." *The American Journal of Sociology* 105, no. 2 (1999): 346–405.

Beniger, James. *The Control Revolution*. Cambridge, MA: Harvard University Press, 1986.

Benjamin, Walter. *Illuminations*. New York: Schocken Books, 1969.

Bennett, Colin. "In Defence of Privacy: The Concept and the Regime." *Surveillance & Society* 8, no. 4 (2011): 486–96.

Berardi, Franco "Bifo." *Soul at Work*. Pasadena, CA: Semiotext(e), 2009.

Bergen, Mark, and Josh Eidelson. "Inside Google's Shadow Workforce." *Bloomberg*, July 25, 2018. https://www.bloomberg.com/news/articles/2018-07-25/in side-google-s-shadow-workforce.

Berker, Selim. "The Normative Insignificance of Neuroscience." *Philosophy and Public Affairs* 37, no. 4 (2009): 293–329.

Berki, R. N. "On the Nature and Origins of Marx's Concept of Labor." *Political Theory* 7, no. 1 (1979): 35–56.

Berlin, Isaiah. "Two Concepts of Liberty." In *Four Essays on Liberty*, 118–73. Oxford, UK: Oxford University Press, 1969.

Berners-Lee, Tim. *Weaving the Web*. London: Harper Collins, 1999.

Bewes, Timothy. *Reification. Or the Anxiety of Late Capitalism*. London, Verso, 2002.

Bhambra, Gurminder. *Connected Sociologies*. London: Bloomsbury, 2014.

Bhola, H. S. *Literacy, Knowledge, Power, and Development*. Springfield, VA: Dyneders, 1992.

Bilbao-Osorio, Beñat, Soumitra Dutta, and Bruno Lanvin. *The Global Information Technology Report 2014: Rewards and Risks of Big Data*. We Forum, 2014. http://www3.weforum.org/docs/WEF_GlobalInformationTechnology_Report _2014.pdf

Bishop, Alan J. "Western Mathematics: The Secret Weapon of Cultural Imperialism." In *The Post-Colonial Studies Reader*, edited by Bill Ashcroft, Gareth Griffiths, and Helen Tiffin, 71–76. London: Routledge, 1995.

Blackburn, Robin. *The Making of New World Slavery*. 2nd ed. London: Verso, 2010.

Blaut, James Morris. *The Colonizer's Model of the World*. New York: Guilford Press, 1993.

Bloomberg. "China Uses Facial Recognition to Fence in Villagers." *Bloomberg*, January 17, 2018. https://www.bloomberg.com/news/articles/2018-01-17/china -said-to-test-facial-recognition-fence-in-muslim-heavy-area.

Blum, Andrew. *Tubes*. New York: Ecco, 2012.

Bogost, Ian. "Welcome to the Age of Privacy Nihilism." *The Atlantic*, August 23, 2018.

Bostrom, Nick. *Superintelligence*. Oxford, UK: Oxford University Press, 2014.

Botsman, Rachel. "Big Data Meets Big Brother as China Moves to Rate Its Citizens." *Wired UK*, October 21, 2017.

Bouk, Dan. "The History and Political Economy of Personal Data over the Last Two Centuries in Three Acts." *Osiris* 32, no. 1 (2017): 85–106.

———. *How Our Days Became Numbered: Risk and the Rise of the Statistical Individual*. Chicago: University of Chicago Press, 2015.

Bourdieu, Pierre. *Language and Symbolic Power*. Cambridge, UK: Polity, 1990.

———. *Outline of a Theory of Practice*. Cambridge, UK: Cambridge University Press, 1977.

Bowcott, Owen. "Uber to Face Stricter EU Regulation after ECJ Rules It Is Transport Form." *Guardian* (UK edition), December 20, 2017.

Bowen, Huw V. *The Business of Empire*. Cambridge, UK: Cambridge University Press, 2008.

Bowker, Geoffrey, and Susan Leigh Star. *Sorting Things Out*. Cambridge, MA: MIT Press, 1999.

———. "Mark Zuckerberg Chides Board Member over "Deeply Upsetting India Comments." *Guardian*, February 10, 2016.

Bowman, Courtney. "Data Localization Laws." *Jurist*, January 6, 2017. http://www .jurist.org/hotline/2017/01/Courtney-Bowman-data-localization.php.

boyd, danah, and Kate Crawford. "Critical Questions for Big Data." *Information, Communication & Society* 15, no. 5 (2012): 662–79.

Bozikovic, Alex. "Google's Sidewalk Labs Signs Deal for 'Smart City' Makeover of Toronto's Waterfront." *The Globe and Mail*, October 17, 2017.

Bradley, Joseph, Joel Barbier and Doug Handler. "Embracing the Internet of Everything to Capture Your Share of $14.4 trillion." Cisco, 2013. https://www.cisco .com/c/dam/en_us/about/ac79/docs/innov/IoE_Economy.pdf.

Brake, David. *Sharing Our Lives Online*. Basingstoke, UK: Palgrave MacMillan, 2014.

Bratton, Benjamin H. *The Stack: On Software and Sovereignty*. Cambridge, MA: MIT Press, 2016.

Brauneis, Robert, and Ellen Goodman. "Algorithmic Transparency for the Smart City." *Social Science Research Network*, April 15, 2018. https://doi.org/10.2139 /ssrn.3012499.

Braverman, Harry. *Labor and Monopoly Capitalism*. New York: Monthly Review Press, (1974) 1998.

Brayne, Sarah. "Big Data Surveillance: The Case of Policing." *American Sociological Review* 82, no. 5 (2017): 977–1008.

Brennan-Marquez, Kiel. "Plausible Cause: Explanatory Standards in the Age of Powerful Machines." *Vanderbilt Law Review* 70, no. 4 (2017): 1249–1301.

Bridges, Khiara. *The Poverty of Privacy Rights*. Stanford, CA: Stanford University Press, 2017.

Brown, Wendy. *Undoing the Demos*. New York: Zone Books, 2015.

Browne, Simone. *Dark Matters*. Durham, NC: Duke University Press, 2015.

Brunton, Finn, and Helen Nissenbaum. *Obfuscation*. Cambridge, MA: MIT Press, 2015.

Brynjolfsson, Erik, and Andrew McAfee. *The Second Machine Age*. New York: W. W. Norton, 2016.

Bucher, Taina. "The Algorithmic Imaginary: Exploring the Ordinary Affects of Facebook Algorithms." *Information Communication and Society* 20, no. 1 (2017): 30–44.

———. "The Friendship Assemblage: Investigating Programmed Sociality on Facebook. *Television & New Media* 14, no. 6 (2013): 479–93.

———. *If . . . Then: Algorithmic Power and Politics*. Oxford, UK: Oxford University Press, 2018.

Budka, Philipp. "Indigenous Articulations in the Digital Age: Reflections on Historical Developments, Activist Engagements and Mundane Practices." Paper presented at the International Communication Association (ICA) 2018 Pre-Conference "Articulating Voice." The Expressivity and Performativity of Media Practice," Prague, CZ, May 24, 2018.

Burri, Mira. "The Regulation of Data Flows through Trade Agreements." *Science Research Network*, August 28, 2017. https://papers.ssrn.com/abstract=3028137.

Butt, Danny. "Global Algorithmic Governance and Neocolonialism." *The Fibreculture Journal* 27 (2016). http://twentyseven.fibreculturejournal.org/2016/03/08/fcj-198-new-international-information-order-niio-revisited-global-algorithmic-governance-and-neocolonialism/.

Caffentzis, George. "Immeasurable Value? An Essay on Marx's Legacy." *The Commoner* 10 (2005): 87–114. http://www.commoner.org.uk/10caffentzis.pdf.

Camerer, Colin. "Neuroeconomics: Using Neuroscience to Make Economic Predictions." *The Economic Journal* 117 (2007): C26–C42.

Camerer, Colin, George Loewenstein, and Drazen Prelec. "Neuroscience: How Neuroeconomics Can Inform Economics." *Journal of Economic Literature* 43, no. 1 (2005): 9–64.

Cameron, Deborah, and Katherine Gibson. "Participatory Action Research in a Poststructuralist Vein." *Geoforum* 36, no. 3 (2005): 315–31.

Carchedi, Guglielmo. "Was the Great Recession a Crisis of Profitability?" *Science & Society* 80, no. 4 (2016): 495–514.

Carchedi, Guglielmo, and Michael Roberts. "The Long Roots of the Present Crisis: Keynesians, Austrians, and Marx's Law." *World Review of Political Economy* 4, no. 1 (2013): 86–115.

Cartwright-Smith, Lisa, and Nancy Lopez. "Law and the Public's Health." *Public Health Reports* 128 (2013): 64–66.

Castells, Manuel. *The Rise of the Network Society.* Oxford, UK: Blackwell, 1996.

Caulfield, Timothy, Sarah Burningham, Yann Joly, Zubin Master, Mahsa Shabani, Pascal Borry, Allan Becker, Michael Burgess, Kathryn Calder, Christine Critchley, Kelly Edwards, Stephanie M. Fullerton, Herbert Gottweis, Robyn Hyde-Lay, Judy Illes, Rosario Isasi, Kazuto Kato, Jane Kaye, Bartha Knoppers, John Lynch, Amy McGuire, Eric Meslin, Dianne Nicol, Kieran O'Doherty, Ubaka Ogbogu, Margaret Otlowski, Daryl Pullman, Nola Ries, Chris Scott, Malcolm Sears, Helen Wallace, and Ma'n H. Zawati. "A Review of the Key Issues Associated with the Commercialization of Biobanks." *Journal of Law and the Biosciences* 1, no. 1 (2014): 94–110.

Césaire, Aimé. *Discourse on Colonialism.* New York: Monthly Review Press, 2001.

Chakrabarty, Dipra. *Provincializing Europe.* Princeton, NJ: Princeton University Press, 2007.

Chatterjee, Partha. *The Nation and Its Fragments.* Princeton, NJ: Princeton University Press, 1993.

Chen, Adrian. "The Laborers Who Keep Dick Pics and Beheadings Out of Your Facebook Feed." *Wired*, October 23, 2014.

Cheney-Lippold, John. *We Are Data*. New York: New York University Press, 2017.

Chibber, Vivek. *Postcolonial Theory and the Specter of Capital*. London: Verso, 2013.

China Copyright and Media. "Next Generation of Artificial Intelligence Development Plan." *China Copyright and Media* (blog), last modified August 1, 2017. https://chinacopyrightandmedia.wordpress.com/2017/07/20/a-next-generation-artificial-intelligence-development-plan/.

———. "Planning Outline for the Construction of a Social Credit System (2014–2020)." *China Copyright and Media* (blog), last modified April 25, 2015. https://chinacopyrightandmedia.wordpress.com/2014/06/14/planning-outline-for-the-construction-of-a-social-credit-system-2014-2020/.

———. "State Council Guiding Opinions Concerning Vigorously Moving Forward the 'Internet Plus' Plan." *China Copyright and Media* (blog), last modified December 17, 2015. https://chinacopyrightandmedia.wordpress.com/2015/07/01/state-council-guiding-opinions-concerning-vigorously-moving-forward-the-internet-plus-plan/.

China Security and Protection Industry Association. "Background of the National 'Sharp Eyes' Project (全国雪亮工程建设背景)." October 13, 2017. http://www.21csp.com.cn/zhanti/xlgcfx/article/article_15369.html.

Christl, Wolfie, and Sarah Spiekermann. "Networks of Control: A Report on Corporate Surveillance, Digital Tracking, Big Data & Privacy." *Cracked Labs*, 2016. http://crackedlabs.org/dl/Christl_Spiekermann_Networks_Of_Control.pdf.

Chun, Rene. "China's New Frontiers in Dystopian Tech." *The Atlantic*, April 2018.

Chun, Wendy. *Programmed Visions*. Cambridge, MA: MIT Press, 2013.

———. *Updating to Remain the Same*. Cambridge, MA: MIT Press, 2016.

Chung, Hyunji, Michaela Iorga, Jeffrey Voas, and Sangjin Lee. "Alexa, Can I Trust You?" *Computer* 50, no. 9 (2017): 100–104.

Clarke, Roger. "Information Technology and Dataveillance." *Communications of the ACM* 31, no. 5 (1988): 498–512.

Cohen, Jean. *Regulating Intimacy*. Princeton, NJ: Princeton University Press, 2002.

Cohen, Julie E. *Between Truth and Power*. Oxford, UK: Oxford University Press, 2019.

———. "The Biopolitical Public Domain: The Legal Construction of the Surveillance Economy." *Philosophy & Technology* 31, no. 2 (2018): 213–33.

———. *Configuring the Networked Self*. New Haven, CT: Yale University Press, 2012.

———. "The Surveillance–Innovation Complex: The Irony of the Participatory Turn." In *The Participatory Condition in the Digital Age*, edited by Darin Barney, Gabriella Coleman, Christine Ross, Jonathan Sterne, and Tamar Tembeck, 207–26. Minneapolis: University of Minnesota Press, 2016.

———. "What Privacy Is For." *Harvard Law Review* 126, no. 7 (2013): 1904–33.

Cohen, Noam. "It's Tracking Your Every Move and You May Not Even Know." *The New York Times*, March 26, 2011.

Coldewey, Devin. "Vermont Passes First Law to Crack Down on Data Brokers." *Techcrunch*, May 30, 2018.

Coleman, Gabriella. *Coding Freedom*. Princeton, NJ: Princeton University Press, 2012.

Connell, Raewyn W. *Southern Theory*. Cambridge, UK: Polity, 2007.

Constantiou, Ioanna D., and Jannis Kallinikos. "New Games, New Rules: Big Data and the Changing Context of Strategy." *Journal of Information Technology* 30, no. 1 (2015): 44–57.

Cooke, Bill. "The Denial of Slavery in Management Studies." *Journal of Management Studies* 40, no. 8 (2003): 1895–1918.

Couldry, Nick. "Inaugural: A Necessary Disenchantment: Myth, Agency and Injustice in a Digital World." *Sociological Review* 62, no. 4 (2014): 880–97.

———. *Why Voice Matters*. London: Sage, 2010.

Couldry, Nick, Aristea Fotopoulou, and Luke Dickens. "Real Social Analytics: A Contribution Towards a Phenomenology of a Digital World." *The British Journal of Sociology* 67, no. 1 (2016): 118–37.

Couldry, Nick, and Andreas Hepp. *The Mediated Construction of Reality*. Cambridge, UK: Polity, 2016.

Couldry, Nick, and Jannis Kallinikos. "Ontology." In *The Sage Handbook of Social Media*, edited by Jean Burgess, Alice Marwick, and Thomas Poell, 146–59. London: Sage, 2017.

Couldry, Nick, and Clemencia Rodriguez (coordinating authors) et al. "International Panel on Social Progress. Chapter 13 on Media and Communications." *International Panel on Social Progress*, October 25, 2017. https://www .ipsp.org/download/chapter-13.

Council of Castile. "Requerimiento." *National Humanities Center*, 1510. https:// nationalhumanitiescenter.org/pds/amerbegin/contact/text7/requirement.pdf.

Cowen, Deborah. *The Deadly Life of Logistics*. Minneapolis: University of Minnesota Press, 2014.

Crain, Matthew. "The Limits of Transparency: Data Brokers and Commodification." *New Media & Society* 20, no. 1 (2016): 88–104.

Crane, Nathalia. *Swear by the Night and Other Poems: With an Introduction*. London: Forgotten Books, 2017.

Crawford, Kate. "The Trouble with Bias." Filmed December 3, 2017 at NIPS Conference. Video. https://www.youtube.com/watch?v=fMym_BKWQzk.

Crawford, Kate, Solon Barocas, Aaron Shapiro, and Hannah Wallach. "The Problem with Bias: Allocative versus Representational Harms in Machine Learning." Presentation to SIGCIS Conference, 2018. http://meetings.sigcis.org/up loads/6/3/6/8/6368912/program.pdf.

Crawford, Kate, and Vladan Joler. "Anatomy of an AI system," September 2018. https://anatomyof.ai/.

Crawford, Kate, Jessa Lingel, and Tero Karppi. "Our Metrics, Ourselves: A Hundred Years of Self-Tracking from the Weight Scale to the Wrist Wearable Device." *European Journal of Cultural Studies* 18, nos. 4–5 (2015): 479–96.

Creemers, Rogier. "Cyber China: Upgrading Propaganda, Public Opinion Work and Social Management for the Twenty-First Century." *Journal of Contemporary China* 26, no. 103 (2017): 85–100.

Crocker, Lawrence. "Marx's Concept of Exploitation." *Social Theory and Practice* 2, no. 2 (1972): 201–15.

Curran, James, Natalie Fenton, and Des Freedman. *Misunderstanding the Internet*. New York: Routledge, 2012.

Dorling, Danny. "Ending the National Census Would Make Us Blind to Our Society." *Guardian*, September 2, 2013.

Dardot, Pierre, and Christian Laval. *The New Way of the World*. London: Verso, 2013.

Davenport, Thomas. *Big Data @ Work*. Cambridge, MA: Harvard Business Review Press, 2014.

Davenport, Thomas, Jeanne G. Harris, and Robert Morison. *Analytics at Work: Smarter Decisions, Better Results*. Boston: Harvard Business School Press, 2010.

Davenport, Thomas, and Laurence Prusak. *Information Ecology*. New York: Oxford University Press, 1997.

Day, Ronald. *Indexing It All*. Cambridge, MA: MIT Press, 2014.

Dayen, David. "Big Tech: The New Predatory Capitalism." *The American Prospect*, December 26, 2017. http://prospect.org/article/big-tech-new-predatory -capitalism.

Dean, Jodi. *Democracy and Other Neoliberal Fantasies*. Cambridge, UK: Polity, 2009.

Debatin, Bernhard, Jennette Lovejoy, Ann-Kathrin Horn, and Brittany Hughes. "Facebook and Online Privacy: Attitudes, Behaviors and Unintended Consequences." *Journal of Computer-Mediated Communication* 15, no. 1 (2009): 83–108.

De Certeau, Michel. *The Practice of Everyday Life*. Berkeley: University of California Press, 1984.

DeCew, Judith Wagner. *In Pursuit of Privacy*. Ithaca, NY: Cornell University Press, 1997.

Degli Espositi, Sara. "When Big Data Meets Dataveillance: The Hidden Side of Analytics." *Surveillance & Society* 12, no. 2 (2014): 209–25.

DeLanda, Manuel. *A New Philosophy of Society.* London: Continuum International Publishing, 2006.

Delbanco, Andrew. "Mysterious, Brilliant Frederick Douglass." *New York Review of Books,* April 7, 2016.

Deleon, A. Review of WaterMinder App (Android version). 2016. Available at https://apprecs.com/android/com.funnmedia.waterminder/waterminder%C2%AE.

Deleuze, Gilles. "Postscript on Control Societies." In *Negotiations,* 177–82. New York: Columbia University Press, 1997.

DeLillo, Don. *Zero K.* New York: Scribner, 2016.

Deloria, Philip J. *Playing Indian.* New Haven, CT: Yale University Press, 1998.

Delphy, Christine. *Close to Home.* London: Verso, 1984.

Denyer, Simon. "Beijing Bets on Facial Recognition in Big Drive for Total Surveillance." *The Washington Post,* January 7, 2018.

———. "China's Watchful Eye." *The Washington Post,* January 7, 2018.

Desrosières, Alain. *The Politics of Large Numbers.* Cambridge, MA: Harvard University Press, 1998.

Dewey, John. *Experience and Education.* New York: Collier Books, 1938.

DiCerbo, Kristen E., and John T. Behrens. "Impacts of the Digital Ocean on Education." Pearson, February 2014. https://www.pearson.com/content/dam/one-dot-com/one-dot-com/global/Files/about-pearson/innovation/open-ideas/DigitalOcean.pdf.

Didžiokaitė, Gabija, Paula Saukko, and Christian Greiffenhagen. "The Mundane Experience of Everyday Calorie Trackers: Beyond the Metaphor of Quantified Self." *New Media & Society* 20, no. 4 (2017): 1470–87.

Dixit, Pranav. "India's Largest Digital Wallet Has Been Accused of Handing Over Users Data to the Government." *Buzzfeed,* May 26, 2018. https://www.buzzfeed.com/amphtml/pranavdixit/india-paytm-data-sharing-government-jammu-kashmir.

DLA Piper. *Data Protection Laws of the World.* 2018. https://www.dlapiperdataprotection.com/.

Doctorow, Cory. "Let's Get Better at Demanding Better from Tech." *Locus,* March 5, 2018. https://locusmag.com/2018/03/cory-doctorow-lets-get-better-at-demanding-better-from-tech/.

Doogan, Kevin. *New Capitalism?* Cambridge, UK: Polity, 2009.

Dressel, Julia, and Hany Farid. "The Accuracy, Fairness, and Limits of Predicting Recidivism." *Science Advances* 4, no. 1 (2018). http://advances.sciencemag.org/content/4/1/eaao5580.

Duarte, Marisa Elena, and Morgan Vigil-Hayes. "#Indigenous: A Technical and Decolonial Analysis of Activist Uses of Hashtags Across Social Movements." *MediaTropes* 7, no. 1 (2017): 166–84.

Du Bois, W. E. B. *The Souls of Black Folk*. New York: Bantam, (1903) 1989.

Duménil, Gérard, and Dominique Lévy. *The Crisis of Neoliberalism*. Cambridge, MA: Harvard University Press, 2013.

Dussel, Enrique. "Europe, Modernity, and Eurocentrism." *Nepantla: Views from South* 1, no. 3 (2000): 465–78.

———. *Philosophy of Liberation*. Eugene, OR: Wipf and Stock, 1985.

Dvorak, Phred, and Yasufumi Saito. "Silicon Valley Powered American Tech Dominance—Now It Has a Challenger." *Wall Street Journal*, April 12, 2018.

Dworkin, Gerald. *The Theory and Practice of Autonomy*. Cambridge, UK: Cambridge University Press, 1988.

Dyer-Witheford, Nick. *Cyber-Marx*. Urbana: University of Illinois Press, 1999.

The Economist. "The World's Most Valuable Resource Is No Longer Oil, but Data." May 6, 2017.

Edelman, Gerald M. *Bright Air, Brilliant Fire*. New York: Basic Books, 1992.

Efrati, Amir. "How Uber Will Combat Rising Driver Churn." *The Information*, April 20, 2017. https://www.theinformation.com/articles/how-uber-will-combat-rising-driver-churn.

Eggers, Dave. *The Circle*. Harmondsworth, UK: Penguin, 2013.

Elan, Priya, Kathryn Bromwich, Corinne Jones, and Aurora Percannella. "Life Inside the New Gig Economy." *Guardian*, November 29, 2015.

Elkin-Koren, Niva, and Eldar Haber. "Governance by Proxy: Cyber Challenges to Civil Liberties." *Brooklyn Law Review* 82, no. 1 (2016): 105–62.

Elmer, Greg. *Profiling Machines*. Cambridge, MA: MIT Press, 2004.

Escobar, Arturo. *Designs for the Pluriverse*. Durham, NC: Duke University Press, 2017.

Espeland, Wendy. "Narrating Numbers." In *The World of Indicators*, edited by Richard Rottenburg, Sally E. Merry, Sung-Joon Park, and Johanna Mugler, 56–75. Cambridge, UK: Cambridge University Press, 2015.

Espeland, Wendy, and Michael Sauder. "Rankings and Reactivity: How Public Measures Recreate Social Worlds." *American Journal of Sociology* 113, no. 1 (2007): 1–40.

Eubanks, Virginia. *Automating Inequality*. New York: St. Martin's, 2018.

Evans, Barbara J. "Barbarians at the Gate: Consumer-Driven Health Data Commons and the Transformation of Citizen Science." *American Journal of Law & Medicine* 42, no. 4 (2016): 651–85.

———. "Much Ado about Data Ownership." *Harvard Journal of Law & Technology* 25, no. 1 (2011): 70–130.

————. "Would Patient Ownership of Health Data Improve Confidentiality?" *Virtual Mentor* 14, no. 9 (2012): 724–32.

Executive Office of the President and President's Council of Advisors on Science and Technology. *Report to the President: Big Data and Privacy, a Technological Perspective*. The White House, May 2014. https://obamawhitehouse.archives.gov/sites/default/files/microsites/ostp/PCAST/pcast_big_data_and_privacy_-_may_2014.pdf.

Fabian, Johannes. *Time and the Other*. New York: Columbia University Press, 2002.

Faden, Ruth R., Nancy E. Kass, Steven N. Goodman, Peter Pronovost, Sean Tunis, and Tom L. Beauchamp. "An Ethics Framework for a Learning Health Care System: A Departure from Traditional Research Ethics and Clinical Ethics." *Ethical Oversight of Learning Health Care Systems, Hastings Center Report Special Report* 43, no. 1 (2013): S16–27.

Fairfield, Joshua. *Owned: Property, Privacy and the New Digital Serfdom*. Cambridge, UK: Cambridge University Press, 2017.

Fals-Borda, Orlando, and Mohammad Anisur Rahman. *Action and Knowledge*. Santa Fé de Bogotá: Rowman & Littlefield, 1991.

Fan, Jiayang. "How E-Commerce Is Transforming Rural China." *New Yorker*, July 16, 2018. https://www.newyorker.com/magazine/2018/07/23/how-e-commerce-is-transforming-rural-china.

Farahany, Nita A. "Searching Secrets." *University of Pennsylvania Law Review* 160, no. 5 (2012): 1239–1308.

Featherstone, Liza. *Selling Women Short*. New York: Basic Books, 2005.

Federal Trade Commission. *Federal Trade Commission Staff Report*. January 2015. https://www.ftc.gov/system/files/documents/reports/federal-trade-commission-staff-report-november-2013-workshop-entitled-internet-things-privacy/150127iotrpt.pdf.

Federici, Silvia. *Wages against Housework*. Bristol, UK: The Power of Women Collective and the Falling Wall Press, 1975.

Feuz, Martin, Matthew Fuller, and Felix Stalder. "Personal Web Searching in the Age of Semantic Capitalism: Diagnosing the Mechanisms of Personalization." *First Monday* 16, no. 2 (2011).

Field, Frank. "Inside the Gig Economy: The 'Vulnerable Human Underbelly' of UK's Labour Market." *Guardian*, August 24, 2017.

Financial Times. "Four Simple Questions Facebook Should Answer." March 19, 2018.

Financial Times Confidential Research. "Data Worry Hinders South-East Asia Social Media Boom." *Financial Times*, July 25, 2018.

Flannery, Patrick. *I Am No One*. London: Atlantic Books, 2016.

Floridi, Luciano. *The Fourth Revolution*. Oxford, UK: Oxford University Press, 2014.

———. "On Human Dignity as a Foundation for The Right to Privacy." *Philosophy & Technology* 29, no. 4 (2016): 307–12.

———, ed. *The Onlife Manifesto*. Cham, CH: Springer International Publishing, 2014.

Foer, Franklin. *World without Mind*. London: Jonathan Cape, 2017.

Foucault, Michel. *The Birth of Biopolitics*. Basingstoke, UK: Palgrave Macmillan, 2008.

———. *Discipline and Punish*. New York: Vintage Books, 1995.

———. *The Order of Things*. London and New York: Routledge, 1994.

Fourcade, Marion, and Kieran Healy. "Classification Situations: Life-Chances in the Neoliberal Era." *Accounting, Organizations and Society* 38, no. 8 (2013): 559–72.

———. "Seeing Like a Market." *Socio-Economic Review* 15, no. 1 (2017): 9–29.

Fox-Brewster, Thomas. "Forget about Backdoors: This Is the Data WhatsApp Actually Hands to Cops." *Forbes*, January 22, 2017. https://www.forbes.com/sites/thomasbrewster/2017/01/22/whatsapp-facebook-backdoor-government-data-request/#12be27ae1030.

Fraser, Nancy. "Expropriation and Exploitation in Racialized Capitalism: A Reply to Michael Dawson." *Critical Historical Studies* 3, no. 1 (2016): 166–78.

———. "Reframing Global Justice." *New Left Review* 36 (2005): 69–90.

———. "A Triple Movement? Parsing the Politics of Crisis after Polanyi." *New Left Review* 81 (2013): 119–32.

Freire, Paulo. *Pedagogy of the Oppressed*. Harmondsworth, UK: Penguin, 1972.

Frey, Carl Benedikt, and Michael A. Osborne. "The Future of Employment: How Susceptible Are Jobs to Computerisation?" *Technological Forecasting and Social Change* 114, C (2017): 254–80.

Fried, Charles. *An Anatomy of Values*. Cambridge, MA: Harvard University Press, 1970.

Frischmann, Brett, and Evan Selinger. *Reengineering Humanity*. Cambridge. UK: Cambridge University Press, 2018.

Fuchs, Christian. *Digital Labour and Karl Marx*. London: Routledge, 2017.

———. "Political Economy and Surveillance Theory." *Critical Sociology* 39, no. 5 (2013): 671–87.

Fuchs, Christian, and Vincent Mosco, eds. *Marx in the Age of Digital Capitalism*. Leiden, NL: Brill, 2017.

Gabrys, Jennifer. *Program Earth*. Minneapolis: University of Minnesota Press, 2016.

Galeano, Eduardo. *Open Veins of Latin America*. New York: New York University Press, 1997.

Galloway, Scott. *The Four: The Hidden DNA of Amazon, Apple, Facebook, and Google*. New York: Random House, 2017.

Gandy, Oscar. *The Panoptic Sort*. Boulder, CO: Westview Press, 1993.

Gandy, Oscar, and Selena Nemorin. "Neuroeconomics, Behavioral Economics and the Political Economy of Nudge." Paper presented at the International Association for Media and Communication Research (IAMCR) 2017 Conference, Cartagena, CO, July 17. http://web.asc.upenn.edu/usr/ogandy/PENudge.pdf.

Gartner. "Gartner Says Worldwide IaaS Public Cloud Services Market Grew 29.5 Percent in 2017." August 1, 2018. https://www.gartner.com/newsroom/id /3884500.

Gebru, Timnit, Jonathan Krause, Yilun Wang, Duyun Chen, Jia Deng, and Li Fei-Fei. "Fine-Grained Car Detection for Visual Census Estimation." *AAAI* 2, no. 5 (2017): 6.

Gehl, Robert W. "What's on Your Mind? Social Media Monopolies and Noopower." *First Monday* 18, no. 3 (2013).

General Data Protection Regulation (GDPR). "Recital 1: Data Protection as a Fundamental Right." 2018. https://gdpr-info.eu/recitals/no-1/.

Generation Libre (Landreau, Isabelle, Gérard Peliks, Nicolas Binctin, and Virginie Pez-Pérard). *My Data Are Mine*. April 2018. https://www.generationlibre.eu /en/personnal-data-ownership/.

Gerlitz, Carolin. "What Counts? Reflections on the Multivalence of Social Media Data." *Digital Culture & Society* 2, no. 2 (2016): 19–38.

Gerlitz, Carolin, and Anne Helmond. "The Like Economy: Social Buttons and the Data-Intensive Web." *New Media & Society* 15, no. 8 (2013): 1348–65.

Gibson-Graham, J. K. *A PostCapitalist Politics*. Minneapolis: Minnesota University Press, 2007.

Giddens, Anthony. *Modernity and Self-Identity*. Stanford, CA: Stanford University Press, 1991.

Gill, Rosalind, and Andy Pratt. "In the Social Factory? Immaterial Labor, Precariousness and Cultural Work." *Theory Culture & Society* 25, nos. 7–8 (2008): 1–30.

Gillespie, Tarleton. *Custodians of the Internet*. New Haven, CT: Yale University Press, 2018.

———. "The Politics of 'Platforms.'" *New Media & Society* 12, no. 3 (2010): 347–64.

Gilliom, John. "A Response to Bennett's 'In Defence of Privacy.'" *Surveillance & Society* 8, no. 4 (2011): 500–504.

Gitelman, Lisa, ed. *"Raw Data" Is an Oxymoron*. Cambridge, MA: MIT Press, 2013.

Global Voices. "Can Facebook Connect the Next Billion?" Advox. July 27, 2017. https://advox.globalvoices.org/2017/07/27/can-facebook-connect-the-next -billion/.

Gomez-Uribe, Carlos. "A Global Approach to Recommendations." *Netflix* (blog), February 17, 2016. https://media.netflix.com/en/company-blog/a-global-ap proach-to-recommendations.

Gray, Mary, and Siddharth Suri. *Ghost Work*. New York: Houghton Mifflin Harcourt, 2019.

Greenberg, Andy. "Apple's Latest Selling Point: How Little It Knows about You." *Wired*, June 8, 2015. https://www.wired.com/2015/06/apples-latest-selling -point-little-knows/.

Greene, Daniel, and Genevieve Patterson, "The Trouble with Trusting AI to Interpret Policy Body-Cam Video." *IEEE Spectrum*, November 21, 2018. https:// spectrum.ieee.org/computing/software/the-trouble-with-trusting-ai-to-inter pret-police-bodycam-video.

Greene, Daniel, and Katie Shilton, "Platform Privacies: Governance, Collaboration, and the Different Meanings of 'Privacy' in iOS and Android Development." *New Media & Society* 20, no. 4 (2017): 1640–57.

Greenfield, Adam. *Radical Technologies*. London: Verso, 2017.

Greeven, Mark, and Wei Wei. "Meet China's New Tech Giants: Alibaba, Baidu, Tencent and Xiaomi." *The Telegraph*, October 17, 2017.

Gregg, Melissa. "The Doublespeak of the Gig Economy." *The Atlantic*, September 11, 2015.

Grewal, David. *Network Power*. New Haven, CT: Yale University Press, 2008.

Griffin, Andrew. "Facebook Is Going to Start Taking User Data from WhatsApp." *The Independent*, August 25, 2016.

Grosfoguel, Ramón. "The Epistemic Decolonial Turn." *Cultural Studies* 21, nos. 2–3 (2007): 211–23.

———. "Del 'Extractivismo Económico' al 'Extractivismo Epistémico' y al 'Extractivismo Ontológico': Una Forma Destructiva de Conocer, Ser y Estar en el Mundo." *Tabula Rasa, Bogotá-Colombia*, 24L (2016): 123–43.

Grosser, Benjamin. "What Do Metrics Want? How Quantification Prescribes Social Interaction on Facebook." *Computational Culture: A Journal of Software Studies* 4 (2014). http://computationalculture.net/what-do-metrics-want/.

Gurumurthy, Anita. "Big Brother Getting Bigger? The Privacy Issues Surrounding Aadhaar Are Worrying." *First Post*, April 3, 2017. http://www.firstpost.com /tech/news-analysis/big-brother-getting-bigger-the-privacy-issues-surround ing-aadhaar-are-worrying-3700365.html.

Gurumurthy, Anita, and Amrita Vasudevan. "Societal Need for Privacy Trumps the Individual." *First Post*, March 26, 2018. https://www.firstpost.com/tech /news-analysis/facebook-cambridge-analytica-row-whether-on-fb-or-aadhaar -societal-need-for-privacy-outweighs-personal-requirement-4405369.html.

Gurumurthy, Anita, Amrita Vasudevan, and Nandini Chami. "The Grand Myth of Cross-Border Data Flows in Trade Deals." *IT for Change*, December 2017.

https://www.itforchange.net/index.php/grand-myth-of-cross-border-data
-flows-trade-deals.

Habermas, Jürgen. *The Theory of Communicative Action*. Vol. 2. Cambridge, UK:
Polity, 1989.

Hacking, Ian. *The Social Construction of What?* Cambridge, MA: Harvard University Press, 1999.

———. *The Taming of Chance*. Cambridge, UK: Cambridge University Press, 1990.

Haggerty, Kevin D., and Richard V. Ericson. "The Surveillant Assemblage." *British
Journal of Sociology* 51, no. 4 (2000): 605–22.

Halavais, Alex. *Search Engine Society*. Cambridge, UK: Polity, 2007.

Halpern, Orit. *Beautiful Data*. Durham, NC: Duke University Press, 2015.

Hamblen, Matt. "Wearables for Workplace Wellness Face Federal Scrutiny."
Computerworld, June 19, 2015. https://www.computerworld.com/article/2937721
/wearables/wearables-for-workplace-wellness-face-federal-scrutiny.html.

Han, Byung-Chul. *Psychopolitics: Neoliberalism and New Technologies of Power*.
New York: Verso Books, 2017.

Hannam, Keshia. "This Chinese Giant Is Now Worth More than Facebook." *Fortune*, November 21, 2017. http://fortune.com/2017/11/21/tencent-market-capi
talization-500-billion-facebook/.

Harding, Sandra. "Postcolonial and Feminist Philosophies of Science and Technology: Convergences and Dissonances." *Postcolonial Studies* 12, no.4 (2009): 401–21.

Hardt, Michael, and Antonio Negri. *Assembly*. Oxford, UK: Oxford University
Press, 2017.

Harris, Cole. "How Did Colonialism Dispossess? Comments from an Edge of
Empire." *Annals of the Association of American Geographers* 94, no. 1 (2004):
165–82.

Harris, Jonathan Gil. "The Untimely Mammet of Verona." Unpublished paper,
2009. http://www.inthemedievalmiddle.com/2009/09/messianic-time-and-un
timely-papers.html.

Harris, Steven J. "Long-Distance Corporations, Big Sciences, and the Geography
of Knowledge." In *The Postcolonial Science and Technology Studies Reader*, edited by Sandra Harding, 61–83. Durham, NC: Duke University Press, 2011.

Harvey, David. *Justice, Nature and the Geography of Difference*. Oxford, UK:
Blackwell, 1996.

———. *Marx, Capital and the Madness of Economic Reason*. London: Profile
Books, 2017.

———. *The New Imperialism*. Oxford, UK: Oxford University Press, 2005.

———. "The 'New' Imperialism: Accumulation by Dispossession." *Socialist Register* 40 (2004): 63–87.

———. *A Short History of Neoliberalism*. New York: Oxford University Press,
2010.

Haupt, Michael. "'Data Is the New Oil'—A Ludicrous Proposition." *Twenty One Hundred*, May 2, 2016. https://medium.com/twenty-one-hundred/data-is-the-new-oil-a-ludicrous-proposition.

Hawkins, Amy. "Beijing's Big Brother Tech Needs African Faces." *Foreign Policy* (blog), July 24, 2018. https://foreignpolicy.com/2018/07/24/beijings-big-brother-tech-needs-african-faces/.

Health and Safety Executive Statistics. "Statistics—Work Related Stress, Depression or Anxiety." 2017. http://www.hse.gov.uk/statistics/causdis/stress/.

Heartfield, James. "Book Review: Andrew Kliman, The Failure of Capitalist Production: Underlying Causes of the Great Recession." *Platypus*, October 26, 2014. https://platypus1917.org/2014/10/26/the-failure-of-the-capitalist-class-and-the-retreat-from-production/.

Hediger, Heinrich. *Man and Animal in the Zoo: Zoo Biology*. London: Routledge, 1970.

Hegel, Georg W. F. *Elements of the Philosophy of Right*. Translated by H. B. Nisbet. Cambridge, UK: Cambridge University Press, (1821) 1921.

———. *Phenomenology of Spirit*. Translated by A. V. Miller. Oxford, UK: Oxford University Press, (1807) 1977.

Heinrich, Michael. "Crisis Theory, the Law of the Tendency of the Profit Rate to Fall, and Marx's Studies in the 1870s." *Monthly Review* 64, no. 11 (2013).

Heller, Nathan. "Is the Gig Economy Working?" *The New Yorker*, May 8, 2017. https://www.newyorker.com/magazine/2017/05/15/is-the-gig-economy-working.

Helmond, Anne. "The Platformization of the Web: Making Web Data Platform Ready." *Social Media & Society* 1, no. 2 (2015). DOI: 10.1177/2056305115603080.

Herzfeld, Michael. "The Absent Presence: Discourses of Crypto-Colonialism." *The South Atlantic Quarterly* 101, no. 4 (2002): 899–926.

Hesmondhalgh, David. "User-Generated Content, Free Labour, and the Cultural Industries." *Ephemera* 10, nos. 3–4 (2010).

Hesmondhalgh, David, and Sarah Baker. "Creative Work and Emotional Labour in the Television Industry." *Theory, Culture & Society* 25, nos. 7–8 (2008): 97–118.

Hildebrandt, Mireille. "Balance or Trade-Off? Online Security Technologies and Fundamental Rights." *Philosophy and Technology* 26, no. 4 (2013): 357–79.

———. *Smart Technologies and the End(s) of Law*. Cheltenham, UK: Edward Elgar Publishing, 2015.

Hildebrandt, Mireille, and Bert-Jaap Koops. "The Challenges of Ambient Law and Legal Protection in the Profiling Era." *Modern Law Review* 73, no. 3 (2010): 428–60.

Hill, Kashmir. "'God View': Uber Allegedly Stalked Users for Party-Goers Viewing Pleasure." *Forbes*, October 3, 2014. http://www.forbes.com/sites/kashmirhill/2014/10/03/god-view-uber-allegedly-stalked-users-for-party-goers-viewing-pleasure.

Hobbes, Thomas. *Leviathan*. Harmondsworth, UK: Penguin, (1651) 1985.

Hoffmann, Anna Lauren, Nicholas Proferes, and Michael Zimmer. "Making the World More Open and Connected: Mark Zuckerberg and the Discursive Construction of Facebook and Its Users." *New Media & Society* 20, no. 1 (2018): 199–218.

Hoffman, Chris. "10 Ridiculous EULA Clauses That You May Have Already Agreed To." *Make Use Of*, April 23, 2012. http://www.makeuseof.com/tag/10 -ridiculous-eula-clauses-agreed/.

Hong, Yu. *Networking China: The Digital Transformation of the Chinese Economy*. Champaign: University of Illinois Press, 2017.

Honneth, Axel. *Freedom's Right*. Cambridge, UK: Polity, 2014.

———. *The I in We*. Cambridge, UK: Polity, 2012.

Hoofnagle, Chris, and Jennifer Urban. "Alan Westin's Privacy *Homo Economicus*." *Wake Forest Law Review* 49 (2014): 261–306.

Hornung, Gerrit, and Christoph Schnabel. "Data Protection in Germany I: The Population Census Decision and the Right to Informational Self-Determination." *Computer Law & Security Review* 25, no. 1 (2009): 84–88.

Hsueh, Vicki. "Cultivating and Challenging the Common: Lockean Property, Indigenous Traditionalisms, and the Problem of Exclusion." *Contemporary Political Theory* 5 (2006): 193–214.

Huateng, Ma. "Open Letter: Seven Key Words to Create 'Digital Ecology Community.'" Internet. Tencent. October 30, 2017. http://tech.qq.com/a/20171030 /009650.htm.

Hull, Gordon. "Successful Failure: What Foucault Can Teach Us about Privacy Self-Management in a World of Facebook and Big Data." *Ethics and Information Technology* 17, no. 2 (2015): 89–101.

Humphreys, Lee. *The Qualified Self*. Cambridge, MA: MIT Press, 2018.

Hunegnaw, David. "The Future of User-Generated Content Is Owned." *AdAge*, January 6, 2017. http://adage.com/article/digitalnext/future-ugc-owned/307322/.

Hvistendahl, Mara. "Inside China's Vast New Experiment in Social Ranking." *Wired*, December 14, 2017.

IBM. *Annual Report 2017*. 2018. Available from http://www.annualreports.co.uk /HostedData/AnnualReports/PDF/NYSE_IBM_2017.pdf.

IBM. "Device Democracy: Saving the Internet of Things." 2014. https://www-935 .ibm.com/services/us/gbs/thoughtleadership/internetofthings/.

IBM. "First IBM Watson Education App for iPad Delivers Personalized Learning for K-12 Teachers and Students." October 19, 2016. http://www-03.ibm.com /press/us/en/pressrelease/50815.wss.

Identity Theft Resource Center. *Annual Data Breach Year-End Review*. 2017. https://www.idtheftcenter.org/2017-data-breaches.

Illich, Ivan. *Tools for Conviviality*. London: Fontana, 1973.

Impero Software and Digital Citizenship Institute. "Digital Citizenship: A Holistic Primer." *Learning Network NZ*. http://www.learningnetwork.ac.nz/shared/professionalReading/DIGCIT.pdf.

Innis, Harold. *A History of the Canadian Pacific Railway*. N.p.: HardPress Publishing, (1923) 2012.

Iyengar, Vinay, and Jeffrey Rayport. "When Consumer Packaged Goods Start Acting Like Software." *Venture Beat*, March 2018. https://venturebeat.com/2018/03/25/when-consumer-packaged-goods-start-acting-like-software/amp/?__twitter_impression=true.

Jais, Nina. "Insuring Shared Value Roundtable—January 19, 2017, Davos." *Shared Value Initiative*, January 27, 2017. https://www.sharedvalue.org/groups/insuring-shared-value.

Jarrett, Kylie. "The Relevance of 'Women's Work': Social Reproduction and Immaterial Labor in Digital Media." *Television & New Media* 15, no. 1 (2014): 14–29.

Jerome, Joseph. "Buying and Selling Privacy: Big Data's Different Burdens and Benefits." *Stanford Law Review Online* 66, no. 47 (2013): 47–53.

Joh, Elizabeth E. "Policing by Numbers: Big Data and the Fourth Amendment." *Washington Law Review* 89, no. 1 (2014): 35–68.

———. "The Undue Influence of Surveillance Technology Companies on Policing." *New York University Law Review* 92 (2017): 101–30.

John, Nicholas A. "The Social Logics of Sharing." *Communication Review* 16, no. 3 (2013): 113–31.

Kahneman, Daniel. *Thinking, Fast and Slow*. New York: Macmillan, 2011.

Kanngieser, Anja. "Tracking and Tracing: Geographies of Logistical Governance and Labouring Bodies." *Environment and Planning D: Society and Space* 31, no. 4 (2013): 594–610.

Kaplan, Bonnie. "Selling Health Data: De-Identification, Privacy, and Speech." *Cambridge Quarterly of Healthcare Ethics* 24, no. 3 (2014): 256–71.

Kaplan, Esther. "The Spy Who Fired Me." *Harper's Magazine*, March 2015. https://harpers.org/archive/2015/03/the-spy-who-fired-me/.

Kaplan, Martha. "Panopticon in Poona: An Essay on Foucault and Colonialism." *Cultural Anthropology* 10, no. 1 (1995): 85–98.

Kaye, Kate. "The $24 Billion Data Business That Telcos Don't Want to Talk About." *AdAge*, October 26, 2015. http://adage.com/article/datadriven-marketing/24-billion-data-business-telcos-discuss/301058/.

Kazmin, Amy. "Indians Sound Alarm Over 'Orwellian' Data Collection System." *Financial Times*, July 30, 2018.

Keen, Andrew. *The Internet Is Not the Answer*. London: Atlantic Books, 2015.

Kelly, Kevin. *The Inevitable*. New York: Penguin, 2016.

———. "New Rules for the New Economy." *Wired*, September 1, 1997.

————. *What Technology Wants*. New York: Penguin, 2010.

Kelman, Steven. "The Political Foundations of American Statistical Policy." In *The Politics of Numbers*, edited by William Alonso and Paul Starr, 275–302. New York: Russell Sage Foundation, 1988.

Kennedy, Helen. *Post, Mine, Repeat*. Basingstoke, UK: Palgrave Macmillan, 2016.

Kerr, Orin. "What's the Status of the Mosaic Theory After Jones?" *The Volokh Conspiracy* (blog), January 23, 2012. http://volokh.com/2012/01/23/whats-the-status-of-the-mosaic-theory-after-jones/.

Khatchadourian, Raffi. "We Know How You Feel." *The New Yorker*, January 12, 2015.

Khosla, Aditya, Byoungkwon An, Joseph J. Lim, and Antonio Torralba. "Looking Beyond the Visible Scene." In *Proceedings of the IEEE Conference on Computer Vision and Pattern Recognition*, Columbus, OH, 2014, 3710–17.

Kirkpatrick, David. *The Facebook Effect*. New York: Simon and Schuster, 2010.

Kitchin, Rob. *The Data Revolution*. London: Sage, 2014.

Kitchin, Rob, and Martin Dodge. *Code/Space*. Cambridge, MA: MIT Press, 2011.

Kitchin, Rob, and Gavin McArdle. "Urban Data and City Dashboards: Six Key Issues." *SocArXiv* (2016). https://osf.io/k2epn/.

Klein, Ezra. "Mark Zuckerberg on Facebook's Hardest Year, and What Comes Next." *Vox*, April 2, 2018. https://www.vox.com/2018/4/2/17185052/mark-zuckerberg-facebook-interview-fake-news-bots-cambridge.

Klein, Naomi. "Dancing the World into Being: A Conversation with Idle No More's Leanne Simpson." *YES! Magazine*, March 5, 2013. http://www.yesmagazine.org/peace-justice/dancing-the-world-into-being-a-conversation-with-idle-no-more-leanne-simpson.

————. *This Changes Everything: Capitalism vs. the Climate*. New York: Simon & Schuster, 2015.

Kliman, Andrew. *The Failure of Capitalist Production*. London: Pluto Press, 2011.

Knight, Will. "China's AI Awakening." *MIT Technology Review*, October 10, 2017. https://www.technologyreview.com/s/609038/chinas-ai-awakening/.

Kobek, Jarett. *I Hate the Internet*. London: Serpent's Tail, 2016.

Kofman, Ava. "Taser Will Use Police Body Camera Videos 'to Anticipate Criminal Activity.'" *The Intercept*, April 30, 2017. https://theintercept.com/2017/04/30/taser-will-use-police-body-camera-videos-to-anticipate-criminal-activity/.

Kollewe, Julia. "Marmite Maker Unilever Threatens to Pull Ads from Facebook and Google." *Guardian*, February 12, 2018.

Krazit, Tom. "Amazon Web Services Backs Deep-Learning Format Introduced by Microsoft and Facebook." *Geekwire*, November 16, 2017. https://www.geekwire.com/2017/amazon-web-services-backs-deep-learning-format-introduced-microsoft-facebook/.

Krishna, Sankaran. *Globalization and Postcolonialism*. Lanham, MD: Rowman & Littlefield Publishers, 2008.

Kuchler, Hannah. "Facebook Investors Wake Up to Era of Slower Growth." *Financial Times*, July 26, 2018.

———. "Max Schrems: The Man Who Took on Facebook—and Won." *Financial Times*, April 5, 2018.

———. "Privacy Pioneers Plan 'Zero Tracking' Rival to Facebook." *Financial Times*, July 17, 2018.

Kücklich, Julian. "Michael Jackson and the Death of Macrofame." *IDC*, June 26, 2009. https://lists.thing.net/pipermail/idc/2009-June/003664.html.

Kunelius, Risto, Heikki Heikkila, Adrienne Russell, and Dmitry Yagodin, eds. *Journalism and the NSA Revelations*. London: I. B. Tauris and Reuters Institute for the Study of Journalism, 2017.

Kurzweil, Raymond. *The Singularity Is Near*. New York: Penguin, 2005.

Laboratory for Systems Medicine. "This Is the Idea: We Extract Meaning from Health Data." 2018. http://labsysmed.org/.

Langfur, Hal. "Myths of Pacification: Brazilian Frontier Settlement and the Subjugation of the Bororo Indians." *Journal of Social History* 32, no. 4 (1999): 879–905.

Lanier, Jaron. *Ten Arguments for Deleting Your Social Media Accounts Right Now*. London: Bodley Head, 2018.

———. *Who Owns the Future?* London: Allen Lane, 2014.

Lardinois, Frederic. "Google Maps Updates Its Local Guides Program with a New Points System and More Levels." *TechCrunch*, June 13, 2017. https://techcrunch.com/2017/06/13/google-maps-updates-it-local-guides-program-with-a-new-points-system-and-more-levels/.

Larmer, Brook. "China's Revealing Spin on the 'Sharing Economy.'" *New York Times*, November 20, 2017.

Latour, Bruno. *Pandora's Hope*. Cambridge, MA: Harvard University Press, 1999.

Lazzarato, Maurizio. *Signs and Machines*. Pasadena, CA: Semiotext(e), 2014.

Lefebvre, Henri. *Critique of Everyday Life*. London, Verso, (1968) 2014.

Lemke, Thomas. "'The Birth of Bio-Politics': Michel Foucault's Lecture at the Collège de France on Neo-Liberal Governmentality." *Economy and Society* 30, no. 2 (2001): 190–207.

Lepore, Jill. "The Hacking of America." *New York Times*, September 17, 2018.

Leslie, Ian. "The Scientist Who Makes Apps Addictive." *1843 Magazine*, October/November, 2016. https://www.1843magazine.com/features/the-scientists-who-make-apps-addictive.

Levy, Karen. "The Contexts of Control: Information, Power, and Truck-Driving Work." *The Information Society* 31, no. 2 (2015): 160–74.

Lewis, Paul. "What If He's Right? Michal Kosinski and the Limits of Modern Surveillance." *Guardian* Weekend Magazine, July 7, 2018, 25–31.

Leys, Ruth. "The Turn to Affect: A Critique." *Critical Inquiry* 37, no. 3 (2011):
434–72.

Lin, Liza, and Josh Chin. "China's Tech Giants Have a Second Job: Helping Beijing
Spy on Its People." *Wall Street Journal*, November 30, 2017.

Loomba, Ania. *Colonialism/Postcolonialism.* London: Routledge, 1998.

Lopez, Linette. "There Are Signs China Is Turning against Alibaba." *Business Insider*, March 21, 2016. http://uk.businessinsider.com/china-turns-against-ali
baba-2016-3.

Lowe, Lisa. *The Intimacies of Four Continents.* Durham, NC: Duke University
Press, 2015.

Lucas, Louise. "Patent Filings Reflect China's Zeal for Facial Recognition Tech."
Financial Times, March 22, 2018.

Luckin, Rose, Wayne Holmes, Mark Griffiths, and Laurie B. Forcier. "Intelligence
Unleashed: An Argument for AI in Education." Pearson and UCL Knowledge
Lab, 2016. https://static.googleusercontent.com/media/edu.google.com/pt-BR
//pdfs/Intelligence-Unleashed-Publication.pdf.

Lugones, Maria. "Heterosexualism and the Colonial/Modern Gender System."
Hypatia 22, no. 1 (2007): 186–219.

Lupton, Deborah. "The Diverse Domains of Quantified Selves: Self-Tracking
Modes and Dataveillance." *Economy and Society* 45, no. 1 (2016): 101–22.

———. *The Quantified Self.* Cambridge, UK: Polity, 2016.

Lupton, Deborah, Sarah Pink, Christine Heyes Lebond and Shanti Sumartojo.
"Personal Data Contexts, Data Sense, and Self-Tracking Cycling." *International Journal of Communication*, 12 (2018): 647–65.

Lyon, David. *Surveillance After Snowden.* Cambridge, UK: Polity, 2015.

———, ed. *Surveillance as Social Sorting.* New York: Routledge, 2002.

Lyotard, Jean-Francois. *The Inhuman.* Cambridge, UK: Polity, 1991.

Ma, Alexandra. "Thousands of People in Sweden Are Embedding Microchips under Their Skin to Replace ID Cards." *Business Insider*, May 14, 2018. http://
businessinsider.com/swedish-people-microchips-under-skin-to-replace-id
-cards-2018-5.

Mac, Ryan, Charlie Warzel, and Alex Kantrowitz. "Growth at Any Cost: Top
Facebook Executive Defended Data Collection in 2016 Memo—and Warned
That Facebook Could Get People Killed." *Buzzfeed*, March 29, 2018. https://
www.buzzfeed.com/ryanmac/growth-at-any-cost-top-facebook-executive
-defended-data?utm_term=.ic6Kk31qJ#.uxg0JqWVP.

MacPherson, C. B. *The Political Theory of Possessive Individualism.* Oxford, UK:
Oxford University Press, 1962.

Madden, Mary, Michelle Gilman, Karen Levy, and Alice Marwick. "Privacy, Poverty and Big Data: A Matrix of Vulnerabilities for Poor Americans." *Washington University Law Review*, 95 (2017): 53–125.

Madden, Mary, and Lee Rainie. "Americans' Attitudes about Privacy, Security and Surveillance." Pew Research Foundation, May 20, 2015. http://www.pewinternet.org/2015/05/20/americans-attitudes-about-privacy-security-and-surveillance/.

Maldonado-Torres, Nelson. "On the Coloniality of Being: Contributions to the Development of a Concept." *Cultural Studies* 21, nos. 2–3 (2007): 240–70.

Maldonado-Torres, Nelson. "Colonialism, Neocolonial, Internal Colonialism, the Postcolonial, Coloniality, and Decoloniality." In *Critical Terms in Caribbean and Latin American Thought*, edited by Yolanda Martínez-San Miguel, Ben Sifuentes-Jáuregui, and Marisa Belausteguigoitia, 67–78. New York: Macmillan, 2016.

Malgieri, Gian Claudio, and Bart Custers. "Pricing Privacy: The Right to Know the Value of Your Personal Data." *Computer Law & Security Review* 34, no. 2 (2018): 289–303.

Manikonda, Lydia, Aditya Deotale, and Subbarao Kambhampati. "What's Up with Privacy?: User Preferences and Privacy Concerns in Intelligent Personal Assistants." *arXiv* preprint, 2017. arXiv:1711.07543.

Manning, Alan. *Monopsony in Motion*. Princeton, NJ: Princeton University Press, 2005.

Manovich, Lev. "100 Billion Data Rows Per Second: Media Analytics in the Early 21st Century." *International Journal of Communication* 12 (2018): 473–88.

Mansell, Robin. *Imagining the Internet: Communications, Innovation and Governance*. Oxford, UK: Oxford University Press, 2012.

Manyika, James, Susan Lund, Jacques Bughin, Jonathan Woetzel, Kalin Stamenov, and Dhruv Dhingra. "Digital Globalization: The New Era of Global Flows." McKinsey, March 2016. http://www.mckinsey.com/business-functions/digital-mckinsey/our-insights/digital-globalization-the-new-era-of-global-flows.

Marazzi, Christian. *Capital and Language*. Los Angeles: Semiotext(e), 2008.

Marshall, Jack. "What Marketers Need to Know About Facebook's Atlas." *The Wall Street Journal*, September 29, 2014.

Martin, Eric, and Andrew Mayeda. "Amazon Would Gain from Trump Push to Boost Cross-Border Retail." *Bloomberg*, October 6, 2017. https://www.bloomberg.com/news/articles/2017-10-06/amazon-would-gain-from-trump-push-to-boost-cross-border-retail.

Martin, Giles. "Microsoft Is Launching a Huge Reorganization to Focus on AI and the Cloud." *MIT Technology Review*, March 29, 2018. https://www.technologyreview.com/the-download/610725/microsoft-is-doing-the-splits-to-focus-on-ai-and-the-cloud/?utm_campaign=add_this&utm_source=twitter&utm_medium=post.

Martin, Neale. *Habit: The 95% of Behaviour Marketers Ignore*. Upper Saddle River, NJ: Pearson Education, 2009.

Martin, Randy. *An Empire of Indifference*. Durham, NC: Duke University Press, 2007.

Marx, Karl. *Capital*. Vol. I. Harmondsworth, UK: Penguin, 1976.

———. *Capital*. Vol. III. Harmondsworth, UK: Penguin, 1993.

———. *Economic and Philosophic Manuscripts of 1844*. London: Lawrence and Wishart, 1973.

———. *Grundrisse*. Harmondsworth, UK: Penguin, 1973.

Marx, Leon. "Closely Watched Trains." *New York Review of Books*, March 15, 1984.

Mason, Paul. *Postcapitalism*. Harmondsworth, UK: Penguin, 2015.

Mattelart, Armand. *Networking the World, 1794–2000*. Minneapolis: University of Minnesota Press, 2000.

Max, D. T. "'SKAM,' the Radical Teen Drama That Unfolds One Post at a Time." *The New Yorker*, June 11, 2018.

Maxwell, Richard, and Toby Miller. *Greening the Media*. Oxford, NY: Oxford University Press, 2012.

Mayer-Schönberger, Viktor, and Kenneth Cukier. *Big Data*. London: John Murray, 2013.

McChesney, Robert. *Digital Disconnect*. New York: The New Press, 2013.

McGee, Chantel. "Only 4 Percent of Uber Drivers Remain After a Year Says Report." *CNBC*, April 20, 2017. https://www.cnbc.com/2017/04/20/only-4-percent-of-uber-drivers-remain-after-a-year-says-report.html.

McIntyre, Niamh, and David Pegg. "Council Algorithms Use Family Data to Predict Child Abuse Risk." *Guardian* (UK edition), September 17, 2018.

McKenna, Erin, and Scott L. Pratt. *American Philosophy: From Wounded Knee to the Present*. London: Bloomsbury, 2015.

McMahon, John. "Behavioral Economics as Neoliberalism: Producing and Governing Homo Economicus." *Contemporary Political Theory* 14, no. 2 (2015): 137–58.

Meiksins Wood, Ellen. "The Uses and Abuses of 'Civil Society.'" *Socialist Register* 26 (March 1990): 60–84. https://socialistregister.com/index.php/srv/article/view/5574.

Mejias, Ulises Ali. *Off the Network*. Minneapolis: University of Minnesota Press, 2013.

Mejias, Ulises Ali, and Nikolai E. Vokuev. "Disinformation and the Media: The Case of Russia and Ukraine." *Media, Culture & Society* 39, no. 7 (2017): 1027–42.

Memmi, Albert. *The Colonizer and the Colonized*. Translated by Susan Gibson Miller. Boston: Beacon Press, 1991.

Meng, Bingchun. *The Politics of Chinese Media*. Basingstoke, UK: Palgrave MacMillan, 2018.

Mezzadra, Sandro, and Brett Neilson. "On the Multiple Frontiers of Extraction: Excavating Contemporary Capitalism." *Cultural Studies* 31, nos. 2–3 (2017): 185–204.

Mignolo, Walter D. *The Darker Side of Western Modernity.* Durham, NC: Duke University Press, 2011.

———. "Delinking: The Rhetoric of Modernity, the Logic of Coloniality and the Grammar of De-Coloniality." *Cultural Studies* 21, nos. 2–3 (2007): 449–514.

Miller, Ron. "Google's Latest Undersea Cable Project Will Connect Japan to Australia." *Techcrunch*, April 4, 2018.

Mirowski, Philip. *Machine Dreams.* Cambridge, UK: Cambridge University Press, 2002.

Mitchell, Stacy. "Amazon Is Trying to Control the Underlying Infrastructure of Our Economy." *Motherboard*, June 25, 2017. https://motherboard.vice.com/en_us/article/7xpgvx/amazons-is-trying-to-control-the-underlying-infrastructure-of-our-economy.

MIT Technology Review. "Social Physics." *MIT Technology Review*, March 4, 2014. https://www.technologyreview.com/s/525341/social-physics.

Montgomerie, Johnna, ed. *Critical Methods in Political and Cultural Economy.* New York: Routledge, 2017.

Moore, Jason W. *Capitalism in the Web of Life.* New York: Verso, 2015.

———. "Sugar and the Expansion of the Early Modern World-Economy." *Review (Fernand Braudel Center)* 23, no. 3 (2000): 409–33.

Moore, Phoebe, and Lukasz Piwek. "Regulating Wellbeing in the Brave New Quantified Workplace." *Employee Relations* 39, no. 3 (2017): 308–16.

Morozov, Evgeny. "After the Facebook Scandal It's Time to Base the Digital Economy on Public v Private Ownership of Data." *The Observer*, April 1, 2018.

———. "Will Tech Giants Move On from the Internet, Now We've All Been Harvested?" *The Observer*, January 28, 2018.

Mosco, Vincent. *Becoming Digital.* Bingley, UK: Emerald Publishing, 2017.

Mosco, Vincent. *To the Cloud.* Boulder, CO: Routledge, 2014.

Mulcahy, Diane. *The Gig Economy.* New York: AMACOM, 2016.

Murphy, Emily R., Judy Illes, and Peter B. Reiner. "Neuroethics of Neuromarketing." *Journal of Consumer Behaviour* 7, nos. 4–5 (2009): 293–302.

Murphy, Raymond. "Exploitation or Exclusion?" *Sociology* 19, no. 2 (1985): 225–43.

Nadella, Satya. *Hit Refresh.* New York: Harper Business Books, 2017.

Nadler, Anthony, and Lee McGuigan. "An Impulse to Exploit: The Behavioral Turn in Data-Driven Marketing." *Critical Studies in Media Communication* 35, no. 2 (2018): 151–65.

Nafus, Dawn, and Jamie Sherman. "This One Does Not Go Up to 11: The Quantified Self as an Alternative Big Data Practice." *International Journal of Communication* 8, no. 11 (2014): 1784–94.

Nandy, Ashis. *The Intimate Enemy*. 2nd ed. Oxford, UK: Oxford University Press, 2010.

Napoli, Philip M. "Automated Media: An Institutional Theory Perspective on Algorithmic Media Production and Consumption." *Communication Theory* 24, no. 3 (2014): 340–60.

NASSCOM. *The IT-BPM Sector in India 2018: Amplify Digital*. March 13, 2018. http://www.nasscom.in/knowledge-center/publications/the-it-bpm-sector -india-2018-amplify-digital.

Naughton, John. "Who's Doing Google and Facebook's Dirty Work?" *Guardian*, December 24, 2017.

Neff, Gina, and Dawn Nafus. *Self-Tracking*. Cambridge, MA: MIT Press, 2016.

Negri, Antonio. *Marx Beyond Marx*. New York: Autonomedia, 1992.

Neuhouser, Frederick. *Foundations of Hegel's Social Theory*. Cambridge, MA: Harvard University Press, 2000.

Newman, Nathan. "UnMarginalizing Workers: How Big Data Drives Lower Wages and How Reframing Labor Law Can Restore Information Equality in the Workplace." *Social Science Research Network*, August 8, 2016. https:// papers.ssrn.com/sol3/papers.cfm?abstract_id=2819142.

Neyland, Daniel, and Norma Möllers. "Algorithmic IF . . . THEN Rules and the Conditions and Consequences of Power." *Information Communication and Society* 20, no. 1 (2017): 45–62.

Nieborg, David, and Thomas Poell. "Platformization of Cultural Production: Theorizing the Contingent Cultural Commodity." *New Media & Society* (2018). DOI: 10.1177/1461444818769694.

Nissenbaum, Helen. "Deregulating Collection: Must Privacy Give Way to Use Regulation?" *Social Science Research Network*, December 28, 2017. https:// papers.ssrn.com/sol3/papers.cfm?abstract_id=3092282.

———. *Privacy in Context*. Stanford, CA: Stanford University Press, 2010.

Noble, Safiya Umoja. *Algorithms of Oppression*. New York: NYU Press, 2018.

Obar, Jonathan A., and Anne Oeldorf-Hirsch. "The Biggest Lie on the Internet: Ignoring the Privacy Policies and Terms of Service Policies of Social Networking Services." *Social Science Research Network*, May 13, 2018. https://papers.ssrn .com/abstract=2757465.

Obermeyer, Ziad, and Ezekiel J. Emanuel. "Predicting the Future: Big Data, Machine Learning, and Clinical Medicine." *New England Journal of Medicine* 375, no. 13 (2016): 1216–19.

Olsen, Porter, and Roopika Risam. "Postcolonial Digital Humanities." In *The Encyclopedia of Postcolonial Studies*, edited by Sangeeta Ray, Henry Schwarz, Jose Luis Villacanas Berlanga, Alberto Moreiras, and April Shemak. London: Wiley-Blackwell, 2016.

Olson, Parmy. "Exclusive: WhatsApp Co-Founder Brian Acton Gives the Inside Story on #DeleteFacebook and Why He Left $850 Million Behind," *Forbes*, September 26, 2018.

O'Neil, Cathy. *Weapons of Math Destruction*. London: Allen Lane, 2016.

O'Neill, Onora. *Autonomy and Trust in Bioethics*. Cambridge UK: Cambridge University Press, 2002.

Ong, Walter. *Orality and Literacy*. London: Methuen, 1982.

Organisation for Economic Co-operation and Development (OECD). "Data-Driven Innovation: Big Data for Growth and Well-Being." October 6, 2015. http://www.oecd.org/sti/ieconomy/data-driven-innovation.htm.

Organisation for Economic Co-operation and Development (OECD). "Share of ICT Investment." 2016. http://www.oecd-ilibrary.org/content/graph/pdtvy-2016 -graph6-en.

Owens, Chante. "Stranger Hacks Family's Baby Monitor and Talks to Child at Night." *San Francisco Globe*, December 17, 2017.

Owens, Trevor. "Sid Meier's Colonization: Is It Offensive Enough?" *Play The Past* (blog), November 30, 2010.

Padios, Jan M. "Mining the Mind: Emotional Extraction, Productivity, and Predictability in the Twenty-First Century." *Cultural Studies* 31, nos. 2–3 (2017): 205–31.

PageFair. *The State of the Blocked Web: 2017 Global Adblock Report*. February 2017. https://pagefair.com/downloads/2017/01/PageFair-2017-Adblock-Report .pdf.

Palmer, Michael. "Data Is the New Oil." *ANA Marketing Maestros*, November 3, 2016. http://ana.blogs.com/maestros/2006/11/data_is_the_new.html.

Panitch, Leo, and Sam Gindin. *The Making of Global Capitalism*. London: Verso, 2013.

Pantzar, Mika, and Minna Ruckenstein. "Living the Metrics: Self-Tracking and Situated Objectivity." *Digital Health* 3 (2017): 1–10.

Parikka, Jussi. *Insect Media*. Minneapolis: University of Minnesota Press, 2010.

Parks, Lisa, and Nicole Starosielski, eds. *Signal Traffic*. Champaign: University of Illinois Press, 2015.

Pasquale, Frank. *The Black Box Society*. Cambridge, MA: Harvard University Press, 2015.

Peña Gangadharan, Seeta. "Digital Inclusion and Data Profiling." *First Monday* 17, no 5 (2012).

Pentland, Alex. *Social Physics*. New York: Penguin, 2014.

Peppet, Scott. "Regulating the Internet of Things: First Steps Toward Managing Discrimination, Privacy, Security and Consent." *Texas Law Review* 93 (2014): 86–176.

Perez, Sarah. "Apple Unveils a New Set of 'Digital Wellness' Features for Better Managing Screen Time." *TechCrunch*, June 4, 2018.

Peterson, Andrea. "Snapchat Agrees to Settle FTC Charges that It Deceived Users." *The Washington Post*, May 24, 2014.

Pfeffer, Fabian T., and Robert F. Schoeni. "How Wealth Inequality Shapes Our Future." *RSF: The Russell Sage Foundation Journal of the Social Sciences* 2, no. 6 (2016): 2–22.

Phillips, Tom. "China Orders GPS Tracking of Every Car in Troubled Region." *Guardian*, February 20, 2017.

Piketty, Thomas. *Capital in the Twenty-First Century*. Cambridge, MA: Harvard University Press, 2017.

Pinkard, Terry. *Hegel's Naturalism*. Oxford, UK: Oxford University Press, 2012.

Pinker, Steven. *Enlightenment Now*. New York, Vintage Books, 2018.

Pippin, Robert. *Hegel's Practical Philosophy*. Cambridge, UK: Cambridge University Press, 2008.

Pitts, Frederick Harry. "Beyond the Fragment: Postoperaismo, Postcapitalism and Marx's 'Notes on Machines,' 45 Years on." *Economy and Society* 46, nos. 3–4 (2017): 324–45.

Plantin, Jean-Christophe. "The Politics of Mapping Platforms: Participatory Radiation Mapping after the Fukushima Daiichi Disaster." *Media, Culture & Society* 37, no. 6 (2015): 904–21.

Plantin, Jean-Christophe, Carl Lagoze, Paul Edwards, and Christian Sandvig. "Infrastructure Studies Meet Platform Studies in the Age of Google and Facebook." *New Media & Society* 20, no. 1 (2016): 293–310.

Pogge, Thomas. *Politics as Usual*. Cambridge, UK: Polity, 2010.

Polanyi, Karl. *The Great Transformation*. Boston: Beacon Press, (1944) 2001.

Pomeranz, Kenneth. *The Great Divergence*. Rev. ed. Princeton, NJ: Princeton University Press, 2001.

Pope Francis. *Encyclical on Climate Change and Inequality*. New York: Melville House, 2015.

Porter, Theodore. *The Rise of Statistical Reasoning 1820–1900*. Princeton, NJ: Princeton University Press, 1986.

———. *Trust in Numbers*. Princeton, NJ: Princeton University Press, 1996.

Posner, Eric, and Glen Weyl. *Radical Markets*. Princeton, NJ: Princeton University Press, 2018.

Posner, Richard. "The Right of Privacy." *Georgia Law Review* 12 (1977): 393–422.

Postone, Moishe. "Rethinking Marx (in a Post-Marxist World)." In *Reclaiming the Sociological Classics*, edited by Charles Camic, 45–80. Oxford, UK: Wiley-Blackwell, 1998.

Prakash, Om. "The English East India Company and India." In *The Worlds of the East India Company*, edited by H. V. Bowen, Margarette Lincoln, and Nigel Rigby, 1–18. Woodbridge, UK: Boydell Press, 2002.

PricewaterhouseCoopers. "The Wearable Future." *PricewaterhouseCoopers*, 2014. https://www.pwc.com/mx/es/industrias/archivo/2014-11-pwc-the-wearable -future.pdf.

Pridmore, Jason, and Detlev Zwick. "Marketing and the Rise of Commercial Consumer Surveillance." *Surveillance & Society* 8, no. 3 (2011): 269–77.

Priestley, Mark. *A Science of Operations*. London: Springer-Verlag, 2011.

PR Newswire. "TASER Makes Two Acquisitions to Create Axon AI." February 9, 2017. https://www.prnewswire.com/news-releases/taser-makes-two-acquisitions -to-create-axon-ai -300404780.

Prosser, William L. "Privacy." *California Law Review* 48 (1960): 383–423.

Pykett, Jessica. "Neurocapitalism and the New Neuros: Using Neuroeconomics, Behavioural Economics and Picoeconomics for Public Policy." *Journal of Economic Geography* 13, no. 5 (2013): 845–69.

Qiu, Jack Linchuan. *Goodbye iSlave*. Champaign: University of Illinois Press, 2016.

Quijano, Aníbal. "Coloniality and Modernity/Rationality." *Cultural Studies* 21, nos. 2–3 (2007): 168–78.

———. "Coloniality of Power, Eurocentrism, and Latin America." *Nepantla: Views from South* 1, no. 3 (2000): 533–80.

Radin, Joanna. "'Digital Natives': How Medical and Indigenous Histories Matter for Big Data." *Osiris*, vol. 32 (2017): 43–64.

Rai, Sonam. "Acxiom Shares Tank after Facebook Cuts Ties with Data Brokers." *Reuters*, March 29, 2018. https://www.reuters.com/article/us-acxiom-stocks /acxiom-shares-tank-after-facebook-cuts-ties-with-data-brokers-idUSKBN 1H520U.

Rainie, Lee, and Maeve Duggan. "Privacy and Information Sharing." Pew Research Foundation, January 14, 2016. http://www.pewinternet.org/2016/01/14 /privacy-and-information-sharing/.

Reuters. "China Chides Tech Firms over Privacy Safeguards." *CNBC*, January 12, 2018. https://www.cnbc.com/2018/01/12/china-chides-alibaba-baidu-over-pri vacy-safeguards.html.

Rhode, Jason. "Apple's Biggest Innovation Isn't Gadgets. It's Dodging Taxes." *Salon*, January 7, 2018. https://www.salon.com/2018/01/07/apples-biggest-innova tion-is-not-gadgets-it-is-dodging-taxes/.

Richards, Neil M. "The Dangers of Surveillance." *Harvard Law Review* 126, no. 7 (2013): 1934–65.

———. *Intellectual Privacy*. Oxford, UK: Oxford University Press, 2015.

Ricoeur, Paul. *Freud and Philosophy*. New Haven, CT: Yale University Press, 1977.

————. *Oneself as Another.* Chicago: University of Chicago Press, 1992.

Rieder, Bernhard. "Big Data and the Paradox of Diversity." *Digital Culture & Society* 2, no. 2 (2016): 39–54.

————. "What Is in PageRank? A Historical and Conceptual Investigation of Recursive Status Index." *Computational Culture: A Journal of Software Studies,* no. 6 (2012): 1–28. http://computationalculture.net/article/what_is_in _pagerank.

Rieder, Bernhard, and Theo Röhle. "Digital Methods: From Challenges to Bildung." In *The Datafied Society,* edited by Mirko Schäfer and Karin Van Es, 109–24. Amsterdam: Amsterdam University Press, 2017.

Rifkin, Jeremy. *The Zero Marginal Cost Society.* New York: St. Martin's Press, 2014.

Roberts, Sarah T. "Social Media's Silent Filter." *The Atlantic,* March 8, 2017.

Rodwin, Marc A. "Patient Data: Property, Privacy & the Public Interest." *American Journal of Law and Medicine* 36, no. 4 (2010): 586–618.

Rooney, Sally. "An App to Cure My Fainting Spells." *The New Yorker,* November 20, 2017.

Rose, Nikolas. *Inventing Our Selves.* Cambridge, UK: Cambridge University Press, 1998.

————. *The Politics of Life Itself.* Princeton, NJ: Princeton University Press, 2009.

————. *Powers of Freedom.* Cambridge, UK: Cambridge University Press, 1999.

————. "Screen and Intervene: Governing Risky Brains." *History of the Human Sciences* 23, no. 1 (2010): 79–105.

Rosenblat, Alex, Tamara Kneese, and danah boyd. "Workplace Surveillance." *Social Science Research Network,* December 14, 2014. https://papers.ssrn.com /abstract=2536605.

Rosenblat, Alex, and Luke Stark. "Algorithmic Labor and Information Asymmetries: A Case Study of Uber's Drivers." *International Journal of Communication* 10 (2016): 3748–84.

Rosenthal, Caitlin. "Slavery's Scientific Management." In *Slavery's Capitalism,* edited by Sven Beckert and Seth Rockman, 62–86. Philadelphia: University of Pennsylvania Press, 2016.

Rossiter, Ned. *Software, Infrastructure, Labor.* New York: Routledge, 2016.

Rössler, Beate. *The Value of Privacy.* Cambridge, UK: Polity, 2005.

Rouvroy, Antoinette. "The End(s) of Critique: Data Behaviourism versus Due Process." In *Privacy, Due Process and the Computational Turn,* edited by Mireille Hildebrandt and Ekaterina de Vries, 143–67. London: Routledge, 2012.

Rouvroy, Antoinette, and Yves Poullet. "The Right to Informational Self-Determination and the Value of Self-Development." In *Reinventing Data Protection?,* edited by Serge Gutwirth, Yves Poullet, Paul de Hert, Cécile de Terwangne, and Sjaak Nouwt, 45–76. New York: Springer, 2009.

Ruppert, Evelyn. "Population Objects: Interpassive Subjects." *Sociology* 45, no. 2 (2011): 218–33.

Russell, Jon. "Alibaba Debuts 'Smile to Pay' Facial Recognition Payments at KFC in China." *TechCrunch*, September 3, 2017. https://techcrunch.com/2017/09/03 /alibaba-debuts-smile-to-day/.

Ryan, Johnny. "Facebook's Hackproof Ads Turned Its Adblocking Problem into a $709 Million Revenue Stream." *PageFair* (blog), November 2, 2017. https:// pagefair.com/blog/2017/facebook-adblock-audience/.

Sacks, Samm. 2018. "New China Data Privacy Standard Looks More Far-Reaching than GDPR." *Center for Strategic and International Studies*, January 29, 2018. https://www.csis.org/analysis/new-china-data-privacy-standard-looks-more -far-reaching-gdpr.

Sa'di, Ahmad H. "Colonialism and Surveillance." In *Routledge Handbook of Surveillance Studies*, edited by Kirstie Ball, Kevin D. Haggerty, and David Lyon, 151–58. New York: Routledge, 2012.

Said, Edward W. *Orientalism*. New York: Vintage, 1979.

Sallomi, Paul, and Paul Lee. "Technology, Media and Telecommunications Predictions, 2017." *Deloitte*, 2017. https://www2.deloitte.com/content/dam/Deloitte /global/Documents/Technology-Media-Telecommunications/gx-deloitte -2017-tmt-predictions.pdf.

Samaddar, Ranabir. *Karl Marx and the Postcolonial Age*. New York: Palgrave Macmillan, 2017.

Sandvig, Christian. "The Facebook 'It's Not Our Fault' Study." *Social Media Collective*, May 7, 2015. https://socialmediacollective.org/2015/05/07/the-facebook -its-not-our-fault-study/.

———. "The Internet as the Anti-Television: Distribution Infrastructure as Culture and Power." In *Signal Traffic*, edited by Lisa Parks and Nicole Starosielski, 225–45. Champaign: University of Illinois Press, 2015.

Sandvig, Christian, Kevin Hamilton, Karrie Karahalios, and Cedric Langbort. "When the Algorithm Itself Is a Racist: Diagnosing Ethical Harm in the Basic Components of Software." *International Journal of Communication* 10 (2016): 4972–90.

Sanjinés, Jorge, Ukamau Group, and Richard Schaaf. *Theory and Practice of a Cinema with the People*. Willimantic, CT: Curbstone Press, 1989.

Santos, Boaventura de Sousa. *Epistemologies of the South*. London: Routledge, 2016.

Sardar, Ziauddin, Ashis Nandy, and Merryl Wyn Davies. *Barbaric Others: A Manifesto on Western Racism*. London: Pluto Press, 1993.

Sarkhel, Aritra, and Neha Alawadhi. "How Data Brokers Are Selling All Your Personal Info for Less than a Rupee to Whoever Wants It." *The Economic Times*, February 28, 2017. https://economictimes.indiatimes.com/tech/internet/how

-data-brokers-are-selling-all-your-personal-info-for-less-than-a-rupee-to
-whoever-wants-it/articleshow/57382192.cms.

Sassen, Saskia. *Expulsions*. Cambridge, MA: Harvard University Press, 2014.

Schiller, Dan. *Digital Capitalism*. Cambridge, MA: MIT Press, 2000.

———. *Digital Depression*. Champaign: University of Illinois Press, 2014.

Schneier, Bruce. "Click Here to Control Everyone." *New York Magazine*, January 27, 2017. https://www.schneier.com/essays/archives/2017/01/click_here_to_kill_e.html.

———. *Click Here to Kill Everybody*. New York: W. W. Norton, 2018.

———. *Data and Goliath*. New York: W. W. Norton, 2014.

———. "The Public-Private Surveillance Partnership." *Bloomberg Business-Week*, July 31, 2013. https://www.bloomberg.com/view/articles/2013-07-31/the-public-private-surveillance-partnership.

Schoeman, Wolfgang. *Privacy and Social Freedom*. Cambridge, UK: Cambridge University Press, 1992.

Scholz, Trebor, ed. *Digital Labor*. Routledge: New York, 2013.

———. *Uberworked and Underpaid*. Cambridge, UK: Polity, 2016.

Scholz, Trebor, and Nathan Schneider, eds. *Ours to Hack and to Own*. New York: OR Books, 2017.

Schüll, Natasha. "Data for Life: Wearable Technology and the Design of Self-Care." *BioSocieties* 11, no. 3 (2016): 317–33.

Schulten, Susan. *Mapping the Nation*. Chicago: University of Chicago Press, 2012.

Schwartz, Paul. "Internet Privacy and the State." *Connecticut Law Review* 32 (1999): 815–59.

Scott, James. *Seeing Like a State*. New Haven, CT: Yale University Press, 1998.

Scott, Mark, and Laurens Cerulus. "Europe's New Data Protection Rules Export Privacy Standards Worldwide." *Politico*, January 31, 2018, https://www.politico.eu/article/europe-data-protection-privacy-standards-gdpr-general-protection-data-regulation.

Selbst, Andrew, and Solon Barocas. "Regulating Inscrutable Systems." Paper presented at the We Robot 2017 Conference in New Haven, United States, March 31. http://www.werobot2017.com/wp-content/uploads/2017/03/Selbst-and-Barocas-Regulating-Inscrutable-Systems-1.pdf.

Sen, Amartya. *Development as Freedom*. Oxford, UK: Oxford University Press, 1999.

———. *Inequality Examined*. Oxford, UK: Oxford University Press, 1992.

———. *Rationality and Freedom*. Cambridge, MA: Harvard University Press, 2002.

Sender, Henny, and Simon Mundy. "Walmart Nears Deal to Take Majority Stake in Flipkart." *Financial Times*, April 24, 2018.

Sewell, William H. *Logics of History*. Chicago: University of Chicago Press, 2005.

Shavel, Michael, Sebastian Vanderzeil, and Emma Currier. "Retail Automation: Stranded Workers? Opportunities and Risk for Labor and Automation." *Investor Responsibility Research Center Institute*, 2017. https://irrcinstitute.org /wp-content/uploads/2017/05/FINAL-Retail-Automation_Stranded-Workers -Final-May-2017.pdf.

Shaw, Jonathan. "The Watchers: Assaults on Privacy in America." *Harvard Magazine*, January–February 2017. https://harvardmagazine.com/2017/01/the -watchers.

Shaw, Tamsin. "Invisible Manipulators of Your Mind." *New York Review of Books*. April 20, 2017.

Shepherd, Tamara."Mapped, Measured and Mined: The Social Graph and Colonial Visuality"." *Social Media + Society* 1, no. 1 (2015). DOI: 10.1177/2056305115578671.

———. "Neocolonial Intimacies." *California Review of Images and Mark Zuckerberg* (2017). http://zuckerbergreview.com/shepherd.html.

Shilliam, Robbie. "Redemptive Political Economy." In *Critical Methods in Political and Cultural Economy*, edited by Johnna Montgomerie, 51–57. New York: Routledge, 2017.

Simpson, Leanne Betasamosake. *As We Have Always Done*. Minneapolis: University of Minnesota Press, 2017.

Singh, Ilina, and Nikolas Rose. "Biomarkers in Psychiatry." *Nature* 460, no. 7252 (2009): 202–7.

Singha, Radhika. "Settle, Mobilize, Verify: Identification Practices in Colonial India." *Studies in History* 16, no. 2 (2017): 151–98.

Skeggs, Bev, and Simon Yuill. "Capital Experimentation with Person/a Formation: How Facebook's Monetization Refigures the Relationship between Property, Personhood and Protest." *Information, Communication & Society* 19, no. 3 (2016): 380–96.

Skinner, Quentin. "Liberty, Liberalism, and Surveillance: A Historic Overview." Interview by Richard Marshall. *Open Democracy*, July 26, 2013. https:// www.opendemocracy.net/ourkingdom/quentin-skinner-richard-marshall /liberty-liberalism-and-surveillance-historic-overview.

Smith, Aaron. "Gig Work, Online Selling and Home Sharing." Pew Research Foundation, November 17, 2016. http://www.pewinternet.org/2016/11/17/gig -work-online-selling-and-home-sharing/.

———. "Shared, Collaborative and On Demand: The New Digital Economy." Pew Research Foundation, May 19, 2016. http://www.pewinternet.org/2016/05/19 /the-new-digital-economy/.

Smith, Linda Tuhiwai. *Decolonizing Methodologies*. 2nd ed. London: Zed Books, 2012.

Smythe, Dallas W. "On the Audience Commodity and Its Work." In *Media and Cultural Studies Keyworks*, edited by Meenakshi Gigi Durham and Douglas Kellner, 230–56. Malden, MA: Blackwell, 2001.

Solon, Olivia. "George Soros: Facebook and Google a Menace to Society." *Guardian*, January 25, 2018.

———. "'It's Digital Colonialism': How Facebook's Free Internet Service Has Failed Its Users." *Guardian*, July 27, 2017.

Solove, Daniel. *Understanding Privacy*. Cambridge, MA: Harvard University Press, 2008.

Soltani, Ashkan, and Craig Timberg. "Apple's Mac Computers Can Automatically Collect Your Location Information." *The Washington Post*, October 20, 2014.

Spivak, Gayatri Chakravorty. "Can the Subaltern Speak?" In *Marxism and the Interpretation of Culture*, edited by Cary Nelson and Lawrence Grossberg, 271–316. Champaign: University of Illinois Press, 1988.

Srnicek, Nick. *Platform Capitalism*. Cambridge, UK: Polity, 2017.

Starosielski, Nicole. *The Undersea Network*. Durham, NC: Duke University Press, 2015.

Starr, Paul, and Ross Corson. "Who Will Have the Numbers? The Rise of the Statistical Services Industry and the Politics of Public Data." In *The Politics of Numbers*, edited by William Alonso and Paul Starr, 415–47. New York: Russell Sage Foundation, 1988.

Statista. "The Leading Companies in the World in 2016, by Net Income." 2016. https://www.statista.com/statistics/269857/most-profitable-companies-worldwide/.

Steel, Emily. "Acxiom to Create 'Master Profiles' Tying Offline and Online Data." *Financial Times*, September 23, 2013.

Stern, Philip J. *The Company-State: Corporate Sovereignty and the Early Modern Foundations of the British Empire in India*. Oxford, UK: Oxford University Press, 2011.

Steward, Helen. *A Metaphysics for Freedom*. Oxford, UK: Oxford University Press, 2012.

Stewart, Kathleen. *A Space on the Side of the Road*. Princeton, NJ: Princeton University Press, 1996.

Stiegler, Bernard. "Relational Ecology and the Digital Pharmakon," *Culture Machine* 13 (2012).

Strandburg, Katherine. "Monitoring, Datafication, and Consent: Legal Approaches to Privacy in the Big Data Context." In *Privacy, Big Data, and the Public Good*, edited by Julia Lane, Victoria Stodden, Stefan Bender, and Helen Nissenbaum, 5–43. Cambridge, UK: Cambridge University Press, 2014.

Streeter, Thomas. *The Net Effect*. New York: New York University Press, 2011.

Stucke, Maurice, and Ariel Ezrachi. "The Subtle Ways Your Digital Assistant Might Manipulate You." *Wired*, November 28, 2016.

Sulmasy, Daniel. "Naked Bodies, Naked Genomes: The Special (but Not Exceptional) Nature of Genomic Information." *Genetics in Medicine* (2014). DOI: 10.1038/gim.2014.11.

Sunstein, Cass R. "The Ethics of Nudging." *Yale Journal on Regulation* 32, no. 2 (2015): 413–50.

Sweeney, Latanya. "Health Data Flows." Paper presented at seminar at the Federal Trade Commission, Washington, DC, May 7, 2014. https://www.ftc.gov /system/files/documents/public_events/195411/consumer-health-data-webcast -slides.pdf.

Taplin, Jonathan. *Move Fast and Break Things*. New York: Little Brown, 2017.

Tashea, Jason. "Should the Public Have Access to Data Police Acquire through Private Companies?" *ABA Journal*, December 2016. http://www.abajournal .com/magazine/article/public_access_police_data_private_company.

Taylor, Charles. *Modern Social Imaginaries*. Durham, NC: Duke University Press, 2004.

Taylor, Paul. "Business Opportunities Come from Big Data." *Financial Times*, December 11, 2012.

Tene, Omer, and Jules Polonetsky. "Big Data for All: Privacy and User Control in the Age of Analytics." *Northwestern Journal of Technology & Intellectual Property* 11, no. 5 (2013): 239–73. https://scholarlycommons.law.northwestern.edu /njtip/vol11/iss5/1.

Terranova, Tiziana. "Attention, Economy and the Brain." *Culture Machine* 13 (2012): 1–19.

———. "Free Labor: Producing Culture for the Digital Economy." *Social Text* 18, no. 2 (2000): 63–88.

Terry, Nicolas. "Big Data Proxies and Health Privacy Exceptionalism." *Health Matrix: The Journal of Law-Medicine* 24, no. 1 (2014): 65–101.

Thaler, Richard, and Cass R. Sunstein. *Nudge*. New Haven, CT: Yale University Press, 2008.

Thatcher, Jim, David O'Sullivan, and Dillon Mahmoudi. "Data Colonialism Through Accumulation by Dispossession: New Metaphors for Daily Data." *Environment and Planning D: Society and Space* 34, no. 6 (2017): 990–1006.

Thornhill, John. "How to Fix Facebook." *Financial Times*, August 5, 2018.

Thornhill, Ted. "Muslim Cleric Declares Selfies a Sin Under Islamic Law." *Daily Mail*, January 27, 2015.

Ticona, Julia, and Alexandra Mateescu. "How Domestic Workers Wager Safety in the Platform Economy." *FastCompany*, March 29, 2018. https://www.fast company.com/40541050/how-domestic-workers-wager-safety-in-the-platform -economy.

Till, Chris. "Exercise as Labour: Quantified Self and the Transformation of Exercise into Labour." *Societies* 4 (2014): 446–62.

Timcke, Scott. *Capital, State, Empire*. London: University of Westminster Press, 2017.

Timoner, Ondi, dir. *We Live in Public*. Pasadena, CA: Interloper Films, 2010. DVD.

Tomich, Dale, and Michael Zeuske. "Introduction, the Second Slavery: Mass Slavery, World-Economy, and Comparative Microhistories." *Review (Fernand Braudel Center)* 31, no. 2 (2008): 91–100. http://www.jstor.org/stable/40241709.

Topol, Eric. *The Patient Will See You Now*. New York: Basic Books, 2015.

Tronti, Mario. *Operai e Capitale*. Turin: Einaudi, 1966.

Tuck, Eve, and K. Wayne Yang. "Decolonization Is Not a Metaphor." *Decolonization: Indigeneity, Education & Society* 1, no. 1 (2012): 1–40.

Tufecki, Zeynep. "We're Building a Dystopia Just to Make People Click on Ads." Published November 17, 2017. *TED* Video. https://m.youtube.com/watch?v=iFTWM7HV2UI.

Turner, Fred. *The Democratic Surround*. Chicago: University of Chicago Press, 2013.

———. *From Counterculture to Cyberculture*. Chicago: University of Chicago Press, 2006.

Turow, Joseph. *The Aisles Have Eyes*. New Haven, CT: Yale University Press, 2017.

———. *The Daily You*. New Haven, CT: Yale University Press, 2012.

Turow, Joseph, Michael Hennessy, and Nora Draper. *The Tradeoff Fallacy: How Marketers Are Misrepresenting American Consumers and Opening Them Up to Exploitation*. Philadelphia: Annenberg School for Communication, University of Pennsylvania, June 6, 2015. https://www.asc.upenn.edu/sites/default/files/TradeoffFallacy_1.pdf.

Turow, Joseph, Michael Hennessy, Nora Draper, Diani Virgilio, and Opa Akebe. *Divided We Feel: Partisan Politics Drive Audiences' Emotions Regarding Surveillance of Low-Income Populations*. Philadelphia: Annenberg School for Communication, University of Pennsylvania, April 2018. https://repository.upenn.edu/cgi/viewcontent.cgi?article=1563&context=asc_papers.

Turow, Joseph, Lee McGuigan, and Elena Maris. "Making Data Mining a Natural Part of Life: Physical Retailing, Customer Surveillance and the 21st Century Social Imaginary." *European Journal of Cultural Studies* 18, nos. 4–5 (2015): 464–78.

Uber. "Earning/Chilling." Filmed in 2016. Video. http://www.ispot.tv/ad/Au3e/uber-earning-chilling.

United Nations. *Big Data for Development*. May 2012. http://www.unglobalpulse.org/sites/default/files/BigDataforDevelopment-UNGlobalPulseJune2012.pdf.

Vaidhyanathan, Siva. *Anti-Social Media*. New York: Oxford University Press, 2018.

Valtysson, Bjarki. "Facebook as a Digital Public Sphere: Processes of Colonization and Emancipation." *Triple C* 10, no. 1 (2012): 77–91.

Van Alsenoy, Brendan, Valerie Verdoodt, Rob Heyman, Ellen Wauters, Jef Ausloos, and Günes Acar. "From Social Media Service to Advertising Network:

A Critical Analysis of Facebook's Revised Policies and Terms." *KU Leuven*, March 31, 2015. https://www.law.kuleuven.be/citip/en/news/item/facebooks-re vised-policies-and-terms-v1-2.pdf.

Van Couvering, Elizabeth. "Search Engines in Practice: Structure and Culture in Technical Development." In *Cultural Technologies*, edited by Goran Bolin, 118–32. London: Routledge, 2012.

Vanderzeil, Sebastian, Emma Currier, and Michael Shavel. "Retail Automation: Stranded Workers? Opportunities and Risks for Labor Automation." *IRRC Institute*, May 18, 2017. https://irrcinstitute.org/reports/retail-automation -stranded-workers-opportunities-and-risks-for-labor-automation/.

Van Dijck, Jose. *The Culture of Connectivity*. Oxford, UK: Oxford University Press, 2013.

———. "Datafication, Dataism and Dataveillance: Big Data between Scientific Paradigm and Ideology." *Surveillance & Society* 12, no. 2 (2014): 197–208.

Varian, Hal. "Beyond Big Data." Paper presented at the NABE Annual Meeting, San Francisco, September 10, 2013. http://people.ischool.berkeley.edu/~hal /Papers/2013/BeyondBigDataPaperFINAL.pdf

Velkova, Julia. "Data That Warms: Waste Heat, Infrastructural Convergence and the Computation Traffic Commodity." *Big Data & Society* 3, no. 2 (2016). http://journals.sagepub.com/doi/full/10.1177/2053951716684144.

Vertesi, Janet. "My Experiment Opting Out of Big Data Made Me Look Like a Criminal." *Time*, May 1, 2014. http://time.com/83200/privacy-internet-big -data-opt-out/.

———. "Seamful Spaces: Heterogeneous Infrastructures in Interaction." *Science, Technology & Human Values* 39, no. 2 (2014): 264–84.

Villasenor, John. "Recording Everything: Digital Storage as an Enabler of Author-itarian Governments." *Brookings Institute*, December 14, 2011. https://www .brookings.edu/research/recording-everything-digital-storage-as-an-enabler -of-authoritarian-governments.

Von Uexküll, Jakob. *Foray into the Worlds of Animals and Humans*. Minneapolis: University of Minnesota Press, (1934/1940), 2010.

Wacquant, Loïc. *Punishing the Poor*. Durham, NC: Duke University Press, 2009.

Wainwright, Joel, and Joe Bryan. "Cartography, Territory, Property: Postcolonial Reflections on Indigenous Counter-Mapping in Nicaragua and Belize." *Cultural Geographies* 16, no. 2 (April 1, 2009): 153–78.

Wakabayashi, Daisuke. "California Passes Sweeping Law to Protect Online Privacy." *The New York Times*, June 28, 2018.

Wallerstein, Immanuel. *Historical Capitalism*. 3rd ed. London: Verso, 2011.

Walmart. *Annual Report 2017*. 2017. http://s2.q4cdn.com/056532643/files/doc_fi nancials/2017/Annual/WMT_2017_AR-(1).pdf.

Walton, Clifford Stevens. *The Civil Law in Spain and Spanish America*. Clark, NJ: The Lawbook Exchange, Ltd., 2003.

Ward, Ben. "The Internet of Things Will Become the Internet of Services." *Silicon*, October 8, 2013. http://www.silicon.co.uk/workspace/internet-of-things-con tributed-feature-mll-telecom-needs-picture-128621.

Warren, Samuel, and Louis Brandeis. "The Right to Privacy." *Harvard Law Review* 4 (1890): 193–220.

Warren, Tom. "Google Starts Testing Chrome's Built-In Ad Blocker." *The Verge*, August 1, 2017. https://www.theverge.com/2017/8/1/16074742/google-chrome -ad-blocker-canary-build-test.

Waters, Richard. "Four Days That Shook the Digital Ad World." *Financial Times*, July 29, 2016.

———. "Google Plays Down Impact of Data Rules." *Financial Times*, April 25, 2018.

———. "Tim Cook Is Right to Kick Facebook over Its Data Privacy Failings." *Financial Times*, March 30, 2018.

Weber, Max. *Economy and Society*. Edited by Roth Guenther and Claus Wittich. Berkeley: University of California Press, 1978.

Weber, Steven. "Data, Development, and Growth." *Business and Politics* 19, no. 3 (2017): 397–423.

Weil, David. *The Fissured Workplace*. Cambridge, MA: Harvard University Press, 2014.

Weise, Karen. "Will a Camera on Every Cop Make Everyone Safer? Taser Thinks So." *Bloomberg Businessweek*, July 12, 2016. https://www.bloomberg.com /news/articles/2016-07-12/will-a-camera-on-every-cop-make-everyone-safer -taser-thinks-so.

Weizenbaum, Joseph. *Computer Power and Human Reason*. New York: W. H. Freeman, 1986.

West, Darrell M. "What Happens If Robots Take the Jobs? The Impact of Emerging Technologies on Employment and Public Policy." *Brookings Institution*, 2015. https://www.brookings.edu/research/what-happens-if-robots-take-the -jobs-the-impact-of-emerging-technologies-on-employment-and-public -policy/.

Westin, Alan F. *Privacy and Freedom*. New York: Athenaeum, 1967.

Wherry, Frederick F. "Relational Accounting: A Cultural Approach." *American Journal of Cultural Sociology* 4, no. 2 (2016): 131–56.

Whitson, Jennifer R. "Gaming the Quantified Self." *Surveillance & Society* 11, nos. 1–2 (2013): 163–76.

Williams, Alex, and Nick Srnicek. "#ACCELERATE MANIFESTO for an Accelerationist Politics." *Critical Legal Thinking*, May 14, 2013. http://criticallegal thinking.com/2013/05/14/accelerate-manifesto-for-an-accelerationist-politics/.

Williams, Chris, Eli Brumbaugh, Jeff Feng, John Bodley, and Michelle Thomas. "Democratizing Data at Airbnb." *Airbnb Engineering & Data Science*, May 12, 2017. https://medium.com/airbnb-engineering/democratizing-data-at-airbnb -852d76c51770.

Williams, Eric. *Capitalism and Slavery*. Chapel Hill: University of North Carolina Press, 1994.

Williamson, Ben. "Calculating Children in the Dataveillance School: Social and Ethical Implications of New Technologies for Children and Young People." In *Surveillance Futures*, edited by Emmeline Taylor and Tonya Rooney, 50–66. London: Routledge, 2016.

Wilson, H. James. "Wearables in the Workplace." *Harvard Business Review*, September 2013. https://hbr.org/2013/09/wearables-in-the-workplace.

Winner, Langdon. "Do Artifacts Have Politics?" *Daedalus* 109, no. 1 (1980): 121–36.

Winseck, Dwayne. "Communication and the Sorrows of Empire: Surveillance and Information Operations 'Blowback' in the Global War on Terrorism." In *Surveillance: Power, Problems, and Politics*, edited by Sean P. Hier and Josh Greenberg, 151–68. Vancouver, BC: UBC Press, 2010.

Wissinger, Elizabeth. "Blood, Sweat, and Tears: Navigating Creepy versus Cool in Wearable Biotech." *Information, Communication & Society* 21, no. 5 (2018): 779–85.

Wolf, Eric. *Europe and the People without History*. 2nd ed. Berkeley: University of California Press, 2010.

Wolf, Gary. "The Data-Driven Life." *The New York Times*, April 28, 2010. http://www.nytimes.com/2010/05/02/magazine/02self-measurement-t.html.

Wong, Julie Carrie. "Social Media Is Ripping Society Apart." *Guardian*, December 12, 2017.

Wood, Allen W. *Hegel's Ethical Thought*. Cambridge, UK: Cambridge University Press, 1990.

World Economic Forum. *Personal Data: The Emergence of a New Asset Class*. Geneva, CH: We Forum, January 2011. http://www3.weforum.org/docs/WEF _ITTC_PersonalDataNewAsset_Report_2011.pdf.

Wright, Joshua D., and Douglas H. Ginsburg. "Behavioral Law and Economics: Its Origins, Fatal Flaws, and Implications for Liberty." *Northwestern University Law Review* 106, no. 3 (2012): 1–58.

Wu, Tim. *The Attention Merchants*. New York: Vintage, 2016.

Wylie, Christopher. "I've Been Getting a Lot of Requests from Indian Journalists . . ." Twitter, March 28, 2018. https://twitter.com/chrisinsilico/status /978921850448371715.

Xu, Alison. "Chinese Judicial Justice on the Cloud: A Future Call or a Pandora's Box? An Analysis of the 'Intelligent Court System' of China." *Information & Communications Technology Law* 26, no. 1 (2017): 59–71.

Yang, Yuan. "China Pours Millions into Facial Recognition Start-Up Face++." *Financial Times*, November 1, 2017.

Yang, Yuan, and Yingzhi Yang. "Smile to Enter: China Embraces Facial-Recognition Technology." *Financial Times*, June 7, 2017.

Yegenoglu, Meyda. *Colonial Fantasies*. Cambridge, UK: Cambridge University Press, 1998.

Yeung, Karen. "The Forms and Limits of Choice Architecture as a Tool of Government." *Law & Police* 38, no. 3 (2016): 186–210.

———. "'Hypernudge': Big Data as a Mode of Regulation by Design." *Information Communication and Society* 20, no. 1 (2017): 118–36.

Yong, Ed. *I Contain Multitudes*. New York: Vintage, 2016.

Young, Robert. *Postcolonialism: An Historical Introduction*. Malden, MA: Wiley-Blackwell, 2001.

Zaretsky, Eli. *Capitalism, the Family, and Personal Life*. New York: Harper Collins, 1986.

Zelizer, Viviana. *Economic Lives*. Princeton, NJ: Princeton University Press, 2010.

Zittrain, Jonathan. *The Future of the Internet—And How to Stop It*. New Haven, CT: Yale University Press, 2008.

Žižek, Slavoj. *Living in the End Times*. 2nd ed. London: Verso, 2011.

Zuboff, Shoshana. "Big Other: Surveillance Capitalism and the Prospects of an Information Civilization." *Journal of Information Technology* 30, no. 1 (2015): 75–89.

Zuboff, Shoshana. *In the Age of the Smart Machine*. New York: Basic Books, 1988.

Zuckerberg, Ethan. "The Internet's Original Sin." *The Atlantic*, August 14, 2014.

Zuckerberg, Mark. "Building Global Community." Facebook, February 16, 2017. https://www.facebook.com/notes/mark-zuckerberg/building-global-community/10154544292806634.

The Zuckerberg Files. "D8 All Things Digital." *Zuckerberg Transcripts* 57, September 17, 2010. http://dc.uwm.edu/zuckerberg_files_transcripts/57/.

———. "F8 2011 Keynote." *Zuckerberg Transcripts* 40, September 24, 2011. http://dc.uwm.edu/zuckerberg_files_transcripts/40/.

Index

Aadhaar unique ID system, 11, 100, 134
Acemoglu, Daron, 238n117
Acosta, Alberto, 90
Actor Network Theory, 142
Acxiom, 14, 17, 53, 228n88
Adsense (Google), 29
Adtech (Facebook), 228n88
advertising and marketing: ad blocking, 11, 225n29; commodification of, 29; Facebook monitoring practice of, 143; global media ad spend by countries, 123, 245n45; ideology of personalization, 16–17, 61; "influencers," 110; outdoor retargeting with, 132; people-based, 21–22
Agre, Philip, 153
AI. *See* artificial intelligence
Airbnb, 61, 106, 195, 236n58, 251n190
Alaimo, Cristina, 131
algorithms: Algorithm Observatory, 210; and autonomy, 160, 172, 183; for Cloud Empire, 56, 59, 62, 65, 68; for data relations, 29–30, 83; and decolonizing data, 194, 198–201, 210; for social knowledge, 115, 120, 129, 131, 134, 143–50. *See also* social knowledge
Alibaba: "ecosystem" of, 262n22; and emerging social order of capital-

ism, 24, 26, 29; internal colonizing and social quantification sector, 55–57; market-capitalization value of, 232n2; social relations colonized by, 13–15
"alibi for capitalism," 102–3
Alimama (Alibaba), 29
Allende, Salvador, 96
Alphabet, 49, 54, 232n2, 236n58. *See also* Google
Amazon: as "Big Five" company, 48–50; data and emerging social order of capitalism, 23; data as colonized resource by, 10; employment by, 236n58; labor surveillance by, 64; market-capitalization value of, 54; mission statement of, 106; Mturk and underpaid labor, 59–60, 108, 145; as new colonial corporation, 15; social knowledge by, 133
Anderson, Chris, 125–27
Andreessen, Marc, 97, 187, 192
Android, 37, 49
Aouragh, Miriyam, 96–97
Appadurai, Arjun, 207, 262n41
Apple: "Appconn," 74; as "Big Five" company, 48–50; data as colonized resource by, 10, 225n29; market-capitalization value of, 54; as new

Richards, Neil, 179
Ricoeur, Paul, 253n10, 254n34
Rieder, Bernhard, 137
Rooney, Sally, xv
Rose, Nikolas, 122
Rosenblat, Alex, 62
Rossiter, Ned, 39, 47
Rössler, Beate, 154, 165
Rotenberg, Marc, 177
Rouvroy, Annette, 127–28, 249n141
Russia, social quantification sector in, 55

sacrifice zones, 90
Safari (Apple), 48–49
Said, Edward, 77, 239n34
Salesforce, 65
Sammadar, Ranabir, 66
Sandvig, Christian, 132
Santos, Boaventura de Sousa, 201, 263n46
Saudi Aramco, 54
Scandia, 153
Schildt, Hakan, 153
Schneier, Bruce, xv, 23–24, 128, 135
Schüll, Natasha Dow, 171–72
seamfulness, Vertesi on, 198–201
seamlessness, Cohen on, 229n106
second-order control, 182–83
"second slavery," 73–74
self: double consciousness of, 157; integrity of, 156–61, 197, 204–5; self-determination, 154–55, 252–53n10; Self versus Other, 239n34; space of the self concept, 156–57, 161–65, 167, 172, 178, 199
self-tracking: as autonomy illusion, 168–73; personal data appropriation spectrum of, 173–76; Quantified Self movement, 168, 171, 257n77; "situated objectivity" of,

256n70; as social knowledge, 128–29, 133; in workplace, 65–66, 153–54
Self-Tracking (Neff, Nafus), 257n77
Sen, Amartya, 201–2
sensors and sensing: biosensors, 141; body sensors, 171; GPS tracking, 29; sensing as model for knowledge, 8; for telematics, 65. *See also* self-tracking
Shared Value, 135
sharing economy (gig economy), 13, 59–63, 108
Shilliam, Robbie, 74
Shotspotter, 134
Sidewalk Labs (Google), 150
Simpson, Leanne Betasamosake, xiv–xv, 90, 195–96, 204
Siri (Apple), 133
Skam (Facebook), 109–10
skin-embedded microchips, 172
Skinner, Quentin, 164
slavery, xvii–xviii, 4, 13, 72–76, 83, 106–7, 167, 225n37. *See also* historical colonialism
smart devices, defined, 50
smart scheduling, 64
Smart Technologies (Hildebrandt), 260n142
Smith, Linda Tuhiwai, 209
Smythe, Dallas, 102
Snapchat, 11, 43, 236n58
Snapshot (Progressive), 145
Snowden, Edward, xvi
social caching: defined, xiii; for social knowledge, 131–38; in social quantification sector, xv–xvi
social factory, Autonomist concept of, 34, 231–32nn138–140
social knowledge, 115–51; as injustice, 150–51, 190–91; overview, 115–18; personalization, 16–17, 61, 132, 175–

CULTURE
AND
ECONOMIC
LIFE

Diverse sets of actors create meaning in markets: consumers and socially engaged actors from below; producers, suppliers, and distributors from above; and the gatekeepers and intermediaries that span these levels. Scholars have studied the interactions of people, objects, and technology; charted networks of innovation and diffusion among producers and consumers; and explored the categories that constrain and enable economic action. This series captures the many angles in which these phenomena have been investigated and serves as a high-profile forum for discussing the evolution, creation, and consequences of commerce and culture.

Lightning Source UK Ltd.
Milton Keynes UK
UKHW010419270120
357609UK00015B/281